Exposition
of
The Westminster Confession of Faith

Exposition
of
The Westminster
Confession
of Faith

Robert Shaw

Christian Heritage

Christian Focus Publications publishes biblically-accurate books for adults and children. The books in the adult range are published in three imprints.

Christian Heritage contains classic writings from the past.

Christian Focus contains popular works including biographies, commentaries, doctrine, and Christian living.

Mentor focuses on books written at a level suitable for Bible College and seminary students, pastors, and others; the imprint includes commentaries, doctrinal studies, examination of current issues, and church history.

For a free catalogue of all our titles, please write to
Christian Focus Publications,
Geanies House, Fearn,
Ross-shire, IV20 1TW, Great Britain

For details of our titles visit us on our web site
http://www.geanies.org.uk/cfp

ISBN 0 906731 04 6
© Christian Focus Publications

This edition published in 1998 by
Christian Focus Publications,
Geanies House, Fearn,
Ross-shire, IV20 1TW, Great Britain
First published in 1845.
First Christian Focus edition 1973
Reprinted 1980, 1992, 1998

Cover design by Donna Macleod

Contents

FOREWORD

The Westminster Confession of Faith is one of the noblest and most influential documents of the Christian Church. It remains the fullest and most carefully constructed brief exposition of the Christian faith ever written. Almost three hundred and fifty years later it continues to be used and loved as a grand summary of biblical teaching.

In past days the Confession was read, pondered and studied by Christians of all levels of education. The crofter and the craftsman might be as familiar with it as the teacher and the theologian. Understanding Christian doctrine and healthy Christian living were then seen as intimate friends. It is hardly surprising that rugged, vigorous, intelligent and self-sacrificing Christianity was the result, for the Confession put calcium into the Christian's spiritual bones.

Of course, the Confession's heyday was in an age in which Christians had little 'leisure-time', no television and few books. We, by contrast, have so many other things to absorb our attention. Yet, it is to our spiritual loss that we – by comparison so well-educated – are so poorly educated in the things which matter most of all, the truths of the gospel. Indeed, opening the Confession may bring us moderns into a world and a vocabulary to which many of us are strangers.

In this setting, we must not make the mistake of either passively accepting the influences of our age, or of wishing we had been born in another era. Instead we must learn to live wholesomely non-conformist Christian lives, increasingly transformed by the renewing of our minds (as Paul puts it in Romans 12:1-2).

Here, Robert Shaw can help us. Taking the chapter of the Confession as a staring point, he warmly and enthusiastically explains its teaching. His work provides a miniature course in theology. More than that, it explains, expounds and applies the whole gospel in a way that will explain the message of Scripture, illumine understanding, stimulate worship and strengthen Christian living. A course of private study with Shaw as teacher and companion will equip us to be intelligent and capable witnesses to Jesus Christ in the modern world – able to give a reason for the hope that the gospel gives us (1 Peter 3:15). This is a considerable return for the modest investment of the price of one book and the expenditure of a little time and study.

If personal testimony is any encouragement, perhaps I may be allowed to place my own on record. I recall, with great gratitude, a period in my later teens when I first became acquainted with the Westminster Confession, and began to study it with the aid of a commentary. Looking back, I think of that as one of the most valuable investments of time and thought I ever made. It took me a stage further in understanding the greatness of God, the glory of Christ, the ministry of the Spirit, the nature of the Christian life, the church and the world to come. I sometimes compare that time of study to the activity of a squirrel gathering nuts which will see him through the winter! So it has proved to be. Let Robert Shaw be your guide, reading him with careful and prayerful thought, discernment and appreciation, and you will know what I mean.

Sinclair B Ferguson
Westminster Theological Seminary
Philadelphia
Pennsylvania
March 1992

PREFACE

In preparing the following Exposition of the Confession of Faith, framed by the Westminster Assembly of Divines, it has been the object of the author to state the truths embraced in each section, to explain the terms employed wherever it seemed necessary, and to illustrate and confirm the doctrines. To avoid swelling the volume to an undue size, the arguments have been stated with the utmost possible brevity; in the illustrations, conciseness combined with perspicuity has been studied, and numerous passages of Scripture, which elucidate the subjects treated of, have been merely referred to, without being quoted at large. It is hoped that the attentive reader will here find the substance of larger works compressed within a small space; that materials for reflection will be suggested; and that an examination of the texts of Scripture marked, will throw much light upon the points to which they refer.

The Westminster Confession of Faith contains a simple exhibition of the truth, based upon the Word of God; but its several propositions are laid in opposition to the heresies and errors which have been disseminated in various ages. It has, therefore, been a prominent object of the author of the Exposition to point out the numerous errors against which the statements in the Confession are directed. The reader will thus find the deliverance of the Westminster Assembly of Divines upon the various errors by which the truth has been corrupted in former times, and will be guarded against modern errors, which are generally only a revival of those that had previously disturbed the Church, and that had been long ago refuted.

To render the work more accessible for reference, a Table of Contents has ben prefixed, and a copious Index added, which will show, at a glance, the various subjects discussed, and the manifold errors that have been noticed, in the course of the work.

To have transcribed the proofs from Scripture annexed to each proposition by the Westminster Assembly of Divines would have extended this volume to an inconvenient size. But the texts have been inserted after each section; and the additional labour of those who will take the trouble of turning to these proofs in their Bibles will be amply compensated. Their scriptural knowledge will be enlarged, and they will be satisfied that every truth set down in the Confession is 'most agreeable to the Word of God'. Of this the author of the Exposition is so completely convinced, that he has not found it necessary to differ from the compilers of the Confession in any one point of doctrine. The language, in some cases, might admit of improvement; but 'as to the truth of the matter' he cordially concurs in the judgment of the General Assembly of the Church of Scotland in 1647, that it is 'most orthodox, and grounded upon the Word of God'. And if the Confession, two hundred years ago, contained a faithful exhibition of the truth, it must do so still; for scriptural truth is, like its divine Author, 'the same yesterday, today, and for ever'.

Whitburn,
May 12, 1845

INTRODUCTORY ESSAY

There have been many objections urged against the use of Creeds and Confessions of Faith, at different periods and with various degrees of skill or plausibility. It is not necessary either to enumerate all these objections or to answer them all, since many of them have sunk into oblivion, and others have already met sufficient refutation. Almost the only objection which is now urged with any degree of confidence is that which accuses Confessions of usurping a position and authority due to divine truth alone. This objection itself has its origin in an erroneous view of what a Confession of Faith really is, and of what it is in which the necessity of a Confession being framed consists. The necessity for the formation of Confessions of Faith does not lie in the nature of the sacred truth revealed to man; but in the nature of the human itself. A Confession of Faith is not a revelation of divine truth – it is 'not even a rule of faith and practice, but a help in both,' to use the words of our own Confession; but it is a declaration of the manner in which any man, or number of men – any Christian or any Church – understands the truth which has been revealed. Its object is, therefore, not to teach divine truth; but to exhibit a clear, systematic and intelligible declaration of our own sentiments, and to furnish the means of ascertaining the opinions of others, especially in religious controversies.

The truth of this view, and the explanation which it gives of the necessity for the existence of Creeds and Confessions, may be easily shown. The human mind is so prone to error, and of such widely diversified capacity in every respect, that when even a simple truth is presented for its reception, that truth may be reproduced in almost as many different aspects as there were different minds to which it was presented. Suppose it a single sentence, uttered in a voice, or written in a language understood by all – each man might understand it in his own way, putting upon it the construction which, to him, seemed the clearest; but it would be impossible to ascertain, whether they all understood it in the same sense or not, by their merely repeating the very words which they had heard or read, unless they were all to state, each in his own words, what they understood it to mean. Each man might then say,

'I believe its meaning was to this effect.' This would be really his Creed, or Confession of Faith, respecting that truth; and when all had thus stated their belief, if anything like a harmonious consent of mind among them could be obtained, it would be their united Confession of Faith with regard to that particular truth so revealed and understood.

But it would be more than this – it would be both a bond of union among themselves on that point, and also a conjoint testimony to all other men; not as absolutely and certainly teaching that truth, but as absolutely and certainly conveying the sense in which these men understood it, so far as their statement was itself distinct and intelligible; and it might prove the term of admission to the body of those who had thus emitted a joint declaration of what they believed to be the meaning of that truth.

To this extent, we think, all intelligent and candid persons will readily concur; and so far, it must be evident that there is no infringement of the natural liberty of any man, nor any attempt to control or overbear his conscientious convictions respecting what he believes to be truth in any given or supposable case. If any man cannot agree with the joint testimony borne by those who are agreed, this may be a cause of mutual regret; but it could neither confer on them any right to compel him to join them, contrary to his convictions, nor entitle him to complain on account of being excluded from a body of men with those opinions he did not concur. No man of strict integrity, indeed, could even wish to become one of a body of men with whom he did not agree on that peculiar point which formed the basis of their association.

Now, let this view be applied to the subject of religious truth – taking care, at the same time, to mark the special points which the idea of religious truth necessarily introduces. Religious truth is the revelation of God's will to man – whether that revelation be conveyed orally, or in a written record. As it comes now to us, it is in a written record. This we believe to be the very Word of the very God of truth. In this respect, it is to every soul the only and the all-sufficient rule of faith, with regard to 'what man is to believe concerning God, and what duty God requires of man'. But the question immediately arises, as above suggested, whether all to whom this revelation of God's will has been made understand it in the same sense? If any man say, that his only rule of faith is the Bible, every man who believes the Bible to be the Word of God will agree in this sentiment; but still the question returns, 'What do you understand the Bible to teach?' It would be no answer to this question merely to repeat a series of texts; for this would give no information in what sense these texts were understood. This must be manifest to every one who reflects for a moment. All who even profess the Christian name, however discordant their opinions may be, at least assume to believe the Bible; but each jarring sectarian gives his own construction to the language of that sacred book; and it is only in consequence of the statement in his own words of what that construction is, that it can be known whether his sentiments accord with, or differ from, those of the majority of professing Christians. This, as before remarked, arises not out of the nature of the truth revealed, but out of the nature of the minds to whom that truth is presented. The question is not, therefore, one respecting God's truth, but respecting man's truth – not respecting the truth of the Bible, but respecting man's apprehension of that truth.

Another element now comes into view. The Bible not only contains a revelation of eternal truth, which it is man's duty to receive and to hold, but it also appoints a body of men to be the depositaries and teachers of that truth – a Church, which is not a voluntary association of men who have ascertained that there is a harmony of sentiment sufficient for a basis of union, but a divine institution, subject directly to God, and having no authority over conscience. And, to complete this idea, let it further be observed, that God, in instituting the Church, has promised to bestow upon it the Holy Spirit, to lead it into the knowledge of the truth. This promise, further, is not to the Church in an aggregate capacity alone, but also to every individual member thereof, so as both to preserve inviolate his own responsibility, and to secure his personal union with God. The realization of this great promise provides what in no other case exists, or can exist – an infallible umpire for the decision of all questions that can arise respecting Christian faith. For it may be confidently maintained that whenever jarring Churches or individual Christians have been enabled to seek the light and guidance of the Holy Spirit in a sincere, humble and earnest spirit, they have obtained such a decision of the point in dispute as to put an end to contention, and to secure the unity of the Spirit in the bonds of peace: and further, notwithstanding all the various aspects in which Christianity has, during the course of many centuries, been externally disguised, there has been still an amount of real harmony of belief, such as none but an infallible teacher and arbiter could have secured.

The Christian Church, as a divine institution, takes the Word of God alone, and the whole Word of God, as her only rule of faith; but she must also frame and promulgate a statement of what she understands the Word of God to teach. This she does, not as arrogating any authority to suppress, change or amend anything that God's Word teaches, but in discharge of the various duties which she owes to God, to the world, and to those of her own communion. Since she has been constituted the depositary of God's truth, it is her duty to him to state, in the most distinct and explicit terms, what she understands that truth to mean. In this manner she not only proclaims what God has said, but also appends her seal that God is true. Thus a Confession of Faith is not the very voice of divine truth, but the echo of that voice from souls that have heard its utterance, felt its power, and are answering to its call.

And, since she has been instituted for the purpose of teaching God's truth to an erring world, her duty to the world requires that she should leave it in no doubt respecting the manner in which she understands the message which she has to deliver. Without doing so the Church would be no teacher, and the world might remain untaught, so far as she was concerned. For when the message had been stated in God's own words, every hearer must attempt, according to the constitution of his own mind, to form some conception of what these words mean; and his conception may be very vague and obscure, or even very erroneous, unless some attempt be made to define, elucidate, and correct them. Nor, indeed, could either the hearers or the teachers know that they understood the truth alike, without mutual statements and explanations with regard to the meaning which they respectively believe it to convey.

Still further, the Church has a duty to discharge to those of its own communion. To them she must produce a form of sound words, in order both to promote and confirm their knowledge, and also to guard them against the hazard of being led into errors; and, as they must be regarded as all agreed, with respect to the main outline of the truths which they believe, they are deeply interested in obtaining some security that those who are to become their teachers in future generations shall continue to teach the same divine and saving truths. The members of any Church must know each other's sentiments – must combine to hold them forth steadily and consistently to the notice of all around them, as witnesses for the same truths; and must do their utmost to secure that the same truths shall be taught by all its ministers, and to all candidates for admission. For all these purposes the formation of a Creed, or Confession of Faith, is imperatively necessary; and thus it appears that a Church cannot adequately discharge its duty to God, to the world, and to its own members, without a Confession of Faith.

There never has been a period in which the Christian Church has been without a Confession of Faith, though these Confessions have varied both in character and in extent. The first and simplest Confession is that of Peter: 'Thou art the Christ, the Son of the living God.' That of the Ethiopian treasurer is similar, and almost identical: 'I believe that Jesus Christ is the Son of God.' This Confession secured admission into the Church; but, without this, admission could not have been obtained.

It was not long till this simple and brief primitive Confession was enlarged; at first, in order to meet the perverse notions of the Judaizing teachers, and next, to exclude those who were beginning to be tainted with the Gnostic heresies. It then became necessary, not only to confess that Jesus Christ was the Son of God, but also that Jesus Christ was come in the flesh, in order to prevent the admission, and to check the teaching, of those who held that Christ's human nature was a mere phantasm or appearance.

In like manner the rise of any heresy rendered it necessary, first, to test the novel tenet by the Word of God and by the decision of the Holy Spirit, and then to add to the existing Confession of Faith a new article, containing the deliverance of the Church respecting each successive heresy. Thus, in the discharge of her duty to God, to the world, and to herself, the Church was constrained to enlarge the Confession of her Faith.

But this unavoidable enlargement ought not to be censured as unnecessarily lengthened and minute; for, let it be observed, that it led to a continually increasing clearness and precision in the testimony of what the Church believes, and tended to the progressive development of sacred truth.

Further, as the need of a Confession arises from the nature of the human mind, and the enlargement of the Confession was caused by the successive appearance and refutation of error, and as the human mind is still the same, and prone to the same erroneous notions, the Confession of Faith, which contains a refutation of past heresies, furnishes, at the same time, to all who understand it, a ready weapon wherewith to encounter any resuscitated heresy. The truth of this view will be most apparent to those who have most carefully studied the various Confessions of Faith framed by the Christian Church. And it must ever be regarded as a matter of no small importance by those who seek admission into any Church, that in its Confession they can obtain a full exhibition of the terms of communion to which they are required to consent. The existence of a Confession of Faith is ever a standing defence against the danger of any Church lapsing unawares into heresy. For although no Church ought to regard her Confession as a standard of faith, in any other than a subordinate sense, still it is a standard of admitted faith, which the Church may not lightly abandon, and a term of communion to its own members, till its articles are accused of being erroneous, and again brought to the final and supreme standard, the Word of God and the teaching of the Holy Spirit, sincerely, humbly, and earnestly sought in faith and prayer.

(2) Quitting the subject of Confessions of Faith in general, we direct our attention to the Confession of Faith framed by the Westminster Assembly of Divines.

The first thing which must strike any thoughtful reader, after having carefully and studiously perused the Westminster Assembly's Confession of Faith, *is the remarkable comprehensiveness and accuracy of its character, viewed as a systematic exhibition of divine truth, or what is termed a system of theology.* In this respect it may be regarded as almost perfect, both in its arrangement and in its completeness. Even a single glance over its table of contents will show with what exquisite skill its arrangement proceeds from the statement of first principles to the regular development and final consummation of the whole scheme of revealed truth. Nothing essential is omitted; and nothing is extended to a length disproportioned to its due importance. Nor do we think that a systematic study of theology could be prosecuted on a better plan than that of the Confession of Faith. Too little attention, perhaps, has been shown to the Confession in this respect; and we are strongly persuaded that it might be most advantageously used in our theological halls as a text-book.

This, at least, may be affirmed, that no private Christian could fail to benefit largely from a deliberate and studious perusal and re-perusal of the Confession of Faith, for the express purpose of obtaining a clear and systematic conception of sacred truth, both as a whole, and with all its parts so arranged as to display their relative importance, and their mutual bearing upon, and illustration of, each other. Such a deliberate perusal would also tend very greatly to fortify the mind against the danger of being led astray by crude notions, or induced to attribute undue importance to some favourite doctrine, to the disparagement of others not less essential, and with serious injury to the harmonious analogy of faith.

There is another characteristic of the Westminster Confession to which still less attention had been generally directed, but which is not less remarkable. Framed, as it was, by men of distinguished learning and ability, who were thoroughly conversant with the history of the Church from the earliest times till the period in which they lived, *it contains the calm and settled judgment of these profound divines on all previous heresies and subjects of controversy which had in any age or country agitated the Church.* This it does without expressly naming even one of these heresies, or entering into mere controversy. Each error is condemned, not by a direct statement and refutation of it, but by a clear, definite and strong statement of the converse truth. There was, in this mode of exhibiting the truth, singular wisdom combined with equally singular modesty. Everything of an irritating nature is suppressed, and the pure and simple truth alone displayed; while there is not only no ostentatious parade of superior learning, but even a concealment of learning the most accurate and profound.

A hasty or superficial reader of the Confession of Faith will scarcely perceive that, in some of its apparently simple propositions, he is perusing an acute and conclusive refutation of the various heresies and controversies that have corrupted and disturbed the Church. Yet, if he will turn to Church history, make himself acquainted with its details, and resume his study of the Confession, he will be often surprised to find in one place the wild theories of the Gnostics dispelled; in another, the Arian and Socinian heresies set aside; in another, the very essence of the Papal system annihilated; and in another, the basis of all Pelagian and Arminian errors removed.

Thus viewed, the Confession of Faith might be so connected with one aspect of Church history as to furnish, if not a textbook according to chronological arrangement in studying the rise and refutation of heresies, yet a valuable arrangement of their relative importance, doctrinally considered. And when we advert to the fact that, owing to the sameness of the human mind, there is a perpetually recurring tendency to reproduce an old and exploded error, as if it were a new discovery of some hitherto unknown or neglected truth, it must be obvious that were the peculiar excellence of our Confession, as a deliverance of all previously existing heresies, better known and more attended to, there would be great reason to hope that their re-appearance would be rendered almost impossible, or, at least, that their growth would be very speedily and effectually checked.

Closely connected with this excellence of the Confession of Faith is *its astonishing precision of thought and language*. The whole mental training of the eminent divines of that period led to this result. They were accustomed to cast every argument into the syllogistic form, and to adjust all its terms with the utmost care and accuracy. Every one who has studied the propositions of the Confession must have remarked their extreme precision; but, without peculiar attention, he may not perceive the astonishing care which these divines must have bestowed on this part of their great work. This may be best shown by an instance. Let us select one from chapter 3, 'On God's Eternal Decree,' sections 3 and 4: 'By the decree of God, for the manifestation of his glory, some men and angels are predestinated unto everlasting life, and others foreordained to everlasting death. These angels and men thus *predestinated* and *foreordained*,' etc.

The expressions to which we wish to draw the reader's attention are the words 'predestinated' and 'foreordained'. A hasty or superficial reader might perceive no difference between these words. But, if so, why are they both used? For there is no instance of mere tautological repetition in the concise language of the Confession. But, further, let it be well remarked that the word 'predestinated' is used only in connection with 'everlasting life', and the word 'foreordained' with 'everlasting death'. And when the compound form of the proposition is assumed, both terms are used to represent each its respective member in the general affirmation. Why is this the case? Because the Westminster Divines did not understand the meaning of the terms *predestination* and *foreordination* to be identical, and therefore never used these words as synonymous. By predestination they meant *a positive decree determining to confer everlasting life*; and this they regarded as the basis of the whole *doctrines of free grace*, arising from nothing in man, but having for its divine origin the character and sovereignty of God. *By foreordination,* on the other hand, they meant *a decree of order, or arrangement, determining that the guilty should be condemned to everlasting death*; and this they regarded as the basis of *judicial procedure*, according to which God 'ordains men to dishonour and wrath for their sin,' and having respect to man's own character and conduct.

Let it be further remarked, that while, according to this view, the term *predestination* could never with propriety be applied to the *lost*, the term *foreordination* might be applied to the *saved*, since they also are the subjects, in one sense, of judicial procedure. Accordingly there is no instance in the Confession of Faith where the term *predestination* is applied to the *lost*, though there are several instances where the term *foreordination*, or a kindred term, is applied to the *saved*. And let this also be marked, that the term *reprobation*, which is so liable to be misunderstood and applied in an offensive sense to the doctrine of predestination, is not even once used in the Confession of Faith and the Larger and Shorter Catechisms. Later writers on that doctrine have indeed employed that word, as older writers had done, and had thereby furnished occasion to the opponents of the doctrine to misrepresent it; but the Westminster Divines cautiously avoided the use of an offensive term, carefully selected such words as were best fitted to convey their meaning, and in every instance used them with the most strict and definite precision.[1]

Many other examples might be given of the remarkable accuracy of thought and language which forms a distinguished characteris-

---

1. In the Exposition it has been found necessary to use the term *reprobation*, in consequence of its frequent occurrence in the writings of the most eminent modern authors; who have, however, been careful to explain it, so as to guard against the harsh misconstruction of its meaning by prejudiced opponents. When so explained it is harmless; but it might have been as well, had a term so liable to be perverted never been employed.

tic of the Confession of Faith; but we must content ourselves with suggesting the line of investigation, leaving it to every reader to prosecute it for himself.

Another decided and great merit of the Confession consists in the clear and well-defined statement which it makes *of the principles on which alone can securely rest the great idea of the co-ordination, yet mutual support, of the civil and the ecclesiastical jurisdictions*. It is but too usual for people to misunderstand those parts of the Confession which treat of these jurisdictions – some accusing those passages of containing Erastian concessions, and others charging them with being either lawless or intolerant. The truth is, they favour no extreme. Proceeding upon the sacred rule – to render to Caesar what is Caesar's, and to God what is God's – they willingly ascribe to the civil magistrate a supreme power in the State: all that belongs to his province, not merely with regard to his due authority over the persons and property of men, but also with regard to what pertains to his own official mode of rendering homage to the King of kings. It is in this latter department of magisterial duty that what is called the power of the civil magistrate – *circa sacra* – *about* religious matters, consists. But there his province ends, and he has no power *in sacris* – *in* religious matters. This is most carefully guarded in the leading proposition of Chapter 30: 'The Lord Jesus Christ, as King and Head of his Church, hath therein appointed a government in the hands of Church Officers, distinct from the Civil Magistrate.'

The leading Erastians of that period, learned and subtle as they were, felt it impossible to evade the force of that proposition, and could but refuse to give to it the sanction of the Legislature. They could not, however, prevail upon the Assembly either to modify or suppress it; and there it remains, and must remain, as the unanswered and unanswerable refutation of the Erastian heresy by the Westminster Assembly of Divines.

In modern times it has been too much the custom of the opponents of Erastianism tacitly to grant the Erastian argument – or, at least, the principle on which it rests – by admitting, or even asserting, that if a Church be established, it must cease to have a separate and independent jurisdiction, and must obey the laws of the State, even in spiritual matters; but then declaring that, as this is evidently wrong, there ought to be no Established Church. There is more peril to both civil and religious liberty in this mode of evading Erastianism that is commonly perceived; for, if it were generally admitted that an Established Church ought to be subject, even in spiritual matters, to the civil jurisdiction of the State, then would civil rulers have a direct and admitted interest in establishing a Church, not for the sake of promoting Christianity, nor with the view of rendering homage to the Prince of the kings of the earth, but for the purpose of employing the Church as a powerful engine of State policy. That they would avail themselves of such an admission is certain; and this would necessarily tend to produce a perilous contest between the defenders of religious liberty and the supporters of arbitrary power; and if the issue should be the triumph of Erastianism, that issue would inevitably involve the loss of both civil and religious liberty in the blending of the two jurisdictions – which is the very essence of absolute despotism.

Of this the framers of our Confession were well aware; and, therefore, they strove to procure the well-adjusted and mutual counterpoise and co-operation of the two jurisdictions, as the best safeguards of both civil and religious liberty, and as founded on the express authority of the Word of God. It never yet has been proved, from either Scripture or reason, that they were wrong, although their views have been much misunderstood and grievously misrepresented. But, instead of prosecuting this topic, we refer to the comment on those chapters which treat of the civil magistrate, of synods, and of Church censures, as giving a very accurate and intelligible explanation of the doctrine of the Confession on these subjects.

The Confession of Faith has often been accused of *advocating intolerant and persecuting principles*. It is, however, in truth, equally free from latitudinarian laxity on the one hand, and intolerance on the other. An intelligent and candid perusal of chapter 20, 'On Christian Liberty, and Liberty of Conscience,' ought of itself to refute all such calumnies. The mind of man never produced a truer or nobler proposition than the following:

'God alone is Lord of the conscience, and hath left if free from the doctrines and commandments of men, which are in anything contrary to his Word, or beside it, in matters of faith or worship.'

The man who can comprehend, entertain, and act upon that principle can never arrogate an overbearing and intolerant authority over the conscience of his fellow-man, much less wield against him the weapons of remorseless persecution.

But there is a very prevalent and yet very false method of thinking, or pretending to think, respecting toleration and liberty of conscience. Many seem to be of the opinion that toleration consists in making no distinction between truth and error, but regarding them with equal favour. This opinion, if carefully analysed, would be found to be essentially of an infidel character. Many seem to think that by liberty of conscience is meant that every man should be at liberty to act in everything according to his own inclination, without regard to the feelings, convictions and rights of other men. This would, indeed, be to convert liberty into lawlessness, and to make conscience of licentiousness.

But the Confession proceeds upon the principle that truth can be distinguished from error, right from wrong; that though conscience cannot be compelled, it may be enlightened; and that when sinful, corrupt and prone to licentiousness, men may be lawfully restrained from the commission of such excesses as are offensive to public feeling, and injurious to the moral welfare of the community. If this be intolerance, it is a kind of intolerance of which none will complain but those who wish to be free from all restraint of law, human or divine. Nothing, in our opinion, but a wilful determination to misrepresent the sentiments expressed in the Confession of Faith, or a culpable degree of wilful ignorance respecting the true meaning of these sentiments, could induce any man to accuse it of favouring intolerant and persecuting principles. Certainly the conduct of those who framed it gave no countenance to such an accusation, though that calumny has been often and most pertinaciously asserted. On this point, also it would be well if people would take the trouble to ascertain what precise meaning the framers of the Confession gave to the words which they employed; for it is not doing justice to them and their work to adopt some modern acceptation of a term used by them in a different sense, and then to charge them with holding the sentiment conveyed by the modern use or misuse of that term. Yet this is the method almost invariably employed by the assailants of the Confession of Faith.

(3) In order to form a right conception of the Confession of Faith, it is absolutely necessary to have some acquaintance with the history of the period in which it was composed. A brief outline, however, is all that our present space can afford.

There was, from the beginning, a very strong and essential difference between the Reformed Churches of England and of Scotland; arising, in a great measure, out of the peculiar elements prevailing at the time in the respective kingdoms. In England, the Reformation was begun, conducted and stopped almost entirely according to the pleasure of the reigning sovereign. In Scotland, it was begun, carried forward and completed in spite of the determined opposition of the sovereign. In England, therefore, the will of the monarch was an essential element from the first, and continued to be so throughout the course of the Reformation; and the Church of England was accordingly based upon, and pervaded by, the evil influence of the Erastian principle, the sovereign being recognised as the supreme judge in causes ecclesiastical as well as in causes civil. The Church of Scotland assumed a very different basis, and gave her undivided allegiance to a far other King: she assumed as the sole rule the Word of God alone, and the whole Word of God, in all matters of doctrine, worship, government and discipline; and paid her allegiance to the Lord Jesus Christ, and to him alone, as the only Head and King of the Church. There was, therefore, in the Church of Scotland, from the first, a degree of spiritual independence, of true religious liberty, to which the Church of England never could attain.

This spiritual independence enjoyed by the Church of Scotland was by no means agreeable to James VI, who set himself to subvert it by every means which fraud (by him called 'king-craft') could devise, or force accomplish. He did not wholly succeed; though, by banishing the faithful and the fearless, and overawing the timid, he did manage to mould it somewhat into conformity with his arbitrary will, and imposed upon it a set of sycophantic and tyrannical prelates. His sterner but less deceitful son, Charles I, urged on by the narrow-minded and cruel Laud, seeking to complete what his father had begun, drove Scotland to the necessity of rising in defence of her liberties, civil and sacred. This gave rise to the great National Covenant of 1638, by which the people of almost the entire kingdom were knit to God and to each other, in a solemn bond for the maintenance and defence of sacred truth and freedom. The contest proceeding, a General Assembly was held at Glasgow towards the close of the same year, in which the system of Prelacy was abolished, and the Presbyterian Church of Scotland restored. In vain did the king attempt to overthrow this second Reformation, even by the extreme measure of an attempted invasion. The tide of war rolled back from the Scottish borders, and the Church and kingdom continued covenanted and free.

But a storm had been long gathering in England, and was ready to burst forth with uncontrollable might. Although the progress of the Reformation in England had been paralysed in all its elements, and stopped short long ere it had reached anything like completeness, still there were many who ardently desired to promote the greater purity of the English Church, by additional reforms in doctrine, worship and discipline. This could not be obtained; but the persevering efforts of these true Reformers gave rise to the Puritan party, as they were designated, and prepared for a more intense and formidable struggle.

On the other hand, while the Puritans were striving for further reform, what may be termed the Court party were receding further and further from the principles of the Reformation, and gradually approximating to those of Rome. The evil genius of the unhappy Laud brought matters to a crisis. His influence urged on the unfortunate king to the adoption of measures formidable alike to both civil and religious liberty.

The free spirit of England was at length aroused; and the contest between the despotic monarch and his free-hearted subjects began to assume the aspect of a civil war. The Parliament declared its own sittings permanent; and regarding the despotic principles and conduct of the bishops as the direct cause of the oppression under which they had so long groaned, passed a bill for the abolition of Prelacy. The king unsheathed the sword of civil war; and the English Parliament sought the assistance of Scotland, as necessary to preserve the liberties of both kingdoms.

The leading Scottish statesmen were well aware, that if the king should succeed in his attempt to overpower the English Parliament, he would immediately assail Scotland with increased power and determination. But at the same time, as their whole contest had been on sacred ground, they could not enter into an offensive and defensive alliance with the English Parliament for any less hallowed cause, or with any less important object in view. Had the king not gone beyond his own province, and invaded that of religion, they would have left his jurisdiction and authority unquestioned and untouched. For such reasons they would not frame with England a civil league, except it were based upon, and pervaded by, a religious covenant. To these views England consented; and the consequence was the formation of THE SOLEMN LEAGUE AND COVENANT – a document which we cannot help regarding as the noblest and best, in its essential nature and principles, of all that are recorded among the international transactions of the world.

A considerable time before this important event took place, the idea had been entertained in England that it would be extremely desirable to call a 'General synod of the most grave, pious, learned, and judicious divines,' for the purpose of deliberating respecting all things necessary for the peace and good government of the Church. This desire had been intimated as early as 1641; while it was not till June 12, 1643, that Parliament issued the Ordinance calling the Assembly. Although, therefore, the Solemn League and Covenant exercised no little influence in the deliberations of that Assembly, it was not the cause of that Assembly being held.

At the time when the Assembly was called together, there was no organized Church in England. Prelacy had been abolished, and no other form of Church government was in existence. It did not meet as a Church court, in any accurate sense of that expression, but was in reality merely an assembly of divines, called together in a case of extreme emergency, to consult, deliberate and advise, but not to exercise directly any judicial or ecclesiastical functions. This it is necessary to bear in mind, not for the purpose of casting any slight upon its character and proceedings, but for the purpose of showing how utterly groundless are the assertions of those who charge it with being constituted on an Erastian principle. It could not have met except under the protection of Parliament. It was not an ecclesiastical court at all; for it had no conformity with either the Episcopalian, Presbyterian or Congregational systems of Church government; it neither ruled the Parliament, nor was ruled by the Parliament; it deliberated, reasoned, voted, formed its own free judgment concerning the important matters before it, and gave the results as its advice to Parliament, to be followed or rejected by that body on its own responsibility. When the members of Parliament, who formed a constituent element of it as lay assessors, strove to introduce Erastian principles into its decisions, it met these attempts with strong, persevering, and invincible opposition – willing rather that its whole protracted labours should be rejected, than that, by any weak and sinful compromise, it should consent to the admission of an evil principle.

The greater part of the divines of whom the Westminster Assembly was composed were of the Puritans; but nearly all of these had been originally Episcopalians, so far, at least, as regarded their ordination, and their having held the ministerial office in connection with the Prelatic Establishment. The Independents were at first only five in number – Goodwin, Nye, Burroughs, Bridge and Simpson – but afterwards increased to about a dozen. There were only two of the divines that entertained Erastian principles – Lightfoot and Coleman. The Scottish commissioners, appointed to consult and deliberate, but not to vote, were six in number, four of whom were ministers – Henderson, Baillie, Rutherford and Gillespie; and two elders – Lord Maitland and Johnston of Warriston. The whole number of the Assembly amounted to one hundred and forty-two divines, and thirty-two lay assessors; but of this number seldom more than from sixty to eighty gave regular attendance. The Assembly was convened for the first time on Saturday, July 1, 1643, and it continued to hold regular meetings till February 22, 1649; when, instead of being formally dissolved, it was formed into a committee for the trial of ministers. In this character it continued to meet occasionally till March 25, 1652, when Cromwell forcibly dissolved the Long Parliament, and put an end to everything to which it had given existence. The number of sessions held by the Westminster Assembly was one thousand one hundred and sixty-three, and the period of its duration five years, six months, and twenty-one days.

The general result of the Westminster Assembly's deliberations was the framing of the Confession of Faith, the Directory for Public Worship, a Form of Church Government and Discipline, and the Catechisms, Larger and Shorter. When these had been completed, the Scottish Commissioners returned to their own country, laid the fruits of those labours in which they had been so long and arduously engaged before the General Assembly of the Church of Scotland, and obtained the ratification of those important productions.

So careful, however, was the Church of Scotland to guard

against the possible admission of anything that could be even suspected to have the slightest taint of Erastianism, that the Assembly, in its Act approving the Confession of Faith, of date August 27, 1647,[2] inserted an explanation of chapter 31, relating to the authority of the civil magistrate to call a synod – restricting that authority to the case of 'Churches not settled or constituted in point of government,' and protecting the right of the Church to hold assemblies on its own authority, 'by the intrinsical power derived from Christ,' even though the civil magistrate should deny his consent.

To this the Scottish Parliament offered no opposition; but the English Parliament refused, or at least declined, to ratify or sanction it, and re-committed certain particulars in discipline. These particulars were Section 4, Chapter 20, 'Of Christian Liberty, and Liberty of Conscience'; Chapter 30, 'Of Church Censures'; and Chapter 31, 'Of Synods and Councils.' Let the intelligent and candid reader peruse carefully the above-named passages, and he cannot but perceive the folly, absurdity, or perverse malevolence of those who accuse the Confession of Faith of being tainted with intolerance and Erastianism; since the very passages on which such persons pretend to found their accusations were those which the decidedly Erastian, and not peculiarly tolerant Parliament of England refused to sanction. It is painful to be constrained even to allude to the continued fabrication of such calumnious charges, and that, too, by some who either do know, or ought to know, that they are utterly untrue. 'What shall I do in order to become famous?' said an ambitious youth to an ancient sophist. 'Kill a man who is famous already, and then your name will be always mentioned along with his,' was the sophist's reply. On some such principle those men seem to act, who charge the Confession of Faith with intolerance, as if that were the ready way to procure renown. But the sophist neglected to draw the distinction between fame and infamy; and it may ultimately appear that those who seek celebrity by attempting to kill the reputation of the Westminster divines have committed a similar mistake.

But it is not necessary here to prosecute the vindication of the Westminster Assembly and the Confession of Faith. That has been effectually done recently by various publications, to which the reader is referred. This only would we further state, with regard to

---

2. The reader will find this Act in Appendix 1.

such accusations, that Presbyterians in general, and Scottish Presbyterians in particular, have long been guilty of the most ungrateful neglect and disregard towards the memories of the truly great and good men by whom the admirable subordinate standards of their Church were framed. It would be absurd to ascribe perfection either to the men or to their works; but it is worse than absurd to permit them to be vilified by assailants of all kinds, certainly in no respect the equals of these men, without uttering one word in their defence. The best mode of defending them, however, is to draw to them the quickened attention of the public mind. Let them be read and studied profoundly; let them be exposed to the most minute and sifting examination; let every proposition be severely tested by the strictest laws of reasoning and by the supreme standard of the Word of God. Whatever cannot endure this investigation, let it be cast aside, as tried in the balance and found wanting; for this is only consistent with its own frank admission, that 'all synods and councils, since the apostles' times, whether general or particular, may err, and many have erred; therefore they are not to be made the rule of faith or practice, but to be used as a help in both.' But so far as it does stand an examination so searching – and of that we have no fear – let it no longer be exposed to the wanton assaults of rude ignorance, guileful calumny, or bitter malevolence. This, and nothing less than this, is due to the memory of the illustrious dead, and to the living Confession of their Faith, and to our own reverential attachment to the sacred doctrines therein stated and maintained.

(4) Our prefatory remarks were begun by directing attention to the necessity for the existence of Creeds and Confessions, and the important purposes subserved by these subordinate standards; and we resume that view for the purpose of stating the inference to which it ought to lead.

Since a Church cannot exist without some Confession or mode of ascertaining that its members are agreed in their general conception of what they understand divine truth to mean; and since the successive rise of heretical opinions, and their successive refutation, necessarily tends to an enlargement of the Confession, and at the same time to an increasing development of the knowledge of divine truth, ought it not to follow, that the various

Confessions of separate Churches would have a constant tendency to approximate, till they should all blend in one harmonious Confession of one Church general?

No-one who has studied a harmony of Protestant Confessions can hesitate to admit that this is a very possible, as it is a most desirable, result. When, further, we rise to that spiritual element to which also our attention has been directed, we may anticipate an increasing degree of enlightenment in the Christian Church, bestowed by the Holy Spirit, in answer to the earnest prayers of sincere and humble faith, which will greatly tend to hasten forward and secure an amount of Christian unity in faith and love far beyond what has existed since the times of the apostles. Entertaining this pleasant idea, we might expect both that the latest Confession of Faith framed by a Protestant Church would be the most perfect, and also that it might form a basis of evangelical union to the whole Church.

To some this may seem a startling, or even an extravagant idea. But let it be remembered, that, owing to a peculiar series of unpropitious circumstances, the Westminster Assembly's Confession of Faith has never yet been adequately known to the Christian Churches. By the Scottish Church alone was it fully received; and in consequence of the various events which have since befallen that Church, comparatively little attention has been paid to the Confession of Faith till recent times. It is now, we trust, in the process of becoming more known and better understood than formerly; and we feel assured that the more it is known and the better it is understood, the more highly will its great and varied excellences be estimated. This will tend, at the same time, to direct to it the attention of other Churches; and we cannot help anticipating the degree of surprise which will be felt by many ingenuous minds, that they had remained so long unacquainted with a production of such remarkable value.

Should this be the case, as we venture to hope, and should any serious objections be entertained by fair and candid minds with regard to some expressions in the Confession, there could be no great difficulty in appending to these some slight verbal explanations, showing what they were intended to mean, and how we understand them; for we are fully persuaded that by far the greater proportion of objections that could be entertained by any evangelical Christian or Church would relate merely to peculiar terms, and would be founded almost entirely on a misconception of what meaning these terms were intended to convey. For our own part, we wish no alteration, even of a single word; but neither do we think it necessary to allow the erroneous interpretation of a word to operate as an obstacle to the reception by other Churches of our Confession of Faith, if, by the explanation of that word, the obstacle might be removed.

Such a result would be the realization of the great idea entertained by the leading members of the Westminster Assembly, and especially by the Scottish commissioners – with whom, indeed, it originated. No narrow and limited object could satisfy the desires and anticipations of these enlightened and large-hearted men. With one comprehensive glance they surveyed the condition of Christendom and the world – marked its necessities, and contemplated the remedy. Thus they formed the great and even sublime idea of a Protestant union throughout Christendom; not merely for the purpose of counterbalancing Popery, but in order to purify, strengthen and unite all true Christian Churches; so that, with combined energy and zeal, they might go forth, in glad compliance with the Redeemer's commands, teaching all nations, and preaching the everlasting gospel to every creature under heaven.

Such was the magnificent conception of men whom it has been too much the fashion to stigmatize as narrow-minded bigots. It is not in the heart of a bigot that a love able to embrace Christendom could be cherished – it is not in the mind of a bigot that an idea of such moral sublimity could be conceived. It may be said, no doubt, that this idea was premature. Premature it was in one sense; for it could not be then realized; but the statement of it was not premature, for it was the statement of the grand result which ought to have been produced by the Reformation. In still another sense it was not premature, any more than it is premature to sow the seed in spring from which we expect to reap the autumnal harvest. The seed must be sown before the harvest can be produced – the idea must be stated before it can be realized. It must then be left to work its way into the mind of man – to grow, and strengthen, and enlarge, till in due time it shall produce its fruit in its season.

May it not be hoped that the fruit-bearing season is at hand? All things seem hastening forward to some mighty change or development. On all sides the elements of evil are mustering with almost preternatural rapidity and power.

Popery has, to an unexpected degree, recovered from its deadly wound and its exhausted weakness, and is putting forth its destructive energies in every quarter of the world.

In England the dread aspect of Laudean Prelacy has re-appeared – called, indeed, by a new name, but displaying all the formidable characteristics of its predecessor – the same in its lofty pretensions, in its Popish tendencies, in its supercilious contempt of every other Church, and in its persecuting spirit.

The civil government appears to be impelled by something like infatuation, and is introducing, or giving countenance to, measures that are darkly ominous to both civil and religious liberty, as if hastening onward to a crisis which all may shudder to contemplate. The masses of the community are in a state ripe for any convulsion, however terrible, having been left for generations uneducated and uninstructed in religious truth.

The Scottish Ecclesiastical Establishment has been rent asunder; its constitution has been changed, or rather subverted; and those who firmly maintained the principles of the Church of Scotland have been constrained to separate from the State, in order to preserve these principles unimpaired. The Church of Scotland is again disestablished, as she has been in former times; but she is free: free to maintain all those sacred principles bequeathed to her by reformers and divines and martyrs; free to offer to all other evangelical Churches the right hand of brotherly love and fellowship; free to engage with them in the formation of a great evangelical union, on the firm basis of sacred and eternal truth.

Surely these concurring events are enough to constrain all who are able to comprehend them, to long for some sure rallying ground on which the defenders of religious truth and liberty may plant their standard. Such rallying ground we think the Confession of Faith would afford, were its principles carefully considered and fully understood. And we would fondly trust we may cherish the hope of at length accomplishing the Christian enterprise for which the Westminster Assembly met together, and of realizing the great idea which filled the minds of its most eminent Christian patriots.

The errors which prevented the success of the Westminster Assembly may be to us beacons, both warning from danger and guiding on to safety. In their case, political influence and intrigue formed one baneful element of deadly power. Let all political influence be distrusted and avoided, and let political intrigue be utterly unknown in all our religious deliberations. In times of trouble and alarm, 'Trust not in princes, nor in the sons of men,' with its divine counterpart, 'Trust in the Lord, and stay yourselves upon your God,' should be the watchword and reply of all true Christian Churches.

Dissensions among brethren, groundless jealousies, and misconstructions, and want of openness and candour, were grievously pernicious to the Westminster Assembly. If the Presbyterians and the Independents could have banished the spirit of dissension, expelled all petty jealousy, and laid their hearts open to each other in godly simplicity and sincerity, all the uniformity that was really necessary might have been easily obtained. And if all truly evangelical Christians – whether they be Presbyterians, or Independents, or Baptists, or Methodists, or Episcopalians, such as some that could be named – would but give full scope to their already existing and strong principles and feelings of faith and hope and love, there could be little difficulty in framing such a Christian union – term it Presbyterian or Evangelical, so that it be truly scriptural – as might be able, by the blessing and the help of God, to stem and bear back the growing and portentous tide of Popery and Infidelity, that threaten, with their proud waves, once more to overwhelm the world.

Has not the time for this great evangelical and scriptural union come? It is impossible for any one to look abroad upon the general aspect of the world with even a hasty glance, without perceiving indications of an almost universal preparation for some great event. The nations of the earth are still – not in peace, but like wearied combatants, resting on their arms a brief breathing space, that, with recovered strength and quickened animosity, they may spring anew to the mortal struggle. During this fallacious repose there has been, and there is, an exertion of the most intense and restless activity, by principles the most fiercely hostile, for the acquisition of partisans. Despotism and Democracy, Superstition and Infidelity, have alike been mustering their powers and calling forth their energies, less apparently for mutual destruction, according to their wont and nature, than in order to form an unnatural coalition and conspiracy against the very existence of free, pure and spiritual Christianity.

Nor, in one point of view, has Christianity been recently lying supine and dormant. Many a noble enterprise for the extension of the gospel at home and abroad has been planned and executed; and the great doctrines of saving truth have been clearly explained and boldly proclaimed, with earnest warmth and uncompromising faithfulness. A time of refreshing also has come from the presence of the Lord – a spirit of revival has been poured forth upon the thirsty Church – and the hearts of Christian brethren have learned to melt and blend with a generous and rejoicing sympathy, to which they had too long been strangers.

Can all these things be beheld and passed lightly over, as leading to nothing, and pretending nothing? That were little short of blind infatuation. What they do fully portend it were presumptuous to say; but it is not difficult to say for what they form an unprecedented preparation. What now prevents a worldwide evangelical and scriptural union? 'All things are prepared, come to the marriage.' 'If ye love ME, love one another.' 'Because HE laid down his life for us, we also ought to lay down our lives for the brethren.' Had these been fully the principles and rules of conduct of the Westminster Assembly, its great idea might have been realized. Let them be those that animate and guide all Christian Churches now. They have been felt in our great unions for prayer; they should be felt by all who venerate and can understand the standards of the Westminster Assembly. And if they be, then may we not only accomplish the object of its Solemn League and Covenant, concur in its Confession of Faith, and realize its great idea of a general evangelical union; but we may also, if such be the will of our Divine Head and King, be mightily instrumental in promoting the universal propagation of the gospel, and drawing down from above the fulfilled answer of that sacred prayer in which we all unite: 'THY KINGDOM COME: THY WILL BE DONE ON EARTH AS IT IS IN HEAVEN.'

CHAPTER 1

THE HOLY SCRIPTURE

Section 1

Although the light of nature, and the works of creation and providence, do so far manifest the goodness, wisdom, and power of God, as to leave men inexcusable (Romans 2:14,15; 1:19,20; Psalm 19:1-3; Romans 1:32; 2:1); yet they are not sufficient to give that knowledge of God, and of his will, which is necessary unto salvation (1 Corinthians 1:21; 2:13,14): therefore it pleased the Lord, at sundry times, and in divers manners, to reveal himself, and to declare that his will unto his Church (Hebrews 1:1); and afterwards, for the better preserving and propagating of the truth, and for the more sure establishment and comfort of the Church against the corruption of the flesh, and the malice of Satan and of the world, to commit the same wholly unto writing (Proverbs 22:19-21; Luke 1:3,4; Romans 15:4; Matthew 4:4,7,10; Isaiah 8:19,20); which maketh the Holy Scripture to be most necessary (2 Timothy 3:15; 2 Peter 1:19); those former ways of God's revealing his will unto his people being now ceased (Hebrews 1:1,2).

Exposition

There are few doctrines of supernatural revelation that have not, in one period or another, been denied or controverted; and it is a peculiar excellence of the Westminster Confession of Faith, that its compilers have stated the several articles in terms the best calculated, not only to convey an accurate idea of sacred truths, but to guard against contrary errors. In opposition, on the one hand, to those who deny the existence of natural religion, and, on the other hand, in opposition to Deists, who maintain the sufficiency of the light of nature to guide men to eternal happiness, this section asserts:

(1) That a knowledge of the existence of God, and a number of his perfections, is attainable by the light of nature, and the works of creation and providence.

(2) That the light of nature is insufficient to give fallen man that knowledge of God, and of his will, which is necessary unto salvation.

(3) That God has been pleased to grant to his Church a supernatural revelation of his will.

(4) That this revelation has been committed to writing, and that the Holy Scripture is most necessary, the ancient modes of God's revealing his will unto his people being now ceased.

First. That there is a God is the first principle of all religion, whether natural or revealed, and we are here taught that the being of God and a number of his perfections may be discovered by the light of nature. By the word 'God' is meant a Being of infinite perfection; self-existent and independent; the Creator, Preserver, and Lord of all things.

> It is true, indeed, that to give a perfect definition of God is impossible, neither can our finite reason hold any proportion with infinity; but yet a sense of this Divinity we have, and the first and common notion of it consists in these three particulars – that it is a Being of itself, and independent from any other; that it is that upon which all things that are made depend; that it governs all things.[1]

When we affirm that the being of God may be discovered by the light of nature, we mean that the senses and the reasoning powers, which belong to the nature of man, are able to give him so much light as to manifest that there is a God. By our senses we are acquainted with his works, and by his works our reason may be led to trace out that more excellent Being who made them. This the Scripture explicitly asserts:

> That which may be known of God is manifest in them (i.e. in men), for God hath showed it unto them. For the invisible things of him from the creation of the world are clearly seen, being understood by the things that are made, even his eternal power and Godhead (Romans 1:19, 20).

The existence of God is not less indubitable than our own existence. Every man knows, with absolute certainty, that he himself exists. He knows also that he had a beginning, and that he derived his being from a succession of creatures like himself. However far back he supposes this succession to be carried, it does not afford a satisfactory account of the cause of his existence. His

---

1. Pearson on the Creed, Art. 1.

ancestors were no more able to make themselves than he was; he must, therefore, ascend to some original Being, who had no beginning, but had life in himself from all eternity, and who gives life and being to all other creatures. This is the Being whom we call God. But

> we are not only conscious of our own existence, we also know that there exists a great variety of other things, both material and spiritual. It is equally inconceivable that these things should have existed from all eternity in their present state, or that they should have fallen into this state by chance; and consequently, as there was a time when they did not exist, and as it was impossible for them to produce themselves, it follows that there were some exterior agent or creator to whom the world owed its beginning and form: that agent or creator we call God.[2]

The amazing works of providence, the regular and unerring motions of the heavenly luminaries for so many thousand years, the never failing return of summer and winter, seed-time and harvest, day and night, and innumerable other wonders, clearly manifest the existence of the Supreme Being, who upholds and governs all things. In the works of creation and providence, too, we see the clearest characters of infinite power, wisdom, and goodness.

> The more that we know of these works, we are the more sensible that in nature there is not only an exertion of power, but an adjustment of means to an end, which is what we call wisdom, and an adjustment of means to the end of distributing happiness to all the creatures, which is the highest conception that we can form of goodness.[3]

As the marks of a Deity are so clearly impressed upon all the works of creation, so we learn from the history of former times, and from the observation of modern travellers, that in every country, and at every period, some idea of a Superior Being, and some species of divine worship, have prevailed. The persuasion of a God is universal, and the most ancient records do not conduct us to a period in the history of any people when it did not exist. That truth must certainly be a dictate of nature, to which all nations have consented. There is much practical Atheism in the world, but it may be questioned whether any have been able entirely to erase from their mind the impression of a Supreme Being. It is, indeed,

---

2. Pretyman's *Elements of Christian Theology*, vol. 2, p. 62.
3. Hill's *Lectures*, vol. 1, p. 9.

affirmed: 'The fool hath said in his heart, There is no God' (Psalm 14:1); but it is rather the wish of the unsanctified affections, than the proper determination of the deliberate judgment, which these words express. Though some may in words disavow the being of God, yet the terrors which they feel in their own breasts, especially upon the commission of some daring wickedness, force upon them the conviction that there is a Supreme Being, who will judge and punish the transgressors of his law. Conscience, indeed, is in the place of a thousand witnesses to this truth. The Apostle Paul, who tells us that 'there is a law written in the hearts of men', adds that 'their conscience bears witness, and their thoughts accuse, or else excuse one another' (Romans 2:15). Conscience reproves, condemns, and scourges a man for his wicked deeds, and anticipates the account which he must give of all his actions, and thus demonstrates that there is a God. The Scriptures, accordingly, take the being of God for granted, and instead of first proving that there is a God, begin with telling us what God did: 'In the beginning God created the heavens and the earth' (Genesis 1:1).

This knowledge of God, which is attainable by the light of nature, serves various useful purposes. It is a testimony of the goodness of God towards all his creatures (Acts 14:17). As it shows men their duty, and convinces them of sin, in many points; so it has had some influence on mankind, at least by the fear of punishment, in restraining them from extreme degrees of wickedness (Romans 2:14, 15). It excites men to seek after a clearer revelation of God, and prepares the way for their receiving the gospel of his grace (Acts 17:27). It serves to vindicate the conduct of God as a righteous governor, in his severe dealing with obstinate sinners, both here and hereafter. This will leave them without excuse in the great day, when God shall judge the secrets of all hearts (Romans 1:20, 21; 2:15, 16). But the knowledge of God by the light of nature being obscure and defective,

The *second* proposition asserts the insufficiency of the light of nature to give fallen man that knowledge of God, and of his will, which is necessary unto salvation. The extent of knowledge, in regard to the things of God, which man is capable of attaining, cannot be ascertained from the writings of modern Deists, who, how much soever they affect to despise supernatural revelation, have derived the greater part of their sentiments respecting God, and moral obligation, from that source. The history of past times

and ancient nations shows, that the greater part of mankind, in
every country destitute of supernatural revelation, knew but little
of the true God, or of their duty towards him. 'The world by
wisdom knew not God'; even the learned Athenians were so
ignorant of the true God that they dedicated an altar 'to the
unknown God'. The heathen world was sunk in the most abominable idolatry and gross superstition. Not only were the heavenly
luminaries deified, but almost every creature on earth was worshipped as a god, and innumerable imaginary beings had divine
honours paid them. Though some heathen philosophers attained
some considerable knowledge of the nature of God, and inculcated
upon their followers several moral virtues, this did not prevent
them from complying with the idolatry of their country, or deter
them from the commission of the most gross and unnatural crimes
(Romans 1:21-28). From the light of nature we may learn that there
is evil both moral and penal in the world; but as to the question how
sin entered into the world, and how deliverance from it may be
obtained, the light of nature is entirely silent. It shows men their sin
and misery, but it discovers not the plain and certain way of
salvation. The Scriptures assure us, that there is no salvation for
sinful men in any other name but that of Jesus Christ – that there
is no salvation through him but by faith, and that there can be no
faith nor knowledge of Christ but by revelation (Acts 4:12; Mark
16:16; Romans 10:14-17). The Scripture affirms, in terms the
most express, that 'where there is no vision,' or revelation, 'the
people perish'; and it describes those who are destitute of divine
revelation, as 'having no hope, and without God in the world'
(Proverbs 29:18; Ephesians 2:12). God does nothing in vain; and
were the light of nature sufficient to guide men to eternal happiness, it cannot be supposed that a divine revelation would have
been given. But –

The *third* proposition asserts, that God has been pleased to
grant to his Church a supernatural revelation of his will. It cannot
be considered as a thing incredible that God should make a
revelation of his mind and will to men. Has he framed men so as
that they should be capable of making known their mind to one
another, by speech and by writing? And shall it be deemed a thing
incredible that he should communicate his mind to them in a
similar way?

It was, indeed, out of infinite love, mercy, and compassion, that God would at all reveal his mind and will unto sinners. He might for ever have locked up the treasures of his wisdom and prudence, wherein he abounds towards us in his Word, in his own eternal breast. He might have left all the sons of men unto that woeful darkness, whereinto by sin they had cast themselves, and kept them, with the angels who sinned before them, under the chains and power of it, unto the judgment of the great day. But from infinite love he condescended to reveal himself and his will unto us.[4]

The mind of God was not revealed to the Church all at once, but by several parts and degrees, as in his infinite wisdom he saw meet. He spake unto the fathers by the prophets 'at sundry times, and in divers manners' (Hebrews 1:1). The 'sundry times' may be understood 'as referring to the matter of ancient revelation, given in different parts, and at different times, thus conveying the idea of the gradual development of truth in different ages, and by different persons'; and the 'divers manners' may be understood 'as indicating the various ways in which these revelations were communicated – by dreams, visions, symbols, Urim and Thummim, prophetic ecstasy, etc.'[5] Under the new dispensation, God has completed the whole revelation of his will by his Son, and no new revelation is to be expected to the end of the world.

The *fourth* proposition asserts, that this revelation has been committed to writing. Until the time of Moses, or for a period of two thousand five hundred years, no part of the sacred books was written. God then communicated his will to the Church by immediate revelation; and the long lives of the patriarchs enabled them to preserve uncorrupted what was so revealed, and to transmit it from generation to generation. Two persons might have conveyed it down from Adam to Abraham; for Methuselah lived above three hundred years while Adam was yet alive, and Shem lived almost a hundred years with Methuselah, and above a hundred years with Abraham. But after the lives of men were shortened, and revelation was greatly enlarged, it pleased God that the whole of his revealed will should be committed to writing, that the Church might have a standing rule of faith and practice, by which all doctrines might be examined, and all actions regulated – that sacred truth might be preserved uncorrupted and entire – that it might be propagated

4. Owen on Hebrews, 1:1.
5. Stuart's Commentary on the Hebrews 1:1.

throughout the several nations of the earth, and might be conveyed down to all succeeding generations. Though, in the infancy of the Church, God taught his people without the written Word, yet now that his former ways of revealing his will to his people have ceased, the Holy Scripture, or written Word, is most necessary. Without this the Church would be left to the uncertainty of tradition and oral teaching; but the written Word is a sure test of doctrines, and a light in a dark place, both of which are most necessary (Isaiah 8:20; 2 Peter 1:19).

Section 2

Under the name of Holy Scripture, or the Word of God written, are now contained all the Books of the Old and New Testaments, which are these:

Of the Old Testament: Genesis, Exodus, Leviticus, Numbers, Deuteronomy, Joshua, Judges, Ruth, 1 Samuel, 2 Samuel, 1 Kings, 2 Kings, 1 Chronicles, 2 Chronicles, Ezra, Nehemiah, Esther, Job, Psalms, Proverbs, Ecclesiastes, The Song of Solomon, Isaiah, Jeremiah, Lamentations, Ezekiel, Daniel, Hosea, Joel, Amos, Obadiah, Jonah, Micah, Nahum, Habakkuk, Zephaniah, Haggai, Zechariah, Malachi.

Of the New Testament: Matthew, Mark, Luke, John, Acts of the Apostles, Epistle to the Romans, 1 Corinthians, 2 Corinthians, Galatians, Ephesians, Philippians, Colossians, 1 Thessalonians, 2 Thessalonians, 1 Timothy, 2 Timothy, Titus, Philemon, Epistle to the Hebrews, Epistle of James, 1 Peter, 2 Peter, 1 John, 2 John, 3 John, Jude, Book of the Revelation.

All which are given by inspiration of God, to be the rule of faith and life (Luke 16:29, 31; Ephesians 2:20; Revelation 22:18, 19; 2 Timothy 3:16).

Section 3

The Books commonly called Apocrypha, not being of divine inspiration, are no part of the canon of the Scripture; and, therefore, are of no authority in the Church of God, nor to be any otherwise approved or made use of, than other human writings (Luke 24:27, 44; Romans 3:2; 2 Peter 1:21).

Exposition

These sections relate to the true canon, and the divine inspiration of the Holy Scriptures. In opposition to the Romish Church, which reckons the apocryphal books of equal authority with the Scriptures, it is asserted that these books are no part of the canon of the Scripture; and in opposition to the Deists, who deny that the Scriptures of the Old and New Testaments are the Word of God, it is affirmed that all the sacred books are given by inspiration of God.

The term *Scriptures* signifies *writings* in general, but is appropriated to the Word of God, which is also, by way of eminency, called the Bible, or *book*, because it is incomparably the best of all books. The sacred books are divided into the Old Testament and the New Testament. The former includes those books which were written under the *old dispensation* of the covenant of grace, or prior to the incarnation of the Son of God; the latter includes those books which were written after the commencement of the *new dispensation*, or posterior to the advent of Christ. The Apostle Paul lays a foundation for this distinction; for he uses the phrases Old Testament and New Testament, and in one instance designates the writings of Moses and the prophets by the former title (2 Corinthians 3:14). The word *canon* literally signifies a rule, and was early used to designate the Inspired Scriptures, which form a perfect rule of faith and life.

The Sacred Scriptures are now collected into one volume, but that volume contains a considerable number of separate books, written by different persons, and in different ages. How, then, do we ascertain the authenticity and genuineness of each of these books, and why do we receive them as canonical, to the exclusion of all others? In determining a question of this kind, we must employ the same method which we follow when the genuineness of any other book is the subject of investigation. How do we know that the books which bear the names of Homer, Horace, Tacitus, and Livy were really composed by them, but by the uniform testimony of all succeeding ages. In the same way do we ascertain that the writings of the Apostles and Evangelists are genuine; we have the testimony of their contemporaries and immediate successors, who are the most competent witnesses in this case. The task of searching the records of antiquity has been undertaken by learned men, and executed with great industry and zeal. The result of their inquiries is, that the books now included in the New Testament were received as inspired by the primitive Church, and numerous passages were quoted from them by the earliest Christian writers; that catalogues of these books, which coincide with ours, are inserted in the works of different authors who flourished in the third and fourth centuries; and that these books were publicly read in Christian congregations, and were continually appealed to by Christian writers, as the standard of faith, and the supreme judge of controversies. The canon of the Old Testament is ascertained by a short process: we know that the Jews arranged their sacred books into three classes, the Law, the Prophets, and the Hagiography, or holy writings. Now, our Lord, just before his ascension, thus addressed his disciples:

> These are the words which I spake unto you, while I was yet with you, that all things must be fulfilled which were written in the law of Moses, and in the prophets, and in the psalms concerning me (Luke 24:44).

The Psalms are here put for the Hagiography, probably because they were the principal book, or occupied the first place in that division. Our Lord, by adopting this common division of the sacred books, which comprehended all the Hebrew Scriptures, ratified the canon of the Old Testament, as it was received by the Jews. This, however, does not determine what particular books were then included in the Sacred Volume; but on this point we have the testimony of the Jewish historian, Josephus, who indeed does not name the books of the Old Testament, but he numbers them, and so describes them that there is scarcely room for any mistake. His testimony is corroborated by that of several of the early Christian fathers, who have furnished us with catalogues of the books of the Old Testament, from which it appears, that the canon then existing was the same as that which we now possess. Besides, a Greek translation of the Old Testament, known by the name of *The Septuagint*, was made two hundred and seventy years before the Christian era, in which are the same books that are at present found in the Hebrew copies.

The books commonly called *Apocrypha*, were never admitted into the list of canonical books, until the Council of Trent, at its fourth session, 1546, placed them in the same rank with the inspired writings. They are rejected by the Protestant Churches for the following reasons:

(1) The Jews, to whom the oracles of God were committed, and who were never blamed for unfaithfulness to their trust, never acknowledged these books to be of divine authority.

(2) They were not written in the Hebrew, but in the Greek language, and the authors of them were posterior to Malachi, in whom, according to the universal testimony of the Jews, the spirit of prophecy ceased.

(3) No part of these books is quoted by Christ or his apostles, nor a single word found in all the New Testament from which it can

be inferred that such books were in existence.

(4) These books contain many things erroneous, superstitious, and immoral; and some of the writers, instead of advancing a claim to inspiration, acknowledge their own weakness, and apologise for their defects.

The Church of England, though she does not receive the apocryphal books as canonical Scripture, and therefore does not 'apply them to establish any doctrine', yet she directs certain portions of them to be read in the church, 'for example of life, and instruction of manners'. Now, as these portions are read promiscuously with the lessons taken from the canonical books, and no notice is given to the people that they are selected from the Apocrypha, they are in reality undistinguished from the inspired writings; and however good and instructive these apocryphal lessons may be, it never can be justified that they should thus be put on a level with the Word of God.

The Holy Scripture is called the *Word of God*, because it is given by inspiration of God.

> The possibility of inspiration seems to be granted by all who profess to be Christians, though there is a great diversity of opinion with respect to its nature and degrees, as applied to the Scriptures. Some are of opinion that the inspiration of the Scriptures amounted to nothing more than a mere superintendence over the minds of the sacred writers, so as to prevent them from publishing gross errors. Others go a little further, and maintain that, besides superintendence, the understanding of the several writers were enlarged – that their conceptions were elevated above the measure of ordinary men – and that with their minds thus elevated, they were left to their own judgment both as to matter and words. The advocates of plenary inspiration, again, maintain that the Holy Spirit suggested to the minds of the persons inspired, not only the matter to be communicated, but also the words in which the communication was to be made. A fourth party are for taking in all these supposed kinds of inspiration now mentioned; and they maintain that the sacred writers sometimes wrote under mere superintendence, sometimes under superintendence accompanied with a high elevation of conception, and at other times under a divine suggestion, or what is called plenary inspiration, according to the nature of the subject on which they wrote.[6]

At no remote period, the plenary and verbal inspiration of the Scriptures was very generally abandoned. Events, however, have

6. Stevenson on the *Offices of Christ*, p. 50-51.

occurred of late years, which have occasioned a more thorough
investigation of the subject; and the most eminent writers who
have treated of it more lately, maintain the plenary inspiration of
the sacred books in opposition to those who hold that it was merely
partial and occasional, and their verbal inspiration, in opposition
to those who hold that only the sentiments or matter, and not the
words, are inspired.

We are humbly of opinion that inspiration, as employed in communicating the sacred oracles to men, *is only of one kind*, and that this is
the inspiration of suggestion, according to which not only the matter,
but the words also, were communicated to the minds of the sacred
writers.

(1) The Scriptures themselves take notice of only one kind of
inspiration, and represent it as extending to all the parts of Scripture
– to those which are historical and moral, as well as to those which are
prophetical and doctrinal (2 Timothy 3:16, 17; 2 Peter 1:21).

(2) There must have been more than an enlargement of the
understanding, and an elevation of conception in inspiration, since a
great many of the things were such as could not have entered into the
hearts of men or of angels, had they not been suggested to the mind
by the Divine Spirit. Of this description were the events foretold by
the sacred writers many years before they took place, and the whole
of the doctrines that relate to the supernatural plan of man's redemption (1 Corinthians 2:9, 10).

(3) For similar reasons we must insist for the suggestion not only
of the ideas, but also of the words of Scripture. To us it is altogether
inconceivable how the sacred writers, who, like other men, were
accustomed to think in words, could have the ideas suggested to their
own minds, except in words; or how they could have written intelli-
gibly about future events, with which they could have had no previous
acquaintance, and on doctrinal subjects, far above their comprehension, had not the language, as well as the matter, been furnished to
them by Divine suggestion (1 Corinthians 2:13).

(4) If what has been called the inspiration of superintendence and
elevation, could in any case be deemed to have been sufficient, it must
have been in cases where the sacred writers may be supposed to have
had a prior acquaintance, from other sources, with the subjects on
which they were called to write; such as subjects of morality and
history. But even in these cases, plenary inspiration seems to have
been absolutely necessary. With regard to moral subjects, it may be
observed, that although the remains of the law of nature furnish man
with certain moral sentiments, yet, in his fallen state, his views of right
and wrong are so dark and confused, that there is not, perhaps, any

case in which plenary inspiration was more necessary than this, in order that man might be furnished with a perfect rule of duty. With respect to history, where the facts recorded may be supposed to have been known by the sacred writers from their own observation, or from other authentic sources, it may be observed, in general, that sacred history differs, in the main ends proposed by it, from profane history.'

While profane history has for its object only the civil and political benefit of individuals and nations, the inspired historians propose a much higher aim – the advancement of salvation in subserviency to the glory of God in Christ – an aim which requires a manner of thinking and writing peculiar to itself.

'Neither does the variety of style found throughout the Scriptures form, in our apprehension, any valid objection to the doctrine of plenary inspiration. Though the inspired penmen were under infallible direction, both in regard to the sentiments to be communicated by them, and the phraseology best adapted to express these sentiments; yet the Holy Spirit, for wise reasons, seems to have accommodated his suggestions, so far as related to mere style, to the age in which they wrote, and their respective talents for composition.

(5) We observe further, in support of plenary inspiration, that unless it be admitted the Bible has no valid claim to be called the Word of God. The Scriptures frequently lay claim to a divine origin in support of their supreme authority as a rule of faith and manners; but if the sacred writers were only under what is called superintendence, we cannot see the justness of that claim. It would be a gross perversion of words, to call a man the author of a book, who had no hand in its composition further than merely guarding its real author from falling into gross error. The designation, *the Word of God*, must suggest to every unprejudiced mind, that the Bible is from God, both in respect of sentiment and expression. Nor does it render the matter any better to tell us, that though some parts of the Bible were written under the mere superintendence of the Spirit, yet others were written by the inspiration of suggestion; for this throws a suspicion over the whole, since it is impossible for us to determine what parts were dictated by plenary inspiration, and what parts were not. The safe way is to hold by the doctrine of the Bible itself, that inspiration is one in kind; that it is not a partial, but a full or plenary inspiration; and that this applies to the whole of the sacred volume. "All Scripture is given by inspiration of God." '[7]

---

7. Stevenson on the Offices of Christ, pp. 51-57. See also the admirable work of Professor Gaussen, on *The Plenary Inspiration of the Holy Scriptures*, which must set this question at rest.

Section 4

The authority of the Holy Scripture, for which it ought to be believed and obeyed, dependeth not upon the testimony of any man or Church, but wholly upon God (who is truth itself), the author thereof; and therefore, it is to be received, because it is the Word of God (2 Peter 1:19, 21; 2 Timothy 3:16; 1 John 5:9; 1 Thessalonians 2:13).

Section 5

We may be moved and induced by the testimony of the Church to an high and reverend esteem of the Holy Scripture (1 Timothy 3:15), and the heavenliness of the matter, the efficacy of the doctrine, the majesty of the style, the consent of all the parts, the scope of the whole, (which is to give all glory to God), the full discovery it makes of the only way of man's salvation, the many other incomparable excellencies, and the entire perfection thereof, are arguments whereby it doth abundantly evidence itself to be the Word of God; yet, notwithstanding our full persuasion and assurance of the infallible truth, and Divine authority thereof, is from the inward work of the Holy Spirit, bearing witness by and with the Word in our hearts (1 John 2:20, 27; John 16:13, 14; 1 Corinthians 2:10-12; Isaiah 59:21).

Exposition

These sections teach us, that the authority of the Scripture depends not upon any man or Church, but wholly upon God, the author thereof, and then points out the evidences that the Scripture is the Word of God. The first of these heads is stated in opposition to the Papists, who maintain that the authority of the Scriptures is derived from the Church. The absurdity of this idea is easily evinced. The true Church of Christ is founded on the Scriptures, and therefore the authority of the Scriptures cannot depend on the Church (Ephesians 2:20).

That the Holy Scripture is the Word of God, is proved both by external and internal evidences.

(1) The *external evidences* are such as these: The character of the sacred penmen – the miracles wrought by them, for the declared purpose of attesting their divine mission and inspiration – the exact accomplishment of numerous prophecies recorded in Scripture – the antiquity of the Scriptures, taken in connection with their wonderful preservation to this day – the effects produced by the Scriptures, effects which could never have been accomplished by the lessons of philosophy, nor the force of human laws – and the influence which the Scriptures have had in civilizing the most

barbarous nations, and in meliorating the condition of society at large, wherever the knowledge of them has been disseminated.

(2) The *internal evidences* are such as these: The incomparable sublimity of the doctrines contained in the Scriptures, and their revealing many truths which could not be discovered by nature or reason – the extent and purity of their precepts – the representation which they give of the character and moral administration of God – the exact adaptation of the revelation they contain to the state and wants of man – the entire harmony of their several parts, though written by different persons, and in different ages – the majesty of their style – and the scope and tendency of the whole to advance the glory of God, and secure the salvation of men. Such arguments as these may produce a rational conviction that the Scriptures are the Word of God; but it is only the Holy Spirit's effectual application of them to the heart, in their self-evidencing light and power, that can produce a cordial and saving persuasion of it. 'He that believeth hath the witness in himself.' Though many who believe are not qualified to demonstrate the inspiration of the Scriptures by rational arguments, yet, by the experience they have of their power and efficacy on their own hearts, they are infallibly assured that they are the Word of God; and they can no more be convinced, by the reasonings and objection of infidels, that the Scriptures are the production of men, than they can be persuaded that men created the sun, whose light they behold, and by whose beams they are cheered.

Section 6
The whole counsel of God, concerning all things necessary for his own glory, man's salvation, faith, and life, is either expressly set down in Scripture, or by good and necessary consequence may be deduced from Scripture: unto which nothing at any time is to be added, whether by new revelations of the Spirit, or traditions of men (2 Timothy 3:15-17; Galatians 1:8, 9; 2 Thessalonians 2:2). Nevertheless, we acknowledge the inward illumination of the Spirit of God to be necessary for the saving understanding of such things as are revealed in the Word (John 6:45; 1 Corinthians 2:9-12); and that there are some circumstances concerning the worship of God, and government of the Church, common to human actions and societies, which are to be ordered by the light of nature and Christian prudence, according to the general rules of the Word, which are always to be observed (1 Corinthians 11:13, 14; 1 Corinthians 14:26, 40).

Section 7

All things in Scripture are not alike plain in themselves, nor alike clear unto all (2 Peter 3:16); yet those things which are necessary to be known, believed, and observed, for salvation, are so clearly propounded and opened in some place of Scripture or other, that not only the learned, but the unlearned, in a due use of the ordinary means, may attain unto a sufficient understanding of them (Psalm 119:105, 130).

Exposition

These sections relate to the perfection and perspicuity of the Scriptures.

(1) In regard to the *perfection*, or sufficiency, of the Scriptures, it is acknowledged that there are some circumstances concerning the worship of God, and government of the Church, in regard to which no express injunctions are given in scripture, and which are to be ordered by the light of nature and Christian prudence, according to the general rules of the Word. The Apostolic rule in such cases is: 'Let all things be done decently and in order' (1 Corinthians 14:40); but this general rule does not authorise the introduction into the Church of rites and ceremonies of human invention, in order to set off the worship of God. This cannot be justified by any plea of expediency, with a view of rendering the services of the Church more attractive, and conciliating those that are without.

And it may be here remarked, that it was one of the first and greatest mistakes into which the Church fell, after inspiration ceased, to make too free a use of this doctrine of expediency. The abuses which have crept in under this specious disguise were not foreseen. The Fathers saw no harm in an indifferent ceremony, to which, perhaps, their new converts were attached from long custom. By adopting things of this kind, the Church, which was at first simple, and unencumbered with rites, became strangely metamorphosed; and in place of her simple robe of white, assumed a gorgeous dress, tricked off with gaudy ornaments and various colours. And this practice of inventing new ceremonies went on increasing, until, in process of time, the burdensome ritual of the Levitical law was not comparable to the liturgy of the Christian Church. Who that now attends a Romish chapel on some 'high day', would suppose that the service performed was connected with the religion of the New Testament?[8]

---

8. Alexander on the *Canon of the Scriptures*.

In maintaining the perfection of the Scriptures, we do not insist that every article of religion is contained in Scripture in so many words; but we hold that conclusions fairly deduced from the declarations of the Word of God are as truly parts of divine revelation as if they were expressly taught in the Sacred Volume. That good and necessary consequences deduced from Scripture are to be received as part of the rule of faith and practice, is evident from the example of our Saviour in proving the doctrine of the resurrection against the Sadducees (Matthew 22:31, 32); and from the example of Paul, who proved that Jesus of Nazareth is the Christ, by reasoning with the Jews out of the Old Testament Scriptures (Acts 17:2, 3). 'All Scripture' is declared to be 'profitable for doctrine, for reproof, for correction, for instruction in righteousness'; but all these ends cannot be obtained, unless by the deduction of consequences. Legitimate consequences, indeed, only bring out the full meaning of the words of Scripture; and as we are endued with the faculty of reason, and commanded to search the Scriptures, it was manifestly intended that we should draw conclusions from what is therein set down in express words.

By the *perfection* of scripture, then, we mean, that the Scripture, including necessary consequences as well as the express words, contains a complete revelation of the will of God, concerning all things necessary for his own glory, man's salvation, faith, and life. The Scripture is represented as *perfect*, fitted to answer every necessary end (Psalm 19:8, 9); it is sufficient to make 'the man of God perfect', and able to make private Christians 'wise unto salvation, through faith which is in Christ Jesus' (2 Timothy 3:15-17). So complete is the Scripture, that its Author has peremptorily prohibited either to add to, or to diminish ought from it (Deuteronomy 4:2; Revelation 22:18, 19).

The perfection of the Scriptures is to be maintained in opposition to those enthusiasts who pretend to new revelations of the Spirit, and in opposition to the Church of Rome, which 'receives traditions with the same veneration that they do the Scriptures'. No *new revelations* are to be added to the oracles of God, for Christ and his apostles have foretold the rise of false prophets, and warned us not to give heed to their pretended revelations (Matthew 24:11, 24). The Apostle Paul denounces a curse upon all who preach any other gospel than that which is contained in the Scriptures (Galatians 1:8, 9). The uncertainty of private revelations furnishes another argument against them. Such is the deceitfulness of the heart, that men are apt to mistake their own fancies and imaginations for revelations of the Spirit, and such is the subtlety of Satan, that he sometimes transforms himself into an angel of light. Private revelations, therefore, must be very uncertain to ourselves, and much more so to others. And it may be observed, that none plead for the authority of private revelations but such as, by the contrariety of their opinions and practices to the Scriptures, manifest themselves to be led by a spirit of delusion.

Neither are the *traditions of men* to be added to the Word of God. Traditions have been a fertile source of corruption in religion, both among Jews and Christians. The Jews pretended that besides what Moses committed to writing, he received from God a variety of revelations, which he communicated verbally to Aaron, and which were orally transmitted from generation to generation. These traditions multiplied exceedingly, especially after the Spirit of prophecy was withdrawn from the Church; and when Christ appeared on earth, he found the Jews so far degenerated, that their religion consisted almost entirely in the observation of such traditions. Hence we find him declaring, 'Ye have made the commandment of God of none effect by your tradition.' 'In vain they do worship me, teaching for doctrines the commandments of men' (Matthew 15:6, 9). In the same way have a multitude of the corruptions in the doctrine and worship of the Romish Church sprung up. They, after the example of the Jews, pretend that Christ and his apostles delivered many things which are not found in the Scriptures, and which have come down to us by tradition. But how can it be shown that those articles of religion, or institutions of worship, which they say have come down by tradition, were really received from the mouth of Christ, or from the teaching of his apostles? Or, supposing that they were derived from this source, how can it be ascertained that they have been conveyed down to us without alteration or corruption? The fact is, many of these traditions, which are called apostolical, can be traced to their commencement, at a period much later than that of the apostles. To admit unwritten traditions would open a door for all the innovations and corruptions which the fancies of men may devise, and would make void the law of God. But as our Lord strongly condemned the Jewish traditions, so we justly reject the mass of traditions received by the Romish Church.

(2) The Scriptures are *clear and perspicuous* in all things necessary to salvation. We allow that there are doctrines revealed in the Scriptures which surpass the comprehension of created beings, such as, the doctrine of the Trinity, the eternal generation and the incarnation of the Son of God. These are mysteries which we cannot comprehend, but the doctrines themselves are plainly taught in the Scriptures, and we must receive them on the divine testimony. We also admit that in the Scriptures there are some things obscure and 'hard to be understood'. But this obscurity is chiefly in history and prophecies, which do not so nearly concern our salvation. As in nature everything necessary for the support of life occurs almost everywhere, and may be found on the most easy search, while other things less necessary, such as its gems and gold, lie concealed in certain places, and can only be discovered and obtained by great exertions and unwearied industry; so there are things in the Scriptures, ignorance of which will not endanger the salvation of the soul, that are abstruse and difficult to be understood, even by those who possess acute minds and great learning. But we maintain, that all those things which are necessary to be known, believed, and observed, for salvation, are so clearly revealed in some place of Scripture or other, that every serious inquirer, in the due use of ordinary means, may understand them. This may be inferred from the fact that their author is God. If he intended them to be a rule of faith and life to men, surely he has adapted them to the understandings of men. There are numerous injunctions to read and search the Scriptures, but these necessarily imply that they are perspicuous and intelligible. Christians are also commended for searching the Scriptures, and trying by the written Word the doctrines delivered to them (Acts 17:11). If the Scriptures were unintelligible to common Christians, and the interpretation of the Church were necessary to discover their meaning, then such Christians would have no foundation upon which a divine faith could rest. Their faith must be ultimately resolved into the testimony of men; but human testimony, being fallible, cannot be the ground of an infallible persuasion.

Notwithstanding the subjective perspicuity of the Scriptures, we acknowledge the inward illumination of the Spirit of God to be necessary for the saving understanding of such things as are revealed in them. This arises from the blindness and perversity of the human understanding, as now corrupted and depraved

(1 Corinthians 2:14). If the enlightening influences of the Holy Spirit were unnecessary, then the greatest adepts in human literature would be best acquainted with the Scriptures; this, however, is not the case (Matthew 11:25). In the promises of God, and in the prayers of the saints, the special illumination of the Spirit is represented as necessary to enable us savingly to understand the things of God (John 14:26; Psalm 118:18, etc.).

Section 8

The Old Testament in Hebrew (which was the native language of the people of God of old), and the New Testament in Greek (which at the time of the writing of it was most generally known to the nations), being immediately inspired by God, and by his singular care and providence kept pure in all ages, are therefore authentical (Matthew 5:18); so as in all controversies of religion the Church is finally to appeal unto them (Isaiah 8:20; Acts 15:15; John 5:39, 46). But because these original tongues are not known to all the people of God, who have right unto and interest in the Scriptures, and are commanded, in the fear of God, to read and search them (John 5:39), therefore they are to be translated into the vulgar language of every nation unto which they come (1 Corinthians 14:6, 9, 11, 12, 24, 27, 28), that the Word of God dwelling plentifully in all, they may worship him in an acceptable manner (Colossians 3:16), and, through patience and comfort of the Scriptures, may have hope (Romans 15:4).

Section 9

The infallible rule of interpretation of Scripture is the Scripture itself; and therefore, when there is a question about the true and full sense of any Scripture (which is not manifold, but one), it must be searched and known by other places that speak more clearly (2 Peter 1:20, 21; Acts 15:15, 16).

Section 10

The Supreme Judge, by which all controversies of religion are to be determined, and all decrees of councils, opinions of ancient writers, doctrines of men, and private spirits, are to be examined, and in whose sentence we are to rest, can be no other but the Holy Spirit speaking in the Scripture (Matthew 22:29, 31; Ephesians 2:20; Acts 28:25).

Exposition

There are four heads embraced in these sections. *First*, That the Scriptures, in the original languages, have come down to us uncorrupted, and are, therefore, authentical. *Secondly*, That the Scriptures are to be translated into the vulgar language of every nation unto which they come. *Thirdly*, That the infallible rule of the interpretation of Scripture is the Scripture itself. *Fourthly*, That the Scriptures are the supreme standard of religious truth, and that the Supreme Judge, by which all controversies in religion are to be determined, is the Holy Spirit speaking to us in the Scriptures.

(1) The Old Testament, except a few passages which were written in *Chaldee*, was originally written in *Hebrew*, the language of the Jews, to whom the prophetical oracles were committed. The passages which were written in *Chaldee* are the eleventh verse of the tenth chapter of the Prophecies of Jeremiah; from the second verse of the fourth chapter of Daniel, to the end of the seventh chapter; and the fourth, fifth, and sixth chapters of Ezra. The New Testament was originally written in *Greek*, the language which, at the time of writing it, was most universally known. The original language of the Gospel according to Matthew is indeed a subject of controversy. The ancients, with one voice, affirm that it was written in Hebrew, and this opinion is supported by many modern critics; others, equally learned, maintain that it was originally composed in Greek. Several of the latest writers on this subject have adopted the opinion that there were two originals, Hebrew and Greek, both written by Matthew himself – the one for the use of the Jews, the other for the use of the Gentiles.

Though the autographs of the inspired writings have long since disappeared, yet there is ample evidence that, by the singular care and providence of God, they have been preserved pure in all ages, and that the copies which we now possess generally coincide with the originals.

The purity of the Old Testament Scriptures is confirmed by the general coincidence of the present Hebrew copies with all the early translations, and particularly with the Septuagint version. It may also be observed, that although our Lord frequently reproved the rulers and teachers of the Jews for their erroneous and false doctrines, yet he never accused them of any corruption in their sacred books; and the Apostle Paul reckons it among the privileges of the Jews, that to them 'were committed the oracles of God', without ever insinuating that they had been unfaithful to their trust. The animosity which has ever since prevailed betwixt Jews and Christians has rendered it impossible for either of them to vitiate these sacred writings without immediate detection.

The corruption of the books of the New Testament is altogether incredible. Had any party entertained a wish to alter them, it would have been impossible for them to succeed. Copies were speedily multiplied; they were early translated into the different languages of the several nations among which the gospel was planted; the Christian fathers embodied numerous quotations from them into their writings; various sects soon arose, keenly opposed to each other, but all receiving the same sacred books, and these became a check upon each other, and rendered corruptions and interpolations impracticable. Every succeeding age increased the difficulty; and though the comparison of a multitude of ancient manuscripts and copies has discovered a vast number of various readings, occasioned by the inadvertency and inaccuracy of transcribers, yet none of these differences affect any one article of the faith and comfort of Christians.

(2) As the Scriptures were originally written in the languages which, at the time of writing them, were most generally understood, God has hereby intimated his will, that they should be translated into the vernacular language of different nations, that every one may read and understand them. This we maintain in opposition to the Church of Rome, which forbids the translation of the Scriptures into the vulgar languages, and declares the indiscriminate reading of them to be highly dangerous. Though the free use of the Scriptures be prohibited by that Church, they were certainly intended by God for all ranks and classes of mankind. All are enjoined to read the Scriptures (John 5:39); and the laity are commended not only for searching them, but for trying the doctrines of their public teachers by them (Acts 17:11). It is, therefore, necessary that the Scriptures should be translated into the language of every nation; and the use of translation is sanctioned by the apostles, who frequently quoted passages of the Old Testament from the Septuagint.

(3) The best and only infallible rule of interpretation of Scripture is the Scripture itself. Some things that are briefly and obscurely handled in one place, are more fully and clearly explained in other places; and, therefore, when we would find out the true sense of Scripture, we must compare one passage with another, that they may illustrate one another; and we must never affix a sense to any particular text, but such as is agreeable to 'the analogy of faith', or the general scheme of divine truth. The compilers of the Confession affirm, that the sense of Scripture is

not manifold, but one. No doubt, many passages of Scripture have a complex meaning – as some prophecies have several steps of fulfilment, in the Jewish nation, the Christian Church, and the heavenly state, and some passages have one thing that is typical of another. Yet these only make up that one and entire sense intended by the Holy Ghost. No Scripture can have two or more meanings properly different, and nowise subordinate one to another, because of the unity of truth, and because of the perspicuity of the Scripture.

(4) That the Scriptures are the supreme standard of religious truth, is asserted in opposition to the Socinians, who maintain that reason is the standard by which we are to judge of the doctrines of revelation, and that we are bound to receive nothing as true which reason does not comprehend. There is, no doubt, much use for the exercise of reason in matters of religion; but, it may be remarked, 'that the office of reason, in reference to a revelation, is not to discuss its contents, to try them by its own standard, and to approve or disapprove, as they agree or disagree with it; for this would be to treat it as if it were not a revelation, at the moment when we acknowledge it to be such; or to insinuate that the Word of God, although known to be his Word, is not entitled to credit, unless it be supported by independent proof. The sole province of reason is to examine the evidence exhibited to show that it is his Word, and to investigate its meaning by rules which are used in determining the sense of any other book. These preliminaries being settled, the state of mind which a revelation demands is faith, implicit faith, to the exclusion of doubts and objections; the subjection of our understanding to the authority of God – entire submission to the dictates of infinite wisdom. The reason is, that his testimony supplies the place of all other evidence.'[9]

That the Supreme Judge, by which all controversies in religion are to be determined, is no other but the Holy Spirit speaking in the Scripture, is asserted in opposition to the Papists, who maintain that the Church is an infallible judge in religious controversies; though they do not agree among themselves whether this infallible authority resides in the Pope, or in a council, or in both together. Now, the Scripture never mentions such an infallible judge on earth. Neither Pope, nor councils, possess the properties requisite to constitute a supreme judge in controversies of religion; for they are fallible, and have often erred, and contradicted one another.

9. Dick's *Lectures on Theology*, vol. 2, p. 5.)

Although the Church or her ministers are the official guardians of the Scriptures, and although it belongs to them to explain and enforce the doctrines and laws contained in the Word of God, yet their authority is only ministerial, and their interpretations and decisions are binding on the conscience only in so far as they accord with the mind of the Spirit in the Scriptures. By this test, the decisions of councils, the opinions of ancient writers, and the doctrines of men at the present time, are to be tried, and by this rule all controversies in religion must be determined (Isaiah 8:20; Matthew 22:29).

CHAPTER 2

GOD AND THE HOLY TRINITY

Section 1

There is but one only[1] living and true God,[2] who is infinite in being and perfection,[3] a most pure spirit,[4] invisible,[5] without body, parts,[6] or passions,[7] immutable,[8] immense,[9] eternal,[10] incomprehensible,[11] almighty,[12] most wise,[13] most holy,[14] most free,[15] most absolute,[16] working all things according to the counsel of his own immutable and most righteous will,[17] for his own glory;[18] most loving,[19] gracious, merciful, longsuffering, abundant in goodness and truth, forgiving iniquity, transgression, and sin;[20] the rewarder of them that diligently seek him;[21] and withal most just and terrible in his judgments;[22] hating all sin,[23] and who will by no means clear the guilty.[24]

Section 2

God hath all life,[25] glory,[26] goodness,[27] blessedness,[28] in and of himself; and is alone in and unto himself all sufficient, not standing in need of any creatures which he hath made,[29] not deriving any glory from them,[30] but only manifesting his own glory, in, by, unto, and upon them: he is the alone fountain of all being, of whom, through whom, and to whom, are all things;[31] and hath most sovereign dominion over them, to do by them, for them, or upon them, whatsoever himself pleaseth.[32] In his sight all things are open and manifest;[33] his knowledge is infinite, infallible, and independent upon the creature,[34] so as nothing is to him contingent or uncertain.[35] He is most holy in all his counsels, in all his works, and in all his commands.[36] To him is due from angels and men, and every other creature, whatsoever worship, service, or obedience, he is pleased to require of them.[37]

1. Deuteronomy 6:4. 1 Corinthians 8:4, 6.
2. 1 Thessalonians 1:9. Jeremiah 10:10.
3. Job 11:7-9; 26:14.
4. John 4:24.
5. 1 Timothy 1:17.
6. Deuteronomy 4:15, 16. John 4:24. Luke 24:39.
7. Acts 14:11, 15.
8. James 1:17. Malachi 3:6.
9. 1 Kings 8:27; Jeremiah 23:23, 24.
10. Psalm 90:2. 1 Timothy 1:17.
11. Psalm 145:3.
12. Genesis 17:1. Revelation 4:8.
13. Romans 16:27.
14. Isaiah 6:3. Revelation 4:8.
15. Psalm 115:3.
16. Exodus 3:14.
17. Ephesians 1:11.
18. Proverbs 16:4; Romans 11:36.
19. 1 John 4:8, 16.
20. Exodus 34:6, 7.
21. Hebrews 11:6.
22. Nehemiah 9:32, 33.
23. Psalm 5:5, 6.
24. Nahum 1:2-3. Exodus 34:7.
25. John 5:26.
26. Acts 7:2.
27. Psalm 119:68.
28. 1 Timothy 6:15; Romans 4:5.
29. Acts 17:24, 25.
30. Job 22:2, 3.
31. Romans 11:36.
32. Revelation 4:11. 1 Timothy 6:15. Daniel 4:25, 35.
33. Hebrews 4:13.
34. Romans 11:33, 34. Psalm 147:5.
35. Acts 15:18. Ezekiel 11:5.
36. Psalm 145:17. Romans 7:12.
37. Revelation 5:12-14.

Exposition
We are here taught: *First*, that there is but one God; *secondly*, that
he is the only living and true God; *thirdly,* that he is a most pure
spirit; *fourthly*, that he is possessed of all possible perfections.

(1) The assertion, that there is but *one* God, does not mean that
there is but *one divine person*, for it is afterwards stated, that 'in the
unity of the Godhead there are three persons'; but it means that the
Divine Being is *numerically one in nature or essence*. This is
affirmed in opposition to the Polytheism of heathen nations, and
to the heresy of the Tritheists, who hold that there are three distinct
Godheads, or that one Godhead is divided into three distinct parts.

The unity of the Divine Being might be discovered by the light
of nature, for the same process of reasoning which leads to the idea
of a God, leads also to the conclusion, that there can be no more
Gods than one. There can be but one first cause, one self-existent,
independent, omnipotent, infinite, and Supreme Being; it is a
contradiction to suppose otherwise. Hence, though the rude un-
thinking multitude among the Pagans adored gods many, and lords
many, yet the wiser of their philosophers had their one supreme
god; and their poets sung of one sovereign deity, whom they called
the *Father of gods and men.* It is unquestionable, however, that the
heathen world received a multiplicity of gods, and the philosophers contented themselves with empty speculations about the
nature of the Deity; and, instead of instructing the vulgar in the
unity of God, confirmed them in their error, by practically complying with the customs of their country.

But divine revelation has firmly established the doctrine of
God's unity. Jehovah solemnly declares, 'I, even I, am he, and
there is no god with me' (Deuteronomy 32:39). 'Before me there
was no god formed, neither shall there be after me' (Isaiah 43:10).
The inspired writers of the Old Testament have said of him, 'The
LORD he is God; there is none else besides him' (Deuteronomy
4:35); and, 'Hear, O Israel: the LORD our God is one LORD'
(Deuteronomy 6:4). Jesus adds his testimony to this great truth; he
told the scribe that came to question him about his religion, 'The
first of all the commandments is, Hear, O Israel: the Lord our God
is one Lord'; and he spoke with high approbation of the answer
returned to this, in which 'the scribe said unto him, Well, Master,
thou hast said the truth: for there is one God; and there is none other

but he' (Mark 12:29, 32). The Apostle Paul often inculcates the same truth: 'We know that an idol is nothing in the world, and that there is none other God but one' (1 Corinthians 8:4); 'There is one God, and one mediator between God and men, the man Christ Jesus' (1 Timothy 2:5).

(2) It is asserted, that this God is the only living and true God. The name of God is, indeed, given in Scripture to various other beings, on account of some resemblance which, in some particular respect, they bear to God. *Angels* are called gods, on account of the excellence of their nature (Psalm 97:7). *Magistrates* are called gods, because, in the execution of their office, they act in God's name, and because we are bound to obey them (Exodus 22:28). *Moses* was a god to Pharaoh, and Aaron was his prophet, because Aaron received the divine messages, which he carried to Pharaoh immediately from Moses; whereas other prophets received their messages to the people immediately from God himself (Exodus 7:1). *Idols* are called gods, because idolaters account them gods, and honour them as such. And Satan is called the god of this world, because he rules over the greater part of the world, and they are his servants, and do his works (2 Corinthians 4:4). But, 'though there be that are called gods, whether in heaven or in earth, yet to us there is but one God', who is the only living and true God. He is styled the *living* God, in order to distinguish him from idols, which are altogether destitute of life. The opposition between the living God and dead idols the Psalmist states and illustrates in a manner the most convincing (Psalm 115:3-7). He is styled the *true* God, in opposition to imaginary and fictitious gods. The heathen, besides worshipping dead idols, worshipped also living creatures (Deuteronomy 32:17). These were only gods in their vain imagination, not in reality. They are called gods, but they were not gods by nature (Galatians 4:8). Between the true God and all rival gods there is an infinite disparity.

(3) It is asserted that this God is a most pure Spirit – that is, he is an incorporeal, immaterial, invisible, and immortal Being, without bodily parts or passions. 'No man hath seen God at any time.' He 'dwelleth in light, which no man can approach unto, whom no man hath seen nor can see'. He is described as 'invisible, incorruptible, and immortal'. The Confession affirms that God is a pure

Spirit, according to the Scriptures, and in opposition to an ancient sect of heretics, who, understanding everything spoken of God in a literal sense, held that God has bodily parts and a human form. These heretics are called *Anthropomorphites*; a name compounded of two Greek words – the one signifying *human*, and the other, *shape* or *form*. That corporeal parts and bodily members – such as eyes, ears, hands and face – are ascribed to God in the Scriptures is certain; but such language is used in accommodation to our capacities, and must be understood in a way suitable to a pure spirit. Were the great God to speak of his essence and perfections as he is in himself, instead of being informed, we would be confounded. He, therefore, employs human properties and actions as emblems of his own spiritual perfections and acts. We become acquainted with persons and things by seeing them or hearing of them; and to intimate the perfect knowledge which God has of his creatures, *eyes* and *ears* are ascribed to him. It is chiefly by our hands that we exert our bodily strength; and *hands* are ascribed to God to denote his irresistible power. We look with an air of complacency and satisfaction on those whom we love; and God's *face* denotes the manifestation of his favour. In the same manner must we explain the several *passions* that are ascribed to God – such as anger, fury, jealousy, revenge, bowels of mercy, etc.

> Passion produces a vehemence of action; so when there is, in the providences of God, such a vehemence as, according to the manner of men, would import a passion, then that passion is ascribed to God. When he punishes men for sin, he is said to be *angry*; when he does that by severe and redoubled strokes, he is said to be full of *fury and revenge*; when he punishes for idolatry, or any dishonour done to himself, he is said to be *jealous*; when he changes the course of his proceedings, he is said to *repent*; when his dispensations of providence are very gentle, and his judgments come slowly from him, he is said to have *bowels*. And thus all the varieties of providence come to be expressed by all that variety of passions which, among men, might give occasion to such a variety of proceeding.[1]

(4) It is asserted that this God is possessed of all possible perfections. The perfections of God are called his *attributes*, because they are ascribed to him as the essential properties of his nature. These attributes are variously, though imperfectly distinguished,

---

1. Burnet on the Thirty-Nine Articles, Art. i.

in our ways of thinking about them. They have been called natural
and moral, incommunicable and communicable attributes – the
latter is the most common distinction. Those attributes are called
incommunicable, of which there is not the least resemblance to be
found among creatures; and those are called communicable, of
which there is some faint, though very imperfect resemblance to
be found among creatures. Without attempting to class the divine
perfections under these two heads, we shall arrange the several
parts of the description of God contained in the two sections now
before us under the following particulars:

(a) God is *infinite*.
To be infinite, according to the literal signification of the word, is
to be unbounded – unlimited. As applied to the other attributes of
God, this term denotes their absolute perfection. He is infinite in
his wisdom, power, holiness, etc. As these perfections must be
considered afterwards, we only notice, at present, that God is
infinite in his *being*, or essence. From this results his *incomprehen-
sibility*, or that supereminent perfection which can be comprehended by none but himself. A perfect knowledge of God is
competent to none but himself, whose understanding is infinite.
'Canst thou by searching find out God? Canst thou find out the
Almighty unto perfection?' (Job 11:7). His infinity, as applied to
his being, also includes his *immensity* and his *omnipresence*.
Betwixt these a distinction may be drawn. His omnipresence has
a relation to creatures actually existing, with every one of which
he is intimately present; but his immensity extends infinitely
beyond the boundaries of all created substance. God fills all places
at once – heaven, and earth, and hell – with his essential presence.
'Am I a God at hand, saith the LORD, and not a God afar off? Can
any hide himself in secret places, that I shall not see him? saith the
LORD. Do not I fill heaven and earth? saith the LORD' (Jeremiah
23:23, 24).

(b) God is *self-existent* and *independent*.
He has all life, glory, and blessedness, in and of himself. His
existence is necessary and underived; for his name is, 'I am that I
am' (Exodus 3:14). His glory and blessedness are likewise underived. His glory necessarily results from, or rather consists in, the
absolute perfection of his own nature, and his blessedness is all

summed up in the possession and enjoyment of his own infinite excellencies. Being thus all-sufficient in and unto himself, he must be independent of any other being. He stands not in need of any creatures which he has made, nor can he derive any glory from them. Every other being receives its all from him, but he receives no advantage from any. 'For his pleasure all things are and were created; but none can be profitable to God, as he that is wise may be profitable to himself; nor is it any gain to him that they make their ways perfect' (Revelation 4:11; Job 22:2, 3).

(c) God is the *fountain of all being*.
As he has life in and of himself, so he is the author of that life which is in every living creature. 'In him we live, and move, and have our being.' All the life of the vegetative, animal, and rational world, the life of grace here, and the life of glory hereafter, are of him, and derived from him. 'With him is the fountain of life' – of all sorts of life. 'Of him, and through him, and to him, are all things' (Romans 11:36). From this it follows, that God has most sovereign dominion over all his creatures, to do by them, for them, or upon them, whatsoever himself pleaseth. He who is the first cause of all things must also be the last end. As he gave being to all creatures, so he must have an absolute right to rule over them, and to dispose of them for the ends of his own glory. Hence we are told, that 'his kingdom ruleth over all,' and that 'he doeth according to his will in the army of heaven, and among the inhabitants of the earth: and none can stay his hand, or say unto him, What doest thou?' (Psalm 103:19; Daniel 4:35). But God has not only a right to exercise sovereign dominion over his creatures, he has also an indisputable claim to their service and obedience. This claim is likewise founded upon his giving them their being. They are not their own, but the Lord's; him, therefore, they are bound to serve. Hence the Confession, with great propriety, affirms, that to God 'is due from angels and men, and every other creature, whatsoever worship, service, or obedience, he is pleased to require of them'.

(d) God is *eternal*.
The word 'eternal' is sometimes used, both in Scripture and in common language, in a restricted sense, for a long time, or for a period whose termination is to us unknown. Sometimes it denotes a duration which, though not without beginning, is without end.

Thus angels and the souls of men are eternal; for though they had a beginning, they will have no end. But eternity, in the strict and proper sense of the word, signifies a duration without beginning, without end, and without succession; and in this sense it is peculiar to the great God. The supposition that there was a period at which God began to be is equally repugnant to reason and to revelation. He that created all things must have existed before any of them began to be; and his existence being underived, he can never cease to exist. The Scripture plainly declares that he is without beginning: 'Before the mountains were brought forth, or ever thou hadst formed the earth and the world, even from everlasting to everlasting, thou art God' (Psalm 90:2). It no less plainly declares that he is without end: 'The LORD shall endure for ever' (Psalm 9:7). That he is without succession is no less explicitly declared: 'One day is with the Lord as a thousand years, and a thousand years as one day' (2 Peter 3:8). There is one passage in which an unbeginning, unending, and unsuccessive duration, is ascribed to God (Psalm 102:25-27). One of his glorious titles is, 'The high and lofty One that inhabiteth eternity'; and he is styled, 'The everlasting God – the Father of eternity – the First and the Last.'

(e) God is *immutable*.

'With him is no variableness, neither shadow of turning.' To this important truth reason and revelation give their united testimony. His immutability necessarily results from his absolute perfection. If he were to change, it must be either to the better or to the worse. He cannot change to the better, for that would imply past imperfection; he cannot change to the worse, for then he would cease to be perfect. He must, therefore, remain invariably the same. To the absolute immutability of God the Scripture gives numerous testimonies (Numbers 23:19; Psalm 33:11; Malachi 3:6).

God is *unchangeable* in his being. 'I am that I am,' is the name by which he made himself known to Moses, a name which conveys the idea not only of self-existence and independence, but also of immutability. He is unchangeable in his glory. Though the manifestation of his glory may vary, yet he is, and ever was, infinitely glorious in himself; for his essential glory is neither capable of increase nor susceptible of diminution. He is unchangeable in his blessedness; for as it consists in the enjoyment of himself, so it can neither be increased nor diminished by anything that creatures can do for or against him (Job 35:5-7). He is unchangeable in his purposes and counsels. He proclaims with divine majesty, 'My counsel shall stand, and I will do all my pleasure: I have spoken it, I will also bring it to pass; I have purposed it, I will also do it' (Isaiah 46:10, 11). He is unchangeable in his covenant, love and promises to his people (Isaiah 54:10). When, therefore, we read in Scripture of God's *repenting*, we must understand such language of an alteration of the outward dispensations of his providence. We are by no means to attribute to him any change of mind; for, in this respect, it is impossible for God to change. 'He is in one mind, and who can turn him?' (Job 23:13).

(f) God is *all-knowing*.
In his sight all things are open and manifest. He has a perfect knowledge of himself, and he only knows himself perfectly. He knows all things besides himself, whether they be past, present, or to come, in our way of measuring them by time. He knows all creatures, from the greatest to the least; he knows all the actions of his creatures, whether secret or open; all their words, thoughts, and intentions. Hence the Scripture declares, 'The eyes of the LORD are in every place, beholding the evil and the good' (Proverbs 15:3). 'He is acquainted with all our ways, there is not a word in our tongue but he knoweth it altogether, and he understandeth our thought afar off' (Psalm 139:2-4). 'Known unto God are all his works from the beginning of the world' (Acts 15:18). Yea, he knows the most contingent events: the actions of free agents, and all events concerned in them, were always known with certainty to him; so that, though they be contingent in their own nature, or ever so uncertain as to us, yet, in reality, nothing is to him contingent or uncertain. We cannot doubt this, when we consider the numerous prophecies, relating to things of this kind, that have received a most exact and circumstantial accomplishment, many ages after the prophecies were announced. It may be remarked, that God knows things, not by information, nor by reasoning and deduction, nor by succession of ideas, but by a single intuitive glance; and he knows them comprehensively, and infallibly.

(g) God is most *free* and most *absolute*.
'He worketh all things after the counsel of his own will' (Ephesians 1:11). His will is infinitely free, and 'he doth according to his will

in the army of heaven, and among the inhabitants of the earth'. He has an absolute right to do whatsoever he pleaseth, and 'none can stay his hand, or say unto him, What doest thou?' (Daniel 4:35).

(h) God is infinitely *wise*.

The wisdom of God is that perfection of his nature by which he directs all things to their proper end – the end for which he gave them being; and this is his own glory: for as he is the most excellent Being, nothing can be so excellent an end as his own glory. How admirably is the wisdom of God displayed in *creation*. Whether we look upward to the heavens, or downward to the earth; whether we survey the mineral, the vegetable, or the animal world, can we forbear to exclaim with the devout Psalmist, 'O LORD, how manifold are thy works! in wisdom thou hast made them all' (Psalm 104:24). When we consider the vast variety of creatures and things which God has produced from the same original matter, the fitness of everything for its intended purpose, the subserviency of one thing to another, and the conspiring of all to a common end – how conspicuous is his wisdom! Nor is the wisdom of God less apparent in the *government* of the world, especially in effecting the most grand and glorious designs by weak and feeble means, and even by the bad dispositions of men – 'making even the wrath of man to praise him, and restraining the remainder thereof.' 'O the depth of the riches both of the wisdom and knowledge of God!' (Romans 11:33). But this perfection of God shines forth with the brightest lustre in the method of our *redemption* by Jesus Christ. Nothing less than wisdom truly divine could have devised a plan whereby 'mercy and truth should meet together, and righteousness and peace should embrace each other'. Here is 'the hidden wisdom of God'. Here 'he has abounded toward us in all wisdom and prudence'; and hence the publication of this contrivance is spoken of as a discovery of 'the manifold wisdom of God' (Ephesians 3:10).

(i) God is infinitely *powerful*, or almighty.

The power of God is that perfection whereby he is able to effect all things that do not imply a contradiction, either to his own perfections, or to the nature of things themselves. 'With God nothing shall be impossible,' said the angel to the Virgin Mary. 'With God all things are possible,' said Jesus to his disciples. How great must be that power which produced the beautiful fabric of the universe out of nothing! 'By the word of the LORD were the heavens made, and all the host of them by the breath of his mouth.' 'For he spake, and it was done; he commanded, and it stood fast' (Psalm 33:6, 9). His power is still exerted in the preservation of the world; for he upholds all creatures in their being and operations by the word of his power. It appears conspicuously in the moral government of the world – especially in restraining wicked men from their purposes; for 'he stilleth the noise of the waves, and the raging of the people'. But it is most eminently displayed in the work of redemption by Jesus Christ; in the formation of his human nature in the womb of the Virgin; in supporting his human nature under that load of wrath which was due to us for our transgressions; and in raising him from the dead. It is also displayed in the production of that wonderful change which takes place in the conversion of a sinner, which in Scripture is termed a new creation; in the preservation of believers in a state of grace; in enabling them to resist and overcome strong temptations, to perform arduous duties, and to bear heavy trials with patience and joyfulness; and it will be signally manifested in raising up their bodies, glorious and immortal, at the last day.

It may be observed, that although there are some things which God cannot do, yet this implies no imperfection in his power. He cannot do what involves a contradiction; for instance, he cannot make a thing to be, and not to be, at the same time; he cannot do what is repugnant to his nature, or his essential perfections; he cannot deny himself – he cannot lie – he cannot look upon sin – he cannot sleep, or suffer, or cease to exist. This, however, argues no defect of power, but arises from his absolute perfection.

(j) God is infinitely *holy*.
The holiness of God is the perfect rectitude of his nature, whereby he is absolutely free from all moral impurity, and, in all that he does, acts like himself, and for the advancement of his own honour; delighting in what accords with, and abhorring what is contrary to, his nature and will. Holiness is, as it were, the lustre and glory of all the divine perfections; hence God is styled 'glorious in holiness'. It is that perfection which those exalted spirits, who are best acquainted with the glories of the divine nature, dwell most upon in their songs of praise; hence, the seraphim cry one to another,

'Holy, holy, holy, is the LORD of hosts' (Isaiah 6:3). God himself puts peculiar honour upon his holiness; for he singles it out as that attribute by which he swears that he will accomplish whatever he hath spoken (Psalm 89:35). The holiness of God is manifest from the original condition of all rational creatures; for, when formed by him, they were perfectly holy. It has been awfully displayed in the judgments which God has executed upon sinners. The expulsion of the rebel angels from heaven – the exclusion of man from paradise, as soon as he became a sinner – the destruction of the old world by water – the overthrow of Sodom and Gomorrah; these, and innumerable other instances, the Scripture records of God's awful displeasure against sin. But nothing affords such a striking demonstration of God's hatred of sin as the sufferings and death of his own Son. God must be of purer eyes than to behold iniquity, since, when our guilt was transferred to his own Son, he spared him not. Could he have overlooked sin in any case, he would certainly have done it in the case of his dear Son. But, though he was the object of his Father's ineffable delight, and though he was personally innocent, yet, when he stood charged with the sins of his people, he could not be excused from suffering and dying. 'It pleased the LORD to bruise him, he hath put him to grief' (Isaiah 53:10).

(k) God is infinitely *just*.

The justice of God is that perfection of his nature according to which he is infinitely righteous in himself, and just and equal in all his proceedings with regard to his creatures. 'A God of truth, and without iniquity, just and right is he' (Deuteronomy 32:4). God is just to himself, by acting in all things agreeably to his nature and perfections, and by maintaining his own rights and prerogatives. He is just to his creatures, by governing them in a way agreeably to their nature, according to a law which he has given them. God's justice has been variously distinguished, according to the various ways in which it is exercised. His *legislative* justice is his giving righteous laws to his creatures, suited to their original abilities, commanding or forbidding such things as are fit for them to do or forbear. Hence, his law is said to be 'holy, and just, and good' (Romans 7:12). His *distributive* justice is his rendering to every one his due, according to law, without respect of persons. This, again, is distinguished by various names. There is *remunerative* justice, whereby God rewards the sincere, though imperfect obedience of those who are accepted in his sight as righteous, through the righteousness of Jesus Christ imputed to them, and received by faith. 'Verily, there is a reward for the righteous.' 'God is not unrighteous, to forget their work and labour of love' (Psalm 58:11; Hebrews 6:10). But this reward is entirely of free grace, and not of debt. There is *punitive* justice whereby God renders to the sinner the punishment due to his crimes. This is nothing else than God's distributive justice, as it regards punishment. It is sometimes called *vindicatory* justice, and sometimes *avenging* justice. This, we hold, in opposition to Socinians, is not an arbitrary effect of the will of God, but an essential perfection of his nature; and, therefore, upon the entrance of sin, its exercise was indispensably necessary. God must inflict the punishment due to sin, either upon the transgressor himself, or upon another as his surety. This appears from the holiness of God, which requires that he should demonstrate his aversion to sin by punishing it according to its demerit. It appears from the threatening of the law, taken in connection with the truth of God. 'In the day thou eatest thereof, thou shalt surely die,' was the penalty annexed to the law, and the faithfulness of God is pledged for the execution of the sentence upon transgressors. This is confirmed by the testimony of conscience in all men, apprehending that punishment will overtake the transgressor: hence, both barbarous and civilized nations have had recourse to sacrifices to appease the anger of the Deity. This appears, further, from God's inflicting remarkable judgments, even in this life, on sinning nations and individuals; and especially from his executing punishment upon his own Son, as the surety of sinners, Christ having substituted himself in the place of sinners, justice exacted of him full satisfaction. And never did justice appear in such terrible majesty, as when God gave it the commission to awake, and smite the man that was his fellow (Zechariah 13:7). Then it was seen that God 'can by no means clear the guilty,' or allow sin to pass with impunity.

Several writers, of late, have attributed to God what they call *public* justice; that is, justice which respects the great general end of government – the public good. But, we apprehend, there is no foundation, either in Scripture or reason, for supposing that this kind of justice has any place in the moral government of God. Such an idea proceeds upon the supposition that the divine government, so far as punishment is concerned, is completely analogous to human governments. There is, however, a wide and obvious distinction between the procedure of human governments and the procedure of the Most High.

(l) God is infinitely *good.*

Though all the perfections of God are his glory, yet this is particularly so called; for when Moses earnestly desired to behold the *glory* of Jehovah, the Lord said, 'I will make all my *goodness* pass before thee, and I will proclaim the name of the LORD before thee.' 'And the LORD passed by before him, and proclaimed, The LORD, the LORD God, merciful and gracious, longsuffering, and abundant in goodness and truth...' (Exodus 33:18, 19; 34:6). The goodness of God is distinguished by different names, according to the different aspects in which it is viewed, or the different objects about which it is exercised. When it relieves the miserable, it is called *mercy*; when it confers favours on the undeserving, or on those who deserve nothing but what is evil, it is called *grace*; when it supplies the want of indigent beings, it is called *bounty*; when it forbears to execute punishment upon provoking rebels, it is called *patience* or *longsuffering.* The *goodness* of God is, therefore, a very comprehensive term; it includes all the forms of his kindness towards men, whether considered as creatures, as sinners, or as saints. But we may describe it generally as that property of the Divine Being which disposes him to communicate happiness to his creatures, as far as is consistent with his other perfections. Innumerable are the instances in which God has manifested his goodness. What but goodness could prompt him to give being to so many creatures, when he stood in no need of them, being infinitely happy in the enjoyment of himself? What goodness does he display in upholding innumerable creatures in existence, and in making ample provision for their wants? But the most astonishing display of this, as well as of all the other perfections of Deity, is in the redemption of sinners. In the contrivance of the plan, and in the execution of it from first to last, God appears good, in a manner and to a degree that astonishes the inhabitants both of earth and of heaven. The goodness of God, as manifested in this work, is usually expressed by the term *love*; and the love herein displayed surpasses knowledge (John 3:16).

The goodness of God may be considered as *absolute* and

relative – as it is in himself, and as it is exercised toward his creatures (Psalm 119:68). It may also be considered as *common* and *special*. Of his goodness, in the former view, his creatures promiscuously are partakers (Psalms 33:5; 145:9). Of his goodness, in the latter view, his chosen people are partakers (Psalm 106:5).

(m) God is infinitely *true* and *faithful*.

The truth of God is that perfection of his nature whereby it is impossible for him not to fulfil whatever he hath spoken. He is 'a God of truth, and without iniquity, just and right is he'. Whatever God hath spoken, whether in a way of promise or of threatening, he will, sooner or later, infallibly accomplish. 'It is impossible for God to lie.' No difficulties can arise to render a performance of his word impracticable; and he is not liable to a change of mind (Numbers 23:19). We may, therefore, be confidently assured, that 'there shall not fail one good word of all that the LORD our God hath spoken'.

How blessed are they who, upon good grounds, can call this all-perfect Being their Father and their God! How miserable those who live 'without God in the world!' and what a 'fearful thing' must it be to 'fall into the hands of the living God!' That we may escape this misery, and possess the happiness of those 'whose God is the Lord', let us unreservedly yield ourselves to God, through Christ, and take him to be our portion for ever. May the unfeigned language of every reader be, 'Whom have I in heaven but thee? and there is none upon earth that I desire besides thee.'

Section 3

In the unity of the Godhead there be three persons, of one substance, power, and eternity; God the Father, God the Son, and God the Holy Ghost (1 John 5:7; Matthew 3:16, 17; 28:19; 2 Corinthians 13:14). The Father is of none, neither begotten nor proceeding; the Son is eternally begotten of the Father (John 1:14, 18); the Holy Ghost eternally proceeding from the Father and the Son (John 15:26; Galatians 4:6).

We are here taught: *first*, that in the one Godhead there are three persons, the Father, the Son and the Holy Ghost; *secondly*, that these three are distinguished by their personal properties; *thirdly*, that each of these persons is truly God.

(1) That in the one Godhead there are three persons is affirmed in opposition to the *Anti-trinitarians*, who maintain that God is one in respect of personality as well as of essence. The term which has

been chosen to express the doctrine now under consideration is *Trinity*. This word is not to be found in Scripture, but it is a very appropriate and happy term to express this profound mystery. It is a compound Latin word, signifying *three in unity*; that is, three distinct persons in one undivided Godhead. The adversaries of this doctrine now call themselves *Unitarians*, by which they mean to intimate their belief of only one God, and insinuate that those who believe the doctrine of the Trinity must admit more than one God. But we maintain, as strongly as they, that there is only one God, and we think it perfectly consistent with this belief to acknowledge three persons in the Godhead. This, indeed, is a mystery, but there is nothing in it absurd, or contradictory to reason. We do not say that *three are one* in the same sense and in the same respect in which they are *three*; that would, no doubt, be a plain contradiction in terms. But we say, they are *three* in one respect, *one* in another respect – *three* in *person*, *one* in *essence*; and there is no absurdity in that at all. It surpasses our reason, indeed, fully to understand it; and so do a thousand things besides, which yet we know are true and real. But, if it be a doctrine clearly revealed in the Sacred Scripture, we are bound to believe it, however incapable we may be of comprehending it.

Before proceeding to establish the doctrine, we must explain the terms employed. The word *Godhead* signifies the divine nature. This is a scriptural term (Romans 1:20; Colossians 2:9). In the Scriptures, and, agreeably to them, in our Confession, Godhead denotes that infinite, eternal and unchangeable nature, or essence, which is not peculiar to the Father, or the Son, or the Holy Ghost, but common to all the three. The distinction in the Godhead is characterised by the word 'person'. This term, in the common acceptation, denotes 'a separate and independent being, whose existence and actions have no necessary connection with the existence and actions of any other being. It has been defined to be a thinking substance, which can act by itself, or an intelligent agent, who is neither a part of, nor sustained by another'. But this term, when applied to the Sacred Three, is not to be understood in exactly the same sense as when applied to creatures. The cases are totally dissimilar.

Three human persons have the same *specific* nature, but three divine persons have the same numerical nature. Anti-trinitarians affirm that, by holding three divine persons, we necessarily make three Gods, because they most unfairly maintain, in the face of our solemn protestations, that we affix the same idea to the word 'person' which it bears when used in reference to men. But we deny that it has this meaning. We do not teach that there are three distinct essences mysteriously conjoined – that the Father, the Son, and the Spirit possess, each of them separately from the others, a divine nature and divine perfections. What we believe is this, that there is a distinction in the Godhead, to which there is nothing similar in creatures, who are one in every sense of the term; and we employ the word 'person' to express that distinction. It may be objectionable, because, being applied to other beings, it is apt to suggest an idea which is inconsistent with the unity of God; but this is the unavoidable consequence of the imperfection of human language; and we endeavour to guard against the abuse by declaring that, in this application, it must be qualified so as to exclude a separate existence. When we say that there are three persons in the Godhead, the word 'person' signifies a distinction which we do not pretend to explain, but which does not intrench upon the unity of essence.[2]

The doctrine of the Trinity is not discoverable by the light of nature, or by unassisted reason. It can only be known by divine revelation, and it is amply confirmed by the Holy Scripture. There are many passages in the Old Testament which prove a *plurality* of persons in the Godhead; such as those passages in which one divine person is introduced as speaking of or to another. To these we can only refer (Genesis 1:26; 3:22; 11:7; Psalm 45:6; 110:1; Isaiah 6:8). All these texts plainly point out a plurality of persons in the Godhead. But it is evident from Scripture, not only that there is a *plurality*, but also that there is a *Trinity*, or only *three persons* in the Godhead. This is plain from Isaiah 61:1, where our Divine Redeemer thus speaks: 'The *Spirit* of the *Lord* GOD is upon *me*; because the *LORD* hath anointed *me*,' etc. Here one divine person is the speaker; he speaks of another divine person, whom he styles the *Spirit*; and of a third divine person, whom he calls the *Lord God*. The work of creation is ascribed to the agency of three distinct persons: 'By the word of the LORD were the heavens made, and all the host of them by the breath of his mouth' (Psalm 33:6). Here three are distinctly pointed out: the *Father*; the *Word*, or the Son of God; and the *breath of his mouth*, which can be no other than the *Holy Spirit*. But in the New Testament this doctrine is still more explicitly revealed. In the history of our Lord's baptism we have

2. Dick's *Lectures on Theology*, vol. ii., pp. 64, 65.

a plain intimation of the mystery of the Trinity (Matthew 3:16, 17). The *Father*, by an audible voice from heaven, bears testimony to the incarnate Redeemer; the *Son*, in human nature, is baptized by John; and the *Holy Spirit* descends upon him in a visible manner. Hence the primitive Christians used to say to any who doubted the truth of this doctrine, 'Go to Jordan, and there you will see the Trinity.' Plainer still is this truth from the form of words appointed to be used in Christian baptism: 'Baptizing them in the name of the Father, and of the Son, and of the Holy Ghost' (Matthew 28:19). To baptize in the name of one, is to baptize by his authority, and dedicate to his service. This is competent only to a divine person. Now, if the Father, in whose name we are baptized, be a person, so must the Son, and the Holy Ghost, for we are baptized in their name, as well as in the name of the Father. The apostolical benediction furnishes another proof of a Trinity: 'The grace of our Lord Jesus Christ, the love of God, and the communion of the Holy Ghost, be with you all' (2 Corinthians 13:14). 'This is evidently a prayer, which it would be impiety and idolatry to address to any other but God. Yet three persons are distinctly addressed, and consequently are recognised as possessed of divine perfections; as knowing our wants, and hearing our requests, and able to do what we ask; as the fountain of all the blessedness implied in the terms, grace, love, and communion.' We have a most explicit testimony to this doctrine: 'There are three that bear record in heaven, the Father, the Word, and the Holy Ghost, and these three are one' (1 John 5:7). The genuineness of this text has been much disputed; but the truth of the doctrine does not rest on a single text, as has been already shown.

Nor is the doctrine of the Trinity a mere speculation. On the contrary, to use the language of Dr Dick, 'without the knowledge of this doctrine it is impossible to understand the grandest of the works of God – redemption – in which the three persons act distinct and conspicuous parts. We are called to contemplate the love of the Father, the condescension of the Son, and the gracious operations of the Spirit. Redemption is not the work of a solitary agent, but of three, all concurring in the salvation of our perishing race. Hence we owe gratitude to each of the persons of the Godhead distinctly, and are bound to give to each the glory to which he is entitled. We are baptized in their name, and consecrated to their service; and our prayers are addressed not to God absolutely considered, but to the

Father, through the Son, and by the assistance of the Holy Ghost. It appears, therefore, that the Christian system of duty is founded upon this doctrine, and that without the belief of it there can be no acceptable religion. So far is it from being useless, that it is the very foundation of practical piety.'

(2) The Sacred Three are distinguished from each other by their personal properties.

It is the personal property of the Father to *beget* the Son (Psalm 2:7). It is the personal property of the Son to be eternally *begotten* of the Father (John 1:14). It is the personal property of the Holy Ghost to *proceed* eternally from the Father and the Son (John 15:26; Galatians 4:6). These are called *personal* properties, to distinguish them from the *essential* perfections of Deity. *Essential* perfections are common to the Father, the Son, and the Holy Spirit, but a *personal* property is something peculiar to each, something which may be affirmed of one, but cannot be affirmed of the other two. Paternity is peculiar to the first person, filiation to the second, and procession to the third. We pretend not to explain these personal properties; here, if in anything, it is safest to abide by the language of Scripture.

(3) Each of the Sacred Three is truly God.

That the Father is God is admitted on all hands; it is, therefore, unnecessary to prove what no one denies. But the Deity of the Son was controverted and denied at an early period of the Christian Church. The Arians, who arose in the beginning of the fourth century, held that the Son had a beginning, and is a creature, though in antiquity and excellency superior to all other creatures. The Socinians, who sprung up towards the close of the sixteenth century, went further than the Arians. They held that the second person had no existence till he was formed in the womb of the Virgin, and that he is called the Son of God because God employed him to propagate divine truth by his ministry, and to confirm it by his death, and advanced him, after his resurrection, to the government of the universe. The modern Socinians, who call themselves Unitarians, the disciples of Dr Priestley, have gone still further in degrading the Son of God. They maintain that Christ is a mere man, that he was the human off-spring of Joseph and Mary, that he is no proper object of religious worship, but only the most excellent of *human* characters – the most eminent of all the prophets of God. They go along with the old Socinians in maintaining that Jesus had no existence prior to his birth, but they disclaim the notion of Socinus, that, since his resurrection, he has been advanced to the government of the universe; and contend that, as he differed in no respect from other men in his mode of coming into the world, so he can have no dominion or superiority over men in the world of spirits. In opposition to adversaries, earlier and later, our Confession asserts that the Son is God, of one substance, power and eternity, with the Father. This might be evinced by a great variety of arguments, which we can only indicate in a very summary manner.

(a) Divine *names* are applied to him. He is expressly called *God* (John 1:1; Romans 4:5); he is called the *mighty* God (Isaiah 4:6); the *true* God (1 John 5:20); the *great* God (Titus 2:13). The *Lord*, or *Jehovah*, the incommunicable name of God, is frequently applied to the Son (Isaiah 6:1), applied to Christ (John 12:41); Isaiah 40:3 is applied to Christ in John 1:23; Numbers 21:6, 7 is applied to Christ in 1 Corinthians 10:9.

(b) Divine *attributes* are ascribed to the Son no less than to the Father. Eternity is ascribed to him (Micah 5:2; Revelation 1:8); omniscience (John 2:24; 21:17); omnipresence (Matthew 28:20); omnipotence (Revelation 1:8; Philippians 3:21); immutability (Psalm 102:25-27, compared with Hebrews 1:10-12 and 13:8).

(c) Divine *works* are ascribed to him. The production of all things out of nothing (John 1:3); the preservation and government of all things (Colossians 1:17; Hebrews 1:3; John 5:17, 27); the purchasing of eternal redemption (Hebrews 9:12); the forgiveness of sins (Mark 2:5); the raising of the dead at the last day (John 5:28, 29); the judging of the world (Romans 14:10).

(d) We are commanded to give the same *divine worship* to the Son that is due to the Father. The established law of worship is, 'Thou shalt worship the Lord thy God, and him *only* shalt thou serve.' But divine worship is expressly commanded to be rendered to the Son (John 5:23). Angels, the highest of created beings, are enjoined to worship him (Hebrews 1:6); and we have numerous instances of divine worship being given to him (Acts 7:59; 2 Corinthians 12:8; 2 Thessalonians 2:16).

(e) As an additional proof that the Son, no less than the Father, is the supreme God, it may be observed that he is expressly affirmed to be *equal* with the Father. He claimed equality with God, and for so doing was accused of blasphemy by the Jews; yet he never charged them with misconstruing his words, but appealed to his works in proof of his claim (John 5:18; 10:30, 38). He thought it no robbery to be equal with God (Philippians 2:6); and his eternal Father acknowledges him to be his fellow and equal (Zechariah 13:7).

We may here observe that when Christ saith that 'his Father is greater than he' (John 14:28), he does not mean that he is greater with respect to his *nature*, but with respect to his *office* as Mediator; in which respect Christ sustains the character of the Father's servant, and acts in virtue of a commission from him (Isaiah 42:1). But as the second person in the undivided Trinity, he is in all respects equal to his Divine Father.

The divinity of the Holy Spirit is also denied by Socinians, but it may be evinced by the same arguments which prove the Deity of the Son.

(a) Divine *names* are ascribed to the Spirit equally with the Father and the Son. He is called *God*. In Acts 5:3, Ananias is said to 'lie unto the Holy Ghost'; and in verse 4 he is said to 'lie unto God'. True Christians are said to be temples of *God*, inasmuch as 'the Spirit of God dwelleth in them' (1 Corinthians 3:16). The name *Jehovah* is also given to him (Isaiah 6:8, 9, compared with Acts 28:25).

(b) Divine *attributes* are ascribed to the Spirit. Eternity is ascribed to him (Genesis 1:1, 2); omnipresence (Psalm 139:7); omniscience (1 Corinthians 2:10, 11). In fine, the apostle attributes to the Spirit the most *sovereign will* and *omnipotent power* (1 Corinthians 12:11).

(c) Divine *works* are ascribed to the Spirit. Creation is ascribed to him, in reference to the world in general, and to man in particular (Genesis 1:2; Job 33:4). The preservation of all things is as much the work of the Spirit as of the Father and the Son (Psalm 104:30). The application of redemption is peculiarly ascribed to the Spirit (Titus 3:5; 1 Corinthians 6:11).

(d) Divine *worship* is ascribed to him. Prayer, one of the most solemn parts of worship, is addressed to him (Revelation 1:4, 5). By the *seven spirits*, in this passage, are not intended any created spirits, but the third person of the Godhead, who is so called on account of the variety and perfection of his gifts and graces. Baptism is administered in the name of the Holy Ghost, as well as in the name of the Father and the Son; and the apostolical benediction is pronounced in his name (2 Corinthians 13:14).

The same glory, then, is due to the undivided Three – to the Son no less than to the Father, and to the Holy Spirit equally with the Father and the Son.

CHAPTER 3

GOD'S ETERNAL DECREE

Section 1
God from all eternity did, by the most wise and holy counsel of his own will, freely and unchangeably ordain whatsoever comes to pass (Ephesians 1:11; Romans 11:33; Hebrews 6:17; Romans 9:15, 18): yet so as thereby neither is God the author of sin (James 1:13, 17; 1 John 1:5), nor is violence offered to the will of the creatures, nor is the liberty or contingency of second causes taken away, but rather established (Acts 2:23; Matthew 17:12; Acts 4:27, 28; John 19:11; Proverbs 16:33).

Section 2
Although God knows whatsoever may or can come to pass upon all supposed conditions (Acts 15:18; 1 Samuel 23:11, 12; Matthew 11:21, 23); yet hath he not decreed anything because he foresaw it as future, or as that which would come to pass upon such conditions (Romans 9:11, 12, 16, 18).

Exposition
By the decree of God is meant his purpose or determination with respect to future things; or, more fully, his determinate counsel, whereby, from all eternity, he fore-ordained whatever he should do, or would permit to be done, in time.

This subject is one of the most abstruse and intricate in theology, and it has been the fruitful source of a variety of controversies in the Christian Church. But whatever diversity of opinion may obtain respecting the details of the doctrine,

> no man will deny that there are divine decrees, who believes that God is an intelligent being, and considers what this character implies. An intelligent being is one who knows and judges, who purposes ends and devises means, who acts from design, conceives a plan, and then proceeds to execute it. Fortune was worshipped as a goddess by the ancient heathens, and was represented as blind, to signify that she was guided by no fixed rule, and distributed her favours at random. Surely no person of common sense, not to say piety, will impute procedure so irrational to the Lord of universal nature. As he knew all things which his power could accomplish, there were, undoubtedly, reasons

which determined him to do one thing, and not to do another; and his choice, which was founded upon those reasons, was his decree.[1]

That God must have decreed all future things, is a conclusion which necessarily flows from his foreknowledge, independence, and immutability.

The foreknowledge of God will necessarily infer a decree; for God could not foreknow that things would be, unless he had decreed they should be; and that because things would not be future, unless he had decreed they should be.[2]

If God be an independent being, all creatures must have an entire dependence upon him; but this dependence proves undeniably that all their acts must be regulated by his sovereign will. If God be of one mind, which none can change, he must have unalterably fixed everything in his purpose which he effects in his providence.

This doctrine is plainly revealed in the Scriptures. They speak of God's foreknowledge, his purpose, his will, the determinate counsel of his will, and his predestination. 'Whom he did foreknow, he also did predestinate' (Romans 8:29). 'He hath made known unto us the mystery of his will, according to his good pleasure, which he hath purposed in himself.' 'He worketh all things after the counsel of his own will' (Ephesians 1:9, 11). 'Christ,' says an apostle, 'was delivered by the determinate counsel and foreknowledge of God ' (Acts 2:23).

The decrees of God relate to all future things, without exception; whatever is done in time was foreordained before the beginning of time. His purpose was concerned with everything, whether great or small, whether good or evil; although, in reference to the latter, it may be necessary to distinguish between appointment and permission. It was concerned with things necessary, free, and contingent; with the movements of matter, which are necessary; with the volitions and actions of intelligent creatures, which are free; and with such things as we call accidents, because they take place undesignedly on our part, and without any cause which we could discover. It was concerned about our life and our death; about our state in time and our state in eternity. In short, the decrees of God are as comprehensive as his government, which extends to all creatures, and to all events.[3]

---

1. Dick's *Lectures on Theology*, vol. ii, p. 167.
2. Edward's *Miscellaneous Observations*, p. 114.
3. Dick's *Lectures on Theology*, vol. ii, p. 170.

The decrees of God are *free*. He was not impelled to decree from any exigence of the divine nature; this would be to deny his self-sufficiency. Neither was he under any external constraint; this would be destructive of his independence. His decrees, therefore, must be the sovereign and free act of his will. By this it is not meant to insinuate that they are arbitrary decisions; but merely that, in making his decrees, he was under no control, and acted according to his own sovereignty.

The decrees of God are most *wise*. They are called 'the counsel of his will' to show that, though his will be free, yet he always acts in a manner consummately wise. He needs not to deliberate, or take counsel with others, but all his decrees are the result of unerring wisdom. 'O the depth of the riches both of the wisdom and knowledge of God! how unsearchable are his judgments, and his ways past finding out!' 'Wisdom is discovered in the selection of the most proper ends, and of the fittest means of accomplishing them. That this character belongs to the decrees of God is evident from what we know of them. They are disclosed to us by their execution; and every proof of wisdom in the works of God is a proof of the wisdom of the plan in conformity to which they are performed.'

The decrees of God are *eternal*. This our Confession explicitly affirms: 'God, *from all eternity*, did ordain whatsoever comes to pass.' This is asserted in opposition to the Socinians, who hold that some, at least, of the decrees of God are temporary. Those decrees which relate to things dependent on the free agency of man, they maintain, are made in time. But what saith the Scripture? It expressly declares, that every thing which has happened, and everything which is to happen, was known to God from everlasting. 'Known unto God are all his works, from the beginning of the world' (Acts 15:18). To suppose any of the divine decrees to be made in time is to suppose the knowledge of the Deity to be limited. If from eternity he knew all things that come to pass, then from eternity he must have ordained them; for if they had not been determined upon, they could not have been foreknown as certain.

The decrees of God are *absolute* and *unconditional*. He has not decreed anything, because he foresaw it as future; and the execution of his decrees is not suspended upon any condition which may or may not be performed. This is the explicit doctrine of our Confession, and it is this principle which chiefly distinguishes

Calvinists from Arminians, who maintain that God's decrees are not absolute but conditional.

> It is granted, that some of the decrees of God are conditional, in this sense, that something is supposed to go before the event which is the object of the decree, and that, this order being established, the one will not take place without the other. He decreed, for example, to save Paul and the companions of his voyage to Italy; but he decreed to save them only on condition that the sailors should remain in the ship (Acts 27). He has decreed to save many from the wrath to come; but he has decreed to save them only if they believe in Christ, and turn by him from the error of their ways. But these decrees are conditional only in appearance. They merely state the order in which the events should be accomplished; they establish a connection between the means and the end, but do not leave the means uncertain. When God decreed to save Paul and his companions, he decreed that the sailors should be prevented from leaving the ship; and accordingly gave Paul previous notice of the preservation of every person on board. When he decreed to save those who should believe, he decreed to give them faith; and, accordingly, we are informed, that those whom he predestinated he also calls into the fellowship of his Son (Romans 8:30). That any decree is conditional in the sense [of Arminians], that it depends upon the will of man, of which he is sovereign master, so that he may will or not will as he pleases, we deny. 'My counsel,' says God, 'shall stand, and I will do all my pleasure' (Isaiah 46:10). But he could not speak so, if his counsel depended upon a condition which might not be performed.[4]

Conditional decrees are inconsistent with the infinite wisdom of God, and are in men the effects of weakness. They are also inconsistent with the independence of God, making them to depend upon the free will or agency of his creatures. The accomplishment of them too would be altogether uncertain; but the Scripture assures us that 'the counsel of the LORD standeth for ever, and the thoughts of his heart to all generations' (Psalm 33:11). All his purposes are unalterably determined, and their execution infallibly certain. 'There are many devices in a man's heart,' which he is unable to accomplish, 'nevertheless the counsel of the LORD, that shall stand' (Proverbs 19:21).

It has been often objected to the doctrine respecting the divine decrees taught in our Confession, that it represents God as the author of sin. But the Confession expressly guards against this inference by declaring that God has so ordained whatsoever comes

---

4. Dick's *Lectures on Theology*, vol. ii, pp. 175, 176, etc.

to pass as that he is not thereby the author of sin. The decree of God is either effective or permissive. His effective decree respects all the good that comes to pass; his permissive decree respects the evil that is in sinful actions. We must also distinguish betwixt an action *purely as such*, and the sinfulness of the action. The decree of God is effective with respect to the action abstractly considered; it is permissive with respect to the *sinfulness* of the action as a moral evil.

It has also been objected that if God has foreordained whatsoever comes to pass, human liberty is taken away. To this it has been commonly replied, that it is sufficient to human liberty, that a man acts without any constraint, and according to his own free choice; that the divine decree is extrinsic to the human mind; and, while it secures the futurition of events, it leaves rational agents to act as freely as if there had been no decree. This answer, it must be acknowledged, merely amounts to an assertion that, notwithstanding the decree of God, man retains his liberty of action. We still wish to know how the divine pre-ordination of the event is consistent with human liberty. 'Upon such a subject,' says Dr Dick, 'no man should be ashamed to acknowledge his ignorance. We are not required to reconcile the divine decrees and human liberty. It is enough to know that God has decreed all things which come to pass, and that men are answerable for their actions. Of both these truths we are assured by the Scriptures; and the latter is confirmed by the testimony of conscience. We feel that, although not independent upon God, we are free; so that we excuse ourselves when we have done our duty, and accuse ourselves when we have neglected it. Sentiments of approbation and disapprobation, in reference to our own conduct or that of other men, would have no existence in our minds if we believed that men are necessary agents. But the tie which connects the divine decrees and human liberty is invisible. "Such knowledge is too wonderful for us; it is high, we cannot attain unto it" (Psalm 139:6).'

It may be further observed, that, although God has unchangeably ordained whatsoever comes to pass, yet this does not take away the contingency of second causes, either in themselves or as to us. Nothing can be more contingent than the decision of the lot – yet 'the lot is cast into the lap; but the whole disposing thereof is of the LORD' (Proverbs 16:33).

Section 3

By the decree of God, for the manifestation of his glory, some men and angels (1 Timothy 5:21; Matthew 25:41) are predestinated unto everlasting life, and others foreordained to everlasting death (Romans 9:22, 23; Ephesians 1:5, 6; Proverbs 16:4).

Section 4

These angels and men, thus predestinated and foreordained, are particularly and unchangeably designed, and their number is so certain and definite, that it cannot be either increased or diminished (2 Timothy 2:19; John 13:18).

Section 5

Those of mankind that are predestinated unto life, God, before the foundation of the world was laid, according to his eternal and immutable purpose, and the secret counsel and good pleasure of his will, hath chosen in Christ unto everlasting glory (1 Ephesians 1:4, 9, 11; Romans 8:30; 2 Timothy 1:9; 1 Thessalonians 5:9), out of his mere free grace and love, without any foresight of faith or good works, or perseverance in either of them, or any other thing in the creature, as conditions, or causes moving him thereunto (Romans 9:11, 13, 16; Ephesians 1:4, 9); and all to the praise of his glorious grace (Ephesians 1:6, 12).

Exposition

The decree of God, with respect to the everlasting state of angels and men, is known by the name of *predestination*; and this consists of two branches, generally distinguished by the names of *election* and *reprobation*.

That part of the angels were elected is inferred from that passage of Scripture in which the *elect angels* are mentioned (1 Timothy 5:21). Of the fallen angels two apostles make express mention (2 Peter 2:4; Jude 6). Thus the election of a part of the angels is explicitly taught in Scripture, and the non-election of others is necessarily implied; for election is a relative term, and necessarily involves the idea of rejection.

Of the decree of election, as it relates to men, the above sections contain a full statement, and a subsequent section states the doctrine of Scripture respecting what is usually termed the decree of reprobation. That there is such a thing as election, in some sense or other, must be admitted by all who believe the Scriptures; but many who retain the word completely explain away the doctrine which the Bible teaches upon the subject.

Some will allow of no election but that of nations, or of whole Churches, in their collective capacity. That the Scripture speaks of such a general election is admitted; but this is not inconsistent with a particular and personal election. The Jews were a chosen generation, separated from among the other nations of the world, to be, in a peculiar manner, the people of God; but our Lord intimates that among them there was a remnant chosen in a superior sense (Matthew 24:22). The Apostle Paul also saith, 'Even at this present time there is a remnant according to the election of grace' (Romans 11:5). That it is of the Jews, the chosen nation, the apostle speaks, and that he distinguishes a remnant from the great body of them, is sufficiently manifest; and he plainly intimates, that the former were chosen in such a sense as the latter were not.

Some allow only of an election to external privileges. Holding that the Scripture speaks solely of an election of communities, they maintain that they are only chosen to the enjoyment of the external means of salvation. But we are assured from Scripture that they who believe 'were ordained to eternal life' and that they were 'chosen to salvation' (Acts 13:48; 2 Thessalonians 2:13).

Some, by election, understand no more than a separation of persons from the world, made in time, and thus identify it with their calling, or conversion. But in Scripture, election and calling are clearly distinguished; and the latter is represented as the effect of the former. Persons are said to be 'called according to God's purpose,' and 'whom he did predestinate, them he also called' (Romans 8:28-30). Now predestination and the purpose of God must be very different from calling, which proceeds from it, unless the cause and the effect are the same thing. To put such interpretations upon the word 'election' is to wrest the language of Scripture, and to impose upon it a sense contrary to its obvious meaning.

It would be tedious, and would serve no good purpose, to enumerate the multifarious opinions which have been held on this subject. It will be sufficient to mention the opinion of the Socinians and of the Arminians. The Socinians deny the certain prescience of future contingencies, such as the determinations of free agents; and, therefore, the only decree respecting the salvation of men which they will admit to have been made from eternity, and to be unchangeable, is a general conditional decree, that such as believe and obey the gospel shall be saved; and, according to them, a special decree concerning particular persons is only made in time, when persons perform the condition contained in the general decree. The Arminians, or Remonstrants as they are also called, are distinguished from the Socinians, by admitting that contingent events, such as the determinations and actions of men, are foreseen by God; but they also deny absolute and unconditional election, and maintain that whatever God has decreed respecting men is founded on the foresight of their conduct. Having foreseen, without any decree, that Adam would involve himself and his posterity in sin and its consequences, he purposed to send his Son to die for them all, and to give them sufficient grace to improve the means of salvation; and knowing beforehand who would believe and persevere to the end, and who would not, he chose the former to eternal life and left the latter in a state of condemnation. There is, however, a diversity of opinion among the holders of this general system; and some of them coincide with Socinians in maintaining that the decrees of God respecting men are not eternal, but are made in time; that men are elected to eternal life after they have believed, and that, if they fall into a state of unbelief and impenitence, the sentence or decree is reversed.

In opposition to these systems, our Confession teaches that God made choice of, and predestinated a certain and definite number of individuals to everlasting life; that he predestinated them unto life before the foundation of the world was laid; that in so doing, he acted according to this sovereign will, and was not influenced by the foresight of their faith or good works, or perseverance in either of them; and that this purpose is immutable, it being impossible that any of the elect should perish. That these doctrines are in accordance with Scripture may be easily evinced.

1. God made choice of, and predestinated, a certain and definite number of individuals to everlasting life. According to the Socinians, God predestinated to eternal life, not any particular individuals of mankind, but a certain sort of description of men; not persons, but characters. The Scripture, however, clearly teaches that God made choice of a certain determinate number of persons from among the rest of the human race, and ordained them to eternal life. It is said, 'The Lord knoweth them that are his' (2 Timothy 2:19). He perfectly knows how many, and who in particular, his elect are. Hence their names are said to be enrolled in a book, called the *Book of Life*; for it is the book in which are

registered the names of all the individuals of mankind who were chosen to everlasting life. A person's name is that whereby he is known and distinguished from others; when, therefore, their names are said to be written in a book, it intimates that God has an exact knowledge of all the individuals whom he had chosen.

2. God predestinated these individuals to life from eternity. According to Socinians, and some Arminians, as has been already noticed, special election only takes place in time, when persons actually believe and obey the gospel. But an election in time is at direct variance with the doctrine of Scripture. It is said, 'God hath chosen us in him *before* the foundation of the world' (Ephesians 1:4); and this emphatical phrase is evidently expressive of eternity. Thus Paul addresses the Thessalonian Christians, 'God hath *from the beginning* chosen you to salvation' (2 Thessalonians 2:13). That the phrase 'from the beginning' denotes eternity is evident from Proverbs 8:23, where Christ is introduced saying, 'I was set up from everlasting, from the beginning, ere ever the earth was.' That the phrase 'from the beginning' is here equivalent to the phrase 'from everlasting' is manifest. Indeed, we cannot conceive of any *new* determinations arising in the divine mind, without supposing the Divine Being defective in knowledge, or mutable in his perfections – suppositions utterly incompatible with the nature of that Being, whose name is JEHOVAH.

3. In making this choice, God acted from his own sovereign will and was not influenced by any foresight of their faith or other qualifications. According to Arminians, God's decree respecting the salvation of men is founded upon their foreseen faith and good works. Thus,

> the decree of God, although prior in time, is posterior in order to the actions of men, and is dependent upon the determination of their will. But to this opinion, so derogatory to the supreme dominion and absolute authority of God, the doctrine of Scripture is directly opposed. Election is ascribed to grace, to the exclusion of works; and these two causes are represented as incompatible and mutually destructive. 'Even so then at this present time, there is a remnant according to the election of grace. And if by grace, then is it no more of works, otherwise grace is no more grace. But if it be of works, then it is no more grace; otherwise work is no more work' (Romans 11:5, 6). How is it possible to reconcile with these words the opinion that the foresight of men's good works was the cause of their election? Besides, it is worthy of particular attention that faith and holiness,

which the advocates of conditional decrees make the causes of election, are expressly said in Scripture to be the effects of it (2 Thessalonians 2:13; Ephesians 1:4). In Romans 9:10-13, Paul produces the case of Jacob and Esau as an illustration of the subject, and traces the predestination of individuals to happiness or misery to the sovereignty of God, without any consideration of their works. As the lot of the two sons of Isaac was settled prior to their personal conduct, so the apostle signifies that the appointment of particular persons to salvation depends solely upon the good pleasure of God.[5]

That election is founded on the good pleasure of God, and not on anything in its objects, is clearly stated in verse 16 of the same chapter: ' It is not of him that willeth, nor of him that runneth, but of God that sheweth mercy'; and also in verse 18: 'Therefore he hath mercy on whom he will ...' Were it otherwise, there would be no shadow of objection to the doctrine.

How could men say it was unjust, if God chose one and rejected another according to their works? And how could any one object, as in verse 19, 'that as the will of God could not be resisted, men were not to be blamed,' if the decision in question did not depend on the will of God, but on that of men? How easy for the apostle to have answered the objector, 'You are mistaken, the choice is not of God, he does not choose whom he wills, but whom he sees will choose him! It is not his will, but man's that decides the point.' Paul does not so answer, but vindicates the doctrine of the divine sovereignty. The fact, therefore, that Paul had to answer the same objections which are now constantly urged against the doctrine of election, goes far to show that that doctrine was his.[6]

4. The purpose of God respecting his elect is immutable. As Arminians hold that saints may fall from a state of grace, so they maintain that a person who is one of the elect today may become one of the reprobate tomorrow. They affirm that 'men may make their election void' – that 'as they change themselves from believers to unbelievers, so the divine determination concerning them changes.' But the Scripture expressly declares, that 'the counsel of the LORD standeth for ever, the thoughts of his heart to all generations' (Psalm 33:11). Besides this general assurance of the immutability of his counsel, it is affirmed that 'the foundation of God standeth sure, having this seal, The Lord knoweth them that

---

5. Dick's *Lectures on Theology*, vol. ii., pp. 189, 190.
6. Hodge's Commentary on the Romans.

are his' (2 Timothy 2:19). The purpose of God, according to election, shall stand; so that the number of the elect can neither be increased nor diminished.

There is one circumstances connected with election that remains to be noticed. The elect are stated to have been 'chosen in Christ,' which, indeed, is the express language of Scripture (Ephesians 1:4). This cannot mean that the mediatory work of Christ was the *cause* of their election; for, as has been already shown, election proceeds from the mere sovereign will of God; and the Scripture represents the mission of our Saviour as the effect of the love of God (John 3:16). The mediation of Christ was necessary in order that the effects of electing love might be bestowed upon God's chosen, in a consistency with the rights and honour of his justice; but election itself originated in divine sovereignty, and had no other cause than the good pleasure of God's will (Ephesians 1:5). The divine purpose is one, embracing the means as well as the end; but according to our conception of the operations of the divine mind, the end is first in intention, and then the means are appointed by which it is to be carried into effect. The phrase 'chosen *in Christ*' signifies therefore, we apprehend, that God had a respect to the mediation of Christ, not as the cause of their election, but as the means by which the purpose of election was to be executed.

Section 6
As God hath appointed the elect unto glory, so hath he, by the eternal and most free purpose of his will, foreordained all the means thereunto (1 Peter 1:2; Ephesians 1:4, 5; 2:10; 2 Thessalonians 2:13). Wherefore they who are elected being fallen in Adam, are redeemed by Christ (1 Thessalonians 5:9, 10; Titus 2:14); are effectually called unto faith in Christ by his Spirit working in due season; are justified, adopted, sanctified (Romans 8:30; Ephesians 1:5; 2 Thessalonians 2:13), and kept by his power through faith unto salvation (1 Peter 1:5). Neither are any other redeemed by Christ, effectually called, justified, adopted, sanctified, and saved, but the elect only (John 17:9; Romans 8:28; John 6:64, 65; 10:26; 8:47; 1 John 2:19).

Exposition
In this section we have first a general statement that, in the divine purpose, the means and the end are inseparably connected. As God appointed the elect to glory, so he appointed them to obtain that glory in and through Christ, and on account of his merits alone

(1 Thessalonians 5:9). He likewise appointed them to all those means which are indispensably necessary to the enjoyment of that glory; such as faith and sanctification, and perseverance therein to the end (2 Thessalonians 2:13). Thus, though the mediation of Christ was not the cause of their election, yet his obedience and death were the grand means appointed for the execution of that gracious purpose; and though the Almighty chose no man to glory because of his future faith and holiness, yet provision was made in the eternal purpose of God for the faith and sanctification of all his chosen, prior to their enjoyment of bliss. It is, therefore, a gross abuse of the doctrine of election for persons to expect that they shall attain the end, while they neglect to use the appointed means. No man acts in this manner in regard to the common affairs of life, and to do so in matters of infinitely higher importance would be the highest presumption and folly.

This section next states more particularly the means by which the elect are brought to glory. They are redeemed by Christ, and his redemption is effectually applied to them by the working of his Spirit. In order to determine the import of the phrase 'redeemed by Christ,' it is necessary to ascertain in what sense the word *redeemed* is here used. The term 'redemption' in Scripture frequently signifies *actual deliverance* from sin and all its penal consequences; but primarily and properly it means a deliverance effected by the *payment of a ransom*. Hence, theologians have usually distinguished between redemption by *price* and redemption by *power*; the latter coincides with *actual deliverance*; the former denotes the *payment of the price*, by which Christ meritoriously procured the deliverance of his people. When the Westminster Confession was compiled, the term 'redemption' was generally used as almost exactly equivalent to the modern term 'atonement'; and, of course, what was then called general and particular redemption corresponds to the modern phrases, general and limited atonement. Some have contended that in this section the term 'redemption' is equivalent, not to the payment of a price, but to the deliverance obtained through the payment of a price; or, that the word *redeemed* is used as equivalent to *saved*. But the section clearly distinguishes between the elect being redeemed and their being saved; and it represents their redemption by Christ as being effected and completed previous to their being effectually called unto faith in Christ. Their justification, adoption, sanctification and final salvation are just the blessings which constitute the deliverance obtained for them through the death of Christ; and, therefore, their redemption by Christ must signify, not the deliverance itself, but the payment of the price which procured their deliverance. Their redemption by Christ is already complete – it was *finished* by Christ on the cross; but their actual deliverance is to be effected *in due season*, namely, when they are united to Christ by faith.

In this section, then, we are taught:

1. That Christ, by his death, did not merely render the salvation of all men possible, or bring them into a salvable state, but purchased and secured a certain salvation to all for whom he died (John 17:4; Hebrews 4:12).

2. That Christ died exclusively for the elect and purchased redemption for them alone; in other words, that Christ made atonement only for the elect, and that in no sense did he die for the rest of the race. Our Confession first asserts, positively, that *the elect are redeemed by Christ*; and then, negatively, that *none other are redeemed by Christ but the elect only*. If this does not affirm the doctrine of particular redemption, or of a limited atonement, we know not what language could express that doctrine more explicitly. It is diametrically opposed to the system of the Arminians, who hold 'that Jesus Christ, by his death and sufferings, made an atonement for the sins of all mankind in general, and of every individual in particular'. It is not less opposed to the doctrine maintained by many, that though the death of Christ had a special reference to the elect, and, in connection with the divine purpose, infallibly secures their salvation, yet that it has also a general reference, and made an equal atonement for all men. The celebrated Richard Baxter, who favoured general redemption, makes the following remark upon this and another section of our Confession:

> Chap. iii. sec. 6, and chap. viii. sec. 8, which speak against universal redemption, I understand not of all redemption, and particularly not of the mere bearing the punishment of man's sins, and satisfying God's justice, but of that special redemption proper to the elect, which was accompanied with an intention of actual application of the saving benefits in time. If I may not be allowed this interpretation, I must herein dissent.[7]

The language of the Confession, in my opinion, will not admit

---

7. Baxter's *Confession of his Faith*, p. 21.

of this interpretation; and, what is more, the Bible is silent about this general redemption, or the general reference of the death of Christ. The Saviour himself declares, 'I lay down my life for the sheep'; and he affirms that the *sheep* for whom he laid down his life are the definite number chosen by God, and given to him in the eternal covenant, and to whom he will eventually give eternal life (John 10:15, 28, 29).

> It is true, the Christian religion being to be distinguished from the Jewish in this main point, that whereas the Jewish was restrained to Abraham's posterity, and confined within one race and nation, the Christian was to be preached to *every creature*, universal words are used concerning the death of Christ; but as the words, 'preaching to every creature,' and to 'all the world,' are not to be understood in the utmost extent – for then they have never been verified, since the gospel has never yet, for aught that appears to us, been preached to every nation under heaven – but are only to be explained generally of a commission not limited to one or more nations, none being excluded from it; the apostles were to execute it, in going from city to city, as they should be inwardly moved to it by the Holy Ghost; so 'Calvinists' think that those large words that are applied to the death of Christ are to be understood in the same qualified manner; that no nation, or sort of men, are excluded from it, and that some of all kinds and sorts shall be saved by him. And this is to be carried no further, without an imputation on the justice of God; for if he has received a sufficient oblation and satisfaction for the sins of the whole world, it is not reconcilable to justice that all should not be saved by it, or should not at least have the offer and promulgation of it made them; that so a trial may be made, whether they will accept of it or not.

3. We are further taught that salvation shall be effectually applied by the Holy Spirit to all those who were chosen of God and redeemed by Christ; and that it shall be effectually applied to them alone. The elect are all in due time, by the power of the Spirit, effectually called unto faith in Christ. 'All that the Father giveth me shall come to me' (John 6:37). 'As many as were ordained to eternal life believed' (Acts 13:48). They are all justified, adopted, sanctified, and shall be enabled to persevere in grace, and at length their salvation shall be consummated in glory. 'Whom he did predestinate, them he also called; and whom he called, them he also justified; and whom he justified, them he also glorified' (Romans 8:30).

---

8. Burnet on the Thirty-Nine Articles, Art. 17.

Thus our Confession, agreeably to Scripture, represents each of the divine persons as acting a distinct part in the glorious work of human redemption, and as entirely concurring in counsel and operation. The Father chose a definite number of mankind sinners to eternal life; the Son laid down his life for those who were chosen in him before the foundation of the world, and obtained for them eternal redemption; and the Holy Spirit applies the purchased redemption to them in due season. Here all is perfect harmony. The Son fulfils the will of the Father, and the Spirit's work is in entire accordance with the purpose of the Father and the mediation of the Son. But according to the scheme of general redemption, or of universal atonement, this harmony is utterly destroyed. The Son sheds his blood for multitudes whom the Father never purposed to save, and the Spirit does not put forth the influence necessary to secure the application of salvation to all for whom Christ died!

Section 7
The rest of mankind, God was pleased, according to the unsearchable counsel of his own will, whereby he extendeth or withholdeth mercy as he pleaseth, for the glory of his sovereign power over his creatures, to pass by, and to ordain them to dishonour and wrath for their sin, to the praise of his glorious justice (Matthew 11:25-26; Romans 9:17-18, 21-22; 2 Timothy 2:19-20; Jude 4; 1 Peter 2:8).

Exposition
This section describes what is usually called the decree of *reprobation*. This term is not used in the Confession, and when it occurs in Scripture bears a different sense from the theological; but for the sake of convenience, it is used to express that act of God's will by which, when he viewed all mankind as involved in guilt and misery, he rejected some, while he chose others. Some who allow of personal and eternal election deny any such thing as reprobation. But the one unavoidably follows from the other; for the choice of some must necessarily imply the rejection of others.

> Election and rejection are co-relative terms; and men impose upon themselves, and imagine that they conceive what it is impossible to conceive, when they admit election and deny reprobation.... There are many passages of Scripture in which this doctrine is taught. We read of some whose names are 'not written', and who, consequently, are opposed to those whose names are written, 'in the Book of Life'; who are 'vessels of wrath fitted to destruction'; who were 'before of old

ordained to condemnation'; who 'stumble at the Word, being disobedient, whereunto also they were appointed'; of persons whom God is said to hate, while others he loves. Let any man carefully and dispassionately read the 9th and the 11th chapters of the Epistle to the Romans, and he will entertain no more doubt that some are ordained to death, than that others are ordained to life.[9]

Our Confession speaks of God's passing by some, and also ordaining them to wrath; and we apprehend there is an important distinction betwixt the two. If the reason be inquired why God *passed by* some of mankind sinners, while he elected others to life, it must be resolved into the counsel of his own will, whereby he extends or withholds mercy as he pleases. No doubt those whom God passed by were considered as fallen and guilty creatures; but if there was sin in them, there was sin also in those who were chosen to salvation; we must, therefore, resolve their opposite allotment into the will of God: 'He hath mercy upon whom he will have mercy, and whom he will he hardeneth' (Romans 9:18). As it would have been just in God to pass by the whole of our race, and to deal with them as he did with the angels who sinned, it must be manifest that, in electing some to life, he did no injustice to the non-elect, whose case would have been just as bad as it is, even supposing the others had *not* been chosen at all. But if the reason be inquired why God *ordained to dishonour and wrath* those whom he passed by, this must be resolved into their own *sin*. In this act God appears as a judge, fixing beforehand the punishment of the guilty; and his decree is only a purpose of acting towards them according to the natural course of justice. Their own sin is the procuring cause of their final ruin, and therefore God does them no wrong. The salvation of the elect is wholly 'to the praise of his glorious grace', and the condemnation of the non-elect is 'to the praise of his glorious justice'.

Section 8
The doctrine of this high mystery of predestination is to be handled with special prudence and care (Romans 9:20; 11:33; Deuteronomy 29:29), that men attending the will of God revealed in his Word, and yielding obedience thereunto, may, from the certainty of their effectual vocation, be assured of their eternal election (2 Peter 1:10). So shall this doctrine afford matter of praise, reverence, and admiration of God (Ephesians 1:6;

9. Dick's *Lectures on Theology*, vol. ii., pp. 197, 198.

Romans 11:33), and of humility, diligence, and abundant consolation, to all that sincerely obey the gospel (Romans 11:5, 6, 20; 2 Peter 1:10; Romans 8:33; Luke 10:20).

Exposition

The doctrine of predestination is, indeed, a high mystery – one of the deep things of God, which our feeble intellects cannot fully comprehend. In our inquiries about it, we ought to repress a vain curiosity, and not attempt to be wise above what is written. But, since the doctrine is revealed by God in his Word, it is a proper subject for sober investigation, and ought to be published from the pulpit and the press. Calvin justly remarks: 'That those things which the Lord hath laid up in secret, we may not search; those things which he hath brought openly abroad, we may not neglect; lest either on the one part we be condemned of vain curiosity, or on the other part, of unthankfulness.' Were this doctrine either dangerous or useless, God would not have revealed it, and for men to attempt to suppress it, is to arraign the wisdom of God, as though he foresaw not the danger which they would arrogantly interpose to prevent. 'Whosoever,' adds Calvin, 'laboureth to bring the doctrine of predestination into misliking, he openly saith evil of God; as though somewhat had unadvisedly slipped from him which is hurtful to the Church.'[10] This doctrine, however, ought to be handled with special judgment and prudence, avoiding human speculations, and adhering to what is plainly revealed in the Scriptures. When prudently discussed, it will neither lead to licentiousness nor to despair; but will eminently conduce to the knowledge, establishment and comfort of Christians.

It ought ever to be remembered that no man can know his election prior to his conversion. Wherefore, instead of prying into the secret purpose of God, he ought to attend to his revealed will, that by making sure his vocation, he may ascertain his election. The order and method in which this knowledge may be attained is pointed out by the Apostle Peter, when he exhorts Christians to 'give all diligence to make their calling and election sure' (2 Peter 1:10). Their eternal election must remain a profound secret until it be discovered to them by their effectual calling in time; but when they have ascertained their calling, they may thence infallibly conclude that they were elected from eternity. Election, then, gives

10. Calvin's *Institutes*, book iii, ch. 21. sec. 4.

no discouragement to any man in reference to obeying the calls and embracing the offers of the gospel. The invitations of the gospel are not addressed to men *as elect*, but as sinners ready to perish; all are under the same obligation to comply with these invitations, and the encouragement from Christ is the same to all – 'Him that cometh to me, I will in no wise cast out.' And the doctrine of election must have a sanctifying and consoling influence on all who sincerely obey the gospel. It is calculated to inspire them with sentiments of reverence and gratitude towards God; to humble their souls in the dust before the eternal Sovereign; to excite them to diligence in the discharge of duty; to afford them strong consolation under the temptations and trials of life; and to animate them with a lively hope of eternal glory.

CHAPTER 4

CREATION

Section 1
It pleased God the Father, Son and Holy Ghost (Hebrews 1:2; John 1:2, 3; Genesis 1:2; Job 26:13; 33:4), for the manifestation of the glory of his eternal power, wisdom and goodness (Romans 1:20; Jeremiah 10:12; Psalm 104:24; 33:5, 6), in the beginning, to create, or make of nothing, the world, and all things therein, whether visible or invisible, in the space of six days, and all very good (Genesis 1; Hebrews 11:3; Colossians 1:16.; Acts 17:24).

Exposition
By the word 'creation' we are to understand the production and formation of all things. I use two words, because creation is twofold – primary and secondary, or immediate and mediate. By the former, is meant the production of something out of nothing; by the latter, the formation of things out of pre-existing matter, but matter naturally indisposed for such productions, and which never could by any power of second causes have been brought into such a form. This section teaches us:

1. That the world had a *beginning*. This will now be considered one of the most obvious truths that can be stated, but it is one that required to be confirmed by divine revelation. That the world existed from eternity was generally maintained by the ancient heathen philosophers. Some of them held, that not only the matter of which the world is framed existed from eternity, but that it subsisted in that beautiful form in which we behold it. Others admitted that the heavens and the earth had a beginning in respect of their present form, but maintained the eternity of the matter of which they are composed. That the world had a beginning is the uniform doctrine of the Scriptures (Genesis 1:1; Psalm 90:2). This is implied in the phrases, 'before the foundation of the world,' 'before the world began' (Ephesians 1:4; 2 Timothy 1:9).

According to the generally received chronology, the Mosaic creation took place 4004 years before the birth of Christ. If, indeed, the accounts of the Egyptians, Hindoos and Chinese were to be credited, we should believe that the universe has existed, in its present form, for many millions of years; but these accounts have been satisfactorily proved to be false. And as a strong presumption that the world has not yet existed 6000 years, it has been often remarked that the invention of arts, and the erection of the earliest empires, are of no great antiquity, and can be traced back to their origin.

2. That creation is the work of *God*. Often does God claim this work as one of the peculiar glories of his Deity, to the exclusion of all others (Isaiah 44:24; 45:12). The work of creation, however, is common to all the three persons of the Trinity. It is ascribed to the Father (1 Corinthians 8:6); to the Son (John 1:3); to the Holy Ghost (Genesis 1:2; Job 26:13). All the three persons are one God. We must not, therefore, suppose that in creation the Father is the principal agent, and the Son and the Holy Ghost inferior agents, or mere instruments. In all external works of Deity, each of the persons of the Godhead equally concur.

3. That creation extends to 'the world, and all things therein, whether visible or invisible'. This is expressly declared in many passages of Scripture: 'God made the world, and all things therein' (Acts 17:24). 'By him were all things created that are in heaven, and that are in earth, visible and invisible' (Colossians 1:16). This certainly includes angels. We have no reason to think that their creation preceded the period of the Mosaic creation; and they are generally supposed to have been created on the first day.

4. That the world, and all things therein, were created 'in the space of six days'. This, also, is the express language of Scripture: 'For in six days the LORD made heaven and earth, the sea, and all that in them is' (Exodus 20:11). The modern discoveries of geologists have led them to assign an earlier origin to the materials of which our globe is composed than the period of the six days, commonly known by the name of the Mosaic creation; and various theories have been adopted in order to reconcile the geological and Mosaic records. Some have held that all the changes which have taken place in the materials of the earth occurred either during the six days of the Mosaic creation, or since that period; but, it is urged, that the facts which geology establishes prove this view to be

utterly untenable. Others have held that a day of creation was not a natural day, composed of twenty-four fours, but a period of an indefinite length. To this it has been objected, that the sacred historian, as if to guard against such a latitude of interpretation, distinctly and pointedly declares of all the days, that each of them had its 'evening and morning' – thus, it should seem, expressly excluding any interpretation which does not imply a natural day. Others hold that the materials of our globe were in existence, and under the active operation of creative powers, for an indefinite period before the creation of man; and that the inspired record, while it gives us no information respecting the pre-existing condition of the earth, leaves ample room for a belief that it did pre-exist, if from any other source traces of this should be discovered by human research. The first verse of the 1st chapter of Genesis, in their opinion, merely asserts that the matter of which the universe is composed was produced out of nothing by the power of the Almighty, but leaves the time altogether indefinite. The subsequent verses of that chapter give an account of the successive process by which the Eternal, in the space of six days, reduced the pre-existing matter to its present form, and gave being to the plants and animals now in existence. This explanation, which leaves room for a long succession of geological events before the creation of the existing races, seems now to be the generally received mode of reconciling geological discoveries with the Mosaic account of the creation.[1]

5. That all things were created *very good*. Everything was good; for it was agreeable to the model which the great Architect had formed in his infinite mind from everlasting; it answered exactly the end of its creation, and was adapted to the purpose for which it was designed.

6. That God made all things for the manifestation of *his own glory*. 'The Lord hath made all things for himself,' for the manifestation of his infinite perfections; and all his works proclaim his almighty power, his unbounded goodness, and his unsearchable wisdom. His glory shines in every part of the material universe; but it would

---

1. The geological opinions of M. Agassiz are consistent with this explanation. See also R. S. Candlish on Genesis 1:20, and Dr Duncan's of Ruthwell, *Geological Lecture to Young Men*. Glasgow, 1842.

have shined in vain, if there had been no creature to contemplate it with an eye of intelligence, and celebrate the praises of the omnipotent Creator. Man, therefore, was introduced into the habitation which had been prepared for him, and of his creation the next section gives an account.

Section 2

After God had made all other creatures, he created man, male and female (Genesis 1:27), with reasonable and immortal souls (Genesis 2:7; Ecclesiastes 12:7; Luke 23:43; Matthew 10:28), endued with knowledge, righteousness, and true holiness, after his own image (Genesis 1:26; Colossians 3:10; Ephesians 4:24), having the law of God written in their hearts (Romans 2:14, 15), and power to fulfil it (Ecclesiastes 7:29); and yet under a possibility of transgressing, being left to the liberty of their own will, which was subject unto change (Genesis 3:6. Ecclesiastes 7:29). Beside this law written in their hearts, they received a command not to eat of the tree of the knowledge of good and evil (Genesis 2:17; 3:8-11, 23); which while they kept, they were happy in their communion with God, and had dominion over the creatures (Genesis 1:26, 28).

Exposition

Man was formed after God had made all other creatures; and this strongly marks the dignity of his character, and the exuberant bounty of his Creator. Before he was brought into existence, the earth, which was designed for his temporary residence, was completely prepared, and amply furnished for his reception. God created man, male and female – one man and one woman – *man* out of the dust of the ground, and *woman* out of a rib taken from man's side. It should seem that of the rest of the creatures God made many couples, but of man he made only one; and from this Christ brings an argument against divorce (Malachi 2:15; Matthew 19:4, 5). Man is a compound existence, made up of two great parts, a soul and a body. His body, though formed of mean materials, is a piece of exquisite workmanship; but his soul is the noblest part of his nature. By his soul he is allied to God and angels; by his body, to the beasts that perish, and to the dust under his feet.

Man was originally created after the *image of God*. This could not consist in a participation of the divine essence; for that is incommunicable to any creature. Neither did it consist in his external form; for God, having no bodily parts, could not be represented by any material resemblance. The image of God

consisted partly in the spirituality of the soul of man. God is a spirit
– an immaterial and immortal being. The soul of man also is a
spirit, though infinitely inferior to the Father of spirits. Thus, in
immateriality and immortality the soul of man bears a resemblance
to God. The image of God in man likewise consisted in the
dominion assigned to him over the creatures, in respect of which
he was the representative and vicegerent of God upon earth. God
is the blessed and only potentate, and he gave to man a delegated
sovereignty over the inferior creatures. He was constituted the
ruler of this lower world, and all the creatures were inspired with
respect for him, and submitted to his government.

But the image of God in man principally consisted in his
conformity to the moral perfections of God, or in the complete
rectitude of his nature. From two passages in the New Testament,
it appears that the image of God, after which man was at first
created, and to which he is restored by the Holy Spirit, consists in
knowledge, righteousness, and holiness (Ephesians 4:25; Colossians 3:10). Man had knowledge in his understanding, righteousness in his will and holiness in his affections. His understanding
was illuminated with all necessary knowledge. He knew God and
his will; he knew himself, his relations to God, his duty to him, and
his dependence upon him.

That he had also an extensive and accurate knowledge of
natural objects may be inferred from his giving distinctive names
to the inferior creatures when they passed in review before him.
His will was in conformity to the will of God. As he knew his duty,
so he was fully disposed to the performance of it. And his
affections were holy and pure; they were placed upon proper
objects, and exercised in a regular manner. There was then no need
that the moral law should be written on tables of stone, for it was
engraven on the heart of man in fair and legible characters. He had
likewise sufficient ability to fulfil it; but his will was entirely free
to act according to his original light and holy inclinations, or to turn
aside to evil.

Besides the natural law written on the hearts of our first parents,
they received a command not to eat of the tree of the knowledge
of good and evil. This prohibition, with the penalty annexed, will
come under our notice in a subsequent chapter; and at present we
only remark that while our first parents retained their original
integrity, and obeyed the positive command which God had

imposed upon them, they were supremely happy. The garden in which they were placed furnished them with every external comfort; they were called to engage in easy and delightful employments; they were exempted from the least degree of languor and of pain; they knew no guilt; they felt no shame; they were strangers to fear; and no angry passions disturbed their souls. But their happiness chiefly consisted in the favour of God, and in the intimate fellowship with him to which they were admitted. What an illustrious creature was man when he came from the hand of his Maker! but how sadly changed now! 'God made man upright; but they have sought out many inventions.'

CHAPTER 5

PROVIDENCE

Section 1

God, the great Creator of all things, doth uphold (Hebrews 1:3), direct, dispose, and govern all creatures, actions and things (Daniel 4:34, 35; Psalm 135:6; Acts 17:25, 26, 28; Job 38-41), from the greatest even to the least (Matthew 10:29-31), by his most wise and holy providence (Proverbs 15:3; Psalm 104:24; 145:17), according to his infallible foreknowledge (Acts 15:18; Psalm 94:8-11), and the free and immutable counsel of his own will (Ephesians 1:11; Psalm 33:10, 11), to the praise of the glory of his wisdom, power, justice, goodness and mercy (Isaiah 63:14; Ephesians 3:10; Romans 9:17; Genesis 45:7; Psalm 145:7).

Exposition

In opposition to Fatalists and others, who maintain that, in the original constitution of the universe, God gave to the material creation physical, and to the intelligent creation moral laws, by which they are sustained and governed, independently of his continued influence; this section teaches that there is a providence, by which God, the great Creator of all things, upholds and governs them all; and that this providence extends to all creatures, actions and things, from the greatest event to the least.

1. That there is a providence may be inferred from the nature and perfections of God; from the dependent nature of the creatures; from the continued order and harmony visible in all parts of the universe; from the remarkable judgments that have been inflicted on wicked men, and the signal deliverances that have been granted to the Church and people of God; and from the prediction of future events, and their exact fulfilment. In the Bible, the providence of God is everywhere asserted. 'His kingdom ruleth over all,' and he 'worketh all things after the counsel of his own will' (Psalm 103:19; Ephesians 1:11).

Two things are included in the notion of providence – the preservation and the government of all things. God *preserves* all things by continuing or upholding them in existence. The Scripture explicitly asserts, that 'he upholds all things by the word of his power,' and that 'by him all things consist' (Hebrews 1:3; Colossians 1:17). He preserves the different species of creatures, and sustains the several creatures in their individual beings; hence he is called 'the Preserver of man and beast' (Job 7:20; Psalm 36:6). God *governs* all things by directing and disposing them to the end for which he designed them. 'Our God is in the heavens, he hath done whatsoever he pleased' (Psalm 115:3). 'He doeth according to his will in the army of heaven, and among the inhabitants of the earth: and none can stay his hand, or say unto him, What doest thou?' (Daniel 4:35). The government of God may be considered in a twofold view – natural and moral. This twofold view of his government arises from the two general classes of creatures which are the objects of it. The irrational and inanimate creatures are the subjects of his *natural* government. The rational part of the creation, or those creatures who are the fit subjects of moral law, as angels and men, are the subjects of his *moral* government.

2. The providence of God extends to all creatures, actions and things, from the greatest even to the least. 'Some,' says Dr Dick, 'maintain only a general providence, which consists in upholding certain general laws, and exclaim against the idea of a particular providence, which takes a concern in individuals and their affairs. It is strange that the latter opinion should be adopted by any person who professes to bow to the authority of Scripture – which declares that a sparrow does not fall to the ground without the knowledge of our heavenly Father, and that the hairs of our head are all numbered – or by any man who has calmly listened to the dictates of reason. If God has certain designs to accomplish with respect to, or by means of, his intelligent creatures, I should wish to know how his intention can be fulfilled without particular attention to their circumstances, their movements, and all the events of their life? ... How can a whole be taken care of without taking care of its parts; or a species be preserved if the individuals are neglected?'

The providence of God extends to the *inanimate* creation. He who fixed the laws of nature, still continues or suspends their operation according to his pleasure; they are dependent on his continued influence, and subject to his control; and to assert the contrary would be to assign to the laws of nature that independence which belongs to God alone (Psalm 119:91; 104:14; Job 38:31-38). The providence of God likewise reaches to the whole *animal* creation. 'The beasts of the forest are his, and the cattle upon a thousand hills.' They are all his creatures, and the subjects of his providence (Psalm 104:27, 28). *Angels*, too, are the subjects of God's providence. The good angels are ever ready to obey his will, and are employed by him in ministering, in various ways, to the saints on earth (Hebrews 1:14). The evil angels are subject to his control, and can do no mischief without his permission (Job 1:12). The providence of God also extends to all human affairs; the affairs of *nations* are under his guidance and control. 'He increaseth the nations, and destroyeth them: he enlargeth the nations, and straiteneth them again. He leadeth princes away spoiled, and overthroweth the mighty' (Job 12:19, 23). This the humbled monarch of Babylon was taught by painful experience, and was constrained to acknowledge 'that the Most High ruleth in the kingdom of men, and giveth it to whomsoever he will' (Daniel 4:25). The providence of God is also to be recognised in the affairs of *families*. 'God setteth the solitary in families,' 'he setteth the poor on high from affliction, and maketh him families like a flock; again they are minished and brought low, through oppression, affliction and sorrow' (Psalms 68:6; 107:39, 41). The providence of God likewise extends to *individuals*, and to their minutest concerns. The birth of each individual, the length of his days, and all the events of his life, are regulated and superintended by the most wise and holy providence of God (Acts 17:28; Job 14:5).

As the doctrine of a particular providence is agreeable both to Scripture and to reason, so it is recommended by its obvious tendency to promote the piety and the consolation of mankind. To a God who governed the world solely by general laws, we might have looked up with reverence, but not with the confidence, and gratitude and hope, which arise from the belief that he superintends its minutest affairs. The thought that he 'compasses our paths and is acquainted with all our ways'; that he watches our steps, and orders all the events in our lot; guides and protects us, and supplies our wants, as it were, with his own hand; this thought awakens a train of sentiments and feelings highly favourable to devotion, and sheds a cheering light upon the path of life. We consider him as our Guardian and our Father; and, reposing upon his care, we are assured that, if we trust in him, no evil shall befal us, and no real blessing shall be withheld.[1]

---

1. Dick's *Lectures on Theology*, vol. 2, p. 302.

Section 2
Although, in relation to the foreknowledge and decree of God, the first cause, all things come to pass immutably and infallibly (Acts 2:23); yet, by the same providence, he ordereth them to fall out according to the nature of second causes, either necessarily, freely, or contingently (Genesis 8:22; Jeremiah 31:35; Exodus 21:13; Deuteronomy 19:5; 1 Kings 22:28, 34; Isaiah 10:6, 7).

Exposition
Since all things were known to God from the beginning of the world, and come to pass according to the immutable counsel of his will, it necessarily follows that, in respect of the foreknowledge and decree of God, all things come to pass infallibly. But, by his providence, he orders them to fall out according to the nature of second causes. Every part of the material world has an immediate dependence on the will and power of God, in respect of every motion and operation, as well as in respect of continued existence; but he governs the material world by certain physical laws – commonly called *the laws of nature*, and in Scripture *the ordinances of heaven* – and agreeably to these laws, so far as relates to second causes, certain effects uniformly and necessarily follow certain causes. The providence of God is also concerned about the volitions and actions of intelligent creatures; but his providential influence is not destructive of their rational liberty, for they are under no compulsion, but act freely; and all the liberty which can belong to rational creatures is that of acting according to their inclinations. Though there is no event contingent with respect to God, 'who declareth the end from the beginning, and from ancient times the things which are not yet done, saying, My counsel shall stand, and I will do all my pleasure'; yet many events are contingent or accidental with regard to us, and also with respect to second causes.

Section 3
God in his ordinary providence maketh use of means (Acts 27:31, 44; Isaiah 55:10, 11; Hosea 2:21, 22), yet is free to work without (Hosea 1:7; Matthew 4:4; Job 34:10), above (Romans 4:19-21), and against them (2 Kings 6:6; Daniel 3:27), at his pleasure.

Exposition
The providence of God is either ordinary or miraculous. In his ordinary providence God works by means, and according to the

general laws established by his own wisdom: we are, therefore, bound to use the means which he has appointed, and if we neglect these, we cannot expect to obtain the end. But though God generally acts according to established laws, yet he may suspend or modify these laws at pleasure. And when, by his immediate agency, an effect is produced above or beside the ordinary course of nature, this we denominate a miracle. The possibility of miracles will be denied by none but Atheists. To maintain that the laws of nature are so absolutely fixed, that they can in no case be deviated from, would be to exclude God from the government of the world – to represent the universe as a vast machine, whose movements are regulated by certain laws which even the great Architect cannot control.

Section 4

The almighty power, unsearchable wisdom, and infinite goodness of God, so far manifest themselves in his providence, that it extendeth itself even to the first fall, and all other sins of angels and men (Romans 11:32-34; 2 Samuel 24:1; 1 Chronicles 21:1; 1 Kings 22:22, 23; 1 Chronicles 10:4, 13, 14; 2 Samuel 16:10; Acts 2:23; 4:27, 28), and that not by a bare permission (Acts 14:16), but such as hath joined with it a most wise and powerful bounding (Psalm 126:10; 2 Kings 19:28), and otherwise ordering and governing of them, in a manifold dispensation, to his own holy ends (Genesis 1:20; Isaiah 10:6, 7, 12); yet so as the sinfulness thereof proceedeth only from the creature, and not from God; who being most holy and righteous, neither is nor can be the author or approver of sin (James 1:13, 14, 17; 1 John 2:16; Psalm 1:21).

Exposition

That the providence of God is concerned about the sinful actions of creatures must be admitted. Joseph's brethren committed a most wicked and unnatural action in selling him to the Midianites; but Joseph thus addressed his brethren: 'Be not grieved, nor angry with yourselves, that ye sold me hither: for God sent me before you to preserve life' (Genesis 45:5). The most atrocious crime ever perpetrated by human hands was the crucifixion of the Lord of glory; yet it is expressly affirmed that God delivered him into those wicked hands which were imbrued in his sacred blood: 'Him, being delivered by the determinate counsel and foreknowledge of God, ye have taken, and by wicked hands have crucified and slain' (Acts 2:23). At the same time, it is indisputable that God cannot be the author nor approver of sin. To solve the difficulty connected with this point, theologians distinguish between an action and its quality. The action, abstractly considered, is from God, for no action can be performed without the concurrence of Providence; but the sinfulness of the action proceeds entirely from the creature. As to the manner in which the providence of God is concerned about the sinful actions of creatures, it is usually stated, that God permits them, that he limits them and that he overrules them for the accomplishment of his own holy ends. But the full elucidation of this abstruse subject, so as to remove every difficulty, surpasses the human faculties. We are certain that God is concerned in all the actions of his creatures; we are equally certain that God cannot be the author of sin; and here we ought to rest.

Section 5

The most wise, righteous, and gracious God, doth oftentimes leave for a season his own children to manifold temptations, and the corruption of their own hearts, to chastise them for their former sins, or to discover unto them the hidden strength of corruption, and deceitfulness of their hearts, that they may be humbled (2 Chronicles 32:25, 26, 31; 2 Samuel 24:1); and to raise them to a more close and constant dependence for their support upon himself, and to make them more watchful against all future occasions of sin, and for sundry other just and holy ends (2 Corinthians 12:7-9; Psalm 73; 77:1, 10, 12; Mark 14:66-72; John 21:15, 17).

Section 6

As for those wicked and ungodly men whom God, as a righteous judge, for former sins doth blind and harden (Romans 1:24, 26, 28; 11:7, 8), from them he not only withholdeth his grace, whereby they might have been enlightened in their understandings, and wrought upon in their hearts (Deuteronomy 29:4), but sometimes also withdraweth the gifts which they had (Matthew 13:12; 25:29), and exposeth them to such objects as their corruption makes occasion of sin (Deuteronomy 2:30. 2 Kings 8:12, 13), and withal, gives them over to their lusts, the temptations of the world, and the power of Satan (Psalm 81:11, 12; 2 Thessalonians 2:10-12); whereby it comes to pass that they harden themselves, even under those means which God useth for the softening of others (Exodus 7:3; 8:15, 32; 2 Corinthians 2:15, 16; Isaiah 8:14; 1 Peter 2:7, 8; Isaiah 6:9, 10; Acts 28:26, 27).

Exposition

God cannot possibly solicit or seduce any man to sin; for this is inconsistent with the purity of his nature (James 1:13, 14). But, in righteous judgment, God sometimes permits persons to fall into one sin for the punishment of another. He deals in this way even with his own dear, but dutiful, children. Sometimes he leaves them for a season to temptations, and to the lusts of their own hearts, for their trial, or to discover to themselves the latent corruptions of their hearts, to humble them, and to excite them to more fervent prayer and remitting watchfulness. Thus, God left Hezekiah to try him, that he might know, or make known, all that was in his heart (2 Chronicles 32:31). Sometimes God deals in this manner with his own children to chastise them for their former sins. Thus, 'The anger of the LORD was kindled against Israel, and he moved David against them to say, Go number Israel and Judah' (2 Samuel 24:1). In Scripture, God is frequently said to harden wicked men for their former sins. This he does, not by infusing any wickedness into their hearts, or by direct and positive influence on their soul in rendering them obdurate, but by withholding his grace, which is necessary to soften their hearts, and which he is free to give or withhold as he pleases; by giving them over to their own hearts' lusts, to the temptations of the world, and the power of Satan; and by providentially placing them in such circumstances, or presenting such objects before them, as their corruption makes an occasion of hardening themselves.

Section 7
As the providence of God doth, in general, reach to all creatures; so, after a most special manner, it taketh care of his Church, and disposeth all things to the good thereof (1 Timothy 4:10; Amos 9:8, 9; Romans 8:28; Isaiah 43:3-5, 14).

Exposition
The providence of God may be considered as *general* and as *special*. His general providence is exercised about all his creatures; his special providence is exercised, in a particular manner, about his Church and people. 'The eyes of the LORD run to and fro throughout the whole earth, to show himself strong in behalf of them whose heart is perfect towards him' (2 Chronicles 16:9). God has the interests of his own people ever in view; he knows what is most conducive to their happiness; and he will make all things, whether prosperous or adverse, to co-operate in promoting their good (Romans 8:28). In all past ages, God has watched over his Church with peculiar and unremitting care; he has sometimes

permitted her to be reduced to a very low condition, but he has also wrought surprising deliverances in her behalf. The very means which her enemies intended for her destruction and ruin have, by an overruling Providence, been rendered subservient to her edification and enlargement (Acts 8:4). The preservation of the Church, in spite of the craft and malice of hell, and of all the pernicious errors and bloody persecutions which have threatened her ruin, is no less wonderful than the spectacle which Moses beheld – *a bush burning* but not *consumed*. And let us still confide and rejoice in the promise of Christ, that the gates of hell shall never prevail against his Church.

CHAPTER 6

THE FALL OF MAN, SIN, AND THE PUNISHMENT THEREOF

Section 1
Our first parents being seduced by the subtilty and temptation of Satan, sinned in eating the forbidden fruit (Genesis 3:13; 2 Corinthians 11:3). This their sin God was pleased, according to his wise and holy counsel, to permit, having purposed to order it to his own glory (Romans 11:32).

Exposition
That man is now in a very corrupt and sinful state, universal experience and observation attest. That he was not originally formed in this degraded state might be inferred from the character of his Maker; and the Scriptures explicitly affirm that he was at first created in the image of God – in a state of perfect rectitude. The question then arises, How was moral evil introduced into the world? To this important question reason can give no satisfactory answer. Pagan philosophers could not fail to observe the degeneracy of human nature; mournful experience taught them that evil had come into the world; but to assign the source of evil was knowledge too wonderful for them; numerous were their conjectures, and all remote from the truth. Divine revelation, however, sets this matter in a clear and certain light; and our Confession, in accordance with the inspired record, traces the entrance of sin to the seduction and disobedience of our first parents. They 'sinned in eating the forbidden fruit.' This supposes that the fruit of a certain tree was prohibited. The moral law was impressed upon the heart of man at his creation, and entire conformity to it was his indispensable duty; but, besides this *natural* law, God was pleased to give man a *positive* law, restricting him from the use of the fruit of a particular tree in the garden. 'The LORD God commanded the man, saying, Of every tree of the garden thou mayest freely eat: but of the tree of the knowledge of good and evil, thou shalt not eat of it' (Genesis 2:16, 17). Without loosening his obligation to yield obedience to the whole moral law, God summed up the duty of man in this single positive injunction, and constituted his abstaining

from the fruit of a certain tree the test of his obedience. The thing forbidden was in its own nature quite indifferent, neither good nor evil; the prohibition was founded solely on the sovereign will of God; it was, therefore, a most proper trial of man's obedience to the divine authority.

The occasion of man's violating this express injunction of his Sovereign was the temptation of Satan. The inspired historian, in the third chapter of Genesis, makes mention only of the serpent as concerned in seducing our first parents; but since we find Satan represented, in manifest allusion to the transactions of the fall, as 'a murderer from the beginning,' and as 'the old serpent and dragon' (John 8:44; Revelation 12:9; 20:2), we are led to the conclusion that Satan was the real tempter, and that he made use of the literal serpent as his instrument in carrying on the temptation. The various methods of fraud and cunning whereby he conducted his plot are stated in the sacred history, and have been illustrated by many eloquent writers. It was not by force or compulsion, but only 'through his subtlety that the serpent beguiled Eve.' Seduced by the tempter, Eve 'took of the fruit, and did eat, and gave also unto her husband with her, and he did eat' (Genesis 3:6). Thus the eating of the forbidden fruit was the first sin actually committed by man in our world. No doubt, our first parents were guilty of sin in their hearts, before they committed it with their hands; but the eating of the forbidden fruit was the *first sin* that was *finished*. 'When lust hath conceived, it bringeth forth sin; and sin, when it is finished, bringeth forth death' (James 1:15).

To some the eating of an apple may appear a very trivial matter, and often have attempts been made to turn this grave subject into ridicule; but, in judging of this act of our first parents, we must remember that they thereby transgressed an express prohibition of the Most High. Their abstaining from the tree of knowledge was the criterion by which their fidelity was to be tried, and their eating of the fruit of that tree was a violation of the whole law; for it was rebellion against the Lawgiver, and a renunciation of his authority. 'This grand transgression,' says a judicious author, 'though in its matter – to wit, eating a little fruit – it may be looked upon as a most mean and insignificant action; yet, if we consider it in its formal nature, as disobedience to an express divine command, which precept was particularly chosen out and enjoined as the test of man's pure love, just gratitude, and absolute obedience to God, it was certainly a most heinous sin. For behold what monstrous infidelity, ingratitude, and diabolical pride, were all at one implied in the same.'[1] 'It was aggravated,' says another, 'by the Being sinned against – a Benefactor so bountiful, a Master so indulgent; by the persons guilty of it, – creatures fresh from God's hand, untainted by sin, and laden with benefits; by the precept violated, – so plain and simple; by the place where it was committed, – a place where every plant, every creature, and every scene, displayed the bounty of the Lord, and proclaimed his goodness; and by its results, which were not to be limited to themselves, but to extend to their descendants, whom, for a momentary gratification, they ruined for ever.'[2]

Is it asked, How could upright man be seduced to commit this great transgression? The answer is, Man, though perfectly holy, was mutable. He had power to stand, but was liable to fall. God left him to the freedom of his own will, and that freedom he abused. No doubt God could have prevented his fall if he had pleased, by giving such influences of his Spirit as would have been absolutely effectual to hinder it; but this he was under no obligation to do. He did not withdraw from man that ability with which he had furnished him for his duty, not did he infuse any vicious inclinations into his heart, – he only withheld that further grace that would have infallibly prevented his fall. If it be inquired, Why God permitted the fall of man to take place? 'Probably the best answer ever given to this question in the present world, is that which was given by Christ concerning one branch of the divine dispensations to mankind: "Even so, Father; for so it seemed good in thy sight." It was a dispensation approved by infinite wisdom, and seen by the Omniscient Eye to be necessary towards that good which God proposed in creating the universe.'[3]

Section 2
By this sin they fell from their original righteousness and communion with God (Genesis 3:6-8; Ecclesiastes 7:29; Romans 3:23), and so became dead in sin (Genesis 2:17; Ephesians 2:1), and wholly defiled in all the faculties and parts of soul and body (Titus 1:15; Genesis 6:5; Jeremiah 17:9; Romans 3:10-18).

---

1. Principal Blackwell's *Sacred Scheme*, p. 199.
2. Belfrage's *Exposition of the Shorter Catechism*, vol. 1, p. 178.
3. Dwight's Theology, Serm. 27.

Exposition

This section points out the consequences of the sin of our first parents in regard to themselves. They 'fell from their original righteousness,' and became wholly corrupted in all the faculties of their souls and members of their bodies. The understanding, once a lamp of light, was now overwhelmed in darkness. The will, once faithful for God, and regulated by his will, now became perverse and rebellious. The affections, once pure and regular, now became vitiated and disordered. The body, too, was corrupted, and its members became instruments of unrighteousness unto sin. Our first parents likewise lost the happiness which they had formerly possessed. They were expelled from that pleasant and delightful abode in which God had placed them, the ground was cursed with barrenness for their sake, they were doomed to lead a life of toil and sorrow, and at last to return to the earth from which they were taken. But this was the least part of the misery into which they fell. They lost communion with God, the chief good; they forfeited his favour, and incurred his righteous displeasure. They became dead in sin – obnoxious to that death which is the wages of sin, and which had been threatened as the penalty of their disobedience. 'In the day thou eatest thereof,' said God, 'thou shalt surely die.' This threatening included *temporal* death, consisting in the dissolution of the union between the soul and the body; *spiritual* death, consisting in the loss of the favour and the image of God; and *eternal* death, consisting in the everlasting separation of both soul and body from God. The very day in which our first parents sinned, the sentence of death, though not immediately executed in its fullest extent, began to lay hold upon them. They became mortal, and were exposed to the disorders of a vitiated constitution; the principle of spiritual life was extinguished in their souls, and they were bound over to eternal wrath; and, had not a Mediator been provided, not only would they have returned to the dust, but they would have been 'punished with everlasting destruction from the presence of the Lord, and from the glory of his power'.

Section 3

They being the root of all mankind, the guilt of this sin was imputed (Genesis 1:27, 28; 2:16, 17; Acts 17:26; Romans 5:12, 15-19; 1 Corinthians 15:21, 22, 45, 49), and the same death in sin and corrupted nature conveyed, to all their posterity, descending from them by ordinary generation (Psalm 51:5; Genesis 5:3; Job 14:4; 15:14).

Section 4

From this original corruption, whereby we are utterly indisposed, disabled, and made opposite to all good (Romans 5:6; 8:7; 7:18; Colossians 1:21), and wholly inclined to all evil (Genesis 6:5; 8:21; Romans 3:10-12), do proceed all actual transgressions (James 1:14, 15; Ephesians 2:2, 3; Matthew 15:19).

Exposition

These sections point out the consequences of the sin of our first parents in regard to their posterity. These consequences are restricted to those 'descending from them by ordinary generation.' This restriction is obviously introduced in order to exclude our Lord Jesus Christ, who, as man, was one of the *posterity* of Adam, but did not descend from him by *ordinary generation*. The genealogy of Christ is traced up to Adam (Luke 3:38), but his human nature was supernaturally framed in the womb of the Virgin, by the power of the Holy Ghost (Luke 1:35). In his birth, therefore, as well as in his life, he was 'holy, harmless, undefiled, and separated from sinners'. But the effects of Adam's first transgression extend to all his *natural posterity*; and, according to our Confession, the guilt of this sin is imputed, and a corrupt nature is conveyed, to them. This is what is commonly called original sin. Though that phrase is often restricted to the corruption of nature derived to us from Adam, yet, in its proper latitude, it includes also the imputation of guilt.

The doctrine of original sin was universally received by the Church of God until the beginning of the fifth century, when it was denied by Pelagius. He maintained 'that the sins of our *first parents* were imputed to *them* alone, and not their *posterity*; that we derive no *corruption* from their fall, but are born as pure and unspotted as Adam came out of the forming hand of his Creator'.[4] This opinion was adopted by Socinus in the sixteenth century, and is held by the modern Socinians. The Arminians, who derive their name from Arminius, a divine of the seventeenth century, may not speak in the same unqualified terms of the purity of the descendants of Adam, but they do not admit that their nature is wholly vitiated, or that they have entirely lost their power to do good. In opposition to such tenets our Confession teaches, that a corrupt nature is conveyed to all the posterity of Adam; and that, by this original corruption, 'we

---

4. Mosheim's *Church History*, cent. 5, p. 2, ch. 5.

are utterly indisposed, disabled, and made opposite to all good, and wholly inclined to all evil'.

It may be proper to remark, that it is not the doctrine of the Scriptures nor of our standards that the corruption of nature of which they speak is any depravation of the soul, nor of any essential attribute, nor the infusion of any positive evil. The Confessions of the Reformers teach 'that original righteousness, as a punishment of Adam's sin, was lost, *and by that defect* the tendency to sin, or corrupt disposition, or corruption of nature, is occasioned. Though they speak of original sin as being, *first*, negative – i.e., the loss of righteousness – and, *secondly*, positive, or corruption of nature, yet by the latter, they state, is to be understood, not the infusion of anything in itself sinful, but an actual tendency or disposition to evil, resulting from the loss of righteousness'.[5] The universal corruption of mankind is amply confirmed by the Scriptures: 'The imagination of man's heart is evil from his youth' (Genesis 8:21). 'Behold, I was shapen in iniquity: and in sin did my mother conceive me' (Psalm 51:5). 'The wicked are estranged from the womb, they go astray as soon as they are born, speaking lies' (Psalm 58:3). 'That which is born of the flesh is flesh' (John 3:6). 'The carnal mind is enmity against God: for it is not subject to the law of God, neither indeed can be' (Romans 8:7). These, with many other places of Scripture, fully show that all mankind are infected with a corrupted nature. And the Scriptures no less clearly ascribe this corruption to the apostasy of Adam. The first man was created in the image of God, but after his fall 'he begat a son in his own likeness' (Genesis 5:3). 'By one man sin entered into the world, and death by sin' (Romans 5:12).

The corruption of human nature, which the Scriptures so clearly teach, may also be inferred from the fact that men, in all countries and in all varieties of situation, are sinners. 'The way we come by the idea of any such thing as disposition or tendency is by observing what is constant or general in event, especially under a great variety of circumstances.' Now, it is a fact, 'that all mankind come into the world in such a state as without fail comes to this issue, namely, the universal commission of sin; so that every one who comes to act in the world as a moral agent, is, in a greater or less degree, guilty of sin.' From this we infer 'that the mind of man has a natural tendency or propensity to that event which so

---

5. Hodge on the Romans, p. 158.

universally and infallibly takes place; and that this is a corrupt or depraved propensity.'[6]

The universal prevalence of sin cannot be accounted for, as Pelagians have alleged, by the influence of bad example; for, as President Edwards has justly argued, 'this is accounting for the corruption of the world by the corruption of the world. There are manifestations of moral depravity so very early in childhood as to anticipate all capacity for observing and following the example of others. There also frequently appear in children propensities towards those vices of which they have seen no examples. Besides, there are many examples of eminent virtue in the world, which yet are not so frequently or easily imitated as those of a vicious nature, which plainly shows an innate tendency towards vice.

Another branch of original sin is the imputation of the guilt of Adam's first transgression. This is rejected by many who admit original corruption.[7] By the *imputation* of Adam's first sin, it is not intended that his personal transgression becomes the personal transgression of his posterity; but that the *guilt* of his transgression is reckoned to their account. And it is only the guilt of his *first* sin, which was committed by him as a public representative, that is imputed to his posterity, and not the guilt of his future sins, after he had ceased to act in that character. The grounds of this imputation are that Adam was both the *natural root* and the *federal head* or representative of all his posterity. The former is the only ground mentioned in this section of the Confession, probably, because the representative character of Adam in the covenant of works has not yet been brought into view; but in the succeeding

---

6. Edwards on *Original Sin*, part 1, sect. 1, 2. This argument, so ably conducted by President Edwards, has been illustrated with his usual eloquence by Dr Chalmers in his *Lectures on the Romans*, vol. 1, pp. 367-370.

7. In the seventeenth century, De la Place affirmed 'that original sin is indirectly, and not directly, imputed to mankind' [Mosheim's *Church History*, cent. 17, sect. 2, p. 2, ch. 2]. By this is meant, that the personal transgression of Adam is not imputed to mankind, but that they derive from him a corrupted nature, and that this corruption is imputed to them. Among recent authors, we may mention Dr Dwight, who denies the imputation of Adam's first sin to his posterity, and limits the consequences of his fall, as regards them, to the conveyance of moral depravity – Serm. 32.)

chapter this is distinctly recognised. And both in the *Larger Catechism* (Question 22), and in the *Shorter* (Question 16), the representative character of Adam in the covenant made with him, is explicitly assigned as the principal ground of the imputation of the guilt of his first sin to all his posterity.

We do not see how the universal corruption of mankind can be accounted for, without admitting that they are involved in the guilt of his first transgression. It must be some sin which God punishes with the deprivation of original righteousness; and that can be no other than the first sin of Adam. The doctrine of imputation is clearly taught in Scripture; particularly in Romans 5, it is so plainly stated, so often repeated, and so formally proved, that it must be acknowledged to be the doctrine of the apostle.

In support of this doctrine, we might appeal to the universality of the effects of sin; especially to the death of infants. The apostle affirms, in the most express terms, that death is the effect of sin (Romans 5:12); and experience as well as Scripture shows that death passes upon all men. It passes even upon those who are incapable of committing actual sin; for 'death reigned from Adam to Moses, even over them that had not sinned after the similitude of Adam's transgression' (Romans 5:14). This is generally understood as referring to infants, who are incapable of sinning personally and actually, as Adam did; and since they have never in their own persons violated any law, their exposure to death can only be accounted for on the ground of the imputation to them of the sin of Adam.

This doctrine also derives confirmation from the analogy betwixt Adam and Christ, as stated by the apostle in the same chapter. In verse 14, he affirms that Adam 'is the figure of him that was to come,' and he traces the analogy in the subsequent verses, particularly in verses 18, 19: 'Therefore, as by the offence of one judgment came upon all men to condemnation; even so by the righteousness of one, the free gift came upon all men unto justification of life. For as by one man's disobedience many were made sinners; so by the obedience of one shall many be made righteous.' 'These verses,' says Dr Chalmers, 'contain the strength of the argument for the imputation of Adam's sin. As the condemnation of Adam comes to us, even so does the justification by Christ come to us. Now we know that the merit of the Saviour is ascribed to us, else no atonement for the past, and no renovation of heart or of life that is ever exemplified in this world for the future, will suffice for our acceptance with God. Even so, then, must the demerit of Adam have been ascribed to us. The analogy affirmed in these verses leads irresistibly to this conclusion. The judgment that we are guilty is transferred to us from the actual guilt of the one representative, even as the judgment that we are righteous is transferred to us from the actual righteousness of the other representative. We are sinners in virtue of one man's disobedience, independently of our own personal sins; and we are righteous in virtue of another's obedience, independently of our own personal qualifications. We do not say, but that through Adam we become personally sinful – inheriting as we do his corrupt nature. Neither do we say, but that through Christ we become personally holy – deriving out of his fullness the very graces which adorned his own character. But, as it is at best a tainted holiness that we have on this side of death, we must have something more than it in which to appear before God; and the righteousness of Christ reckoned unto us and rewarded in us, is that something. The something which corresponds to this in Adam, is his guilt reckoned unto us and punished in us – so that, to complete the analogy, as from him we get the infusion of his depravity, so from him also do we get the imputation of his demerit.'[8] 'Adam is not merely the corrupt parent of a corrupt offspring, who sin because of the depravity wherewith he has tainted all the families of the earth; but who have sinned in him, to use the language of our old divines, as their federal head – as the representative of a covenant which God made with him, and through him with all his posterity.'[9]

Section 5
This corruption of nature, during this life, doth remain in those that are regenerated (1 John 1:8, 10; Romans 7:14, 17, 18, 23; James 3:2; Proverbs 20:9; Ecclesiastes 7:20), and although it be through Christ pardoned and mortified, yet both itself, and all the motions thereof, are truly and properly sin (Romans 7:5, 7, 8, 25; Galatians 5:17).

Exposition
This section teaches us that corruption of nature remains in those that are regenerated, and is commensurate with this life. This

8. Chalmers' *Lectures on the Romans*, vol. 2, pp. 22, 23.
9. *Ibid.* vol. 1, p. 422.

condemns the tenet of *Christian perfection*; and it is supported by the plainest declarations of Scripture. 'If we say that we have no sin, we deceive ourselves, and the truth is not in us' (1 John 1:8). Paul himself says, 'Sin dwelleth in me,' and affirms, that 'when he would do good, evil is present with him' (Romans 7:17-21). It has, indeed, been disputed, whether Paul, in that chapter, describes his own feelings, or personates another. We have no doubt that Paul speaks of himself as regenerated, and describes his own state, and consequently the state of every regenerated person; but we do not rest the doctrine upon this single passage, for the conflict there described is represented in other places in language which, by common consent, can only be applied to true Christians. We shall only refer to Galatians 5:17: 'The flesh lusteth against the Spirit, and the Spirit against the flesh: and these are contrary the one to the other; so that ye cannot do the things that ye would.'

This section affirms that, even in the regenerated, this corruption, and all the motions thereof, are truly and properly sin. The guilt of it is, no doubt, removed by the blood of Christ, and the power of it subdued by his Spirit and grace; but, in itself, it retains the character of sin. This is affirmed in opposition to a tenet of the Church of Rome. That universal propensity to sin, which we call the corruption of nature, Roman Catholic writers denominate *concupiscence*; and this, they maintain, is no part of original sin, and is not in itself sinful. As they believe that original sin is taken away by baptism, and nevertheless find that this corrupt disposition remains in the regenerated, they conclude that it is no part of original sin, but that it is the natural state in which Adam was made at first; only, that in us it is without the restraint of supernatural assistance which was given to him, and which, in consequence of his transgression, was withdrawn from him and his posterity. In answer to this, it is argued that lust or concupiscence is, in several places of the New Testament, spoken of as sin; particularly in Romans 7:17, Paul declares that 'he had not known *sin* but by the law'; he then gives an instance of this – 'he had not known *lust*, except the law had said, Thou shalt no covet.' Here he expressly asserts that *lust* is *sin*.[10]

---

10. Burnet on *the Thirty-Nine Articles*, Art. 9. Hill's *Lectures in Divinity*, vol. 2, p. 16.

Section 6
Every sin, both original and actual, being a transgression of the righteous law of God, and contrary thereunto (1 John 3:4), doth, in its own nature, bring guilt upon the sinner (Romans 2:15; 3:9:19), whereby he is bound over to the wrath of God (Ephesians 2:3), and curse of the law (Galatians 3:10), and so made subject to death (Romans 6:23), with all miseries spiritual (Ephesians 4:18), temporal (Romans 8:20; Lamentations 3:39), and eternal (Matthew 25:41; 2 Thessalonians 1:9).

Exposition
This section relates to the *desert* of sin. Being a transgression of the law of God, it must, in its own nature, bring guilt upon the sinner, or render him liable to punishment. It exposes him to the *wrath* of God, for 'the children of disobedience' are also 'children of wrath,' i.e. they deserve and are obnoxious to the wrath of God. It subjects him to the curse of the law, by which we may understand the condemnatory sentence of the broken law, which binds over the guilty sinner to all the direful effects of the wrath of God. It likewise subjects him to *death*, or the dissolution of the mysterious union between the soul and the body. Pelagians and Socinians hold that death is not the punishment of sin – that Adam was mortal from the beginning; and for this reason, those who are born of him must also be mortal. Others, again, both in former and later times, have held that temporal death was the only penalty threatened to Adam, and that this is the only death which results from his sin. Both these opinions are so plainly contradictory to the express declarations of the Word of God, that they are unworthy of serious refutation. In addition to this, our Confession states, that sin exposes the sinner to numerous *miseries*, both in this life, and in that which is to come. Among the *spiritual* or inward miseries to which it renders the sinner liable in this world, the compilers of our Confession elsewhere mention 'blindness of mind, a reprobate sense, strong delusions, hardness of heart, horror of conscience, and vile affections'; and among the *temporal* or outward miseries, they mention 'the curse of God upon the creatures for our sakes, and all other evils that befall us in our bodies, names, relations and employments' (*The Larger Catechism*, Question 28.) And the miseries to which sin exposes in the world to come, they sum up in 'everlasting separation from the comfortable presence of God, and most grievous torments in soul and body, without intermission, in hell-fire for ever' (*The Larger Catechism*, Question 29.)

When we reflect on the loss which Adam sustained by his fall, and on the guilty and corrupted state in which we are thereby involved, and on the manifold miseries to which we are liable, both here and hereafter, let us be deeply impressed with a sense of the dreadful malignity and demerit of sin – the source of all our woe. Let us not dare to repine against God, or to impeach his goodness or equity, for permitting sin to enter into the world, and making us responsible for the transgression of the first Adam; but rather let us admire the divine wisdom and grace displayed in providing the second Adam, by whose obedience we may be made righteous, as by the disobedience of the first we were made sinners. Let us cordially receive the Lord Jesus Christ, that, being found in him, we may not only be acquitted from the guilt of the first man's transgression, but may be brought, through 'the abundance of grace, and of the gift of righteousness, to reign in life by one,' even by Jesus Christ, our Lord.

CHAPTER 7

GOD'S COVENANT WITH MAN

Section 1
The distance between God and the creature is so great, that although reasonable creatures do owe obedience unto him as their Creator, yet they could never have any fruition of him as their blessedness and reward, but by some voluntary condescension on God's part, which he hath been pleased to express by way of covenant (Isaiah 40:13-17; Job 9:32, 33; 1 Samuel 2:25; Psalm 113:5, 6; 100:2, 3; Job 22:2, 3; 35:7, 8; Luke 17:10; Acts 17:24, 25).

Section 2
The first covenant made with man was a covenant of works (Galatians 3:12), wherein life was promised to Adam, and in him to his posterity (Romans 10:5; 5:12-20), upon condition of perfect and personal obedience (Genesis 2:17; Galatians 3:10).

Exposition
Man is naturally and necessarily under a law to God. This results from the necessary and unalterable relation subsisting between God and man, as the one is the Creator, and the other his creature. God might, therefore, if he had pleased, demanded all possible obedience of man, without making any promise securing his establishment in a state of innocence and enjoyment, and his advancement to a state of still higher felicity, as the reward of his disobedience. And though man had gone through a long course of obedience, without a single failure, he could not have laid his Creator under any obligation to him, or been entitled to any recompense. But God graciously condescended to deal with man by way of covenant, and thus gave him an opportunity to secure his happiness by acquiring a right to it – a right founded upon stipulation, or upon the promise. 'Man,' says the celebrated Witsius, 'upon his accepting the covenant, and performing the condition, does acquire some right to demand of God the promise; for God has, by his promises, made himself a debtor to man; or, to speak in a manner more becoming God, he was pleased to make his performing his promises a debt due to himself – to his goodness,

justice and veracity. And to man, in covenant, and continuing steadfast to it, he granted the right of expecting and requiring that God should satisfy the demands of his goodness, justice and truth, by the performance of the promises.'[1]

A covenant is generally defined to be an agreement between two parties, on certain terms. In every covenant there must be two parties, and consequently two parts – a conditionary and a promissory; the one to be performed by the one party, and the other to be fulfilled by the other party. If either of the parties be fallible, a penalty is often added; but this is not essential to a covenant.

There are two important truths to which our attention is here directed. *First*, That God entered into a covenant with Adam, promising him life upon condition of his perfect and personal obedience. *Secondly,* That this covenant was made with Adam, not only for himself, but for all his natural posterity.

1. That God entered into a covenant with Adam in his state of innocence, appears from Genesis 2:16, 17: 'The LORD God commanded the man, saying, Of every tree of the garden thou mayest freely eat: but of the tree of the knowledge of good and evil, thou shalt not eat of it: for in the day that thou eatest thereof, thou shalt surely die.' Here, indeed, there is no express mention of a covenant; but we find all the essential requisites of a proper covenant. In this transaction there are *two parties*; the *Lord God* on the one hand, and *man* on the other. There is a *condition* expressly stated, in the positive precept respecting the tree of knowledge of good and evil, which God was pleased to make the test of man's obedience. There is a *penalty* subjoined: 'In the day thou eatest thereof, thou shalt surely die.' There is also a *promise*, not distinctly expressed, but implied in the threatening; for, if death was to be the consequence of disobedience, it clearly follows that life was to be the reward of obedience. That a promise of life was annexed to man's obedience, may also be inferred from the description which Moses gives of the righteousness of the law: 'The man that doeth these things shall live by them' (Romans 10:5); from our Lord's answer to the young man who inquired what he should do to inherit eternal life: 'If thou wilt enter into life, keep the commandments' (Matthew 19:17); and from the

1. Witsius on the *Economy of the Covenants*, book 1, ch. 1, sect. 14.

declaration of the apostle, that 'the commandment was ordained to life' (Romans 7:10). We are, therefore, warranted to call the transaction between God and Adam a *covenant*. We may even allege, for the use of this term, the language of Scripture. In Hosea 6:7 (margin), we read, 'They, *like Adam*, have transgressed the covenant.' This necessarily implies that a covenant was made with Adam, and that he violated it.

2. That this covenant was made with Adam, not only for himself, but also for all his natural posterity, is a doctrine which has met with much opposition. It is denied by Pelagians and Socinians, who maintain that he acted for himself alone, and that the effects of his fall terminated upon himself. Arminians admit that the whole human race is injured by the first sin, but at the same time controvert the proposition, that Adam was their proper representative. This truth, however, may be easily established. The Scripture represents Adam as a figure or type of Christ (Romans 5:14); and wherein does the resemblance between them consist? Simply in this, that as Christ was a federal head, representing all his spiritual seed in the covenant of grace, so Adam was a federal head representing all his natural seed in the covenant of works. In 1 Corinthians 15:45, 47, the one is called the *first Adam*, the other, the *last Adam*; the one the *first man*, the other the *second man*. Now, Christ was not the *second* man in any other sense, but as being the federal head or representative of his seed; and, therefore, the *first* man must have sustained a similar character, as being the federal head or representative of all his natural posterity. The extension of the effects of Adam's first sin to all his descendants, is another strong proof of his having represented them in the covenant made with him. That he has transmitted sin and death to all his posterity, is clearly taught in the 5th chapter of the Epistle to the Romans; and unless his public character, as a representative in the covenant, be admitted, no satisfactory reason can be assigned why we are affected by the first sin in a way that we are not affected by his subsequent transgressions, or the transgressions of our more immediate progenitors. We know that 'the son shall not bear the iniquity of the father' (Ezekiel 18:20); and had Adam been merely a private person, his sin could have affected us no more than that of our immediate parents. The conclusion is inevitable – that, in the

covenant of works, our first parent not only acted for himself, but represented all his natural posterity.

Often has this part of the divine procedure been arraigned by presumptuous man. The supposition that God called Adam to represent us in a covenant, into which he entered with him long before we had a being, and to the making of which we could not personally consent, is, it has been alleged, inconsistent with the divine goodness, and contrary to moral justice and equity. To this it might be sufficient to reply, that this transaction being the proposal and deed of God, it must be fit and equitable. 'Shall not the Judge of all the earth do right?' 'He is a God of truth, and without iniquity, just and right is he.' But though we ought to acquiesce in the propriety of this transaction, simply because it was the will of God, yet it might be evinced, by various considerations, that it was not only consistent with equity, but manifested much of the divine goodness. If Adam had fulfilled the condition of the covenant, and thus secured happiness, not only to himself, but also to all his posterity, no one, certainly, would have complained that Adam was constituted his representative; and why should that transaction, which, in this event, would have been deemed just, be pronounced unjust on the contrary event? Adam, being made after the image of God, was as capable of keeping the covenant as any of his posterity could ever be supposed to be; that he should fulfil it was as much his personal interest as that of any of his descendants, his own felicity, no less than theirs, being at stake; and he was intimately related to the persons whom he represented, and had the strongest inducement to take care of his numerous offspring, as well as of himself. Adam having such peculiar advantages and inducements to perform the demanded obedience, it may be fairly presumed, that, had it been possible for us to be present when the federal transaction was entered into, we would have readily agreed that it was more eligible and safe for us to have our everlasting felicity insured by the obedience of our first parent, as our covenant head, than that it should depend upon our own personal behaviour. And who would complain of his being represented by Adam in the covenant of works, since God has opened up a way for our recovery from the consequences of the breach of that covenant, by another and a superior covenant?

Section 3

Man, by his fall, having made himself incapable of life by that covenant, the Lord was pleased to make a second (Galatians 3:21; Romans 8:3; 3:20, 21; Genesis 3:15; Isaiah 42:6), commonly called the Covenant of Grace: whereby he freely offereth unto sinners life and salvation by Jesus Christ, requiring of them faith in him, that they may be saved (Mark 16:15, 16; John 3:16; Romans 10:6, 9; Galatians 3:11); and promising to give unto all those that are ordained unto life his Holy Spirit, to make them willing and able to believe (Ezekiel 36:26, 27; John 6:44, 45).

Exposition

In entering upon the exposition of this section, it is proper to remark, that, at the period when our Confession was framed, it was generally held by the most eminent divines, that there are two covenants connected with the salvation of men, which they called the covenant of *redemption*, and the covenant of *grace*; the former made with Christ from everlasting, the latter made with sinners in time; the righteousness of Christ being the condition of the former, and faith the condition of the latter covenant. This distinction, we conceive, has no foundation in the Sacred Scriptures, and it has long since been abandoned by all evangelical divines. The first Adam is said to have been a *figure* of Christ, who is called the *second* Adam. Now, there was not one covenant made with Adam, the condition of which he was to perform, and another made with his posterity, the condition of which they were to fulfil; but one covenant included both him and them. It was made with him as their representative, and with them as represented in and by him. In like manner, one covenant includes Christ and his spiritual seed. The Scriptures, accordingly, everywhere speak of it as *one* covenant, and the blood of Christ is repeatedly called 'the blood of the covenant,' not of the covenants, as we may presume it would have been called, if it had been the condition of a covenant of redemption and the foundation of a covenant of grace (Hebrews 10:29; 13:20). By the blood of the same covenant Christ made satisfaction, and we obtain deliverance (Zechariah 9:11). We hold, therefore, that there is only one covenant for the salvation of fallen men, and that this covenant was made with Christ before the foundation of the world.[2] The

---

2. The distinction between the covenant of redemption and the covenant of grace was maintained by Owen, Charnock, Flavel and many others.

Scriptures, indeed, frequently speak of God making a covenant with believers, but this language admits of an easy explication, in consistency with the unity of the covenant. 'The covenant of grace,' says a judicious writer, 'was made with Christ in a strict and proper sense, as he was the party-contractor in it, and undertook to fulfil the condition of it. It is made with believers in an improper sense, when they are taken into the bond of it, and come actually to enjoy the benefit of it. How it is made with them may be learned from the words of the apostle: "I will give you the sure mercies of David" (Acts 13:34) which is a kind of paraphrase upon Isaiah 55:3: "I will make an everlasting covenant with you, even the sure mercies of David." God makes the covenant with them, not by requiring anything of them in order to entitle them or lay a foundation for their claim to the blessings of it, but by making these over to them as a free gift, and putting them in possession of them, as far as their present state will admit, by a faith of his own operations.'[3]

The supposition of two covenants for the salvation of mankind sinners, is encumbered with various difficulties. One is obvious. In every proper covenant, there are two *essential* parts – a conditionary and promissory. If, therefore, there be a covenant made with sinners, different from the covenant made with Christ, it must have a condition which they themselves must perform. But though our old divines called faith the condition of the covenant made with sinners, they did not assign any merit to faith, but simply precedence. 'The truth is,' as Dr Dick has remarked, 'that what these divines call the covenant of grace, is merely the administration of what they call the covenant of redemption, for the purpose of communicating its blessings to those for whom they were intended; and cannot be properly considered as a covenant, because it is not suspended upon a proper condition.' The Westminster Assembly, in this section, appear to describe what

---

By them it was explained in a sense consistent with the perfections and grace of God. But by others, the covenant of redemption has been represented as the foundation for God's entering into another covenant with sinners, of which faith, repentance, and sincere obedience, are made the terms. That the covenant made with Christ and with believers is one and the same covenant, has been maintained by Boston, R. and E. Erskine, Adam Gib, Hill of London, Brown of Haddington, Dick, Belfrage, and, indeed, by all modern evangelical divines.)
3. Wilson's (of London) Sermons, p. 72.

was then usually designated the covenant of grace, as distinguished from the covenant of redemption. But, though they viewed the covenant under a twofold consideration, as made with the Surety from everlasting, and as made with sinners in time, they certainly regarded it as one and the same covenant. 'The covenant of grace,' say they, 'was made with Christ as the second Adam, and in him with all the elect as his seed' (*The Larger Catechism*, Question 31). The doctrine of our standards on this deeply interesting subject, may be summed up in the following propositions:

1. That a covenant was entered into between Jehovah the Father and his co-eternal Son, respecting the salvation of sinners of mankind. The reality of this federal transaction, appears from Psalm 89:3: 'I have made a covenant with my chosen, I have sworn unto David my servant.' The speaker, in this passage, can be no other but the *Lord*, who is mentioned in the beginning of the Psalm; and it cannot reasonably be questioned, that the words spoken have their ultimate and principal fulfilment in Jesus Christ, and assert a covenant made with him, of which the covenant of royalty made with David, King of Israel, was typical. In other places of Scripture, though the word covenant does not occur, we have a plain intimation of all the essential parts of a proper covenant. In Isaiah 53:10, we have the two great parts of the covenant – the conditionary and the promissory; and the two glorious contracting parties – the one undertaking for the performance of its arduous condition – the other engaging for the fulfilment of its precious promises: 'If his soul shall make a propitiatory sacrifice, he shall see a seed which shall prolong their days; and the gracious purpose of Jehovah shall prosper in his hands' (Bishop Lowth's Translation.)

2. That this covenant was made with Christ, as the head, or representative, of his spiritual seed. This is confirmed by the comparison between Christ and Adam, which is stated by the apostle (Romans 5; 1 Corinthians 15:45, 47); which clearly establishes the truth, that Adam and Christ severally sustained a public character, as the federal heads of their respective seeds. Christ and his spiritual seed are called by the same name (Isaiah 49:3) – a plain evidence of God's dealing with him as their representative in the covenant. Christ is likewise called the Surety

of the covenant (Hebrews 7:22); and the promises of the covenant were primarily made to him (Galatians 3:16; Titus 1:2).

3. That this covenant originated in the free grace and sovereign will of God. The Scriptures uniformly ascribe this transaction to the good pleasure of Him who worketh all things according to the counsel of his own will, and represent it as conducing to the praise of the glory of his grace (Ephesians 1:3-6). On this account this covenant is, with great propriety, called the covenant of grace, because it originated in the free grace of God, and conveys the blessings of salvation to sinners in a manner the most gratuitous.

4. That this covenant was established from eternity. The covenant of grace is called the *second* covenant, as distinguished from the covenant of works made with Adam; but though the second in respect of manifestation and execution, yet, with respect either to the period or the order in which it was made, it is the first covenant. The Head of this covenant is introduced (Proverbs 8:23), saying 'I was set up from everlasting, from the beginning, ere ever the earth was'; *i.e.*, he was set apart to his mediatory office and work – in other words, to be the head of his spiritual seed in the covenant of grace from everlasting. The promise of eternal life is said to have been given us in Christ 'before the world began' (Titus 1:2); and the covenant is frequently styled an *everlasting* covenant (Hebrews 13:20).

5. In the administration of this covenant, God 'freely offereth unto sinners life and salvation by Jesus Christ, requiring of them faith in him, that they may be saved'. Though Christ, in this covenant, represented only a definite number of mankind, who were 'chosen in him before the foundation of the world', yet, in the administration of the covenant, a free offer of salvation by Jesus Christ is addressed to sinners of mankind indefinitely and universally (John 6:32; Isaiah 55:1; Revelation 22:17). This offer is not restricted, as Baxterians allege, to sensible sinners, or those who are convinced of their sin, and their need of the Saviour; for it is addressed to persons sunk in total insensibility as to their own miseries and wants (Revelation 3:17, 18). This offer is made as really to those who eventually reject it, as it is to those who eventually receive it; for if this were not the case, the former class

of gospel-hearers could not be condemned for their unbelief (John 3:18, 19).

That God 'requires of sinners faith in Christ that they may be saved,' admits of no dispute. The part assigned to faith, however, has been much controverted. Many excellent divines, in consequence of the distinction which they made between the covenant of redemption and the covenant of grace, were led to speak of faith as the *condition* of the latter covenant. But the term, as used by them, signifies not a meritorious or procuring cause, but simply something which goes before, and without which the other cannot be obtained. They consider faith merely as a condition of *order* or *connection*, as it has been styled, and as an instrument or means of obtaining an interest in the salvation offered in the gospel. This is very different from the meaning attached to the term by Arminians and Neonomians, who represent faith as a condition on the fulfilment of which the promise is suspended.[4] The Westminster Assembly elsewhere affirm, that God requires of sinners faith in Christ, 'as the condition to interest them in him' (*The Larger Catechism*, Question 32). But this is very different from affirming that faith is the condition of the covenant of grace. That faith is indispensably necessary as the instrument by which we are savingly interested in Christ, and personally instated in the covenant, is a most important truth, and this is all that is intended by the Westminster divines. They seem to have used the term *condition* as synonymous with *instrument*; for, while in one place they speak of faith as the condition to interest sinners in the Mediator, in other places they affirm, that 'faith is the alone *instrument* of justification' (*Confession*, chapter 11, 2.), and teach, that 'faith justifies a sinner in the sight of God, only as it is an instrument by which he receiveth and applieth Christ and his righteousness' (*The Larger Catechism*, Question 73). As the word *condition* is ambiguous, apt to be misunderstood, and is frequently employed in an unsound and dangerous sense, it is now disused by evangelical divines.

---

4. The sentiments of different writers on this important point are stated by Dr Fraser, in his excellent notes on Witsius' *Dissertations on the Apostles' Creed*, vol. i, note 44. To the writers mentioned by him may be added, Boston, *View of the Covenant of Grace*, head iii., sect. 1; Wilson of London, *Sermons*, p. 71); and Dr Dick *Lectures*, vol. ii., p. 434.

6. That God promises his Holy Spirit to work in his elect that faith by which they come to have a special interest in the blessings of this covenant. This implies, that a certain definite number were ordained to eternal life, and that all these shall in due time be brought to believe in Christ (Acts 13:48). It also implies, that they are in themselves unwilling and unable to believe (John 6:44); but God promises to give them the Holy Spirit to make them willing and able (Ezekiel 36:26). Faith, therefore, instead of being the condition of the covenant of grace, belongs to the promissory part of the covenant (Romans 15:12). It is the gift of God, who worketh in us both to will and to do of his good pleasure (Ephesians 2:8; Philippians 2:13).

Section 4
This covenant of grace is frequently set forth in the Scripture by the name of a Testament, in reference to the death of Jesus Christ the testator, and to the everlasting inheritance, with all things belonging to it, therein bequeathed (Hebrews 9:15-17; 7:22; Luke 22:20; 1 Corinthians 11:25).

Exposition
In the Authorised Version of the New Testament, the covenant of grace is frequently designated a testament; and it is generally admitted, that the original word signifies both a covenant and a testament. There is, at least, one passage in which it is most properly rendered *testament*, namely, Hebrews 9:16, 17. Some learned critics, indeed, have strenuously contended against the use of that term even in this passage; but the great majority allow that the common translation is unexceptionable.[5]

Section 5
This covenant was differently administered in the time of the law, and in the time of the gospel (2 Corinthians 3:6-9): under the law it was administered by promises, prophecies, sacrifices, circumcision, the paschal lamb, and other types and ordinances delivered to the people of

---

5. The reader will find a summary of the views of critics on this subject in a long and able article by Dr Fraser, appended to his Translation of Witsius' *Dissertations on the Apostles' Creed*, vol. i., note 42. The learned Professor Stuart of Andover (in his Commentary on the Hebrews) also mentions the commentators who prefer the word covenant in the passage referred to, and declares that 'his difficulties in admitting it are insuperable.'

the Jews, all fore-signifying Christ to come (Hebrews 8; 9; 10; Romans 4:11; Colossians 2:11, 12; 1 Corinthians 5:7), which were for that time sufficient and efficacious, through the operation of the Spirit, to instruct and build up the elect in faith in the promised Messiah (1 Corinthians 10:1-4; Hebrews 11:13; John 8:56), by whom they had full remission of sins, and eternal salvation; and is called the Old Testament (Galatians 3:7-9, 14).

Section 6

Under the gospel, when Christ the substance (Colossians 2:17), was exhibited, the ordinances in which this covenant is dispensed are, the preaching of the Word, and the administration of the sacraments of Baptism and the Lord's Supper (Matthew 28:19, 20; 1 Corinthians 11:23-25); which though fewer in number, and administered with more simplicity and less outward glory, yet in them it is held forth in more fulness, evidence, and spiritual efficacy (Hebrews 12:22-27; Jeremiah 31:33, 34), to all nations, both Jews and Gentiles (Matthew 28:19; Ephesians 2:15-19); and is called the New Testament (Luke 22:20). There are not, therefore, two covenants of grace differing in substance, but one and the same under various dispensations (Galatians 3:14, 16. Acts 15:11. Romans 3:21-23, 30. Psalm 32:1 Romans 4:3, 6, 16, 17, 23, 24. Hebrews 13:8).

Exposition

The doctrines laid down in these sections are the following:

1. That there are not two covenants of grace, differing in substance, but that the Old and New Testament economies are only two dispensations of the same covenant. The Jewish and the Christian dispensation are meant by the first and second – the old and new covenant (Hebrews 8:7, 13).

2. That believers who lived under the old dispensation, as well as those who live under the gospel, were saved by faith in Christ, and lived and died in the hope of a blessed immorality.

3. That the New Testament dispensation of the covenant of grace is, in many respects, superior to that which preceded the coming of Christ in the flesh. The present dispensation exceeds the past, in the superior clearness of its manifestations – in its substantial ratification by the death of Christ – in the more abundant outpouring of the Holy Spirit – in the introduction of a more spiritual

form of worship, and in its extension to all nations.[6]

In concluding this chapter, let us reflect how admirably adapted the covenant of grace is to the situation of those who are ruined by the violation of the first covenant. Its condition being fulfilled by the glorious Surety, a full salvation is freely offered to the chief of sinners. But what will it avail us that this gracious covenant has been revealed, unless we obtain a personal interest in it, and are made partakers of its invaluable blessings? Let us, therefore, 'take hold of God's covenant,' and let us labour after the fullest evidence of our interest in this blessed covenant. Then, amid all the troubles of life, we may 'encourage ourselves in the Lord our God'; and, even when all other things fail us, we may experience that strong consolation which David enjoyed under his complicated trials, and in the immediate prospect of dissolution; and to which he gave utterance in these his last words: 'Although my house be not so with God, yet he hath made with me an everlasting covenant, ordered in all things, and sure; this is all my salvation, and all my desire.'

---

6. The sameness of the covenant of grace under both dispensations, the blessings and defects of the Old Testament, and the superior advantages of the New, are fully discussed by Calvin, *Institutes*, book ii, ch. 9-11, and by Witsius, *Economy of the Covenants*, book iv., ch. 11, 12, 13, 15.

CHAPTER 8

CHRIST THE MEDIATOR

Section 1

It pleased God, in his eternal purpose, to choose and ordain the Lord
Jesus, his only begotten Son, to be the Mediator between God and man
(Isaiah 42:1; 1 Peter 1:19, 20; John 3:16; 1 Timothy 2:5):the Prophet
(Acts 3:22), Priest (Hebrews 5:5, 6), and King (Psalm 2:6; Luke 1:33);
the Head and Saviour of his Church (Ephesians 5:23); the Heir of all
things (Hebrews 1:2); and Judge of the world (Acts 17:31): unto whom
he did from all eternity give a people to be his seed (John 17:6; Psalm
22:30; Isaiah 53:10), and to be by him in time redeemed, called, justified,
sanctified and glorified (1 Timothy 2:6; Isaiah 55:4, 5; 1 Corinthians
1:30).

Exposition

A mediator is one who interposes between two parties at variance, to procure a reconciliation. Before the fall, there was no
need of a mediator between God and man; for, though there was
an infinite distance in nature, yet, there was no variance between
these parties. But upon the fall the case was altered; God was
dishonoured, and highly offended; man was alienated from God,
and subjected to his judicial displeasure; and as man was unable
to satisfy the claims of the divine law which he had violated, if he
was to be restored to the favour of his offended sovereign, the
interposition of another person was requisite, to atone for his guilt,
and lay the foundation of peace. This is the office and work assigned to Jesus Christ, the one mediator between God and man;
and the present section relates to his divine appointment to this
office, and the donation of a people to him as his seed.

1. It pleased God, from all eternity, to choose and ordain the Lord
Jesus, his only begotten Son, to be the mediator between God and
man. God being the party offended by the sin of man, to him
belonged the right of admitting satisfaction by another in the room
of the personal transgressors. But he not only admitted of a vicarious satisfaction; he also, in the exercise of boundless grace
and unsolicited love, provided one equal to the arduous undertaking, in the appointment of his own Son to his mediatory office.

Our Lord did not engage in the work of mediation without a special call and commission from his Father. From eternity he was chosen and appointed to execute the office of mediator between God and man; hence he is said to be 'set up from everlasting,' and 'foreordained before the foundation of the world' (Proverbs 8:23; 1 Peter 1:20). When he was on earth he often declared, that what he did in accomplishing the work of our redemption, he did by a special commission from the Father, and in obedience to his will (John 6:38). The divine appointment of Christ to his mediatory office affords a striking proof of the love of the Father, who 'sent his only begotten Son ... to be the propitiation for our sins' (1 John 4:9-10), and lays a firm foundation for our trust in Christ. Without the appointment of his Father, his work would not have been valid in law for our redemption; but this appointment assures us, that the whole work of his mediation is most acceptable to God, and affords us the highest encouragement to rely upon his finished work for our eternal salvation.

2. The Father, from all eternity, gave to Christ a people to be his seed, and to be by him brought to glory. That a definite number of mankind, who were chosen by God in the exercise of rich and sovereign grace, were given to Christ, is manifest from the distinction made betwixt them and the world. Christ designated them 'the men that were given him out of the world,' and declares that he prayed 'not for the world, but for them whom the Father had given him' (John 17:6, 9). In these passages *the world* is opposed to those that were given to Christ, and this must convince every unprejudiced mind that the persons given to Christ are a definite number, selected by God from the world of mankind. They were given to Christ to be his seed. It was not left uncertain whether Christ, as the reward of his mediatory work, would have a people to serve him; it was stipulated that he should have a seed, in whom he would see the travail of his soul (Isaiah 53:10, 11). They were given to him that he might redeem them, and bring them to glory. He was not merely to procure for them a possibility of salvation, but to secure for them a full and final salvation; and none that were given to him shall be lost. 'This is the Father's will which hath sent me,' says Christ, 'that of all which he hath given me I should lose nothing, but should raise it up again at the last day' (John 6:39).

Section 2
The Son of God, the second person in the Trinity, being very and eternal God, of one substance, and equal with the Father, did, when the fulness of time was come, take upon him man's nature (John 1:1, 14; 1 John 5:20; Philippians 2:6; Galatians 4:4), with all the essential properties and common infirmities thereof, yet without sin (Hebrews 2:14, 16, 17; 4:15); being convinced by the power of the Holy Ghost, in the womb of the Virgin Mary, of her substance (Luke 1:27, 31, 35; Galatians 4:4). So that two whole, perfect, and distinct natures, the Godhead and the manhood, were inseparably joined together in one person, without conversion, composition or confusion (Luke 1:35; Colossians 2:9; Romans 9:5; 1 Peter 3:18; 1 Timothy 3:16). Which person is very God and very man, yet one Christ, the only Mediator between God and man (Romans 1:3, 4; 1 Timothy 2:5).

Exposition
This section relates to the constitution of the person of the Mediator. In opposition to Socinians and Unitarians, who maintain that Christ was merely a man, and had no existence before he was born of Mary; and in opposition to Arians, who, though they admit the pre-existence of Christ, maintain that he is a creature, and existed prior to his incarnation only as a super-angelic spirit; our Confession teaches, that Christ not only existed before his incarnation, but was from all eternity the Son of God, of one substance, and equal with the Father; and that, in the fulness of time, he assumed a complete human nature into union with the divine, so that he is both very God and very man, having two distinct natures, yet but one person.

1. Jesus Christ not only existed prior to his incarnation, but is the eternal Son of God, of one substance and equal with the Father. The pre-existence of Christ is confirmed by numerous testimonies of Scripture. That he existed before John the Baptist, is affirmed by John himself, who 'bare witness of him,' saying, 'He that cometh after me is preferred before me: for he was before me' (John 1:15). That he existed before Abraham is affirmed by Christ himself, who told the Jews, 'Before Abraham was, I am' (John 8:58). That he existed before the flood is evident from the words of the Apostle Peter, who affirms that by the Spirit Christ 'went and preached unto the spirits in prison; which sometime were disobedient, when once the longsuffering of God waited in

the days of Noah, while the ark was a-preparing' (1 Peter 3:19, 20). That he existed before the foundation of the world is no less evident, for the Scripture teaches us that all things were created by him, and in his valedictory prayer he thus expressed himself: 'Now, O Father, glorify thou me with thine own self with the glory which I had with thee before the world was' (John 17:5). Christ also declares that he 'came down from heaven,' and speaks of his ascending up where he was before (John 3:15; 6:62); which clearly imports, that he had a residence in heaven before he took our nature.[1]

We are not left to conjecture what that nature was in which Christ subsisted prior to his incarnation. We are assured that 'he was in the form of God, and thought it not robbery to be equal with God' (Philippians 2:6); that 'in the beginning was the Word, and the Word was with God, and the Word was God' (John 1:1). But the supreme Deity of Christ has been established in a preceding chapter, and we shall not now resume that subject. It will be proper, however, in this place, to offer a few remarks concerning the Sonship of Christ. The title of sons of God is applied in Scripture to various orders of beings, but Christ is styled the Son of God in a sense altogether peculiar to himself; hence he is called God's own Son – his proper Son – the only begotten of the Father. His Sonship is not founded upon his mission, nor upon his miraculous conception, nor upon his resurrection, as is supposed by many; but he is the Son of God by an eternal, necessary and ineffable generation. This truth is confirmed by many passages of Scripture, the application of which to the eternal generation of the Son of God has been vindicated by many learned divines.[2] We can only refer the reader to Psalm 2:7; Proverbs 8:24, 25; Micah 5:2; John 1:14. The denial of our Lord's eternal Sonship tends to subvert the doctrine of the Trinity; it also throws a veil over the glory of the work of redemption; for the grace of the second person in becoming incarnate, obeying, and suffering – the love of the first in sending him, and delivering him up to sufferings and death for us – and the infinite value of his atonement, are all in Scripture

---

1. The pre-existence of Christ is ably treated in Archbishop Magee's celebrated work on *Atonement – Illustrations, No. 1*; Hill's Lectures, vol. i, p. 289; Wilson on the *Person of Christ*, ch. 11.)
2. See Witsius on the *Creed*, Diss. 12; Gib's *Contemplations*, pp. 207-227.

made to turn upon his essential dignity as the Son of God. We cannot pretend to explain the manner of the eternal generation of the Son; but to deny it upon the ground that it is incomprehensible by us would be preposterous; for, upon the same ground, we might as well deny the subsistence of three distinct persons in one Godhead. Though the eternal generation of the Son be to us an inconceivable mystery, yet of one thing we are certain, that it necessarily implies the Son's equality with the Father. The Jews understood our Lord's claim to Sonship as a claim to equality with the Father, and consequently to proper Deity; and he sanctioned the interpretation which they put upon his words, by declaring, 'I and my Father are one' (John 10:30, 33).

2. In the fulness of time, the Son of God assumed a complete human nature into union with his divine person. This article of our faith has been opposed by heretics of various descriptions, and the statements of our Confession are intended to meet the heresies which have been broached in different periods.

1. The Son of God took upon him man's nature – a real and perfect humanity. In the primitive times of Christian Church this was denied by various sects, called Docetae, who held that Christ had not a real, but a mere shadowy body; while others, in later times, affirmed that Christ had a body, but not a soul.[3] But the Scriptures declare that 'the Word was made flesh' (John 1:14) – that 'God sent forth his Son, made of a woman' (Galatians 4:4) – and that, 'forasmuch as the children are partakers of flesh and blood, he himself likewise took part of the same' (Hebrews 2:14). It would be impossible to find language that could more explicitly assert the reality of Christ's human nature. His apostles, who were admitted to familiar converse with him, were certain that it was not a mere phantom which they beheld, and were as fully persuaded of the reality of his body as of their own. 'We have looked upon, and our hands have handled the Word of life'

3.The Arians and Eunomians held that Christ had no part of the human nature, except merely the flesh; but that the place of the soul was supplied by the indwelling of the Word. The Appollinarians distinguished man into three parts – the body, the sensible soul, and the rational soul; the latter they held Christ did not possess, but the Word was substituted in its place – Newlands, *Analysis of the Thirty-Nine Articles*, p. 57.

(1 John 1:1). That Christ had a human soul is equally unquestion-able. He 'increased in wisdom and stature' (Luke 2:52); the one in respect of his body, the other in respect of his soul. In his agony, he said, 'My soul is exceeding sorrowful, even unto death' (Mark 14:34); and on the cross, he committed it to his Father, saying, 'Father, into thy hands I commend my spirit' (Luke 23:46).

2. Christ was subject to the common infirmities of our nature, but was altogether without sin. He was subject to hunger and thirst, to weariness and pain, and other natural infirmities. On this ac-count, he is said to have been sent into the world 'in the likeness of sinful flesh' (Romans 8:3). But it was only the *likeness* of sin-ful flesh, for he had no sin in reality; hence he is called 'the holy one,' 'the holy child Jesus,' and 'a lamb without blemish and without spot.' The perfect purity of our Lord's human nature was necessary to qualify him for his mediatory work; for if he had been himself a sinner, he could not have satisfied for the sins of others. 'Such an high priest became us, who is holy, harmless, undefiled and separate from sinners' (Hebrews 7:26).

3. The human nature of Christ was conceived by the power of the Holy Ghost in the womb of the Virgin Mary, and was formed of her substance. The body of Christ was not created out of nothing, neither did it descend from heaven, but was formed, by the agency of the Holy Spirit, of the substance of the Virgin; hence Mary is called the *mother* of Jesus, and he is called 'the fruit of her womb,' and 'the seed of the woman' (Luke 1:42, 43; Genesis 3:15).[4]

4. The Son of God assumed the human nature into union with the divine, so that two distinct natures, the Godhead and the manhood, are inseparably joined together in one person. This is asserted in opposition to certain errors which were broached in the fifth century. The Nestorians held that in Christ 'there were *two persons*, of which the one was *divine*, even the eternal Word; and the other, which was *human*, was the man Jesus.' A strong aversion to this error led the Eutychians into the opposite extreme. They taught

---

4. Besides some ancient heretics, certain Anabaptists, who appeared in England about the time of the Reformation, asserted that Christ brought down his human nature from heaven, and that it only passed through Mary, as the beams of the sun through glass.

that in Christ 'there was but one nature'; his human nature being absorbed by the divine.[5] That the Godhead and the manhood are united in the one person of Christ is confirmed by all those passages of Scripture which speak of two natures as belonging to our Saviour (e.g. Isaiah 4:6; Romans 4:5; Matthew 1:18). The human nature of Christ never had a separate subsistence or personality of its own, but, from its first formation, was united to, and subsisted in, the person of the Son of God. This is called the hypostatical or personal union. Though this is an intimate union, yet the two natures are not confounded, but each retains its own essential properties. But, in consequence of this union, the attributes and acts which are proper to one nature are ascribed to the person of Christ. He could only obey and suffer in the human nature, but his obedience and sufferings are predicated of him as the Son of God – as the Lord of glory (Hebrews 5:8; 1 Corinthians 2:8). To represent our Saviour as having a human person distinct from his Godhead, is to divest his obedience and sufferings of their inherent value, and consequently, to subvert the grand doctrine of the redemption of the Church by his blood. It is, therefore, a most important article of our faith, that our blessed Saviour is 'very God and very man, yet one Christ.'[6] To this it is subjoined, that he is 'the one mediator between God and man'. The Papists would associate saints and angels with Christ in the work of mediation. They allow, indeed, that Christ is the only mediator of redemption, but they allege that there are other mediators of intercession. But the Scripture makes no such distinction; on the contrary, it expressly asserts that there is only one mediator, as there is only one God (1 Timothy 2:5).

Section 3
The Lord Jesus, in his human nature thus united to the divine, was sanctified and anointed with the Holy Spirit above measure (Psalm 45:7; John 3:34); having in him all the treasures of wisdom and knowledge (Colossians 2:3); in whom it pleased the Father that all fulness should dwell (Colossians 1:19): to the end, that being holy, harmless, undefiled, and full of grace and truth (Hebrews 7:26; John 1:14), he might be thoroughly furnished to execute the office of a Mediator and Surety

---

5. Mosheim's Eccl. Hist. cent. v., p. 2. ch. 5.
6. On this subject the reader may consult Hurrion's Sermons, vol i.; and Owen on the Person of Christ, chap. xviii.

(Acts 10:38; Hebrews 12:24; 7:22). Which office he took not unto himself, but was thereunto called by his Father (Hebrews 5:4, 5); who put all power and judgment into his hand and gave him commandment to execute the same (John 5:22, 27; Matthew 28:18; Acts 2:36).

Exposition

This section relates to the qualification of Christ for his mediatory work. The Father, who called him to this work, furnished him with all requisite qualifications for its performance. Not only did he 'prepare a body for him,' that he might be capable of suffering and dying; he also conferred upon his human nature the gifts and graces of the Holy Spirit in an immeasurable degree, that he might be thoroughly furnished to execute his mediatorial office. 'God giveth not the Spirit by measure unto him' (John 3:34). In his miraculous conception, his human nature was formed by the Holy Spirit, with initial grace in its highest degree of perfection; and when about to enter upon his public ministry in our nature, to seal his commission, and to qualify him in that nature of his work, the Spirit descended upon him in a bodily shape (Luke 3:21, 22).[7]

Section 4

This office the Lord Jesus did most willingly undertake (Psalm 40:7, 8; Hebrews 10:5-10; John 10:18; Philippians 2:8); which that he might discharge, he was made under the law (Galatians 4:4), and did perfectly fulfil it (Matthew 3:15; 5:17); endured most grievous torments immediately in his soul (Matthew 26:37, 38; Luke 22:44; Matthew 27:46), and most painful sufferings in his body (Matthew 26; 27); was crucified, and died (Philippians 2:8); was buried, and remained under the power of death, yet saw no corruption (Acts 2:23, 24, 27; Acts 13:37; Romans 6:9). On the third day he arose from the dead (1 Corinthians 15:3-5), with the same body in which he suffered (John 20:25, 27); with which also he ascended into heaven, and there sitteth at the right hand of his Father (Mark 16:19), making intercession (Romans 8:34; Hebrews 9:24; 7:25); and shall return to judge men and angels at the end of the world (Romans 14:9, 10; Acts 1:11; 10:42; Matthew 13:40-42; Jude 6; 2 Peter 2:4).

Exposition

It demands our special attention, that Christ 'engaged his heart to approach unto God' as the *surety* of sinners – not, indeed, of man-

---

7. See Owen on the Holy Spirit, Book 2, chapter 4.

kind sinners universally, but only of those whom the Father gave
to him, and whom he received as his spiritual seed. The present
section is closely connected with the preceding, and affirms that
Christ willingly undertook the office, not only of a mediator, but
also of a *surety*. A surety is one who engages to pay a debt, or to
suffer a penalty, incurred by another. Such a surety is our Lord
Jesus Christ. He undertook, in the everlasting covenant, to be responsible to the law and justice of God for that boundless debt
which his elect were bound to pay. And having become their surety,
by his Father's appointment and his own voluntary engagement,
their guilt was legally transferred to him, and all his obedience
and sufferings in their nature were vicarious, or in the room of
those whom he represented before God.

> 'Our Lord's surety is denied by the Socinians, who maintain, that he
> did not suffer and die in our stead, but only for our good; or to con-
> firm his doctrine, and to leave us an example of patience and resig-
> nation to the will of God under our sufferings. His proper suretyship
> is also denied by the Neonomians, who maintain, that "he only satis-
> fied divine justice for sinners, in so far as it was necessary to render
> it consistent with God's honour to enter into lower terms of salva-
> tion with them". And it is likewise denied by all those who are op-
> posed to the doctrine of the imputation of our sins to Christ, and are
> advocates of a general and indefinite atonement.'[8]

They may speak of Christ as the *substitute* of sinners, and of his
sufferings as *vicarious*, but the doctrine of his proper *suretyship*,
which necessarily involves the imputation to him of the guilt of
his people, and his endurance of the punishment which they had
incurred, can have no place in their system. In Scripture, however, the term surety is expressly applied to Christ (Hebrews 7:22).
And he is not, as Socinians allege, a surety *for God*, to secure the
performance of his promises to us, but a surety *to God* for elect
sinners; and, as such, engaged to pay the debt of obedience which
they owed to the law, as a covenant of works, and the debt of
punishment which they had contracted by sin. That the sins of his
people were imputed to him, is plainly affirmed: 'The LORD laid
on him the iniquity of us all' (Isaiah 53:6). It is declared, that
Christ suffered, for sins, for the unjust, for the transgressions of
his people; which necessarily supposes that he was charged with

8. Stevenson on the *Offices of Christ*, p. 140.

their guilt (1 Peter 3:18; Isaiah 53:8). All the sacrifices offered by divine appointment, under the legal dispensation, were typical of the death of Christ; but all the legal sacrifices were vicarious – the guilt of the offender was transferred to the sin-offering, which was signified by laying his hands on the head of the victim; and, to show that the type is realized in our Lord's substitution in the room of his people, he is said to have borne their sins in his body on the tree (1 Peter 2:24). It is impossible to account for the sufferings and death of Christ, in consistency with the goodness and equity of God, in any other way than by admitting the doctrine of his suretyship; for he had no sin of his own, and must, therefore, have suffered in the stead of others, that he might make a proper satisfaction to divine justice for their sins. This alone lays a foundation for the imputation of Christ's satisfaction to his people. He obeyed and suffered as their surety: and, upon this ground, what he did and suffered is placed to their account, and becomes effectual for their salvation (2 Corinthians 5:21). From this it necessarily follows, that Christ suffered and died only for the definite number of our race that were given to him by the Father, unless we embrace the system of universal salvation. If Christ stood as the surety of every individual of the human race, the conclusion is inevitable, either that all mankind must be saved, or that Christ has failed in accomplishing the work which he undertook.

This section further states what Christ did in the discharge of his mediatory office, and that both in his humbled and in his exalted state. In the former state:

1. *He was made under the law, and did perfectly fulfil it*. The law under which Christ was made was the moral law, not as a rule of life, but under the form of a covenant, demanding perfect obedience as the condition of life, and full satisfaction for man's transgression. Christ was not originally a debtor to the law, but he voluntarily came into a state of subjection to it, as the surety of sinners; and he both fulfilled its precept and endured its penalty. All his obedience and sufferings, as the subject of law, were in no respect for himself, but entirely in the stead of his people; and by his service, the law was not merely fulfilled, but magnified and made honourable (Isaiah 42:21).

2. *He suffered both in soul and in body.* His sufferings were various in kind, and extreme in degree. Throughout his life, he was 'a man of sorrows, and acquainted with grief.' He suffered much from men, not only from avowed enemies, but also from pretended friends, and even from his own disciples. He was also assailed by Satan's temptations. But, besides what he endured by the agency of creatures, he suffered from the more immediate hand of God himself as a rectoral judge. 'It pleased the LORD to bruise him, and to put him to grief.' As Socinians deny the penal nature of our Lord's sufferings, so they limit them to what he endured through the agency of creatures; but unless we admit that he suffered in his soul from the immediate hand of God, as an offended judge, exacting of him satisfaction for the sins of those whose cause he had undertaken, we cannot account for his dreadful agony in the garden of Gethsemane, and for his bitter lamentation on the cross. He sustained, for a season, the loss of the sensible manifestations of his Father's love, and the awful pressure of God's judicial displeasure on account of sin. This it was that drew from him these doleful complaints: 'My soul is exceeding sorrowful, even unto death'; 'My God, my God, why hast thou forsaken me?'

3. *He was crucified, and died.* Death was the penalty of the law, and the just wages of sin; death, therefore, behoved to be endured by the surety of sinners. Though Christ had obeyed the precept of the law, and endured the most exquisite sufferings in the course of his life, yet, had he not submitted to death, all had been unavailing for our redemption. But, 'he became obedient unto death'; and the death to which he was subjected was, of all others, the most lingering, the most painful, and the most ignominious, 'even the death of the cross.' It was also an accursed death; for it was written in the Jewish law, 'He that is hanged is accursed of God' (Deuteronomy 21:23). A curse seems to have been annexed to this mode of execution, in order to signify beforehand the curse under which Christ lay when he underwent this kind of death (Galatians 3:10). His death was violent, in respect of the instrumentality of men, who 'slew him with wicked hands'; but, on his own part, it was voluntary (John 10:18). And, let us never forget, that his death was vicarious; for, if it had not possessed this character, we could have derived no higher benefit from his death

than from that of prophets, apostles, and martyrs. 'Christ died for our sins, according to the Scriptures' (1 Corinthians 15:3).

4. *He was buried, and remained under the power of death for a time.* Had he revived as soon as he was taken down from the cross, his enemies might have pretended that he was not really dead, and his friends would not have had sufficient evidence that he was actually dead. Therefore, to prove the reality of his death, upon which the hopes and happiness of his people depend, he was laid in a sepulchre, and continued under the power of death for three days and three nights. He was buried, also, to sanctify the grave to his followers, that it might be to them a place of repose, where their bodies may rest till the resurrection.

Let us think of the dreadful malignity and awful desert of sin, which was the procuring cause of the sufferings and death of our Saviour. Let us admire 'the grace of our Lord Jesus Christ, who, though he was rich, yet for our sakes became poor, that we through his poverty might be rich.' And though it was only in the human nature that he was capable of suffering and dying, let us never forget the dignity of his person. He who was crucified on Calvary was 'the Lord of glory,' and when he lay in Joseph's tomb, he was still 'the Lord' (1 Corinthians 2:8; Matthew 28:6).

The Spirit of Christ in the Old Testament prophets, testified beforehand the suffering of Christ, and the glory that should follow; his humiliation was, accordingly, succeeded by a glorious exaltation, both that he might receive inconceivable glory for himself, as the reward of his work on earth, and also that he might continue to exercise all his mediatory offices for the good of his Church. The several steps of his exaltation are here enumerated, on each of which we shall offer a few brief remarks.

(1) *He rose from the dead on the third day.* The resurrection of Christ was necessary, that ancient predictions might be fulfilled, and ancient types realized; and, also that we might be assured of the perfection of that satisfaction and righteousness which he finished upon the cross. His resurrection is a well attested fact. The number of the witnesses was amply sufficient – they could not be themselves deceived, and it is equally incredible that they could intend to deceive others – they gave the best proof men could give that they firmly believed what they testified; for they published the fact at the hazard of their lives, and many of them sealed

their testimony with their blood. Christ rose with the same body that had been crucified and laid in the grave; this was evinced by its bearing the marks of the wounds which he received by the nails and the spear (John 20:20). The disciples were glad when they saw the Lord, and his resurrection is a source of unspeakable joy to his followers in every age. His supreme Deity was thereby vindicated – his divine mission and the truth of the doctrine which he taught was fully confirmed – the sufficiency and acceptableness of the sacrifice which he offered up was attested – incontestable evidence was given of his decisive victory over death and the grave – and believers have now a certain pledge and infallible assurance of their joyful resurrection to eternal life.

(2) *He ascended into heaven.* After his resurrection, he continued forty days on earth, that he might afford his disciples infallible proofs of his being alive after his passion, and that he might instruct them in the things pertaining to the kingdom of God. He then ascended from the mount called Olivet, in the presence of his disciples, attended by a glorious retinue of angels, by a local translation of his human nature from earth to heaven, into which he was welcomed by the shouts and acclamations of its inhabitants (Psalm 47:5). He ascended on high, that he might take possession of the glory which he had so justly merited; that he might send down the Holy Spirit in his miraculous gifts and sanctifying influences upon his Church and people; that he might rule, govern, and defend his people, as their exalted king; that he might make powerful intercession for them; and that he might prepare a place for them, and take possession of the heavenly inheritance in their name.

(3) *He sitteth at the right hand of God.* This phrase must obviously be understood in a figurative sense; for God, being a spirit, has no bodily parts. Among men, the right hand is the place of honour and respect, and Christ is represented as set down at the right hand of God, to denote the inconceivable dignity and glory to which, as God-man, he is now advanced, and the sovereign authority and dominion with which he is invested (Ephesians 1:20, 22). His *sitting* at the right hand of God implies the perfection of his rest, his security from all adversaries, and the everlasting continuance of his glorious state (Hebrews 10:12).

Is Christ so highly exalted? Then we have no reason to be ashamed of the cross of Christ; for he who 'endured the cross is now set down at the right hand of the throne of God.' We may be assured of the preservation of his Church on earth, and that all the plots of his and her enemies must prove vain devices (Psalm 2:1-4). And, as Christ ascended and sat down at the right hand of God, as the head and representative of his people, in his exaltation they may behold the pledge and pattern of their own exaltation (Ephesians 2:6).

(4) *He is now making intercession for his people.* His intercession consists in his appearing before God in the nature and name of his people, presenting the merit of his atoning sacrifice as the ground of his pleadings in their behalf, and intimating his desire to the Father, in a manner suited to his exalted state, that the blessings which he has purchased for them may be enjoyed by them. He intercedes, 'not for the world, but for them which the Father hath given him'; and he pleads for every one of them particularly, in a suitableness to their diversified circumstances (John 17:9; Luke 22:32). His intercession is as extensive as the promises of the new covenant, and the blessings which he hath purchased by his death; particularly, he prays that those who are not yet converted may be brought to the knowledge of the truth; that the converted may be preserved in a state of grace, and upheld in the hour of temptation; that their persons and services may be accepted with God; that they may be progressively sanctified; and that they may, in due time, be glorified (John 17). His intercession is ever prevalent and successful (Psalm 21:2; John 11:42). The prevalent efficacy of his intercession may be inferred from the dignity of his person, and the endearing relation in which he stands to the Father. Not only is the advocate dear to the Father, but the clients for whom he pleads are also the objects of the Father's special love (John 16:27). Christ's pleadings in their behalf are always conformable to his Father's will – they are founded upon the sacrifice which he offered up, with which the Father has declared himself well pleased; the Father has also bound himself by promise to grant unto Christ all his requests, and his covenant shall stand fast with him, and his faithfulness shall not fail. This should engage us to love Christ with a supreme affection; it should attract our hearts from earth to heaven, and fix our affections and desires on things above; it should encourage us to 'come boldly to the throne of grace'; and it should constrain us to live to Christ, to plead his cause, and promote his interests on earth.

(5) *He shall return to judge men and angels at the end of the world.* This is a truth clearly revealed, and fully attested in the Sacred Records. Enoch, the seventh from Adam, foretold it in solemn language (Jude 14). The Old Testament Scriptures abound with promises of the second as well as of the first coming of Christ (Psalms 50:3; 96:13; 98:9). The apostles, with one voice, proclaim this truth (1 Thessalonians 4:16; 2 Thessalonians 1:7-9). Angels bear witness to the same truth (Acts 1:11). It is confirmed by the infallible testimony of Christ himself (Matthew 26:64; Revelation 22:7, 12, 20). He will come personally and visibly – with great power and glory. The time of his coming, though fixed in the councils of heaven, is to us unknown; but it will be sudden and unexpected, and should be regarded by us as near at hand (Matthew 25:13; James 5:8, 9). The great end of his coming is to judge the world, when he will pronounce the final doom of angels and men, and will consummate the salvation of his people (Hebrews 9:28).

We should accustom ourselves to frequent and serious thoughts about the coming of our Lord; for it is an event in which we are deeply interested, since 'we must all appear before the judgment-seat of Christ; that every one may receive the things done in his body, according to that he hath done, whether it be good or bad' (2 Corinthians 5:10). We should occupy our talents till our Lord come, that we may receive from him that best of plaudits: 'Well done, good and faithful servant, enter thou into the joy of thy Lord.' Let us endeavour to maintain the Christian graces in lively and vigorous exercise, and to be always in a posture of preparation for the coming of Christ (Luke 12:35, 26). And, let us 'abide in him, that when he shall appear, we may have confidence, and not be ashamed before him at his coming' (1 John 2:28).[10]

Section 5
The Lord Jesus, by his perfect obedience and sacrifice of himself, which he through the eternal Spirit once offered up unto God, hath fully satisfied the justice of his Father (Romans 5:19; Hebrews 9:14, 16; 10:14; Ephesians 5:2; Romans 3:25, 26); and purchased not only reconciliation, but an everlasting inheritance in the kingdom of heaven, for all those whom the Father hath given unto him (Daniel 9:24, 26; Colossians 1:19, 20; Ephesians 1:11, 14; John 17:2; Hebrews 9:12, 15).

---

10. See Hurrion's Sermons, vol. ii.

Exposition

This section relates to the ends gained, or the effects accomplished, by the obedience and sacrifice of Christ. It is affirmed:

1. *That he hath fully satisfied the justice of his Father.* Retributive justice is essential to God, as a moral governor; and the exercise of it, upon the entrance of sin, was indispensably necessary. Christ, as the surety of those whom the Father had given unto him, made a true and proper satisfaction to divine justice, by enduring in their stead the very punishment which their sins deserved. 'He put away sin by the sacrifice of himself' (Hebrews 9:26). 'He finished transgression, made an end of sins, and made reconciliation for iniquity' (Daniel 9:24). 'He hath redeemed us from the curse of the law, being made a curse for us' (Galatians 3:13).

'Our Lord's sufferings, as our surety, possessed everything requisite to a true and proper satisfaction for sin; he suffered by the appointment of God, who alone had a right to admit of the death of a surety in the room of transgressors; he suffered in the same nature that had sinned; his sufferings were voluntary and obediential, and therefore possessed a moral fitness for making reparation to the injured honours of the divine law; he was Lord of his own life, and had a right to lay it down in the room of others; and his sufferings were, from the dignity of his person, of infinite value for the expiation of our sins.'

That the sacrifice of Christ was fully satisfactory to divine justice, cannot be questioned. An apostle testifies that the sacrifice which Christ offered up was 'for a sweet-smelling savour unto God' (Ephesians 5:2). Christ himself announced that the satisfaction was complete, when, on the cross, he proclaimed, 'It is finished.' And we have a most decisive proof of the satisfactory nature of his sacrifice, in his resurrection from the dead and his glorious exaltation in heaven.

2. *He purchased reconciliation for his people.* This necessarily flows from the former; for if justice is fully satisfied, God's judicial displeasure must be turned away. It is sin which separates between God and sinners; and, therefore, Christ made reconciliation by satisfying divine justice for sin – the cause of the separation. God was not merely rendered reconcileable, but fully reconciled, by the death of Christ. If God were only reconcileable, then some

acts of our own must be the proper ground of our reconciliation. But such a sentiment is subversive of the gospel, which everywhere declares, that Christ made reconciliation by his death (Romans 5:10). From this, however, it will by no means follow, that the elect are in a state of actual reconciliation, either from the time of Christ's death, or from the first moment of their existence. The Scripture represents them as being 'by nature children of wrath, even as others.' A sure foundation for their reconciliation was laid by the death of Christ; but they are only actually reconciled to God when, by that faith which is of divine operation, they accept of pardon and peace as obtained by Christ, and freely exhibited to them in the gospel. 'We joy in God,' says the apostle, 'through our Lord Jesus Christ, by whom we have now received the atonement,' or rather the 'reconciliation' (Romans 5:11).

3. *He purchased for his elect an everlasting inheritance in the kingdom of heaven.* Christ not only sustained the full infliction of the penalty of the law, to obtain for his people deliverance from condemnation, but also perfectly fulfilled its precept, to procure for them a title to the eternal inheritance. Indeed, his endurance of the penalty, and his obedience to the precept of the law, though they may be distinguished, cannot be separated, and constitute that one righteousness which is meritorious of their complete salvation. 'Grace reigns through righteousness unto eternal life, by Jesus Christ our Lord' (Romans 5:21). 'By Christ's satisfaction,' says the accurate Witsius, 'deliverance from sin, and all the happy effects of that immunity, were purchased at once for all the elect in general.'[11]

Section 6
Although the work of redemption was not actually wrought by Christ till after his incarnation, yet the virtue, efficacy, and benefits thereof, were communicated unto the elect in all ages successively from the beginning of the world, in and by those promises, types, and sacrifices, wherein he was revealed and signified to be the Seed of the woman which should bruise the serpent's head, and the Lamb slain from the beginning of the world, being yesterday and today the same, and for ever (Galatians 4:4, 5; Genesis 3:15; Revelation 13:8; Hebrews 13:8).

---

11. Witsius on the *Economy of the Covenants*, book ii., ch. 7. See also the excellent *Dissertations* of Turretin, vol. iv – *De Satisfactione Christi.*

Exposition

This section asserts the efficacy of the death of Christ for the salvation of sinners before, as well as since, he actually laid down his life. Though four thousand years elapsed before he actually appeared in the flesh, and put away sin by the sacrifice of himself, yet he was exhibited from the beginning of the world, in promises, predictions, and types; and believers under the Old Testament were saved by the merit of his sacrifice, as well as those under the New. Abraham 'rejoiced to see his day', and was justified by faith in him. 'His death is not more efficacious now, nor will be to eternity, than it was before; for he is the same in point of virtue *yesterday* in the ages past, as he is *today* at present, and will be in the ages *to come*' (Hebrews 13:8).[11] Let us rejoice that his death still possesses the same virtue and efficacy that ever it had; nothing more is required but the application of faith for the communication to us of its fruits and effects.

Section 7

Christ, in the work of mediation, acteth according to both natures; by each nature doing that which is proper to itself (Hebrews 9:14; 1 Peter 3:18): yet, by reason of the unity of the person, that which is proper to one nature is sometimes in Scripture attributed to the person denominated by the other nature (Acts 20:28; John 3:13; 1 John 3:16).

Exposition

In opposition to Roman Catholics, who maintain that Christ is mediator only as man, this section asserts that Christ, as mediator, acteth according to both natures. The Scriptures teach us that he acted as mediator prior to his assumption of human nature. It is a mediatorial act – the act of a prophet, to reveal the will of God; and it cannot be questioned that Christ was the author of revelation under the old as well as the new dispensation. It is a mediatorial act to intercede for the Church; but this Christ did long before his incarnation (Zechariah 1:12). And since his incarnation the mediator acts as God-man, and the works peculiar to each nature are ascribed to the person of Christ, in which both natures are united. The human nature alone could suffer and die; yet it is said, 'The Lord of glory was crucified'; and, 'God purchased the church with his own blood' (1 Corinthians 2:8; Acts 20:28). This

11. Charnock's Works, vol. ii., p. 563.

claims our special attention; for upon the communion of the two natures in the person of Christ, in all mediatory acts, especially as a surety, the inherent value of his work principally depends.

Section 8
To all those for whom Christ hath purchased redemption, he doth certainly and effectually apply and communicate the same (John 6:37, 39; 10:15, 16); making intercession for them (1 John 2:1, 2; Romans 8:34); and revealing unto them, in and by the Word, the mysteries of salvation (John 15:13, 15; Ephesians 1:7-9; John 17:6); effectually persuading them by his Spirit to believe and obey; and governing their hearts by his Word and Spirit (John 14:16; Hebrews 12:2; 2 Corinthians 4:13; Romans 8:9, 14; 15:18, 19; John 17:17); overcoming all their enemies by his almighty power and wisdom, in such manner and ways as are most consonant to his wonderful and unsearchable dispensation (Psalm 110:1; 1 Corinthians 15:25, 26; Malachi 4:2, 3; Colossians 2:15).

Exposition
This section relates to the extent of Christ's death with respect to its objects, and in opposition to the Arminian tenet, that Christ died for all men – for those who shall finally perish, as well as for those who shall be eventually saved; it affirms that the purchase and application of redemption are exactly of the same extent. In the fifth section we were taught that Christ purchased redemption only for 'those whom the Father hath given unto him'; and here it is asserted, that, 'to all those for whom Christ hath purchased redemption, he doth certainly and effectually apply and communicate the same.' It was formerly remarked, that, at the period when the Confession was framed, the phrase to *purchase redemption* was nearly synonymous with the phrase to *make atonement* for sin. What language, then, could affirm more explicitly than that here employed, that the atonement of Christ is specific and limited – that it is neither universal nor indefinite, but restricted to the elect, who shall be saved from wrath through him?

The sacrifice of Christ derived infinite value from the dignity of his person; it must, therefore, have been intrinsically sufficient to expiate the sins of the whole human race had it been so intended; but, in the designation of the Father, and in the intention of Christ himself, it was limited to a definite number, who shall ultimately obtain salvation. This important truth may be confirmed by the following arguments:

1. Restrictive terms are frequently employed in Scripture to express the objects of the death of Christ: 'He bare the sin of *many*'; 'He gave his life a ransom for *many*' (Isaiah 53:12; Matthew 20:28). Does not this intimate that Christ died, not for *all* men, but only for *many*?

2. Those for whom Christ died are distinguished from others by discriminating characters. They are called the *sheep* (John 10:15); the *church* (Ephesians 5:25); God's *elect* (Romans 8:33); the *children of God* (John 11:52).

3. Those whom Christ redeemed by his blood are said to be 'redeemed *from among* men' (Revelation 14:4), which, if Christ had redeemed *all* men, would be an unmeaning and inconsistent phrase; they are also said to be 'redeemed *out of* every kindred', etc. (Revelation 5:9), which certainly implies that only *some* of every kindred are redeemed.

4. The redemption obtained by Christ is restricted to those who were 'chosen in him', and whom the Father gave to him to redeem by his death (Ephesians 1:4, 7; John 17:2).

5. Christ died in the character of a surety, and therefore he laid down his life only for those whom he represented, or for his spiritual seed (Isaiah 53:10).

6. The intention of Christ in laying down his life was, not merely to obtain for those for whom he died a possibility of salvation, but actually to save them – to bring them to the real possession and enjoyment of eternal salvation (Ephesians 5:25, 26; Titus 2:14; 1 Peter 3:18; 1 Thessalonians 5:10). From this, it inevitably follows, that Christ died only for those who shall be saved in him with an everlasting salvation.

7. The intercession of Christ proceeds upon the ground of his atoning sacrifice; they must, therefore, be of the same extent with regard to their objects; but he does not pray for the world, but only for those who were given him out of the world; his sacrifice must, therefore, be restricted to that definite number (1 John 2:1, 2; John 17:9).

8. An apostle infers from the greatness of God's love in delivering up his Son to death for sinners, that he will not withhold from them any of the blessings of salvation; we must, therefore, conclude that Christ did not die for all mankind (Romans 8:32).

9. The same apostle infers the certainty of our salvation by the life of Christ, from our reconciliation to God by his death; now,

since all are not saved by his life, we must conclude that all were not reconciled by his death (Romans 5:10).

10. Christ, by his death, procured for his people not only salvation, but all the means leading to the enjoyment of it; consequently, his intention in dying must be limited to those who do repent and believe, and not extended to the whole human race.

11. The doctrine that Christ died for all men leads to many absurd consequences, such as: That Christ shed his blood for many in vain, since all are not saved; that he laid down his life in absolute uncertainty whether any of the human race would be eventually saved; that he shed his blood for millions who, at the very moment of his death, were consigned to the pit of everlasting destruction; that he died for those for whom he does not intercede; that he died for those to whom he never sent the means of salvation, yea, to some of whom he even forbade his gospel to be preached (Matthew 10:5; Romans 10:14); and that God acts unjustly in inflicting everlasting punishment upon men for those very transgressions for which he has already received full satisfaction by the death of Christ. To affirm any of these things would be blasphemous in the highest degree; and, therefore, that doctrine which involves such consequences must be unscriptural.

Universal terms are sometimes used in scripture in reference to the death of Christ; but reason and common sense demand that *general* phrases be explained and defined by those that are *special*, and which can only admit of one interpretation. The meaning in each case may usually be ascertained from the context; and one obvious reason for the use of indefinite and universal terms in relation to the death of Christ is, to intimate that the saving effects of his death extend to some of all nations – to Gentiles as well as Jews – to all classes and descriptions of men.[12]

---

12. On this topic numerous publications have lately appeared; among the earlier productions, we would refer to Hurrion's Four Sermons in the Limestreet Lectures, and especially to Dr Owen's Treatise, *Salus Electorum, Sanguis Jesu*, which, in fact, exhausts the subject.

CHAPTER 9

FREE WILL

Section 1
God hath endued the will of man with that natural liberty that it is neither forced, nor by any absolute necessity of nature determined, to good or evil (Matthew 17:12; James 1:14; Deuteronomy 30:19).

Exposition
The decision of most of the points in controversy between Calvinists and Arminians, as President Edwards has observed, depends on the determination of the question: *Wherein consists that freedom of will which is requisite to moral agency?* According to Arminians three things belong to the freedom of the will:

1. That the will has a *self-determining power*, or a certain sovereignty over itself, and its own acts, whereby it determines its own volitions.

2. A state of *indifference*, or that *equilibrium*, whereby the will is without all antecedent bias, and left entirely free from any prepossessing inclination to one side or the other.

3. That the volitions, or acts of the will, are *contingent*, not only as opposed to all constraint, but to all *necessity*, or any fixed and certain connection with some previous ground or reason of their existence.

Calvinists, on the other hand, contend that a power in the will to determine its own determinations, is either unmeaning, or supposes, contrary to the first principles of philosophy, something to arise without a cause; that the idea of the soul exerting an act of choice or preference, while, at the same time, the will is in a perfect equilibrium, or state of indifference, is full of absurdity and self-contradiction; and that, as nothing can ever come to pass without a cause, the acts of the will are never contingent, or without necessity – understanding by *necessity*, a *necessity of consequence,* or an infallible connection with something foregoing.[1]

According to Calvinists, the liberty of a moral agent consists in the power of acting according to his choice; and those actions

---

1. See Edwards' *Inquiry into Freedom of Will.*

are free which are performed without any external compulsion or restraint, in consequence of the determinations of his own mind.

'The necessity of man's willing and acting in conformity to his apprehensions and dispositions, is, in their opinion, fully consistent with all the liberty which can belong to a rational nature. The infinite Being necessarily wills and acts according to the absolute perfection of his nature, yet with the highest liberty. Angels necessarily will and act according to the perfection of their natures, yet with full liberty; for this sort of necessity is so far from interfering with liberty of will, that the perfection of the will's liberty lies in such a necessity. The very essence of its liberty lies in acting consciously, choosing or refusing without any external compulsion or constraint, but according to inward principles of rational apprehension and natural disposition.'[2]

Section 2
Man, in his state of innocency, had freedom and power to will and to do that which is good and well pleasing to God (Ecclesiastes 7:29; Genesis 1:26); but yet mutably, so that he might fall from it (Genesis 2:16, 17; 3:6).

Section 3
Man, by his fall into a state of sin, hath wholly lost all ability of will to any spiritual good accompanying salvation (Romans 5:6; 8:7; John 15:5); so as a natural man, being altogether averse from that good (Romans 3:10, 12), and dead in sin (Ephesians 2:1, 5; Colossians 2:13), is not able, by his own strength, to convert himself, or to prepare himself thereunto (John 6:44, 65; Ephesians 2:2-5; 1 Corinthians 2:14; Titus 3:3-5).

Section 4
When God converts a sinner, and translates him into the state of grace, he freeth him from his natural bondage under sin (Colossians 1:13; John 8:34, 36), and by his grace alone enables him freely to will and to do that which is spiritually good (Philippians 2:13; Romans 6:18, 22); yet so as that, by reason of his remaining corruption, he doth not perfectly not only will that which is good, but doth also will that which is evil (Galatians 5:17; Romans 7:15, 18, 19, 21, 23).

Section 5
The will of man is made perfectly and immutably free to do good alone in the state of glory only (Ephesians 4:13; Hebrews 12:23; 1 John 3:2; Jude 24).

---

2. Adam Gib on *Liberty and Necessity; Contemplations*, p. 484.

Exposition

The human *will* is not a distinct agent, but only a power of the rational soul. It is essential to a soul to have a *moral disposition,* good or bad, or a mixture of both; and, according to what is the prevailing moral disposition of the soul, must be the moral acting of the will. Hence there is a great difference in regard to the freedom of the will in the different states of man.

In the state of innocence, the natural inclination of man's will was only to good; but it was liable to change through the power of temptation, and therefore free to choose evil.

In his natural corrupt state, man freely chooses evil, without any compulsion or constraint on his will; and he cannot do otherwise, being under the bondage of sin.

In the state of grace, he has a free will partly to good and partly to evil. In this state there is a mixture of two opposite moral dispositions, and as sometimes the one, and sometimes the other, prevails, so the will sometimes chooses that which is good, and sometimes that which is evil.

In the state of glory, the blessed freely choose what is good; and, being confirmed in a state of perfect holiness, they can only will what is good.

The important truth laid down in the third section concerning man's inability, in his fallen state, to will or do that which is spiritually good, claims some further notice. It has been opposed by various sects. The Pelagians maintained 'that mankind are capable of repentance and amendment, and of arriving to the highest degrees of piety and virtue by the use of their natural faculties and powers'. The Semi-Pelagians, though they allowed that assisting grace is necessary to enable a man to *continue* in a course of religious duties, yet they held 'that *inward preventing grace* was not necessary to form in the soul the *first beginnings* of true repentance and amendment; that every man was capable of producing these by the mere power of his natural faculties; as also of exercising faith in Christ, and forming the purposes of a holy and sincere obedience.'[3] The Arminians, in words, ascribe the conversion of the sinner to the grace of God; yet they ultimately resolve it into the free-will of man.

In opposition to these various forms of error, our Confession asserts that man, in his natural corrupt state, 'has lost all ability of

---

3. Mosheim, cent. v., p. 2. ch. 5.

will to any spiritual good accompanying salvation,' and that 'a natural man is not able, by his own strength, to convert himself, or to prepare himself thereunto'. This may be confirmed:

1. By the representations given in Scripture of the natural condition of mankind sinners. They are said to be 'dead in trespasses and sins'; to be not only blind, but 'darkness' itself; to be 'the servants of sin'; to be 'enemies of God', who are not, and cannot be subject to his law (Ephesians 2:1; 5:8; Romans 6:17; Colossians 1:21; Romans 8:7).

2. The Scripture contains explicit declarations of man's inability to exercise faith in Christ, or to do anything spiritually good (John 6:44; 15:5).

3. God claims the conversion of sinners as his own work, which he promises to accomplish (Ezekiel 11:19, 20; 36:26, 27; Jeremiah 31:33).

4. The conversion of sinners is uniformly ascribed to the efficacy of divine grace (Acts 16:14; 1 Thessalonians 1:5).

5. The conversion of the soul is described in Scripture by such figurative terms as imply that it is a divine work. It is called a creation (Ephesians 2:10); a resurrection (John 5:21); a new birth (John 1:13).

6. If the sinner could convert himself, then he would have something of which he might boast – something which he had not received (1 Corinthians 1:29, 30; 4:7).

7. The increase of Christians in faith and holiness is spoken of as the work of God; which must more strongly imply that the first *beginnings* of it is to be ascribed to him (Philippians 1:6; 2:13; Hebrews 13:20, 21).

We only add, that man's incapacity of willing or doing that which is spiritually good, being a *moral inability*, is not inconsistent with his responsibility.

CHAPTER 10

EFFECTUAL CALLING

Section 1
All those whom God hath predestinated unto life, and those only, he is pleased, in his appointed and accepted time, effectually to call (Romans 8:30; 11:7; Ephesians 1:10, 11), by his Word and Spirit (2 Thessalonians 2:13, 14; 2 Corinthians 3:3, 6), out of that state of sin and death in which they are by nature, to grace and salvation by Jesus Christ (Romans 8:2; Ephesians 2:1-5; 2 Timothy 1:9, 10); enlightening their minds spiritually and savingly to understand the things of God (Acts 26:18; 1 Corinthians 2:10, 12; Ephesians 1:17, 18); taking away their heart of stone, and giving unto them an heart of flesh (Ezekiel 36:26); renewing their wills, and by his almighty power determining them to that which is good (Ezekiel 11:19; Philippians 2:13; Deuteronomy 30:6; Ezekiel 36:27), and effectually drawing them to Jesus Christ (Ephesians 1:19); yet so as they come most freely, being made willing by his grace (Canticles 1. 4).

Section 2
This effectual call is of God's free and special grace alone, not from anything at all foreseen in man (2 Timothy 1:9; Titus 3:4, 5; Ephesians 2:4, 5, 8, 9; Romans 9:11); who is altogether passive therein, until, being quickened and renewed by the Holy Spirit (1 Corinthians 2:14; Romans 8:7; Ephesians 2:5), he is thereby enabled to answer this call, and to embrace the grace offered and conveyed in it (John 6:37; Ezekiel 36:27; John 5:25).

Exposition
There is an *external* call of the gospel, whereby all who hear it are called to the fellowship of Christ, and to receive a full salvation in him, without money and without price (Isaiah 55:1). This call is not confined to the elect, nor restricted to those who are sensible of their sins, and feel their need of a Saviour, or who possess some good qualifications to distinguish them from others; but it is addressed to mankind sinners as such, without distinction, and without exception. All who come under the general denomination of *men*, whatever be their character and state, have this call directed to them: 'To you, O men, I call, and my voice is to the

sons of men' (Proverbs 8:4). 'Look unto me, and be ye saved, all the ends of the earth' – sinners of every nation, of every rank, and condition (Isaiah 45:22). To reconcile the unlimited call of the gospel with the doctrines of particular election and a definite atonement, seems to exceed the efforts of the human mind. But though we cannot discover the principle which reconciles them, the doctrines themselves are clearly taught in the Word of God; and are, therefore, to be received with unhesitating confidence. That the call of the gospel is indefinite and universal, that God is sincere in addressing this call to all to whom the gospel comes, and that none who comply with the call shall be disappointed; these are unquestionable truths. But the outward call by the Word is of itself ineffectual. Though all without exception are thus called, yet multitudes refuse to hearken, and in this respect 'many are called, but few are chosen'; that is, few are determined effectually to embrace the call.

But there is also an *internal* call, in which the Holy Spirit accompanies the external call with power and efficacy upon the soul; and this call is always effectual. This effectual work of the Spirit is termed a *calling*, because men are naturally at a distance from Christ, and are hereby brought into fellowship with him. They are called 'out of that state of sin and death in which they are by nature, to grace and salvation by Jesus Christ' – out of darkness into marvellous light – out of the world that lieth in wickedness into the family of God – from a state of bondage into a state of glorious liberty – from a state of sin unto holiness – and from a state of wrath unto the hope of eternal glory. Concerning this calling we are here taught:

1. That the *elect* alone are partakers of it: 'All those whom God hath predestinated unto life, and those only, he is pleased effectually to call.' The subjects of this work are said to be 'called according to God's purpose,' and 'whom he did predestinate, them he also called' (Romans 8:28, 30; 2 Timothy 1:9). Those who dispense the Word know not who are included in 'the election of grace' and must, therefore, address the calls and invitations of the gospel to men indiscriminately. They draw the bow at a venture, but the Lord, who 'knoweth them that are his', directs the arrow, so as to cause it to strike home to the hearts of those whom he 'hath chosen in Christ before the foundation of the world.'

2. That this calling is under the direction of the sovereign will

and pleasure of God as to the *time* of it. He is pleased to call his elect 'in his appointed and accepted time'. Some are called into the vineyard at the third hour, some at the sixth, some at the ninth, and some even at the eleventh hour of the day. Some, like good Obadiah, have feared the Lord from their youth; others, like Saul of Tarsus, have been born, as it were, out of due time. There is also a diversity with respect to the *manner* of this calling. Some, like Lydia, have been secretly and sweetly allured to the Saviour, and could hardly declare the time or manner in which the happy change began; others, like the Philippian jailer, have for a season suffered the terrors of the Lord, and been made to cry out, trembling and astonished, 'What shall I do to be saved?' (Acts 16).

3. *That this calling is effected by the Word and Spirit.* The Word is usually the outward means employed, and the Holy Spirit is always the efficient agent, in calling men into the kingdom of grace. If, in any instance, the call of the gospel proves successful, it is not owing to the piety or persuasive eloquence of those who dispense the gospel (1 Corinthians 3:7); neither is it on account of one making a better use than another of his own free will (Romans 9:16); it is solely to be ascribed to the power of the Divine Spirit accompanying the outward call of the Word (1 Thessalonians 1:5).

By means of the law, the Spirit convinces them of their sinfulness, shows them the danger to which they are exposed, and discovers to them the utter insufficiency of their own works of righteousness as the ground of their hope and trust for acceptance before God. By means of the gospel, he enlightens their minds in the knowledge of Christ – discovers to them the glory of his person, the perfection of his righteousness, the suitableness of his offices, and the fulness of his grace; shows them his ability to save to the uttermost, his suitableness to their condition, and his willingness to receive all that come to him. He also takes away their heart of stone, and gives unto them an heart of flesh – renews their wills, and effectually determines and enables them to embrace Christ as their own Saviour.

4. *That in this calling no violence is offered to the will.* While the Spirit effectually draws sinners to Christ, he deals with them in a way agreeable to their rational nature, 'so as they come most freely, being made willing by his grace.' The liberty of the will is not invaded, for that would destroy its very nature; but its obstinacy

is overcome, its perverseness taken away, and the whole soul powerfully, yet sweetly, attracted to the Saviour. The compliance of the soul is voluntary, while the energy of the Spirit is efficient and almighty: 'Thy people shall be willing in the day of thy power' (Psalm 110:3).

5. *That in this calling the operations of the Holy Spirit are invincible.* As Arminians and others maintain that God gives sufficient grace to all men, upon the due improvement of which they may be saved, if it is not their own fault, so they also hold that there are no operations of the Spirit in conversion which do not leave the sinner in such a state as that he may either comply with them or not. It is obvious that this opinion makes the success of the Spirit's work to depend on the sinner's free will, so that those who do actually obey the call of the gospel are not more indebted to God than those who reject it, but may take praise to themselves for having made a better use of their power, in direct opposition to Scripture, which declares that 'it is not of him that willeth, but of God that showeth mercy'. We admit that there are common operations of the Spirit which do not issue in the conversion of the sinner; but we maintain that the *special* operations of the Spirit overcome all opposition, and effectually determine the sinner to embrace Jesus Christ as he is offered in the gospel. If the special operations of the Spirit were not invincible, but might be effectually resisted, then it would be uncertain whether any would believe or not, and consequently possible that all which Christ had done and suffered in the work of redemption might have been done and suffered in vain.

6. *That this calling proceeds from the free grace of God.* The term *grace* is sometimes used to denote the influence of the Holy Spirit on the heart, and sometimes to denote the free favour of God, as opposed to all merit on the part of his creatures. It is to be understood in the latter sense when this effectual call is said to be 'of God's free and special grace alone, not from anything at all foreseen in man'. Previous to their vocation, men can perform no work that is spiritually good; and, after their conversation, their best works are imperfect, and cannot entitle them to any reward. God is not, therefore, influenced to call them on account of any good works which they have already done, nor from the foresight of anything to be afterwards done by them (2 Timothy 1:9; Titus 3:5). To manifest that this call is entirely owing to the free grace

of God, and to display the exceeding riches of his grace, God is sometimes pleased to call the very chief of sinners.

7. *That in this calling the sinner is altogether passive, until he is quickened and renewed by the Holy Spirit.* Here it is proper to distinguish between regeneration and conversion; in the former the sinner is passive, in the latter he is active, or co-operates with the grace of God. In regeneration a principle of grace is implanted in the soul, and previous to this the sinner is incapable of moral activity; for, in the language of inspiration, he is 'dead in trespasses and sins'. In conversion the soul turns to God, which imports activity; but still the sinner only acts as he is acted upon by God, who 'worketh in him both to will and to do'.

Section 3
Elect infants, dying in infancy, are regenerated and saved by Christ through the Spirit (Luke 18:15, 16; Acts 2:38, 39; John 3:3, 5; 1 John 5:12; Romans 8:9), who worketh when, and where, and how he pleaseth (John 3:8). So also are all other elect persons, who are incapable of being outwardly called by the ministry of the Word (1 John 5:12. Acts 4:12).

Exposition
The Holy Spirit usually works by means; and the Word, read or preached, is the ordinary means which he renders effectual to the salvation of sinners. But he has immediate access to the hearts of men, and can produce a saving change in them without the use of ordinary means. 'As infants are not fit subjects of instruction, their regeneration must be effected without means, by the immediate agency of the Holy Spirit on their souls. There are adult persons, too, to whom the use of reason has been denied. It would be harsh and unwarrantable to suppose that they are, on this account, excluded from salvation; and to such of them as God has chosen, it may be applied in the same manner as to infants.'[1]

Section 4
Others not elected, although they may be called by the ministry of the Word (Matthew 22:14), and may have some common operations of the Spirit (Matthew 7:22; 13:20, 21; Hebrews 6:4, 5), yet they never truly come unto Christ, and therefore cannot be saved (John 6:64-66; 8:24): much less can men not professing the Christian religion be saved in any

---

1. Dick's *Lectures on Theology*, vol. iii., p. 265.

other way whatsoever, be they ever so diligent to frame their lives according to the light of nature and the law of that religion they do profess (Acts 4:12; John 14:6; Ephesians 2:12; John 4:22; 17:3); and to assert and maintain that they may, is very pernicious, and to be detested (2 John 9-11; 1 Corinthians 16:22; Galatians 1:6-8).

Exposition

The doctrines stated in this section are the following:

1. That though those who are not elected have the external call of the gospel addressed to them, in common with those who are elected, yet 'they never truly come to Christ, and therefore cannot be saved'.

2. That there are 'common operations of the Spirit,' which produce conviction of sin, by means of the law in the conscience; and joyous emotions, by means of the gospel, in the affections of men in their natural state; which do not issue in conversion.

3. That those cannot be saved who are totally destitute of revelation. 'Though the invitation which nature gives to seek God be sufficient to render them *without excuse* who do not comply with it (Romans 1:20), yet it is not sufficient, even objectively, for salvation; for it does not afford that lively hope which maketh not ashamed, for this is only revealed by the gospel; whence the Gentiles are said to have been *without hope in the world* (Ephesians 2:12). It does not show the true way to the enjoyment of God, which is no other than faith in Christ. It does not sufficiently instruct us about the manner in which we ought to worship and please God, and do what is *acceptable* to him. In short, this call by nature never did, nor is it even possible that it ever can, bring any to the saving knowledge of God; the gospel alone is the 'power of God unto salvation, to every one that believeth' (Romans 1:16). We are persuaded there is no salvation without Christ (Acts 4:12); no communion of adult persons with Christ, but by faith in him (Ephesians 3:17); no faith in Christ without the knowledge of him (John 17:3); no knowledge but by the preaching of the gospel (Romans 10:14); no preaching of the gospel in the works of nature; for it is that *mystery which was kept secret since the world began* (Romans 16:25).[2]

Let us be thankful that we are favoured with the revelation and free offer of Christ in the gospel. Let us give all diligence to

---

2. Witsius' *Economy of the Covenants*, book iii., ch. 5, sect. 13, 14.

make sure our election, by making sure our calling; and if we have, indeed, been made 'partakers of the heavenly calling,' let us 'walk worthy of the vocation wherewith we are called,' and 'worthy of God, who hath called us unto his kingdom and glory'.

CHAPTER 11

JUSTIFICATION

Section 1
Those whom God effectually calleth he also freely justifieth (Romans 8:30; 3:24); not by infusing righteousness into them, but by pardoning their sins, and by accounting and accepting their persons as righteous: not for any thing wrought in them, or done by them, but for Christ's sake alone: not by imputing faith itself, the act of believing, or any other evangelical obedience, to them as their righteousness; but by imputing the obedience and satisfaction of Christ unto them (Romans 4:5-8; 2 Corinthians 5:19, 21; Romans 3:22, 24, 25, 27, 28; Titus 3:5, 7; Ephesians 1:7; Jeremiah 23:6; 1 Corinthians 1:30, 31; Romans 5:17-19), they receiving and resting on him and his righteousness by faith: which faith they have not of themselves; it is the gift of God (Acts 10:44; Galatians 2:16; Philippians 3:9; Acts 13:38, 39; Ephesians 2:7, 8).

Section 2
Faith, thus receiving and resting on Christ and his righteousness, is the alone instrument of justification (John 1:12; Romans 3:28; 5:1); yet is it not alone in the person justified, but is ever accompanied with all other saving graces, and is no dead faith, but worketh by love (James 2:17, 22, 26. Galatians 5:6).

Exposition
The doctrine of justification by faith holds a most important place in the Christian system. It was justly termed by Luther, *articulus stantis vel cadentis ecclesioe* – the test of a standing or of a falling Church. In the Church of Rome this doctrine was most grossly corrupted; and it was eminently through the preaching of the scriptural doctrine of justification that the reformation from Popery was effected. Even in the Protestant Churches, however, pernicious errors in regard to this subject have been widely disseminated, and at different periods have produced much acrimonious controversy. In our Confession, the scriptural doctrine of justification is accurately discriminated from the various forms of error; and, in the progress of our exposition, we shall point out the errors to which the statements of the Confession are opposed.

1. *Justification is a judicial act of God, and is not a change of nature, but a change of the sinner's state in relation to the law.* The Church of Rome confounds justification with sanctification, and represents justification as a physical act, consisting in the infusion of righteousness into the souls of men, making them internally and personally just. But though justification and sanctification be inseparably connected, yet they are totally distinct, and the blending of them together perverts both the law and the gospel. Justification, according to the use of the word in Scripture, must be understood forensically; it is a law term, derived from human courts of judicature, and signifies, not the making of a person righteous, but the holding and declaring him to be righteous in law. The *forensic* sense of the word is manifest from its being frequently opposed to *condemnation* (e.g. Deuteronomy 25:1; Proverbs 17:15; Romans 5:16; 8:33, 34). Condemnation lies not in infusing wickedness into a criminal, or in making him guilty, but in judicially pronouncing sentence upon him according to his transgression of the law; so justification does not lie in infusing righteousness into a person, but in declaring him to be righteous on legal grounds; and, like the sentence of a judge, it is completed at once.

Socinians, and some others, represent justification as consisting only in the pardon of sin. In opposition to this, our Confession declares that God justifies those whom he effectually calls, not only 'by pardoning their sins', but also 'by accounting and accepting their persons as righteous'. The pardon of sin is unquestionably one important part of justification. It consists in the removal of guilt, or the absolution of the sinner from the obligation to punishment which he lay under by virtue of the sentence of the violated law. The pardon which God bestows is full and complete. It includes *all sins*, be they ever so numerous, and extends to all their aggravations, be they ever so enormous. Thus saith the Lord, 'I will pardon all their iniquities whereby they have sinned, and whereby they have transgressed against me' (Jeremiah 33:8). All the sins of the believer are at once pardoned in his justification; his past sins are formally forgiven, and his future sins will not be imputed, so that he cannot come into condemnation (Psalm 32:1, 2; John 5:24). But the pardon of sin alone would only restore the believer to such a state of probation as that from which Adam fell; he would be under no legal charge of guilt, but still he would have no legal title to eternal life. But when God justifies a sinner, he does not merely absolve him from guilt, or from a liableness to eternal death; he also pronounces him righteous, and, as such, entitled to eternal life. Hence, it is called 'the justification of life'; and they who 'receive the gift of righteousness, shall reign in life by one, Jesus Christ' (Romans 5:17, 18).

2. *No man can be justified before God, in whole or in part, on the ground of a personal righteousness of any kind.* Romanists, Socinians, and Pelagians, maintain that we are justified either by a personal inherent righteousness, or by our own works.[1]

In opposition to this, our Confession teaches that persons are not justified 'for anything wrought in them, or done by them, but for Christ's sake alone'. That we cannot be justified by an *inherent righteousness*, is manifest:

1. Because we can only be justified on the ground of a perfect righteousness, and our inherent righteousness is imperfect; for the Scripture saith, 'There is no man that sinneth not' (1 Kings 8:46).

2. Because the righteousness by which we are justified is not our own (Philippians 3:9).

3. Because the sentence of justification must, in the order of nature, though not of time, precede the implantation of inherent holiness.

4. Because, if we were justified by an inherent righteousness, it could not be said that God 'justifieth the *ungodly*' (Romans 4:5).

That we cannot be justified by our own *works* is no less manifest:

1. Because our personal obedience falls far short of the requirements of the law. The law demands obedience in all respects perfect; but 'in many things we offend all' (James 3:2).

2. Because our obedience, though it were commensurate to

---

1. The Church of Rome pleads for a double justification. The *first*, consisting in the remission of sin and the renovation of the inward man, is said to be by faith, in a sense, however, which does not exclude merit and predisposing qualifications; the *second*, whereby we are adjudged to everlasting life, is said to be by inherent righteousness and by works, performed by the aid of that grace which was infused in the first. Concil. Trident., sess. vi., *de justificatione.*

the high demands of the law, could not satisfy for our past transgressions. The law requires not only the fulfilment of its precept,
but also the endurance of its penalty: 'Without shedding of blood
there is no remission' (Hebrews 9:22).

3. Because we are justified freely by grace, and grace and works
are diametrically opposed (Romans 3:24; 11:6).

4. Because justification by works not only makes void the grace
of God, but also renders the death of Christ useless, and of no
effect (Galatians 2:21).[2]

5. Because we are justified in such a way as excludes all boast-
ing (Romans 3:27).

6. Because justification by works is in direct contradiction to
the uniform testimony of Scripture. The Apostle Paul fully dis-
cusses the subject of justification in his Epistles to the Romans
and to the Galatians; and in both of these Epistles he explicitly
declares, that 'by the deeds of the law there shall no flesh be justified in the sight of God' (Romans 3:20; Galatians 2:16).

In answer to this argument, it has been often urged, that the
works which the apostle excludes from the ground of the sinner's
justification before God, are only works of the *ceremonial*, not of
the *moral*, law. This 'witty shift', Calvin says, the 'wrangling
disputants' of his time borrowed from Origen and some of the old
writers; and he declares it is 'very foolish and absurd', and calls
upon his readers to maintain this for a certain truth, that the whole
law is spoken of, when the power of justifying is taken away from
the law.'[3]

The reference is to every law that God has given to man, whether
expressed in words or imprinted in the heart. It is that law which the
Gentiles have transgressed, which they have naturally inscribed in
their hearts. It is that law which the Jews have violated, when they
committed theft, adulteries, and sacrileges, which convicted them of
impiety, of evil speaking, of calumny, of murder, or injustice. In one
word, it is that law which shuts the mouth of the whole world, as had
been said in the preceding verse, and brings in all men guilty before
God.[4]

2. See the excellent Sermons of Robert Traill on this text.
3. Calvin's *Institutes*, book iii., ch. 11, sect. 19.
4. Robert Haldane on the Romans, vol. i., p. 261. On this point, see also
Owen on *Justification*, ch. 14; Jonathan Edwards' *Sermons*, pp. 33-52;
Rawlin on *Justification*, p. 39; and Chalmers on the *Romans*, pp. 193-199.

Others have contended that the works which the apostle excludes from any share in our justification are merely works not *performed in faith*. This allegation is equally groundless; for the apostle excludes works in general – works of every sort, without distinction or exception (Ephesians 2:9, 10); and the most eminent saints disclaim all dependence upon their own works, and deprecate being dealt with according to their best performances (Psalm 143:2; Philippians 3:8, 9).

Arminians maintain that faith itself, or the act of believing, is accepted as our justifying righteousness. In opposition to this our Confession teaches, that God does not justify us 'by imputing faith itself, the act of believing, as our righteousness'. And in confirmation of this, we observe, that faith, as an act performed by us, is as much a work of obedience to the law as any other; and, therefore, to be justified by the act of faith, would be to be justified by a work. But this is contrary to the express declarations of Scripture, which exclude all sorts of works from the affair of justification (Galatians 2:16). Besides, faith is plainly distinguished from that righteousness by which we are justified. We read of 'the *righteousness of God* which is *by faith* of Jesus Christ', and of 'the *righteousness* which is of God by *faith*' (Romans 3:22; Philippians 3:9). No language could more clearly show that righteousness and faith are two different things. 'Nothing,' says Mr Haldane, 'can be a greater corruption of the truth than to represent faith itself as accepted instead of righteousness, or to be the righteousness that saves the sinner. Faith is not righteousness. Righteousness is the fulfilling of the law.'[5]

Neonomians allege, that though we cannot fulfil that *perfect* obedience which the law of works demanded, yet God has been graciously pleased, for Christ's sake, to give us a *new law*; according to which, *sincere obedience*, or faith, repentance, and sincere obedience, are accepted as our justifying righteousness. It may be here remarked that the Scripture nowhere gives the slightest intimation that a new and milder law has been substituted in place of the law of works originally given to man. Christ came 'not to destroy the law, but to fulfil it'. The gospel was never designed to teach sinners that God will now accept of a *sincere* instead of a *perfect* obedience, but to direct them to Jesus Christ as 'the end of the law for righteousness to every one that believeth'.

---

5. Haldane on the *Romans*, vol. i., p. 350.

The idea of a *new law*, adapted to the present condition of human nature, reflects the greatest dishonour both upon the law and the Lawgiver; for it assumes that the Lawgiver is mutable, and that the law first given to man demanded too much.

3. The righteousness of Jesus Christ is the sole ground of a sinner's justification before God. It is not his *essential* righteousness as God that we intend,[6] for that is incommunicable; but his mediatory or surety-righteousness, which, according to our Confession, consists of his 'obedience and satisfaction'. That sinners are justified only on this ground might be demonstrated by the multiplicity of proofs. None can be justified without a *perfect* righteousness; for the demands of the law cannot be set aside or relaxed. The judgment of God, in pronouncing the sinner righteous, would not be according to truth, unless the sentence were founded upon a righteousness adequate to the requirements of the law. In the Old Testament, the Messiah is mentioned under this endearing name, 'The Lord our Righteousness' (Jeremiah 23:6); and it is predicted that he should 'bring in everlasting righteousness' (Daniel 9:21). In the New Testament, Christ is said to be 'made unto us righteousness'; and we are said to be 'made the righteousness of God in him' (1 Corinthians 1:30; 2 Corinthians 5:21). It is declared that 'by the obedience of one shall many be made righteous', and that 'by the righteousness of one, the free gift comes upon all men unto justification of life' (Romans 5:18, 19).

4. *Sinners obtain an interest in the righteousness of Christ, for their justification, by God imputing it to them, and their receiving it by faith.* The doctrine of the *imputation* of Christ's righteousness is rejected, not only by Romanists and Socinians, but by several authors of widely different sentiments.[7] Let it be observed, that we plead for the imputation of the righteousness of Christ itself, and not merely of its effects. 'To say that the righteousness of Christ, that is, his obedience and sufferings, are imputed to us

---

6. This was the opinion of Osiander, a learned man, who appeared in Germany in the beginning of the Reformation, and who gave Luther and Melancthon much annoyance with his notions. See Mosheim, cent. xvi., sect. 3, p. 2, ch. i., c. 35.
7. Among the authors here referred to, Dr Dwight and Professor Stuart may be mentioned.

only as to their effects, is to say, that we have the benefit of them, and no more; but imputation itself is denied. So say the Socinians; but they know well enough, and ingenuously grant, that they overthrow all true, real imputation thereby.'[8] The effects of Christ's righteousness are communicated to us upon the ground of the imputation of his righteousness itself; but they are really *imparted*, and not imputed to us. Many, we apprehend, oppose the doctrine of imputation, owing to their misconception of its proper nature. It does not signify the infusion of holy dispositions, or the actual transference of the righteousness of Christ to believers, so that it becomes inherently and subjectively theirs – that is impossible, in the nature of things; but the meaning is, that God reckons the righteousness of Christ to their account, and, in consideration of it, treats them as if they were righteous. God does not reckon that they performed it themselves, for that would be a judgment not according to truth; but he accounts it to them for their justification.

> There are certain technical terms in theology which are used so currently, that they fail to impress their own meaning on the thinking principle. The term 'impute' is one of them. It may hold forth a revelation of its plain sense to you, when it is barely mentioned that the term impute in the 6th verse (Romans 4) is the same in the original with what is employed in that verse of Philemon where Paul says, 'If he hath wronged thee, or oweth thee ought, put that on mine account.' To impute righteousness to a man without works, is simply to put righteousness down to his account, though he has not performed the works of righteousness.[9]

The doctrine of the imputation of Christ's righteousness is clearly taught in Scripture. We are represented as being constituted righteous by the obedience of Christ, as we are constituted sinners by the disobedience of Adam; and this can only be by imputation (Romans 5:19). We are also said to be made the righteousness of God in Christ, as he was made sin for us; and this, likewise, could only be by imputation (2 Corinthians 5:21). We are expressly told that God imputeth righteousness without works (Romans 4:6). This imputation proceeds upon the grounds of the believer's *federal* union with Christ from eternity, and of his *vital* union

8. Owen on Justification, ch. 7.
9. Chalmers' Lectures on the *Romans*, vol. i., p. 208.

with him in time. Christ, as the surety of his spiritual seed, engaged from everlasting to fulfil this righteousness for them; he fulfilled it in their nature, and in their room; and when they become vitally united to him by the Spirit and by faith, God graciously accounts his righteousness to them for their justification.

5. *Faith is the alone instrument of the sinner's justification.* That we are justified by faith is so frequently and expressly declared in the Scriptures, that no one who professes to receive the Word of God as the rule of his faith can venture to deny it. There are very different opinions, however, in regard to the office of faith in the justification of a sinner.

Some say that a sinner is justified by faith, as it is an act performed by him; as if faith came in the room of perfect obedience, required by the law. This we have already disproved; and 'it is well known,' says Witsius, 'that the Reformed Churches condemned Arminius and his followers for saying that faith comes to be considered, in the matter of justification, as a work or act of ours.'[10]

Some have said, that faith is to be considered as the *condition* of our justification. The 'condition' of anything usually signifies that which, being done, gives us a right and title to it, because it possesses either intrinsic or conventional merit. To call faith, in this sense, the condition of our justification, would introduce human merit, to the dishonour of divine grace, and would entirely subvert the gospel. Some worthy divines have called faith a condition, who were far from being of opinion that it is a condition properly so called, on the performance of which men should, according to the gracious covenant of God, have a right to justification as their reward. They merely intended, that without faith we cannot be justified – that faith must precede justification in the order of time or of nature. But as the term 'condition' is very ambiguous, and calculated to mislead the ignorant, it should be avoided.

Others have said that faith justifies, as it is informed and animated by charity. This is the language of the Romanists; and here we may fitly use the words of the heroic champion of the Reformation. Commenting on Galatians 2:16, he says:

---

10. Witsius on the *Economy of the Covenants*, book viii., ch. 3, sec. 51.

This is the true mean of becoming a Christian, even to be justified by faith in Jesus Christ, and not by the works of the law. Here we must stand, not upon the wicked gloss of the schoolmen, which say, that faith justifieth when charity and good works are joined withal. With this pestilent gloss, the sophisters have darkened and corrupted this and other like sentences in Paul, wherein he manifestly attributeth justification to faith only in Christ. But when a man heareth that he ought to believe in Christ, and yet, notwithstanding, faith justifieth not except it be formed and furnished with charity, by and by he falleth from faith, and thus he thinketh: If faith without charity alone justifieth not, then is faith in vain and unprofitable, and charity alone justifieth; for except faith be formed with charity it is nothing ....Wherefore we must avoid this gloss as a most deadly and devilish poison, and conclude with Paul, 'that we are justified, not by faith furnished with charity, but by faith only and alone.'[11]

In opposition to these various views of the relation which faith bears to justification, our Confession teaches that 'faith, receiving and resting on Christ and his righteousness, is the *alone instrument* of justification'. Some have misrepresented this expression, as if it meant that faith is the instrument wherewith God justifies. But it was never intended that faith is an instrument on the part of God, but on our part. Some have also inaccurately spoken of faith as the instrument by which we receive justification. Faith is more properly the instrument by which we receive Christ and his righteousness.[12] This, according to Mr Traill, is 'the plain old Protestant doctrine, That the place of faith is only that of a hand or instrument receiving the righteousness of Christ, for which only we are justified.'[13]

The language of modern evangelical divines entirely accords with this 'old Protestant doctrine'. 'Faith,' says Mr Haldane, 'does not justify as an act of righteousness, but as the instrument by which we receive Christ and his righteousness.'[14] 'When we read that we are justified by faith,' says Dr Chalmers, 'one should understand that faith is simply the instrument by which we lay hold of this great privilege.'[15] 'As the hand is said to nourish,' says Dr

---

11. Luther's *Commentary on the Galatians*. 'A book,' says Mr Traill, 'that hath more plain sound gospel, than many volumes of some other divines.'
12 See Edwards' Sermon, p. 13. 13. Traill's *Works*, vol. i., p. 298.
14. Haldane on the *Romans*, vol. i., p. 333.
15. Chalmers on the *Romans*, vol. i., p. 272.

Colquhoun, 'because it is the instrument of applying food to the body; so faith justifies, as the hand or instrument of applying the Redeemer's righteousness to the soul.'[16]

It is to be carefully observed, that our Confession not merely describes faith as the *instrument*, but as the *alone* instrument of justification. This is directed against an error of the Romanists, who hold that hope, and love, and repentance, are included in faith as justifying, and concur with faith, strictly so called, to justification. That we are justified by faith *alone* is proved by such arguments as these: We are justified by faith, in opposition to works (Romans 4:2, 3) – faith alone receives and applies the righteousness of Christ; we are justified freely by grace, and therefore by faith alone – because this alone is consistent with its being by grace (Romans 3:24; 4:16); Abraham obtained the blessing of justification by faith alone, and he was designed as a pattern of the way in which all others, in succeeding ages, were to be justified (Galatians 3:6-9).

The advocates of the doctrine of justification by faith *alone* were grossly calumniated, as if they had denied the necessity of good works. To guard against this injurious misrepresentation, our Confession teaches, that though 'faith is the alone instrument of justification, yet it is not alone in the person justified'. The faith that justifies is a living and active principle, which works by love, purifies the heart, and excites to universal obedience. It is accompanied with every Christian grace, and productive of good works. 'Works,' says Luther, 'are not taken into consideration when the question respects justification. But true faith will no more fail to produce them, than the sun can cease to give light.' This suggests a distinction, which enables us to remove the apparent discrepancy between the Apostles Paul and James; but we forbear entering on that subject.[17]

Section 3

Christ, by his obedience and death, did fully discharge the debt of all those that are thus justified, and did make a proper, real, and full satisfaction, to his Father's justice in their behalf (Romans 5:8-10, 19; 1

---

16. Colquhoun's Sermons, p. 147.

17. See Owen on *Justification*, ch. xx.; Dick's *Lectures*, vol. iii., pp 380-385; Hill's *Lectures*, vol. ii., pp. 284, 285; Turretin's *Inst. Theo.*, L. 16, Q. 8; also Turretin's *Exerc. Theol.* text – *De Concord. Paul et Jac.*

Timothy 5, 6; Hebrews 10:10, 14; Daniel 9:24, 26; Isaiah 53:4-6, 10-
12). Yet, inasmuch as he was given by the Father for them (Romans
8:32), and his obedience and satisfaction accepted in their stead (2 Corinthians 5:21; Matthew 3:17; Ephesians 5:2), and both freely, not for
anything in them, their justification is only of free grace (Romans 3:24;
Ephesians 1:7); that both the exact justice and rich grace of God might
be glorified in the justification of sinners (Romans 3:26; Ephesians 2:7).

Exposition
Socinians deny that Christ made any real and proper satisfaction
to divine justice in behalf of his people; and their grand objection
to this doctrine is, that it leaves no room for the exercise of grace
in the salvation of sinners. Many modern writers, of a different
class, deny that Christ satisfied *retributive* justice, and insist that
he only satisfied *public* justice; consequently they must maintain,
that he neither discharged the debt of those who are justified, nor
made a proper satisfaction in their behalf. Indeed, they hold that a
debt of obedience or a debt of punishment, is, in its nature,
intransferable; of course, neither was transferred to Christ, and
neither was paid by him. The demands of the law, in respect both
of obedience and satisfaction, instead of being exacted by Jehovah,
and fulfilled by Christ, are, in their opinion, by an act of divine
sovereignty, 'suspended, superceded, overruled'. And the chief
argument which they urge against the doctrine of 'a proper, real,
and full satisfaction' to divine justice is, 'its excluding anything
of the nature of grace from every part of the process of a sinner's
salvation, excepting the original appointment of the Surety.'

The statement of our Confession, in this section, is directly
opposed to these views; and in confirmation of it, we need only
refer to the explicit testimony of the Scriptures. 'By the obedience
of one shall many be made righteous' (Romans 5:19). What
stronger proof could we desire that Christ discharged the debt of
obedience due by those who are justified? 'By his knowledge
shall my righteous servant justify many; for he shall bear their
iniquities' (Isaiah 53:11). 'Christ hath redeemed us from the curse
of the law, being made a curse for us' (Galatians 3:13). What
words could more clearly convey the sentiment, that Christ
endured the very penalty of the broken law, and thereby made 'a
proper, real and full satisfaction to his Father's justice', in behalf
of all whom he represented? But the justification of sinners,
'through the redemption that is in Christ Jesus,' instead of

excluding or obscuring, serves rather to illustrate the glory of the *grace* displayed in it. Grace shines in God's condescending to accept of the righteousness of a surety; still more in his providing the surety; above all, in giving his only begotten Son to be the propitiation for our sins. Besides, that faith by which we receive the righteousness of Christ is the gift of God (Ephesians 2:8).

> The glory of the gospel is, that *grace reigns through righteousness.* Salvation is of grace; but this grace comes to us in a way of right-eousness. It is grace to us; but it was brought about in such a way that all our debt was paid. This exhibits God as just as well as merci-ful. Just, in requiring full compensation to justice; and merciful, be-cause it was he, and not the sinner, who provided the ransom.[18]

Section 4

God did, from all eternity, decree to justify all the elect (Galatians 3:8; 1 Peter 1:2, 19, 20; Romans 8:30); and Christ did, in the fulness of time, die for their sins, and rise again for their justification (Galatians 4:4; 1 Timothy 2:6; Romans 4:25): nevertheless they are not justified, until the Holy Spirit doth in due time actually apply Christ unto them (Colossians 1:21, 22; Galatians 2:16; Titus 3:4-7).

Exposition

This section is directed against the Antinomian error, that the elect were justified from eternity, or when the price of their redemption was paid by Christ. It is readily admitted that God, from eternity, decreed to justify the elect; but till the period of effectual calling they are in a state of wrath and condemnation (Ephesians 2:3; John 3:18). The righteousness by which they are justified was perfected in Christ's death, and the perfection of it was declared by his resurrection, and they may be said to have been *virtually* justified when Christ was acquitted and discharged as their head and representative; nevertheless, they are not *actually* and *formally* justified until they are vitally united to Christ by faith.

Section 5

God doth continue to forgive the sins of those that are justified (Mat-thew 6:12; 1 John 1:7, 9; 2:1, 2): and although they can never fall from the state of justification (Luke 22:32; John 10:28; Hebrews 10:14), yet they may by their sins fall under God's fatherly displeasure, and not have the light of his countenance restored unto them, until they humble

---

18. Haldane on the *Romans*, vol. i., p. 320.

themselves, confess their sins, beg pardon, and renew their faith and repentance (Psalms 89:31-33; 51:7-12; 32:5; Matthew 26:75; 1 Corinthians 11:30, 32; Luke 1:20).

Exposition

As justification is an act completed at once, so those who are justified cannot come into condemnation: 'There is now no condemnation to them that are in Christ Jesus' (Romans 8:1). The sins which they afterwards commit cannot revoke the pardon which God has graciously given them; but they may subject them to his fatherly displeasure, and to temporary chastisements (Psalm 89:30-33). Here we must advert to the well-known distinction between judicial and fatherly forgiveness. Though God, in the capacity of a judge, pardons all the sins of believers, in the most free and unconditional manner, in the day of their justification, yet that forgiveness which, as a father, he bestows upon his justified and adopted children, is not, in general, vouchsafed without suitable preparation on their part for receiving and improving the privilege. They ought, therefore, to humble themselves before God, make ingenuous confession of their offences, renew their faith and repentance, and earnestly supplicate the removal of his fatherly displeasure, and the restoration of his paternal smiles.

Section 6

The justification of believers under the Old Testament was, in all these respects, one and the same with the justification of believers under the New Testament (Galatians 3:9, 13, 14; Romans 4:22-24; Hebrews 13:8).

Exposition

The reverse of this is maintained by Socinians. We shall only observe, that though 'the righteousness of God' is now more clearly manifested by the gospel, yet it was 'witnessed by the law and the prophets' (Romans 3:21). And those, under the Old Testament, who laid hold upon that righteousness by faith, were as really and fully justified as believers under the New Testament. Paul, accordingly, adduces the justification of Abraham as an example of the method in which believers in all ages must be justified (Romans 4:3). Though the everlasting righteousness was not actually brought in until Christ 'became obedient unto death', yet the efficacy of his death extended to believers under the former as well as under the present dispensation.

What an invaluable and transcendently glorious privilege is justification! How unspeakably blessed is the man to whom God imputeth righteousness without works! Delivered from the awful curse of the broken law, and introduced into a state of acceptance and favour with God, all penal evil is extracted out of the cup of his affliction, death itself is divested of its sting, and all things shall work together for his good. Adorned with the glorious robe of the Redeemer's righteousness, he shall stand before the judgment-seat undismayed, while the exalted Saviour and Judge shall bid him welcome to that state of final and everlasting blessedness which God hath prepared for him, saying, 'Come, ye blessed of my Father, inherit the kingdom prepared for you from the foundation of the world.'

But where will the sinner and the ungodly appear in that day when the Son of man shall sit upon the throne of his glory, and summon them before his august tribunal to receive their final doom? How will the impenitent and unbelieving – all who have not submitted to the righteousness of God – then 'call to the mountains and rocks to fall upon them and hide them from the face of him that sitteth on the throne, and from the wrath of the Lamb'.

Let those who have hitherto been labouring to establish their own righteousness cease from the vain attempt – let them receive the gift of righteousness which is presented for their acceptance in the offer of the gospel – and let them plead this perfect and glorious righteousness, and improve it by faith, as the sole ground of all their expectations from a God of grace either in time of through eternity. Renouncing all dependence on their own works of righteousness, let them, like Paul, desire to 'win Christ, and be found in him, not having their own righteousness, but that which is through the faith of Christ, the righteousness which is of God by faith.'

CHAPTER 12

ADOPTION

All those that are justified, God vouchsafeth, in and for his only Son Jesus Christ, to make partakers of the grace of adoption (Ephesians 1:5; Galatians 4:4, 5): by which they are taken into the number, and enjoy the liberties and privileges of the children of God (Romans 8:17; John 1:12); have his name put upon them (Jeremiah 14:9; 2 Corinthians 6:18; Revelation 3:12), receive the Spirit of adoption (Romans 8:15); have access to the throne of grace with boldness (Ephesians 3:12; Romans 5:2); are enabled to cry, Abba, Father (Galatians 4:6); are pitied (Galatians 4:6); protected (Proverbs 14:26), provided for (Matthew 6:30, 32; 1 Peter 5:7), and chastened by him as by a father (Hebrews 12:6); yet never cast off (Lamentations 3:31), but sealed to the day of redemption (Ephesians 4:30), and inherit the promises (Hebrews 6:12), as heirs of everlasting salvation (1 Peter 1:3, 4. Hebrews 1:14).

Exposition

All men are the children of God in respect of their creation; for 'we are all his offspring'. 'Have we not all one Father? hath not one God created us?' (Malachi 2:10). The members of the visible Church are the children of God in respect of an external federal relation. They are the visible family of God on earth, and enjoy peculiar privileges. At a very early period, the professors of the true religion were denominated 'the sons of God' (Genesis 6:2). God having chosen Israel for his peculiar people, and conferred upon them many privileges which he did not vouchsafe to other nations, and the knowledge and worship of the true God being maintained amongst them, while all other nations were sunk in ignorance and idolatry, they were called 'the sons of God'. The Lord commanded Pharaoh to be told concerning Israel, 'He is my son, even my first-born' (Exodus 4:22). This is a great blessing; but many who enjoy it are not really the children of God, and shall at last be cast out into utter darkness (John 8:44; Matthew 8:12).

In a far higher sense are all those that are justified the children of God. They are made partakers of the grace of *adoption*. Among men, adoption signifies that act by which a person takes the child of another into the place, and entitles him to the privileges, of his own son. Spiritual adoption is that act by which God receives sinners into his family, and gives them a right to all the privileges of his children. Sinners are naturally 'the children of the devil', aliens to the family of God, and heirs of wrath; by adoption they are translated out of the family of Satan into the family of Heaven, and thus admitted to fellowship with Jesus Christ, the only begotten Son of God, as their elder brother, with all the holy angels, and with all the saints – both those on earth and those in heaven.

Thus far there is a resemblance between civil and spiritual adoption; but there are also important points in which they differ. Men adopt a stranger to supply a defect, but God had no such inducement to adopt any of the children of Adam; for he is infinitely blessed in himself, and he had 'a well-beloved Son', who was the object of his ineffable delight. Men usually adopt only *one* to be their son and heir, but God receives an innumerable multitude into his family, and 'brings *many* sons to glory'. Men are always influenced by some real or supposed excellence in the person to whom they show this kindness; but those whom God adopts are altogether destitute of any good qualifications to recommend them to his favour.

Adoption, being a change of state, is completed at once, and is equally the privilege of all that truly believe in Christ (Galatians 3:26, 28). Some of the children of God may excel others in gifts and gracious qualities; but the filial relation to God is the same in all. This high privilege entirely flows from the free and sovereign grace of God. In the bestowment of this blessing there is a display of love and grace which surpasses expression, and calls forth the admiration of all who are partakers of it. 'Behold, what manner of love the Father hath bestowed upon us, that we should be called the sons of God' (1 John 3:1).

But divine grace could only be dispensed to the guilty in a way consistent with the claims of justice, and the honour of the law. Had God received such rebels into his favour and family without demanding a satisfaction for their offences, this would have sullied the glory of his perfections, and dishonoured the law which they had violated. This privilege, therefore, is bestowed on the ground of the obedience and satisfaction of Christ, as the meritorious cause thereof. 'When the fulness of the time was come, God sent forth his Son, made of a woman, made under the law, to redeem them that were under the law, that we might receive the adoption of sons' (Galatians 4:4, 5). How amazing the condescension and grace of our Lord Jesus Christ, who endured the curse of the law, that the forfeiture of our sonship might be reversed! As he procured this privilege for us by an invaluable price, so it is only when we are united to him by faith that we become actually interested in it. 'As many as received him, to them gave he power to become the sons of God, even to them that believe on his name' (John 1:12).

We shall now take a cursory view of the inestimable privileges of the children of God.

1. *They obtain a new name.* A stranger taken into the family of another, received the name of the adopter, and those whom God adopts 'are called by a new name, which the mouth of the Lord hath named,' even by the honourable and endearing name of 'the sons and daughters of the Lord Almighty' (Isaiah 62:2; 2 Corinthians 6:18).

2. *They receive the spirit of adoption* (Romans 8:15; Galatians 4:6). The Spirit implants in them the dispositions of children, and transforms them into the image of God's dear Son; he witnesseth with their spirits that they are the sons of God; he seals them to the day of redemption, and is the earnest of their inheritance until the redemption of the purchased possession (Romans 8:16; Ephesians 1:13, 14).

3. *They have access to the throne of grace with boldness.* God allows his children to draw near to him with freedom, to pour out their hearts before him, to make all their requests known to him; and they may cherish this confidence, that if they ask anything according to his will, he heareth them (1 John 5:14).

4. *They are the objects of God's fatherly sympathy and pity.* He knows their frame, and remembers that they are but dust; and when he sees it necessary to correct them, he feels for them with the bowels of parental compassion (Psalm 103:13).

5. *They enjoy the protection of their heavenly Father.* Numerous are their spiritual enemies, and manifold the dangers to which they are exposed; but he who neither slumbers nor sleeps, watches over them with unwearied care. He gives his angels charge concerning them, who encamp around them, and, in ways unknown to us, perform many kind offices for them (Psalm 34:7; Hebrews 1:14).

6. *They are provided for by their heavenly Father*. He knows they need his providential favours in this world, and these he does not withhold (Matthew 6:30-32; Psalm 34:9, 10). For their souls he has made suitable provision in his Word, and he communicates to them supplies of grace according to their diversified circumstances (Philippians 4:19).

7. *Paternal correction is not withheld when necessary* (Hebrews 12:6). This, indeed, they are apt to regard as a punishment rather than a privilege; but it is the fruit of paternal love, it is intended for their profit, and is promised as a blessing (Psalm 89:30-34). These corrections, though not for the present joyous, but grievous, promote their spiritual advantage; and many of God's children have acknowledged from their happy experience, that it was good for them to be afflicted (Psalms 94:12; 119:67, 71; Job 5:17).

8. *Unfailing establishment in their state of sonship, and in all the privileges connected with that state*. As their heavenly Father will never cast them off, so he secures that they shall not totally and finally depart from him (Jeremiah 32:40).

9. *They are heirs of all the promises*. These are exceeding great and precious; they are adapted to every condition in which the children of God can be placed; and faithful is he who hath promised (Hebrews 6:12, 17).

10. *They are heirs of a rich and glorious inheritance*, which is reserved for them in heaven (1 Peter 1:4). They are said to be 'heirs of salvation' (Hebrews 1:14); 'heirs of the grace of life' (1 Peter 3:7); 'heirs of the kingdom' (James 2:5); and 'heirs of God' (Romans 8:17).

How dignified are all true believers! What character so honourable as that of the sons of God! True, the dignity to which they are advanced is not conspicuous to the world, nor always discerned by themselves; but the day of revelation of Jesus Christ will be the day of 'the manifestation of the sons of God' (Romans 8:19). Then will Christ acknowledge them as his brethren before the assembled world, and put them in full possession of that inheritance which he has gone to prepare for them. Let them, therefore, look for his glorious appearing; and, in the meantime, let them act in accordance with their high character and their exalted prospects – walking as the sons of God, harmless and without rebuke, and shining as lights in the world.

CHAPTER 13

SANCTIFICATION

Section 1
They who are effectually called and regenerated, having a new heart and a new spirit created in them, are further sanctified really and personally, through the virtue of Christ's death and resurrection (1 Corinthians 6:11; Acts 20:32; Philippians 3:10; Romans 6:5, 6), by his Word and Spirit dwelling in them (John 17:17; Ephesians 5:26; 2 Thessalonians 2:13); the dominion of the whole body of sin is destroyed (Romans 6:6, 14), and the several lusts thereof are more and more weakened and mortified (Galatians 5:24; Romans 8:13), and they more and more quickened and strengthened in all saving graces (Colossians 1:11; Ephesians 3:16-19), to the practice of true holiness, without which no man shall see the Lord (2 Corinthians 7:1; Hebrews 12:14).

Section 2
This sanctification is throughout in the whole man (1 Thessalonians 5:23), yet imperfect in this life; there abideth still some remnants of corruption in every part (1 John 1:10; Romans 7:18, 23; Philippians 3:12): whence ariseth a continual and irreconcileable war; the flesh lusting against the Spirit, and the Spirit against the flesh (Galatians 5:17; 1 Peter 2:11).

Section 3
In which war, although the remaining corruption for a time may much prevail (Romans 7:23), yet, through the continual supply of strength from the sanctifying Spirit of Christ, the regenerate part doth overcome (Romans 6:14; 1 John 5:4; Ephesians 4:15, 16): and so the saints grow in grace (2 Peter 3:18; 2 Corinthians 3:18), perfecting holiness in the fear of God (2 Corinthians 7:1).

Exposition
In Scripture, the word *sanctification* bears a variety of senses. It signifies *separation* from a common to a sacred use, or *dedication* to the service of God. Thus the altar, temple, priests, and all the sacred utensils, were sanctified. It also signifies *purification* from ceremonial defilement (Hebrews 9:13). But the sanctification of believers, of which this chapter treats, consists in their purification from the pollution of sin, and the renovation of their nature after the image of God.

Antinomians maintain, that believers are sanctified only by the holiness of Christ being imputed to them, and that there is no inherent holiness infused into them, nor required of them. This is a great and dangerous error; and, in opposition to it, our Confession asserts, that believers are *really* and *personally* sanctified. Their sanctification includes 'the mortification of sin in their members'. It includes also 'the fruits of the Spirit, as love, joy, peace, long-suffering, gentleness, goodness, faith, meekness, temperance' (Galatians 5:22). These are personal things; they are wrought in the hearts of believers, and produced in their tempers and lives. It is absurd to say they are in Christ, and imputed to believers; they are the effects of the Holy Spirit imparted to us, whose operations are compared, by Christ himself, to 'a well of water within us, springing up unto everlasting life'.

Romanists, as we formerly noticed, confound justification with sanctification; and, as this leads to various dangerous mistakes, we shall mention several points in which they differ. They differ in their *nature*: justification is a relative change of state; sanctification is a real change of the whole man, soul and body. They differ in their *order*: justification, in the order of nature, though not of time, precedes sanctification; for righteousness imputed is, in the order of nature, prior to holiness, implanted and inherent. They differ in their *matter*: the matter of justification is the righteousness of Christ imputed; the matter of sanctification is an inherent righteousness communicated. They differ in their *form*: justification is a judicial act by which the sinner is pronounced righteous; sanctification is a physical or moral act, or rather a series of acts, by which a change is effected in the qualities of the soul. They differ in their *properties*; justification is perfected at once, and is equal in all believers; sanctification is imperfect at first, and exists in different degrees of advancement in different individuals; hence the former is called an *act*, and the latter a *work*. Other points of difference might be mentioned, but we only add, that in justification we receive a *title* to heaven; sanctification gives us a *meetness* for, and a capacity of, enjoying it.

Sanctification is both a *privilege* and a *duty*. In the one view it is the work of God, and in the other it is the work of man, assisted by supernatural grace. As a privilege, it is graciously promised in the gospel (Ezekiel 36:27). As a duty, it is required by the law; hence we are called to 'make' to ourselves a 'new heart', and 'to cleanse ourselves from all filthiness of the flesh and spirit, perfecting holiness in the fear of God' (Ezekiel 18:31; 2 Corinthians 7:1).

Sanctification may be considered as *initial* and *progressive*. Initial sanctification is the same as regeneration, whereby we become 'new creatures' – 'old things being done away, and all things becoming new'. In progressive sanctification, the several lusts of the old man are more and more weakened and mortified. In initial sanctification, the Spirit of Christ enters the heart with all his train of graces, and implants them there. In progressive sanctification, these graces are more and more quickened and strengthened. In initial sanctification, a principle of spiritual life is implanted, and the lineaments of the divine image faintly impressed upon the soul. In progressive sanctification, the spiritual life is increased, and the outlines of the divine image gradually filled up. In short, the same work which is begun in regeneration is carried on in sanctification, until the new creature attains to the full stature of a perfect man in Christ (Philippians 1:6).

Sanctification extends to *the whole man*, including all the faculties of the soul, and all the members of the body (1 Thessalonians 5:23). Our entire nature was originally created in the image of God; by the entrance of sin this image was utterly defaced and lost; hence corrupted and depraved nature is called 'the old man', because it infects the whole man, and defiles both soul and body. Now, as original corruption pervades the whole man, so sanctifying grace extends to every part; hence our nature, as renewed after the image of God, is called 'the new man', because the holiness communicated in sanctification possesses and ennobles the whole man.

Sanctification is *imperfect* in this life. There have been men, and there still are, who maintain, that sinless perfection is attainable in this life. This is held by Antinomians, who profess that the perfect holiness of Christ is imputed to believers. It is held likewise by Romanists, Socinians, and others, who affirm that believers have, or may attain, a perfect inherent holiness.[1] The doctrine of sinless perfection was also held by the founder of the Methodists; and the same opinion is still held by his followers.[2] In opposition to such views, our Confession decidedly affirms that sanctification

---

1. For a fuller account of these opinions, see Hill's *Lectures*, p. 303.
2. Richard Watson's *Theol. Institutes*, vol. iv., p. 140.

is 'imperfect in this life'. Though it extends to the whole man, yet 'there abideth still some remnants of corruption in every part'. The Scriptures abound with the most explicit testimonies against the doctrine of sinless perfection (Ecclesiastes 7:20; James 3:2; Proverbs 20:9; 1 John 1:8). The epithet *perfect* is indeed applied to several saints, but it must be understood either comparatively, in which sense 'Noah was perfect in his generation'; or, as synonymous with sincerity or uprightness, in which sense God said to Abraham, 'Walk before me, and be thou perfect.' That the most eminent saints mentioned in Scripture were not free from sin is evident from the defects and blemishes which are discovered in their conduct. They were far from imagining that they had attained to sinless perfection (Job 9:20; Psalm 19:12; Philippians 3:12). Every real Christian will certainly aspire after perfection; but none can attain to absolute perfection in this life.

As there is both grace and the remainders of corruption in every saint, it follows that there will be 'a continual and irreconcilable war' between these two opposite principles. This conflict is described in a very striking manner (Romans 7; Galatians 5:17). Sometimes the one principle prevails, and sometimes the other; but grace will finally overcome.

The *impulsive* or moving cause of sanctification is the free grace of God (Titus 3:5). The *meritorious* cause is the blood and righteousness of Christ (Titus 2:14). The *efficient* cause is the Holy Spirit (1 Peter 1:2; 2 Thessalonians 2:13; 1 Corinthians 6:11). The *instrumental* cause is faith in Christ (Acts 15:9; 26:18). The external *means* are the Word read and preached, the sacraments, and prayer (John 17:17; 1 Peter 2:2). Providences, especially afflictive dispensations, are also blessed for promoting the sanctification of believers (Romans 8:28; 5:4-5).

Holiness, though it cannot give us a title to heaven, is indispensably necessary. It is necessary by a divine and unalterable constitution; for 'without holiness no man shall see the Lord' (Hebrews 12:14). God has enacted it as an immutable law, that nothing which defileth shall enter into the heavenly city (Revelation 21:27). It is necessary, also, as a preparative for heaven. It is the evidence of our title, and constitutes our meetness for enjoying the pleasures and engaging in the work of the heavenly world. 'Blessed are the pure in heart; for they shall see God' (Matthew 5:8).

Let us, then, in the diligent use of appointed means, earnestly 'follow holiness'. 'This is the will of God, even our sanctification.' This is his express command: 'Be ye holy; for I am holy'. Those whom he ordained to glory as the end, he chose to holiness as the means, without which none shall ever attain that end (Ephesians 1:4). This is, also, the end of our redemption by Jesus Christ (Ephesians 5:25, 26). He died not only to save us from wrath, but to save us from our sins. Holiness was the primeval glory of our nature, and shall we not endeavour to recover that glory – to be restored to the image of him who created us? Holiness is eminently the glory of God; and shall we not seek to resemble him in sanctity? Holiness is necessary to make us 'meet for being partakers of the inheritance of the saints in light'. Presumptuous and delusive is that hope of seeing Christ hereafter, which does not produce an ardent desire and earnest endeavour to be conformed to him here. 'Every man that hath this hope in him purifieth himself, even as he is pure' (1 John 3:3).

CHAPTER 14

SAVING FAITH

Section 1

The grace of faith, whereby the elect are enabled to believe to the saving of their souls (Hebrews 10:39), is the work of the Spirit of Christ in their hearts (2 Corinthians 4:13; Ephesians 1:17-19; 2:8), and is ordinarily wrought by the ministry of the Word (Romans 10:14, 17): by which also, and by the administration of the sacraments, and prayer, it is increased and strengthened (1 Peter 2:2; Acts 20:32; Romans 4:11; Luke 17:5; Romans 1:16, 17).

Exposition

'He that believeth, and is baptized, shall be saved; but he that believeth not shall be damned' is the solemn announcement of the Saviour himself. The place thus assigned to faith in the matter of salvation, shows that the subject of this chapter possesses the deepest interest. If a Saviour was necessary to the recovery of lost sinners, faith in that Saviour is no less necessary to the actual enjoyment of salvation. The vast importance of having scriptural views of the nature of saving faith must therefore be obvious. The present section teaches us:

1. That the subjects of this faith are *elect sinners*. All whom God from eternity elected to everlasting life are in time brought to believe to the saving of their souls. An apostle affirms: 'As many as were ordained to eternal life believed'; and Christ himself declares: 'All that the Father giveth me shall come to me' (Acts 13:48; John 6:37). 'The faith of God's elect' differs from every other sort of faith. Saving faith is supernatural – the act of a renewed soul – a living principle, which purifies the heart, works by love, and overcomes the world; it must, therefore, be widely different from a natural, a dead, or a common faith. It is denominated 'precious faith', 'faith unfeigned', 'the faith of the operation of God'; and that faith to which the Scripture applies so many discriminating epithets must surely possess some quality peculiar to itself. Accordingly, we read in Scripture of many who believed, and yet did not possess saving faith. Simon the sorcerer believed; Agrippa believed; the hearers compared to the stony ground

believed; and many believed in the name of Jesus, when they saw the miracles which he did; 'but he did not commit himself unto them, because he knew all men.' It is manifest, then, that 'they do not speak accurately, cautiously, or safely, who represent all sorts of faith to be of the same specific nature; because they may all agree in some bare simple act or persuasion of the mind. It must be a great and dangerous mistake to think that the belief of any ordinary fact upon human testimony, and every assent given by men, or even devils, to any doctrines or facts recorded in Scripture, is of the very same kind with that which is saving, although wanting so many things essential to the latter, of which so much is spoken, and which is so highly celebrated in the Book of God.'[1]

2. That this faith is wrought in the hearts of the elect *by the Holy Spirit*. Some unequivocally affirm that every man has perfect power to believe the gospel, independently of the Spirit's influences; and others, who seem to recognise the necessity of divine influence, do yet deny that any direct special influence is either needed or bestowed; and therefore ultimately ascribe the existence of faith in one rather than another to the free-will of man. That man, in his fallen state, 'has lost all ability of will to any spiritual good accompanying salvation', we have formerly endeavoured to establish,[2] and shall only now appeal to the explicit testimony of Scripture. Faith is declared to be 'the gift of God' – to be of 'the operation of God' – and to require the exertion of 'mighty power, like that which wrought in Christ when God raised him from the dead' (Ephesians 1:19, 2:18; Colossians 2:12). The

---

1. The late Professor Bruce's (of Whitburn) *Evangelical Discourses*, p. 106. There are some excellent remarks on this point in the 'Miscellaneous Observations' of President Edwards. After adducing several arguments to prove 'that saving faith differs from common faith in nature and essence', he says: 'Beware how you entertain any such doctrine as that there is no essential difference between common and saving faith; and that both consist in a mere assent of the understanding to the doctrines of religion. That this doctrine is false, appears by what has been said; and if it be false, it must needs be exceedingly dangerous.' A desire to simplify the notion of faith has led some late writers to represent saving faith as a simple belief of the truth – as nowise different, in respect of *act*, from the belief of any ordinary historical fact. Those who are disposed to adopt this view of faith, would do well to weigh the arguments of the acute Edwards.
2. See pages 158-159.

Holy Ghost is called 'the Spirit of faith' (2 Corinthians 4:13); and faith is mentioned among 'the fruits of the Spirit' (Galatians 5:22); because the production of faith in the hearts of the elect peculiarly belongs to him, as the applier of the redemption purchased by Christ.

3. That faith is ordinarily wrought in the hearts of the elect by *the ministry of the Word.* 'Faith cometh by hearing, and hearing by the Word of God' (Romans 10:17). Some allow of no other influence in this matter but the outward means. They explain away the plain import of those passages of Scripture which ascribe the production of faith to an immediate divine influence, as if no more were intended than that God furnishes men with the truth and its evidence. According to their interpretation, that emphatic declaration of Christ, 'No man can come to me except the Father *draw* him,' simply means that the Father gives them the Scriptures. This is to substitute the means in the place of the efficient agent; and if the work is effected simply by the external means, there can be no propriety in speaking of the Holy Spirit as having anything to do in the production of faith. But our Confession clearly distinguishes between the work of the Holy Spirit and the ministry of the Word. There is a distinct and immediate influence of the Spirit on the heart; but the Spirit usually works by means, and the Word read or preached is the divinely appointed means by which he usually communicates his influence. Lydia, in common with others, heard the Word preached by Paul; but 'the Lord opened her heart'. The apostle clearly distinguishes between the gospel and the power which renders it successful: 'Our gospel came not unto you in word only, but also in power, and in the Holy Ghost...' (1 Thessalonians 1:5).

Section 2
By this faith, a Christian believeth to be true whatsoever is revealed in the Word, for the authority of God himself speaking therein (John 4:42; 1 Thessalonians 2:13; 1 John 5:10; Acts 24:14); and acteth differently upon that which each peculiar passage thereof containeth; yielding obedience to the commands (Romans 16:26), trembling at the threatenings (Isaiah 66:2), and embracing the promises of God for this life and that which is to come (Hebrews 11:13; 1 Timothy 4:8). But the principal acts of saving faith are, accepting, receiving, and resting upon Christ alone for justification, sanctification, and eternal life, by virtue of the covenant of grace (John 1:12; Acts 16:31; Galatians 20; Acts 15:11).

Exposition

1. *The general object of divine faith is the whole Word of God.* As faith, in general, is an assent to truth upon testimony, so divine faith is an assent to divine truth upon divine testimony. Saving faith, therefore, includes an assent of the heart to all the truths revealed in the Word of God, whether they relate to the law or to the gospel; and that, not upon the testimony of any man or Church, nor because they appear agreeable to the dictates of natural reason, but on the ground of the truth and authority of God himself, speaking in the Scriptures, and evidencing themselves, by their own distinguishing light and power, to the mind.[3]

2. *The special and personal object of saving faith is the Lord Jesus Christ.* To know Christ, and God as manifested in him, is comprehensive to all saving knowledge – a term by which faith is sometimes expressed (John 17:3). Hence, this faith is called 'the faith of Jesus Christ', and the scope of the apostle's doctrine is thus described: 'Testifying both to the Jews and the Greeks repentance toward God, and faith toward our Lord Jesus Christ.'

> This faith consists in believing the testimony of God concerning his Son, and the life that is in him for men. It respects him in his person and whole character, according to the revelation made of him, and according to the measure of knowledge a person has of him as thus revealed, especially as now manifested, and more clearly exhibited, and freely offered in the gospel. It views him in his supreme Deity as 'Immanuel, God with us'; as vested with all saving offices, so as to bear, in the highest sense, the name Jesus or Saviour, Lord or King, the great High Priest, Messias, or the Christ; and as exercising all his offices for the benefit of mankind sinners, with whom he entered into near affinity, by the assumption of their nature, that he might be capable of acting the part of a surety in obeying, dying, meriting, and mediating for them.[4]

It will not do to limit the object of saving faith to any one doctrinal proposition – such as, that Jesus is the Son of God, or that Jesus Christ is come in the flesh, or that Christ died for our sins according to the Scriptures. This, at the utmost, would only be giving credit to a certain *doctrine*; but saving faith is a believing on the *person* of Christ, or an appropriating of Christ himself,

---

3. Owen's *Treatise on the Reason of Faith*, and Halyburton's *Essay on Faith*.
4. Professor Bruce's *Evangelical Discourses*, p. 108.

with all the benefits and blessings included in him.[5]

3. *The principal acts of saving faith are, accepting, receiving, and resting upon Christ.* Romanists make faith to be nothing more than 'a bare naked assent to the truth revealed in the Word'. This notion was strenuously opposed by our Reformers, and is renounced in the National Covenant of Scotland, under the name of a 'general and doubtsome faith'; yet, many Protestants, in modern times, represent saving faith as nothing more than a simple assent to the doctrinal truths recorded in Scripture, and as exclusively an act of the understanding. But, although saving faith gives full credit to the whole Word of God, and particularly to the testimony of God concerning his Son Jesus Christ, as has been already stated, yet, its principal acts are 'accepting, receiving, and resting upon Christ'. True faith is the belief of a testimony; but it must correspond to the nature of the testimony believed. Were the gospel a mere statement of speculative truths, or a record of facts in which we have no personal interest, then, a simple assent of the mind to these truths, the mere crediting of these facts, would constitute the faith of the gospel. But the gospel is not a mere statement of historical facts, or of abstract doctrines respecting the Saviour; it contains in it a free offer of Christ, and of salvation through him, to sinners of every class, who hear it, for their acceptance. Saving faith, therefore, that it may correspond to the testimony believed, must include the cordial acceptance or reception of Christ, as tendered to us in the gospel.

As Christ is exhibited in Scripture under various characters and similitudes, so faith in him is variously denominated. It is expressed by *coming* to him, by *looking* unto him, by *fleeing* to him for refuge, by *eating* his flesh and *drinking* his blood, by *receiving* him, and by *resting* upon him. It is to be observed, that the terms employed in our Confession do not denote different acts of faith, but are only different expressions of the same act. Believing on Christ is called a *receiving* of him, in reference to his being presented to poor sinners, as the *gift* of God to them; and it is styled a *resting* on him, because he is revealed in the

---

5. Curworth's *Aphorisms on the Assurance of Faith.* An edition was published in 1829, with a Recommendation by the late Rev. John Brown of Whitburn, along with two Essays on Faith by American Divines; and they have been recently published along with Treatises on Faith by E. Erskine and Dr. Anderson of America.

gospel as a *sure foundation*, on which a sinner may lay the weight of his eternal salvation with the firmest confidence. It is manifest, that all the figurative descriptions of saving faith in Scripture imply a particular application of Christ by the soul, or a trusting in Christ for salvation to one's self in particular; and this is what some have called the *appropriation* of faith. It is no less evident, that in the phraseology of Scripture, faith is not simply an assent of the understanding, but implies an act of volition, accepting the Saviour and relying on him for salvation. This does not proceed upon any previous knowledge which the sinner has of his election; nor upon any persuasion that Christ died intentionally for him more than for others, for it is impossible to come to the knowledge of these things prior to believing; nor does it proceed upon the persuasion that Christ died equally for all men, and therefore for him in particular; nor upon the perception of any good qualities in himself to distinguish him from others; but it proceeds solely upon the free, unlimited offer and promise of the gospel to the chief of sinners.

4. *That the true believer receives and rests upon Christ* alone *for salvation.* This distinguishes the true believer from such as rest their hope of salvation on the general mercy of God, without any respect to the mediation of Christ, or upon their own works of righteousness, or upon the righteousness of Christ and their own works conjoined.

5. That the true believer receives and rests upon Christ for a *complete salvation.* He trusts in Christ for salvation not only from wrath, but also from sin – not only for salvation from the guilt of sin, but also from its pollution and power – not only for happiness hereafter, but also for holiness here. In the language of the Confession, he rests upon Christ 'for justification, sanctification, and eternal life'; and that 'by virtue of the covenant of grace'; that is, as these blessings are exhibited and secured in that covenant.

Section 3
This faith is different in degrees, weak or strong (Hebrews 5:13, 14; Romans 4:19, 20; Matthew 6:30; 8:10); may be often and many ways assailed and weakened, but gets the victory (Luke 22:31, 32; Ephesians 6:16; 1 John 5:4, 5); growing up in many to the attainment of a full assurance through Christ (Hebrews 6:11, 12; 10:22; Colossians 2:2); who is both the author and finisher of our faith (Hebrews 12:2).

Exposition

Different interpretations have been put on this section. Some have maintained, that 'assurance is here plainly made a fruit and consequent of saving faith, and not an essential act'.[6] Others have held that assurance is here supposed to be essential to saving faith, and that it belongs, in some degree, to every believer, strong or weak, but is always in proportion to the degree of his faith. 'How faith,' says the illustrious Boston, 'can *grow* in any to a *full* assurance, if there be no assurance in the nature of it, I cannot comprehend.' And another, amplifying this idea, says: 'If there was not *some* degree of assurance in the nature of faith, it could never grow up to *full* assurance. To what degree soever anything may grow, it cannot, by its growth, assume a different nature. It may increase to a higher degree of the same kind, but not into another kind.'[7]

Perhaps this difference of opinion has arisen from attaching a different meaning to the word *assurance*. Those who deny that assurance belongs to the nature of faith, understand, by that word, an assurance that a person is already in a state of salvation; but this sense of the term is disavowed by those who maintain that assurance is essential to faith. Says one of the latter class of divines:

> It would greatly conduce to clear views of this subject were the distinction between the assurance of *faith* and the assurance of *sense* rightly understood and inculcated. When we speak of assurance as essential to faith, many suppose we teach that none can be real Christians who do not feel that they have passed from death unto life, and have not unclouded and triumphant views of their own interest in Christ, so as to joy under the manifestations of his love. 'My beloved is mine, and I am his.' But God forbid that we should thus offend against the generation of his children. That many of them want such an assurance may not be questioned. This, however, is the assurance, not of faith, but of sense; and vastly different they are. The object of the former is Christ revealed in the *Word*; the object of the latter, Christ revealed in the *heart*. The ground of the former is the testimony of God *without us*; that of the latter, the work of the Spirit *within us*. The one embraces the promise, looking at nothing but the veracity of the promiser; the other enjoys the promise in the sweetness of its actual accomplishment. Faith trusts for pardon to

6. Principal Hadow's Sermon on 1 John 5:11, 12, preached before the Synod of Fife, 1719, p. 33.
7. Colquhoun's *View of Saving Faith*, p. 247.

SAVING FAITH 197

the blood of Christ; sense asserts pardon from the comfortable intimations of it to the soul. By faith, we take the Lord Jesus for salvation; by sense, we feel that we are saved, from the Spirit's shining on his own gracious work in our hearts.[8]

The distinction between these two kinds of assurance has been accurately drawn by Dr M'Crie, and extremes on both hands judiciously pointed out.

Assurance is of two kinds, which have been designed the assurance of faith and the assurance of sense. The former is direct, the latter indirect. The former is founded on the testimony of God; the latter, on experience. The object of the former is entirely without us; the object of the latter is chiefly within us. 'God hath spoken in his holiness, I will rejoice,' is the language of the former; 'We are his workmanship, created anew in Christ Jesus,' is the language of the latter. When a man gives me his promissory-note, I have the assurance of faith; when he gives me a pledge, or pays the interest regularly, I have the assurance of sense. They are perfectly consistent with one another, may exist in the soul at the same time, and their combination carries assurance to the highest point.

Those who deny the assurance of faith, appear to labour under a mistake, both as to the gospel and as to believing. The gospel does not consist of general doctrines merely; but also of promises indefinitely proposed to all who hear it; to be enjoyed, not on the condition of believing, but in the way of believing. 'I, even I, am he that blotteth out thy transgressions, for mine own sake, and will not remember thy sins.' 'I will sprinkle clean water upon you, and ye shall be clean.' 'I will put my laws into their mind, and write them in their hearts.' 'Behold, I bring you glad tidings of great joy, which shall be to all people.' Can a person believe these promises, truly and with understanding, without having some assurance of the blessings promised? There appears also to be a mistake as to the nature of faith, and the place which it holds in the application of redemption. It is a trusting in Christ, a relying upon him for salvation upon the ground of the divine testimony respecting him; and does not this always imply some degree of assurance or confidence?

Others go to an opposite extreme. They maintain, that every true Christian always enjoys an absolute and unwavering certainty as to his final happiness – that he is a true believer, and in a state of salvation; and they dwell on the assurance of faith, to the neglect of

8. *Essay on Saving Faith*, by the Rev. Dr. Mason, New York; published along with Cudworth's *Aphorisms*, pp. 105, 106.

the evidence which arises from Christian experience and growth in holiness. This is apt to cherish a spirit of presumption, on the one hand, and to throw persons into a state of despondency, on the other. There are various degrees of assurance, and in some genuine believers it may be scarcely perceptible. He who is the author and finisher of our faith, was careful not to break the bruised reed, or quench the smoking flax. While he rebuked the unbelief and unreasonable doubts of his disciples, he never called in question the reality of their faith. He received the man who said, 'Lord, I believe; help thou mine unbelief.' While he said to Peter, 'O thou of little faith, wherefore didst thou doubt?' he took him by the hand and lifted him out of the water. Grant that doubting is sinful; is there a just man on earth that doeth good and sinneth not? Are not the love and patience, and other gracious dispositions of a Christian, also sinfully defective? Urge the admonition, 'Be not faithless, but believing'; but neglect not to urge also, 'Be ye holy, for I am holy.' 'Be perfect as your Father in heaven is perfect.' Would it not be dangerous to the interest of holiness, and discreditable to religion, if a person were supposed to be in possession of perfect assurance, while subject to imperfection in every other respect? Is there not a proportional growth in all the members of the spiritual man? Would he not otherwise be a monstrous creature? Or is the exploded doctrine of sinless perfection in this life to be revived among us? He whose faith is faultless, and his assurance perfect and unvarying, sees Christ as he is, and is already completely like him. He would not be a fit inhabitant of earth; and the only prayer he could put up would be, 'Now lettest thou thy servant depart in peace.'[9]

---

9. M'Crie's *Sermons*, pp. 281-283.

CHAPTER 15

REPENTANCE UNTO LIFE

Section 1
Repentance unto life is an evangelical grace (Zechariah 12:10; Acts 11:18), the doctrine whereof is to be preached by every minister of the gospel, as well as that of faith in Christ (Luke 24:47; Mark 1:15; Acts 20:21).

Section 2
By it a sinner, out of the sight and sense, not only of the danger, but also of the filthiness and odiousness of his sins, as contrary to the holy nature and righteous law of God, and upon the apprehension of his mercy in Christ to such as are penitent, so grieves for and hates his sins, as to turn from them all unto God (Ezekiel 18:30, 31; 36:31; Isaiah 30:22; Psalm 51:4; Jeremiah 31:18, 19; Joel 2:12, 13; Amos 5:15; Psalm 119:128; 2 Corinthians 7:11), purposing and endeavouring to walk with him in all the ways of his commandments (Psalm 119:6, 59, 106; Luke 1:6; 2 Kings 23:25).

Exposition
The repentance described in this chapter is called *repentance unto life*, because it is inseparably connected with the enjoyment of eternal life, and to distinguish it from the sorrow of the world, which worketh death. It is styled a *grace*, because it is the free *gift* of God, and is wrought in the heart by the operation of his Spirit. 'Then hath God also to the Gentiles *granted* repentance unto life' (Acts 11:18). 'Turn thou me, and I shall be turned; surely after that I was turned, I repented' (Jeremiah 31:18, 19). This repentance is also denominated an *evangelical* grace, to distinguish it from *legal* repentance. The latter flows from a dread of God's wrath; the former, from faith in God's mercy. In the latter, the sinner is chiefly affected with the punishment to which his sin exposes him; in the former, he mourns for his sin as offensive and dishonouring to God. Cain and Judas repented, but it was on account of the consequences of sin to themselves; whereas the true penitent mourns after a godly sort, with a godly sorrow, or a sorrow which directly regards God (2 Corinthians 7:9, 10).

That the doctrine of repentance is to be preached by every

minister of the gospel, as well as that of faith in Christ, is asserted in opposition to a gross heresy of the Antinomians, who maintain that repentance ought not to be preached by any minister of the gospel; alleging that it leads us away from Christ, and proves most hurtful and dangerous. How opposite is such a sentiment to the example and command of Christ himself! He preached the doctrine of repentance to those who attended his public ministry. 'Repent,' said he, 'and believe the gospel' (Mark 1:15). And in the instruction which he delivered to the apostles, when he commissioned them to preach the gospel, it was expressly enjoined that 'repentance and remission of sins should be preached in his name among all nations' (Luke 24:47). The apostles, accordingly, inculcated the necessity of repentance both on Jews and Gentiles (Acts 2:38; 3:19; 14:15). The Apostle Paul speaks of 'repentance from dead works' as one of the first principles of the doctrine of Christ (Hebrews 6:1); and, when giving a summary of his doctrine before the elders of Ephesus, he comprehends the whole under the two great articles of repentance and faith: 'Testifying both to the Jews, and also to the Greeks, repentance towards God, and faith towards our Lord Jesus Christ' (Acts 20:21).

A *sinner* is the only subject capable of repentance. Christ 'came not to call the righteous, but sinners to repentance'; and he intimated that 'just men need no repentance'. But 'all have sinned, and come short of the glory of God'. Repentance, therefore, must be universally necessary. 'God now commandeth all men everywhere to repent' (Acts 17:30); and Jesus Christ, the faithful and true witness, has solemnly declared 'Except ye repent, ye shall all likewise perish' (Luke 13:3).

1. True repentance springs from *a sight and sense* of sin. All men will readily acknowledge, in general terms, that they are sinners; but no man can have a clear sight and a feeling sense of his sins, until the Holy Spirit becomes his teacher. It is his work to convince of sin (John 16:8). This he does by means of the law; for 'by the law is the knowledge of sin' (Romans 3:20). When the Spirit enlightens the mind of the sinner to discern the purity, spirituality, and vast extent of the divine law, he sees sin to be 'exceeding sinful'. He views it as not only dangerous, but as odious in itself, on account of its contrariety to the holy nature and righteous law of God.

2. True repentance flows from *an apprehension of the mercy*

of God in Christ to such as are penitent. Had we reason to regard God as an inexorable judge, we might, like Adam, attempt to flee from his presence, and escape the sword of his avenging justice; but never would we return to him as sincere penitents. Blessed be God! we have the firmest grounds on which to rest our faith of his pardoning mercy. He has proclaimed his name as 'The LORD, the LORD God, merciful and gracious, forgiving iniquity, and transgression, and sin' (Exodus 34:6, 7). The wicked is invited to 'forsake his way, and return unto the LORD', encouraged by the assurance that 'he will have mercy upon him, and will abundantly pardon' (Isaiah 55:7). 'Jesus Christ is set forth to be a propitiation, through faith in his blood' (Romans 3:25); 'through his name is preached unto us the forgiveness of sins' (Acts 13:38); and we are assured, 'that through his name whosoever believeth in him shall receive remission of sins' (Acts 10:43). Now, it is an apprehension of the mercy of God in Christ, by faith, that melts the heart into penitential sorrow of sin. Of so generous a nature is evangelical repentance, that the penitent soul is never so deeply humbled and grieved for sin, as when it has reason to hope that a gracious God has freely forgiven it. This generous temper is assigned to the true penitent in the Sacred Scripture: 'Thou shalt remember, and be confounded, and never open thy mouth any more, because of thy shame, *when* I am pacified toward thee, for all that thou hast done, saith the Lord GOD' (Ezekiel 16:63).

With regard to the *order* of faith and repentance, it may be remarked, that we can form no conception of a moment of time when the one exists in the soul separate from the other. In point of *time*, then, faith and repentance necessarily accompany each other; but in the order of *nature*, faith must precede repentance. Evangelical repentance is a turning from sin to God; but there can be no turning to God, except through Christ; and no coming to Christ, but by believing in him (John 14:6; 6:35). Besides, evangelical repentance flows from love to God; but the exercise of unfeigned love to him proceeds from the exercise of true faith (1 Timothy 1:5). Add to this, it is only by looking on him whom we have pierced, that we can mourn after a godly sort, according to that remarkable promise: 'They shall look on me whom they have pierced, and they shall mourn for him' (Zechariah 12:10). There is, indeed, a conviction of the person's guilt and misery, accompanied with a kind of sorrow for sin, and resolutions to forsake it, because it exposes him to everlasting punishment, which, in the nature of things, must precede the exercise of faith in Christ; but this is very different from evangelical repentance.[1]

3. True repentance includes *grief,* or deep contrition and godly sorrow for sin. There is a false sorrow, which many mistake for the genuine. Many are grieved for their sin, merely on account of the punishment it is like to bring upon themselves; and those who are most deeply affected with this kind of sorrow, if they succeed in allaying their fears, often return to a course of sinning with greater freedom and impetuosity than before. But the sorrow of a true penitent is *for sin* as committed against God – as rebellion against his rightful authority – as a violation of his holy law, and as a most base, ungrateful return for all his goodness (Psalm 51:4).

4. True repentance includes *hatred* of sin, not only as that which exposes us to death, but as hateful in itself, as the abominable thing which God hates, and as that which renders us vile and loathsome in his sight. If this hatred of sin is genuine, it will lead us to loathe and abhor ourselves, and it will extend to *all* sin in ourselves and others (Job 42:6; Ezekiel 36; Jeremiah 31:19; Psalm 119:128, 136).

5. True repentance includes *a turning from sin unto God, with a sincere purpose, and endeavour to walk with him in all the ways of his commandments.* This is the crowning act and the grand test of genuine repentance. Paul preached both to Jews and Gentiles 'that they should repent and turn to God, and do works meet for repentance' (Acts 26:20). True penitents forsake sin, with a firm resolution to have no more to do with idols. They are converted from the love as well as from the practice of sin. They particularly guard against those sins to which they were formerly most addicted, and before whose influence they are most ready to fall (Psalm 18:23). They assiduously watch against all occasions of sin, and earnestly long for complete deliverance from it. They return to God as their rightful Lord and Master, resolving, in dependence upon his grace, to 'serve him in holiness and righteousness all the days of their lives'. They form a steady and unshaken purpose in their hearts, and sedulously endeavour, by watchfulness and diligence, in the constant use of all means, to

1. Boston's *Miscellany Questions*, Quest. 3; Colquhoun's *View of Saving Faith*, p. 303; Wilson's (of London) *Sermons*, p. 390; Anderson's (of America) *Precious Truth*, p. 180; Black's *Sermons*, p. 87.

avoid all sin, and to practise universal holiness. It is not meant
that true penitents have attained to sinless perfection; for 'there is
no man that liveth and sinneth not'. They will, therefore, find
occasion every day for the renewed exercise of repentance. All
tears will not be wiped from their eyes until all sin is perfectly
removed from their souls.

Section 3
Although repentance be not to be rested in, as any satisfaction for sin, or
any cause of the pardon thereof (Ezekiel 36:31, 32; 16:61-63), which is
the act of God's free grace in Christ (Hosea 14:2, 4; Romans 3:24; Ephesians 1:7); yet is it of such necessity to all sinners, that none may expect pardon without it (Luke 13:3, 5; Acts 17:30, 31).

Exposition
1. In opposition to the Romanists, who make satisfaction one of
the essential parts of repentance, and conceive that certain acts or
penances, performed by an offender, constitute a compensation
for his transgression, in consideration of which it is forgiven; and
also in opposition to Socinians, who deny the atonement for sin
by the death of Christ, and maintain that repentance is the only
atonement required; our Confession asserts, that repentance is not
to be rested in as any satisfaction for sin, or a cause of the pardon
thereof. It has already been shown, that it must always be the duty
of every sinner to repent; now, the discharge of a present duty can
never atone for past crimes. Repentance is never supposed to be a
legal ground for remitting the punishment due to crimes committed against a civil State. How unreasonable, then, to suppose that
it can form a sufficient ground for the pardon of sin as committed
against God! Christ has fully satisfied the justice of God by the
sacrifice of himself, and his blood alone cleanseth us from all sin
(1 John 1:7). To us the pardon of sin is wholly gratuitous – 'an act
of God's free grace in Christ' – and, if it be of grace, then it is no
more of works; and, therefore, not by repentance, as a satisfaction for sin.

2. *True repentance and pardon are inseparably connected.*
Though no one is pardoned for his repentance, yet repentance is
of such indispensable necessity, that an impenitent sinner cannot
be a pardoned sinner.

'They are connected in the economy of salvation, not as cause and
effect, but to show the consistency of a gratuitous pardon with the

interest of holiness. For any government to acquit a criminal, and restore him to society without some evidence of a change of disposition, would be little else than granting him a license to commit crimes with impunity. But if this would be unworthy of a human, how much more a divine government! God, for the vindication of the honour of the plan of mercy, has so connected pardon with repentance and confession – the expression of repentance – that they are the only certain evidences that we are in a pardoned state; while pardon and repentance are equally the gift of God through Jesus Christ our Lord.'[2]

Section 4
As there is no sin so small but it deserves damnation (Romans 6:23; 5:12; Matthew 12:36); so there is no sin so great that it can bring damnation upon those who truly repent (Isaiah 55:7; Romans 8:1; Isaiah 1:16, 18).

Exposition
In opposition, on the one hand, to the Church of Rome, which holds that some sins are mortal, and others venial – that is, of so trifling a nature, that they may be expiated by some temporal infliction – our Confession asserts, that 'there is no sin so small but it deserves damnation'; and, on the other hand, in opposition to certain Anabaptists, and some others, who have held that if persons, after baptism and grace received, fall into grievous sins, there is no pardon remaining for them, even though they should repent, our Confession asserts, that 'there is no sin so great that it can bring damnation upon those who truly repent'. We admit that a great variety in the degree of guilt attaches to different sins; but we maintain that every sin is worthy of death. Most explicit are the declarations of an inspired apostle: 'The wages of sin is death' (Romans 6:23). 'Cursed is every one that continueth not in all things which are written in the book of the law to do them' (Galatians 3:10). Both these texts are unquestionably applicable to sin of every kind. The chief of sinners, however, may obtain mercy; and those who, after grace received, have fallen into grievous sins, may truly repent, and obtain forgiveness. David, after his 'great transgression', and Peter, after his denial of his Master, repented and were pardoned (2 Samuel 12:13; John 21:19).

---

2. Stevenson on the *Offices of Christ*, p. 244.

Section 5
Men ought not to content themselves with a general repentance, but it is every man's duty to endeavour to repent of his particular sins particularly (Psalm 19:13; Luke 19:8; 1 Timothy 1:13, 15).

Exposition
No man can reckon up all his sins in order; for 'who can understand his errors?' But it is not enough to acknowledge in general terms that we are sinners; we should, by a strict and impartial examination of our hearts and ways, endeavour to obtain a discovery of those particular sins by which we have offended and dishonoured God and should 'mourn, every one for his iniquity'. Thus, when David was brought to the exercise of true repentance, he not only acknowledged in general that he had sinned, but he had his eye upon that particular sin by which he had in a special manner dishonoured God: 'My sin is ever before me. Against thee, thee only, have I sinned, and done *this* evil in thy sight' (Psalm 51:3, 4). 'I will declare *mine* iniquity; I will be sorry for *my* sin' (Psalm 38:18).

Section 6
As every man is bound to make private confession of his sins to God, praying for the pardon thereof (Psalms 51:4, 5, 7, 9, 14; 32:5, 6); upon which, and the forsaking of them, he shall find mercy (Proverbs 28:13; 1 John 1:9); so he that scandalizeth his brother, or the Church of Christ, ought to be willing, by a private or public confession and sorrow for his sin, to declare his repentance to those that are offended (James 5:16; Luke 17:3, 4; Joshua 7:19; Psalm 51); who are thereupon to be reconciled to him, and in love to receive him (2 Corinthians 2:8).

Exposition
In this section we are taught:

1. *That every man ought to make private confession of his sins to God.* We cannot discover to God anything that was previously concealed from his omniscient eye; but by confessing our sins we give glory to God, as well as take shame to ourselves. Hence Joshua said unto Achan: 'My son, give, I pray thee, glory to the LORD God of Israel, and make confession unto him' (Joshua 7:19). To cover our sins is to dishonour God, as if he either did not see, or could not punish them; whereas, to confess our sins is to honour God's holy law, which we have violated – to honour his omniscience, which beheld all our transgressions – to honour his

justice, which might have taken vengeance upon them – and to honour his patience and long-suffering, which have forborne to execute the merited punishment.

2. That those who privately confess their sins to God, and forsake them, shall find mercy, *though they do not also confess all their sins to a priest*. This is amply confirmed by that inspired declaration: 'He that covereth his sins shall not prosper; but whoso confesseth and forsaketh them shall have mercy' (Proverbs 28:13). The experience of David corresponded to this declaration (Psalm 32:5). But the Church of Rome holds that the auricular confession of sins to a priest, and his absolution thereupon obtained, is the only means appointed by God for the procuring of pardon of all mortal sins committed after baptism.[3] For such a confession there is neither example nor command in Scripture. The text on which Romanists chiefly rely (John 20:23) says nothing of the confession of sins in the ears of a priest; and the ministers of religion can only remit sins *declaratively*, not *authoritatively*. They can absolve from the censures of the Church, but not from the guilt of sin, as committed against God. In one place we are enjoined to 'confess our faults one to another' (James 5:16); but this confession is mutual, not a confession by the people to the priest. Christians ought to confess their faults to those whom they have injured; but the confession of all their sins in private to a priest, as required by the Church of Rome, is wholly unauthorised by Scripture, and it has been the occasion of flagrant abuse.

'Not only is auricular confession productive of much inconvenience to society, by giving the ministers of religion an undue and dangerous influence over the minds of the people in their most secret affairs; but it perverts their notions of the justification of a sinner, and it provides a method of quieting their consciences, which is so easy of access that it encourages them to sin with little fear.'[4]

3. Though Christians are only required to confess their secret sins to God, who seeth in secret, yet, if they have wronged a Christian brother, in his property or good name, they are bound to

3. Some of the grossest corruptions of the Church of Rome respect the doctrine of repentance. According to the tenets avowed in the standards of that Church, repentance consists of three acts – confession of sins to a priest, contrition, or attrition, and satisfaction.
4. Hill's *Lectures in Divinity*, pp. 292, 293.

confess their offence to him, and to make all the reparation in their power for the injury they have done to him; and upon their repentance he is bound to forgive them (Matthew 5:23, 24; Luke 17:3, 4). When Christians fall into public scandal, they should be willing to make a more public confession of their offence, that they may openly honour that God by their confession, whom they have openly dishonoured by their conduct; and the Church, upon their repentance, ought in love to receive them, and restore them to all their Christian privileges. The Novatians maintained that such as had fallen into grievous transgressions, especially those who had apostatized from the faith, in a time of persecution, were not to be again received into the bosom of the Church.[5] But this opinion is contrary both to the precepts and examples of Scripture. If a man be overtaken in a fault, they who are spiritual are enjoined to restore such an one in the spirit of meekness, considering themselves, lest they also be tempted (Galatians 6:1). The church at Corinth was required to forgive the incestuous person, upon his repentance, and receive him again into communion, lest he should be swallowed up with over much sorrow (2 Corinthians 2:7, 8).

---

5. Mosheim's *Eccl. Hist.*, cent. iii., ch. 5, p. 2, c. 17, 18.

CHAPTER 16

GOOD WORKS

Section 1
Good works are only such as God hath commanded in his Holy Word (Micah 6:8; Romans 12:2; Hebrews 13:21), and not such as, without the warrant thereof, are devised by men, out of blind zeal, or upon any pretence of good intention (Matthew 15:9; Isaiah 29:13; 1 Peter 1:18; Romans 10:2; John 16:2; 1 Samuel 15:21-23).

Exposition
This section states what is necessary to constitute an action a good work, as considered in itself. It must be *such as God has commanded in his holy Word*. The law of God is the sole rule of man's obedience, and no action, how specious soever in appearance, can be properly called good, unless required by the supreme legislator. No command of man can make a good work, unless it be, at the same time, virtually or explicitly commanded by God. Those actions which have no warrant from the Word of God, but are devised by men, out of blind zeal, cannot be reckoned good works. On this ground Christ rejected those services of the Pharisees, which had no other authority than the traditions of the elders, or their own enactments, saying: 'Who hath required this at your hands.' And, on the same ground, those works of superstition and will-worship, which are only enjoined by the commandments of men, in the Church of Rome, must be rejected. 'In vain,' said our Saviour, 'do they worship me, teaching for doctrines the commandments of men' (Matthew 15:9).

Actions which God has not commanded cannot be transformed into good works, (as is maintained by the Church of Rome), by the *good intention* of the agent. Many have pretended to act from a good intention, when they were acting in direct opposition to the revealed will of God (1 Samuel 13:13; 15:17-23). Men have thought that they were doing God good service, when they were committing the most atrocious crimes (John 16:2; Acts 26:9).

A work commanded by God is good, considered in itself; but something more is requisite to make it good as performed by us. And no action is a good work in the sight of God, except it be *formally* as well as *materially* good. What things are necessary to render a work *formally* good, may be learned from the subsequent sections of this chapter; but we judge it proper to state them briefly in this place.

1. They must be performed by a person who is justified by the righteousness of Christ, and renewed by his Spirit.

2. They must be done from a right principle – faith working by love. There must be faith or persuasion that what we do is commanded by God; and we must perform it from a respect to his authority (Romans 14:23). There must also be a faith of the acceptance of our works only through the mediation of Christ. Our obedience must likewise flow from love to God (1 John 5:3).

3. They must be performed in a right manner. They must be done in the strength of promised grace, and in dependence upon the righteousness of Christ for acceptance – in the exercise of gratitude to God for all his benefits, and under a deep sense of our own unworthiness.

4. They must be directed to a right end. Our works cannot be accounted good, except our chief and ultimate end in doing them be the glory of God (1 Corinthians 10:31).

Section 2

These good works, done in obedience to God's commandments, are the fruits and evidences of a true and lively faith (James 2:18, 22): and by them believers manifest their thankfulness (Psalm 116:12, 13; 1 Peter 2:9), strengthen their assurance (1 John 2:3, 5; 2 Peter 1:5-10), edify their brethren (2 Corinthians 9:2; Matthew 5:16), adorn the profession of the gospel (Titus 2:5. 9-12; 1 Timothy 6:1), stop the mouths of the adversaries (1 Peter 2:15), and glorify God (1 Peter 2:12; Philippians 1:11; John 15:8), whose workmanship they are, created in Christ Jesus thereunto (Ephesians 2:10); that, having their fruit unto holiness, they may have the end eternal life (Romans 6:22).

Exposition

Our good works cannot be profitable to God; for he is infinitely perfect and all-sufficient in himself, and no addition can be made to his essential glory or felicity (Job 22:2; 35:7). Neither can our good works have any influence upon our justification before God; for 'by the deeds of the law there shall no flesh be justified in his sight' (Romans 3:20). Nor can our good works be the ground of our title to heaven, or to eternal life; for 'eternal life is the gift of

God, through Jesus Christ our Lord' (Romans 6:23). Still, however, the performance of good works must be constantly inculcated and earnestly urged upon all Christians; and they serve many valuable purposes. Hence the solemn injunction which Paul laid upon Titus, and in him upon all other ministers of the gospel: 'This is a faithful saying, and these things I will that thou affirm constantly, that they which have believed in God might be careful to maintain good works: these things are good and profitable unto men' (Titus 3:8). Several of the important uses of good works are here specified.

1. They are the *fruits and evidences of a true and lively faith.* An inoperative faith, which produces not the fruits of righteousness, is pronounced by the Apostle James to be *dead* (James 2:2, 6). Of a living faith good works are the native *fruits*, and they are the proper *evidences* that faith is unfeigned. 'Show me,' says the same apostle, 'thy faith without thy works, and I will show thee my faith *by* my works' (James 2:18).

2. Good works are suitable *expressions of gratitude to God.* None can render any proper recompense to God for his inestimable blessings; but all Christians are indispensably bound to glorify him by a universal and cheerful obedience to his commandments; and their good works are, as it were, thank-offerings to God for his benefits bestowed upon them.

3. Good works *strengthen the assurance* of believers. They both confirm their assurance of faith, and increase their assurance of personal interest in Christ, and his great salvation. 'Hereby we do know that we know him,' says the beloved disciple, 'if we keep his commandments' (1 John 2:3).

4. The good works of believers *edify their fellow-Christians.* Those who are careful to maintain good works become patterns to others, and stir them up to a holy emulation. Hence the Apostle Paul informed the believers at Corinth, that their zeal, in contributing for the poor saints at Jerusalem, 'had provoked very many' (2 Corinthians 9:2).

5. They *adorn the profession of the gospel.* Practical godliness is the brightest ornament of the Christian religion. Hence Christians are exhorted by the faithful discharge of the duties of their station and relation, to 'adorn the doctrine of God our Saviour in all things' (Titus 2:10).

6. They *stop the mouths of adversaries.* When professing

Christians have 'a conversation becoming the gospel', and are 'ready to every good work', they recommend religion to others, silence the adversaries of the truth, and convince them of the injustice of those reproaches which have been cast upon the gospel, as having a tendency to licentiousness. 'So is the will of God,' says an apostle, 'that with well-doing ye may put to silence the ignorance of foolish men' (1 Peter 2:15).

7. They *glorify God*. The more fruitful believers are in good works, the more is God glorified; for 'herein' says our Lord, 'is my Father glorified, that ye bear much fruit' (John 15:8). By their good works Christians not only glorify God themselves, but may lead others to glorify him also. 'Let your light so shine before men,' says our Saviour, 'that they may see your good works, and glorify your Father who is in heaven' (Matthew 5:16).

8. Good works *are essentially prerequisite to an admission into heaven*. Though they do not merit everlasting life, yet they are indispensably necessary in all who are 'heirs of the grace of life'. Believers, 'being made free from sin, have their fruit unto holiness, and the end everlasting life' (Romans 6:22).

Section 3
Their ability to do good works is not at all of themselves, but wholly from the Spirit of Christ (John 15:4-6; Ezekiel 36:26, 27). And that they may be enabled thereunto, besides the graces they have already received, there is required an actual influence of the same Holy Spirit to work in them to will and to do of his good pleasure (Philippians 2:13; 4:13; 2 Corinthians 3:5): yet are they not hereupon to grow negligent, as if they were not bound to perform any duty unless upon a special motion of the Spirit; but they ought to be diligent in stirring up the grace that is in them (Philippians 2:12; Hebrews 6:11, 12; 2 Peter 1:3, 5, 10, 11; Isaiah 64:7; 2 Timothy 1:6; Acts 26:6, 7; Jude 20, 21).

Exposition
In opposition to Pelagians, Romanists and Arminians, our Confession asserts, that the ability of believers to do good works is not of themselves, but wholly from the Spirit of Christ. It is to be carefully observed, that a supernatural habit, or vital principle of grace, is infused or implanted in the souls of all true believers, in the day of their regeneration, whereby they are disposed and enabled to perform acts of holy obedience (Ezekiel 36:26, 27). But, notwithstanding this power or ability, which believers have

212 EXPOSITION OF THE WESTMINSTER CONFESSION OF FAITH

received by habitual grace, there is required an actual influence of the Holy Spirit unto their performance of every single gracious holy act. Whatever furniture of habitual grace they may have received, there is an actual operation of the Holy Spirit in them necessary unto the actual gracious performance of every duty of obedience. This is confirmed:

1. By the express declaration of our Saviour: 'Without me ye can do nothing' (John 15:5). Here our Saviour explicitly affirms that believers, who are made partakers of habitual grace, cannot of themselves, by virtue of any grace they have already received, or without new supplies of grace from him, do anything that is spiritually good or acceptable to God.

2. By the acknowledgement of Paul, speaking in the name of believers: 'Not that we are sufficient of ourselves, to think any thing as of ourselves: but our sufficiency is of God' (2 Corinthians 3:5).

3. By the prayers of the saints for new supplies of grace, to enable them to do the will of God. Paul prays on behalf of the Hebrews: 'The God of peace make you perfect in every good work to do his will, working in you that which is well-pleasing in his sight' (Hebrews 13:20, 21). The necessity, and the efficiency of actual grace unto every acceptable act of holy obedience, cannot be more directly expressed.[1]

In opposition, on the other hand, to certain enthusiasts, who maintain that believers ought not to perform any duty in religion, unless the Spirit within move and excite them to these duties, our Confession asserts, that believers ought not to 'grow negligent, as if they were not bound to perform any duty unless upon a special motion of the Spirit; but they ought to be diligent in stirring up the grace of God that is in them.' This is so amply confirmed by the passages of Scripture to which the compilers of our Confession refer, that we feel it quite unnecessary to dwell upon it.

Section 4

They who in their obedience attain to the greatest height which is possible in this life, are so far from being able to supererogate, and to do more than God requires, as that they fall short of much which in duty they are bound to do (Luke 17:10; Nehemiah 13:22; Job 9:2, 3; Galatians 5:17).

---

1. Owen's *Discourse concerning the Holy Spirit*, Book 4, chapters 6, 7.

Exposition

This section is levelled against the doctrine of the Church of Rome, respecting works of supererogation. That Church teaches, that besides those precepts which are binding on all, and which none can disobey without sin, there are 'counsels of perfection' given in the New Testament, which men are at liberty to neglect if they please; and, therefore, those who comply with these counsels, perform more than they are bound to do, and have, consequently, a superfluous degree of merit, that may be transferred to others for their benefit. In the progress of the corruptions of that Church, it was taught and believed, that the whole stock of superfluous merit, arising out of the good works of those who comply with the counsels of perfection, is committed to the management of the Pope, to be parcelled out according to his pleasure, in such dispensations and indulgences as the sins and infirmities of other members of the Church appear to him to stand in need of. The enormous abuses of this discretionary power with which the Pope was invested, were the immediate cause of the Reformation.[2]

In opposition to this blasphemous doctrine, Protestants maintain that there is not the slightest foundation in the Scripture for what the Papists call 'counsels of perfection'. This is evident from the nature of the commands which devolve upon all men. We are required 'to love God with all our heart, and with all our soul, and with all our strength, and with all our mind; and our neighbours as ourself' (Luke 10:27). What more can be conceived than is implied in these two commands? Works of supererogation have no existence but in the vain imaginations of ignorant and self-righteous men. So far are the most eminent saints from exceeding the measure of their duty, that they fall far short of what they are in duty bound to do. 'In many things we offend all.' 'If we say that we have no sin, we deceive ourselves, and the truth is not in us' (James 3:2; 1 John 1:8). Our Saviour has taught us to pray daily that our trespasses may be forgiven; which necessarily implies that we offend every day.

Section 5

We cannot, by our best works, merit pardon of sin, or eternal life, at the hand of God, by reason of the great disproportion that is between them and the glory to come, and the infinite distance that is between us and

---

2. Hill's *Lectures in Divinity*, vol. ii., p. 302.

God, whom by them we can neither profit nor satisfy for the debt of our former sins (Romans 3:20; 4:2, 4, 6; Ephesians 2:8, 9; Titus 3:5-7; Romans 8:18; Psalm 16:2; Job 22:2, 3; 35:7, 8); but when we have done all we can, we have done but our duty, and are unprofitable servants (Luke 17:10); and because, as they are good, they proceed from his Spirit (Galatians 5:22, 23); and as they are wrought by us, they are defiled and mixed with so much weakness and imperfection, that they cannot endure the severity of God's judgment (Isaiah 64:6; Galatians 5:17; Romans 7:15, 18; Psalms 143:2; 130:3).

Exposition

This section is also directed against an error of the Church of Rome, which teaches that the good works of the saints are meritorious of eternal life.[3] That we cannot, by our best works, merit pardon of sin, or eternal life, at the hand of God, appears from the following considerations:

1. Our Saviour declares (Luke 17:10), that when we have done all those things which are commanded us, we are unprofitable servants, and have only done that which was our duty.

2. Our best works cannot be profitable to God, and therefore can merit nothing at his hand (Psalm 16:2).

3. All our works, as they are good, proceed from the almighty agency of the Spirit of grace (Philippians 2:13); and as they are not performed in our own *strength*, they can merit no reward.

4. Our best works, as they are wrought by us, have such a mixture of sin in them, that, instead of meriting anything at the hand of God, they cannot endure the severity of God's judgment (Psalm 143:2).

5. Our best works bear no proportion to the inestimable blessing of eternal life (2 Corinthians 4:17); accordingly, the reward is represented 'as of grace, not of debt'; and we are directed to 'look for the *mercy* of our Lord Jesus Christ unto eternal life' (Jude 21).

---

3. The schoolmen in the Church of Rome spake of *meritum de congruo* – a merit of congruity; and *meritum de condigno* – a merit of condignity. By the former, they meant the value of good works previous to justification, which it was fit or congruous for God to reward by infusing his grace. By the latter, they meant the value of good works performed after justification in consequence of grace infused. These, although performed by the grace of God, were conceived to have that intrinsic worth which merits a reward, and to which eternal life is as much due as a wage is to the servant by whom it is earned – Hill's *Lectures*, vol. ii., p. 301.

Section 6

Yet, notwithstanding, the persons of believers being accepted through Christ, their good works also are accepted in him (Ephesians 1:6; 1 Peter 2:5; Exodus 28:38; Genesis 4:4; Hebrews 11:4); not as though they were in this life wholly unblameable and unreprovable in God's sight (Job 9:20; Psalm 143:2); but that he, looking upon them in his Son, is pleased to accept and reward that which is sincere, although accompanied with many weaknesses and imperfections (Hebrews 13:20, 21; 2 Corinthians 8:12; Hebrews 6:10; Matthew 25:21, 23).

Exposition

This section teaches us that the good works of believers, although not meritorious, are yet accepted of God, through Christ. Here it is only necessary to offer two remarks.

First, that our persons must be accepted, before our works of obedience can be accepted with God. 'The LORD had respect unto Abel, and to his offering' (Genesis 4:4). In accepting of his offering, God testified that he had respect unto his person; i.e. that he esteemed and accounted him righteous (Hebrews 11:4).

Second, that the best of our works are not accepted as they are ours, but only upon account of the merit and mediation of Christ. As our persons are 'accepted in the Beloved', so our works are only 'acceptable to God by Jesus Christ' (1 Peter 2:5).

Section 7

Works done by unregenerate men, although, for the matter of them, they may be things which God commands, and of good use both to themselves and others (2 Kings 10:30, 31; 1 Kings 21:27, 29; Philippians 1:15, 16, 18); yet, because they proceed not from an heart purified by faith (Genesis 4:5; Hebrews 11:4, 6); nor are done in a right manner, according to the Word (1 Corinthians 13:3; Isaiah 1:12); nor to a right end, the glory of God (Matthew 6:2, 5, 16); they are therefore sinful, and cannot please God, or make a man meet to receive grace from God (Haggai 2:14; Titus 1:15; Amos 5:21, 22; Hosea 1:4; Romans 9:16; Titus 3:5). And yet their neglect of them is more sinful, and displeasing unto God (Psalms 14:4; 36:3; Job 21:14, 15; Matthew 25:41-43, 45; 23:23).

Exposition

This section is again levelled against the errors of the Church of Rome. The writers of that Church hold that the actions of men in an unregenerate state can be so pure as to be free from all sin, and to merit at God's hand by what they call the merit of *congruity*. We have formerly made a distinction respecting good works, which claims attention here. An action may be *materially*, and yet not *formally*, good. Prayer, reading and hearing the Word of God, distributing to the poor, are actions materially good; but unless these actions are done by persons who are 'accepted in the Beloved', and 'created anew in Christ Jesus' – unless they flow from a right principle, are performed in a right manner, and directed to a right end, they are not formally good. Now, unregenerate men may do many things that are good, for the matter of them, because they are things which God commands, and of good use to themselves and others; but, as performed by them, they are destitute of everything that can render an action 'good and acceptable in the sight of God'. Explicit is the declaration of the Apostle Paul: 'They that are in the flesh cannot please God' (Romans 8:8). To be *in the flesh* is to be in a natural, corrupt, depraved state; and, as a polluted fountain cannot send forth pure streams, nor a corrupt tree bring forth good fruit, so they that are in the flesh cannot perform any work that is spiritually good and acceptable to God. Instead of pleasing God, and making them meet to receive grace from him, all the works of unregenerate men are sinful, and therefore deserve the wrath and curse of God.

> 'All unconverted persons are said in Scripture to be sinners, or workers of iniquity (Psalm 53:4); and their works, how advantageous soever many of them may be to themselves or others, are all, notwithstanding, represented as *sins*, in the account of an infinitely holy God (Proverbs 21:4); for although many of them may be *materially* good, yet *all* of them are *formally* evil, and therefore they are an abomination to him' (Proverbs 15:8).[4]

It must not, however, be inferred, that unregenerate men may live in the neglect of any duty which God has commanded. Though their prayers, for example, cannot be acceptable to God, yet their neglect of prayer would be more sinful and displeasing to him. This neglect is always represented in Scripture as highly criminal: 'The wicked, through the pride of his countenance, will not seek after God' (Psalm 10:4). And as this is their sin, so the wrath of God is denounced against them: 'Pour out thy fury upon the heathen, that know thee not, and upon the families that call not upon thy name' (Jeremiah 10:25).

In concluding this chapter, we would impress upon the reader,

---

4. Colquhoun's *Treatise on the Law and the Gospel*, p. 333.

that the gospel is 'a doctrine according to godliness'. 'The grace of God, that bringeth salvation, hath appeared to all men; teaching us that, denying ungodliness and worldly lusts, we should live soberly, righteously, and godly in this present world.' Nothing but the most deplorable ignorance, or the most determined enmity against the truth, could ever have led men to set the gospel and morality in opposition to each other, or to allege that the doctrine of grace tends to licentiousness. Such men know not what they say, nor whereof they affirm. It is by inculcating morality upon gospel principles that we establish it upon the firmest basis. 'Do we make void the law through faith? God forbid: yea, we establish the law.' Though good works are excluded from having any meritorious influence in the matter of salvation, yet, as we have seen, they are of indispensable necessity, and serve many valuable purposes. Let it, therefore, be the study of all who 'name the name of Christ' to be 'fruitful in good works', that so they may silence the adversaries of the truth, recommend religion to all within the sphere of their influence, glorify their Father who is in heaven, and promote their own comfort and happiness.

CHAPTER 17

THE PERSEVERANCE OF THE SAINTS

Section 1
They whom God hath accepted in his Beloved, effectually called and sanctified by his Spirit, can neither totally nor finally fall away from the state of grace; but shall certainly persevere therein to the end and be eternally saved (Philippians 1:6; 2 Peter 1:10; John 10:28, 29; 1 John 3:9; 1 Peter 1:5, 9).

Section 2
This perseverance of the saints depends not upon their own free will, but upon the immutability of the decree of election, flowing from the free and unchangeable love of God the Father (2 Tim. 2:18, 19. Jer. 31:3); upon the efficacy of the merit and intercession of Jesus Christ (Heb. 10:10, 14; 13:20, 21; 9:12-15. Rom. 8:33-39. John 17:11, 24. Luke 22:32. Heb. 7:25); the abiding of the Spirit, and of the seed of God within them (John 14:16, 17. 1 John 2:27; 3:9); and the nature of the covenant of grace (Jer. 32:40); from all which ariseth also the certainty and infallibility thereof (John 10:28. 2 Thess. 3:3. 1 John 2:19).

Section 3
Nevertheless they may, through the temptations of Satan and of the world, the prevalency of corruption remaining in them, and the neglect of the means of their preservation, fall into grievous sins (Matt. 26:70, 72, 74); and for a time continue therein (Ps. 51:14): whereby they incur God's displeasure (Isa. 64:5, 7, 9. 2 Sam. 11:27), and grieve his Holy Spirit (Eph. 4:30); come to be deprived of some measure of their graces and comforts (Ps. 51:8, 10, 12. Rev. 2:4. Cant. 5:2-4, 6); have their hearts hardened (Isa. 63:17. Mark 6:52; 16:14), and their consciences wounded (Ps. 32:3, 4; 51:8); hurt and scandalize others (2 Sam. 12:14), and bring temporal judgments upon themselves (Ps. 89:31, 32; 1 Cor. 11:32).

Exposition
The perseverance of the saints is one of the articles by which the creed of the followers of Calvin is distinguished from that of the followers of Arminius. The latter hold that true believers may fall into sins inconsistent with a state of grace, and may continue in apostasy to the end of life, and consequently may finally fall into perdition. The same doctrine is avowedly supported by the Church

of Rome; for the Council of Trent has decreed, that 'If any person shall say that a man who has been justified cannot lose grace, and that, therefore, he who falls and sins was never truly justified, he shall be accursed.'[1] In opposition to this tenet, our Confession affirms, that true believers 'can neither totally nor finally fall away from a state of grace; but shall certainly persevere therein to the end, and be eternally saved'. There may seem to be a redundancy of language in this statement; for, if believers cannot fall *totally*, it follows that they cannot fall *finally*. Both terms, however, are employed with the utmost propriety.

> 'They are intended to oppose the doctrine of Arminians, who affirm, that although a saint may fall totally from grace, he may be restored by repentance; but that since this is uncertain, and does not always take place, he may also fall finally, and die in his sins. Now, we affirm, that the total apostasy of believers is impossible, not in the nature of things, but by divine constitution; and, consequently, that no man who has been once received into the divine favour can be ultimately deprived of salvation.'[2]

For the purpose of explaining the doctrine of the perseverance of the saints, and obviating objections against it, we offer the following observations, which will be found embodied in the several propositions of our Confession:

1. *The privilege of final perseverance is peculiar to true believers.* It is restricted in our Confession 'to those whom God hath accepted in his Beloved, effectually called, and sanctified by his Spirit'. Many in the visible Church are merely nominal Christians. They are joined to the Church by an external profession; but they are not united to the Head of the Church by the Spirit of grace, and by a living faith. They assume the form of godliness, but are strangers to its power. They may have a name to live, but they are spiritually dead. Now, it is readily granted that such seeming Christians may finally apostatize. They never knew the grace of God in truth, and may, in a season of trial, discover their real character by open apostasy. They might have a splendid profession of religion, and be possessed of eminent gifts, and might thus deceive themselves and impose upon others; but they had not 'the root of the matter'

1. *Decret. of Justificatione*, canon xxiii.
2. Dick's *Lectures on Theology*, vol. iii. p. 516.

in them. And we may assuredly conclude of all those who fall totally and finally away, that they were never really 'rooted and grounded in Christ'. An inspired apostle declares, concerning such persons: 'They went out from us, but they were not of us: for if they had been of us, they would no doubt have continued with us; but they went out, that they might be made manifest, that they were not all of us' (1 John 2:19).

This enables us to explain the several examples of apostasy mentioned in Scripture, in perfect consistency with the final perseverance of the saints. The stony-ground hearers, who received the Word with joy, and afterwards fell away, are expressly said to have *no root* in themselves, and so endured only for a while (Matthew 13:21). In Hebrews 6:4-6, some are said to be enlightened, and to have tasted of the heavenly gift, and to be made partakers of the Holy Ghost, and to have tasted the good Word of God, and the powers of the world to come, and yet it is supposed they may fall away and never be restored again; but it is evident, that notwithstanding the high things ascribed to them, they never had the truth of grace; for there are better things, even things that accompany salvation, expressly mentioned (verse 9) in contradistinction to their attainments. Those mentioned by another apostle (2 Peter 2:20), who had escaped the pollutions of the world, and were again entangled therein, and overcome, had evidently never experienced a real change of their impure nature, though they had an outward reformation. Such examples, or the fall of such mere professors of religion as Hymeneus, Philetus, and Demas, do not in the least invalidate the doctrine of the final perseverance of true saints.

It may here be remarked, that as the privilege of perseverance is limited to *true believers,* so it must be extended to *every one of them.* If one of them could be lost, this would sap the foundation of the comfort of the whole; for the condition of all would be insecure. Not only those who have a high degree of grace, but all who have true grace, though but like a grain of mustard seed – not only the strong and flourishing, but such as are like 'the smoking flax and bruised reed', shall be enabled to 'hold on their way', and shall grow stronger and stronger. The same reasons hold for the perseverance of all, as of any who have 'obtained like precious faith'; and we must either erase this entirely from the catalogue of the believer's privileges, or maintain that it extends to every one of them.

2. The perseverance of the saints is *not owing to their inherent strength, or to any measure of grace they have already received, but solely to divine grace.* We readily acknowledge, that in themselves they are utterly weak, and wholly insufficient to withstand the numerous and formidable enemies that are combined against them; such as Satan, the world, and the corruptions of their own hearts. If left to contend with their spiritual adversaries in their own strength, they would be easily overcome. If their perseverance depended on their own resolution, their faith would soon fail. How strikingly is this humbling truth exemplified in the case of Peter! He said with confidence: 'Though all men should be offended because of thee, yet will I never be offended' ... 'Though I should die with thee, yet will I not deny thee' (Matthew 26:33, 35). But how soon was his fortitude shaken! How soon was his good resolution forgotten, and given to the winds! He trusted too much in his own strength, and was left to feel his weakness. He was brought to the trial, and his presumed strength was gone. He trembled at the voice of a maid, and denied his Lord with dreadful oaths and horrid imprecations. What but the prevalent prayer, and upholding grace of the Divine Redeemer, prevented him from becoming, like Judas, a perfidious apostate! But such are the best of saints, considered in themselves. Their perseverance, therefore, as our Confession states, 'depends not upon their own free will'. They have no might in themselves to resist and overcome the powerful foes united against them, and they are safest when most deeply sensible of their own weakness, and most entirely dependent upon divine grace; for 'when they are weak, then are they strong'.

3. The perseverance of the saints does *not secure them from partial falls, but from total and final apostasy.* Our Confession admits, that believers may 'through the temptations of Satan, and of the world, the prevalency of corruption remaining in them, and the neglect of the means of their preservation, fall into grievous sins, and for a time continue therein.' The caution addressed to 'him that thinketh he standeth, to take heed lest he fall,' and the ardent prayers of the saints, that God would 'cleanse them from secret faults, and keep them back from presumptuous sins,' manifest, that though none of the saints can fall from a state of grace, yet they may fall into very great sins. And the Scriptures furnish many

instances of partial falls in the most eminent saints.

The patient Job cursed the day of his birth. The man Moses, who was 'meek above all men which were upon the face of the earth', spake unadvisedly with his lips. David, the man after God's own heart, was guilty of an atrocious and a complicated sin. Solomon, though the wisest of men, 'did evil in the sight of the LORD, and went not fully after the LORD, as did David his father.' Peter, a bold and zealous disciple, denied his Lord in the most aggravated manner. But though true saints may fall very low, so low that themselves and others may have little hope of their recovery, yet they shall not be utterly lost; for the hand of the Lord still in a measure sustains them. 'Though a good man fall, he shall not be utterly cast down; for the LORD upholdeth him with his hand' (Psalm 37:24). 'A just man falleth seven times, and riseth up again' (Proverbs 24:16). Though David fell into very grievous sins, and appears to have remained in a state of great insensibility till he was awakened by the Prophet Nathan, yet, it is manifest that he had not lost entirely what was wrought in him by the Spirit of God. For we find him afterwards praying: 'Cast me not away from thy presence, and take not thy Holy Spirit from me' (Psalm 51:11); which implies that he had then some experience of God's presence, and that the Holy Spirit had never wholly departed from him. When it is said of Solomon, that 'he went not fully after the LORD, as did David his father' (1 Kings 11:6), it seems manifest that his declension is to be understood of an abatement of his former zeal, and not of a total and final apostasy. God, as still his Father, 'chastened him with the rod of men, and with the stripes of the children of men'; but never suffered 'his mercy to depart away from him' (2 Samuel 7:14, 15). Peter, too, was recovered from his lamentable fall. When Christ 'turned and looked upon him, he went out, and wept bitterly' (Luke 22:61, 62). When his Lord afterwards questioned him respecting his love, he could appeal to him as the searcher of hearts, that he did love him in sincerity; and Christ having renewed his commission, he laboured zealously and faithfully in his Master's service.

The fact, then, that true saints may fall into grievous sins is by no means incompatible with their final perseverance. The Lord promises to 'heal their backslidings' (Hosea 14:4); and while this promise implies that they may fall partially, it secures that they shall not fall totally and finally.

4. The perseverance of the saints *secures the preservation of the principle of grace in their souls, though it may greatly decay as to its exercise.* In regard to the acting or exercise of grace, the believer may sometimes be in a very languishing condition; but the principle of grace shall never be entirely eradicated. He may appear like a tree almost killed by a long and severe winter. He may seem to be without fruit, without verdure; yea, even without life. But, under all the witherings of the believer, 'his seed remaineth in him'; otherwise the promise would fail in which it is engaged, that 'the root of the righteous shall not be moved' (Proverbs 12:3).

We see this exemplified in the case of Peter. Christ said to him: 'I have prayed for thee, that thy faith fail not' (Luke 22:32). We cannot doubt that Peter's faith, as to its *exercise*, did fail, and that in a most lamentable manner. But to suppose that his faith failed as to its *principle* or *habit*, would be altogether inconsistent with the success of Christ's prayer, which we are sure is always prevalent. As a tree in winter has still life in the root, though its branches wither, and it appears to be dead; so the believer, in his most decayed and languishing condition, has still a vital principle of grace within. And as the tree revives and flourishes as soon as the spring returns, so the believer's graces revive, and act with renewed vigour when 'the Sun of Righteousness' returns with his refreshing influences. The exercise of grace may be interrupted, but the principle of grace, once implanted, shall never be entirely extirpated. The believer may fall into a very languid condition, but he shall never fall away from a state of grace. He shall be enabled to persevere until grace shall be consummated in glory.

Having explained the doctrine of the perseverance of the saints, as it is exhibited in our Confession, the arguments by which it is supported may now be stated. These are arranged, in the second section, in the following order:

(1) The perseverance of the saints is secured by *the immutability of the decree of election.* That a certain definite number of mankind sinners were, in sovereign mercy, chosen of God, and appointed unto glory, before the foundation of the world, is a truth attested by many express declarations of Scripture (Ephesians 1:4; 2 Thessalonians 2:13; Acts 13:48). This purpose of God finally to bestow salvation or eternal life upon his chosen, necessarily includes a determination to do all that is requisite to make them

meet for the enjoyment of it, and to preserve them amidst all snares and temptations to the full possession of it. Now, if one included in the election of grace should finally perish, the purpose of God would, in that instance, be frustrated, and in every instance in which such an event should take place. But his purpose, originating from himself, and being altogether independent of his creatures, must be unchangeable as his nature. Hence he proclaims, with divine majesty: 'I am the Lord; I change not.' 'My counsel shall stand, and I will do all my pleasure.' Our Saviour himself, from the election of believers, infers the impossibility of their being seduced into a perishing condition. 'There shall arise false Christs, and false prophets, and shall show great signs and wonders, insomuch that (if it were possible) they shall deceive the very elect' (Matthew 24:24). It is evident that, in this passage, our Lord treats of the elect after being brought to the knowledge of the truth, and that he speaks not of any seduction whatsoever, but that which is total and final. Now, the words, 'If it were possible,' imply a real impossibility of their being so seduced.

(2) It is secured by *the merit of Christ's sufferings and death*. Christ 'purchased the Church with his own blood'. The 'iniquities' of all his people 'were laid upon him', and, as their Surety, 'he bore their sins in his own body on the tree'. He sustained the full infliction of the curse which they deserved, and 'obtained for them eternal redemption'.

> Now, as a surety stands in the room of the person whom he represents, the latter reaps all the benefit of what the surety has done in his name; so that, if his debt has been paid by the surety, the creditor cannot demand the payment of it from him. If Christ made satisfaction on the cross for the sins of his people – not for some of them only, but for them all, as we are expressly assured – it would be contrary to justice to subject them also to the punishment. But, if the saints may fall from a state of grace, and perish in their sins, satisfaction will be twice exacted – first, from the surety; and secondly, from them. Either Christ did, or did not, make an atonement for the sins of his people. If he did not make an atonement for them, they must satisfy for themselves; if he did answer the demands of justice in their room, it is impossible that, under the righteous administration of Heaven, they should, by any cause, or for any reason, come into condemnation. Accordingly, the new covenant promises to believers complete and irrevocable pardon. I will 'be merciful to their

unrighteousness, and their sins and their iniquities will I remember
no more' (Hebrews 8:12). But if the doctrine of the defectibility of
the saints is true, the promise is false; for their sins may be
remembered again. Nay, if this doctrine is true, Christ might have
died in vain; for, as one saint may fall from a state of grace as well as
another, it might happen that not a single sinner should be actually
redeemed by his blood from everlasting destruction.[3]

(3) It is secured by *the perpetuity and prevalence of Christ's
intercession.* As Christ purchased his people by the merit of his
own blood, so 'he ever liveth to make intercession' for them. And
what is the matter of his intercession on their behalf? He prays
for every one of them, as he did for Peter, 'that their faith fail
not'. In those petitions which he offered up for his followers, while
he was yet on earth, we have a specimen of his pleadings before
the throne. Now, he prayed once and again for their preservation:
'Holy Father, keep through thine own name those whom thou
hast given me'; 'I pray not that thou shouldest take them out of
the world, but that thou shouldest keep them from the evil' (John
17:11, 15). Lest any should confine these petitions to his immediate disciples, or to such as already believed on him, he adds (verse
20): 'Neither pray I for these alone, but for them also which shall
believe on me through their word.' If, then, there is any efficacy
in the intercession of Christ, the perseverance of all who believe
on him is infallibly secured. But his intercession, being founded
on his satisfactory death and meritorious righteousness, must be
prevalent and effectual to obtain for his people all that he asks on
their behalf. Him the Father always heareth (John 11:42).

(4) It is secured by *the constant inhabitation of the Spirit.* When
our Lord was about to depart out of this world, he consoled the
hearts of his disciples by the promise of the Spirit. 'I will pray the
Father,' said he, 'and he shall give you another Comforter, that he
may abide with you for ever' (John 14:16). That the gift of the
Spirit was not peculiar to the apostles, but is the happy privilege
of every real Christian, is evident from the inspired declaration:
'If any man have not the Spirit of Christ, he is none of his' (Romans
8:9). Now, the Spirit does not enter into the hearts of believers as
a transient visitant, but 'to make his abode with them.' Hence
they are called 'the temple of God, because the Spirit of God
dwelleth in them.' And the constant residence of the Spirit in

3. Dick's *Lectures on Theology*, vol. iii, p. 521.

believers effectually secures their perseverance; for his gracious purpose in taking up his residence in them is, to make them meet for the inheritance of the saints in light, to guard them through life, and conduct them to glory. By him they are *sealed* to the day of redemption, and he is the *earnest* of their future inheritance (2 Corinthians 1:22; Ephesians 1:13, 14). An earnest is a part given as a security for the future possession of the whole; and as the Holy Spirit is to believers the earnest of the heavenly inheritance, this must imply the utmost certainty of their future bliss. If any who have received the Spirit were left to fall totally and finally from a state of grace, and to come short of the heavenly inheritance, then, shocking thought ! the Spirit of truth would be a precarious and fallacious earnest.

(5) It is secured by *the unchangeable nature of the covenant of grace*. This covenant, being founded in the grace of God, and not in our obedience, is 'ordered in all things, and sure.' The tenor of this covenant is clearly expressed: 'I will make an everlasting covenant with them, that I will not turn away from them, to do them good; but I will put my fear in their hearts, that they shall not depart from me' (Jeremiah 32:40). It is worthy of remark, that here is not only a promise of the constant affection of God towards his people, so that he will never turn away from them to do them good, but also a promise that he will put his fear in their hearts, so that they shall not depart from him. God not only promises that he will continue to be gracious to them, if they continue to fear him, but he also pledges himself to put his fear in their hearts, or to grant to them such communications of his grace as shall preserve them from falling away. The certainty of the saints' perseverance could not possibly be expressed in stronger terms.

In addition to these arguments, which are specified in the Confession, we may state that the perseverance of the saints is also evident:

1. From manifold divine promises (Isaiah 54:10; John 10:27-30; Hebrews 13:5).

2. From the various divine perfections.

3. From the connection between the effectual calling and the glorification of believers (Romans 8:30).

4. From the character of perfection that belongs to all the works of God (Philippians 1:6).

5. From the intimate and indissoluble union that subsists

between Christ and believers (John 15:5; 1 Corinthians 12:12; John 14:19, 20).[4]

The doctrine of the saints' perseverance has been sometimes represented as unfriendly to the interests of holiness. But how it can have this effect, it is not easy to perceive. Although believers 'shall certainly persevere in grace to the end, and be eternally saved'; yet, if they fall into grievous sins, they thereby 'incur God's displeasure, and grieve his Holy Spirit – come to be deprived of some measure of their graces and comforts – have their hearts hardened, and their consciences wounded – hurt and scandalize others, and bring temporal judgment upon themselves'. If, then, the saints feel any concern about the glory of their heavenly Father, the edification of others, and their own comfort, they have the strongest motives to 'abstain from all appearance of evil', and to endeavour to be found 'walking in all the commandments and ordinances of the Lord blameless'. Besides, the perseverance for which we plead is a perseverance *in holiness* to the end; and how can this doctrine have any tendency to make men careless about the commission of sin? Add to this, that the more firmly the believer is persuaded that nothing shall be able to separate him from the love of God, and the more he feels the love of God shed abroad in his heart, the more powerfully will he be *constrained* to live so as to promote the glory of God (2 Corinthians 5:14, 15).

The certainty of the saints' perseverance affords no encouragement to any to neglect the means which God has appointed for their preservation. 'Watch and pray,' said our Saviour, 'that ye enter not into temptation.' 'Beware lest ye fall from your own stedfastness,' said his apostle. 'Look to yourselves, that ye lose not those things which ye have wrought.' The Scriptures abound with such exhortations and admonitions; and they are greatly mistaken who infer from them that the saints may fall totally and finally away from grace. God deals with his people as rational creatures, and these exhortations and admonitions are the very means which he employs, and which he renders effectual, for preventing their apostasy, and for promoting their final

---

4. This subject is treated by all systematic writers. It is also fully discussed in the following works: Lime Street Lectures, Ser. 9; Berry Street *Sermons*, Ser. 24; Elisha Coles on *God's Sovereignty*; Sam. Wilson's *Sermons*, Ser. 11-15; and President Edwards' *Remarks on Important Theological Controversies*, chap. v.

perseverance. God works in believers, both to will and to do; but he requires them to do their part while he is doing his. Let every Christian, therefore, be 'stedfast, unmoveable, always abounding in the work of the Lord, forasmuch as he knows that his labour is not in vain in the Lord'.

CHAPTER 18

ASSURANCE OF
GRACE AND SALVATION

Section 1
Although hypocrites, and other unregenerate men, may vainly deceive themselves with false hopes and carnal presumptions of being in the favour of God and estate of salvation (Job 8:13, 14; Micah 3:11; Deuteronomy 29:19; John 8:41); which hope of theirs shall perish (Matthew 7:22, 23); yet such as truly believe in the Lord Jesus, and love him in sincerity, endeavouring to walk in all good conscience before him, may in this life be certainly assured that they are in a state of grace (John 2:3; 3:14, 18, 19, 21, 24; 5:13), and may rejoice in the hope of the glory of God; which hope shall never make then ashamed (Romans 5:2, 5).

Section 2
This certainty is not a bare conjectural and probable persuasion, grounded upon a fallible hope (Hebrews 6:11, 19); but an infallible assurance of faith, founded upon the divine truth of the promises of salvation (Hebrews 6:17, 18), the inward evidence of those graces unto which these promises are made (2 Peter 1:4, 5, 10, 11; 1 John 2:3; 3:14; 2 Corinthians 1:12), the testimony of the Spirit of adoption witnessing with our spirits that we are the children of God (Romans 8:15, 16): which Spirit is the earnest of our inheritance, whereby we are sealed to the day of redemption (Ephesians 1:13, 14; 4:30; 2 Corinthians 1:21, 22).

Exposition
By the 'assurance of grace and salvation', treated of in this chapter, is meant the believer's assurance that he is 'in the state of grace', and has a personal interest in the salvation of Christ. The statements on this subject are directed against certain errors of the Church of Rome, and of the Arminians. The Church of Rome deny that it is possible for any man in this life to attain more than a conjectural and probable persuasion of salvation, except by extraordinary revelation; and they build some of the most gainful parts of their traffic upon that perpetual doubt and uncertainty, with respect to their final salvation, in which they keep their votaries, and which they profess in some degree to remove by the prayers of the Church, the merits of saints and martyrs, and the absolution which

the priests pronounce in the name of God. The Arminians, in consistency with their denial of the certainty of the saints' final perseverance, hold that it is not possible for any man to attain a greater certainty of salvation than this, that, if he shall persevere in the faith to the end, he shall be saved.

1. In opposition to these errors, our Confession teaches, that the saints, without any special or immediate revelation, in the due use of ordinary means, may attain, not merely a conjectural or probable persuasion, but a certain assurance of their being in a state of grace, and of their final salvation. This is confirmed by such considerations as the following:

1. In the Scriptures, Christians are enjoined to examine themselves, and give all diligence to attain this assurance. The Apostle Paul exhorts the Corinthians to 'examine themselves whether they be in the faith', and speaks of it as an argument of something very blameable in them, not to know whether Jesus Christ be in them or not (2 Corinthians 13:5). The Apostle Peter directs *all* Christians to 'give all diligence to make their calling and election sure', not to others, but to themselves; and informs them how they may do this (2 Peter 1:5-11). The exhortation is addressed to them that have 'obtained precious faith through the righteousness of God, even our Saviour Jesus Christ'; they are directed to 'add to their faith, virtue; and to virtue, knowledge,' etc; and they are informed, that by so doing, they would attain a certain assurance of their calling and election, and have a certain admission into the everlasting kingdom of God in heaven. This direction is of the same nature with the exhortation of the Apostle Paul to the Hebrews (6:11): 'We desire that every one of you do show the same diligence, to the full assurance of hope unto the end.' These exhortations make it manifest that Christians have the means, without any special revelation, of assuring themselves of their present piety and future safety.

2. The Scriptures exhibit many marks or characters of genuine believers, by which they may be certainly assured that they have believed to the saving of their souls. 'Hereby we do know that we know him, if we keep his commandments'; 'Whoso keepeth his word, in him verily is the love of God perfected; hereby know we that we are in him' (1 John 2:3, 5). 'We know that we have passed from death unto life, because we love the brethren'; 'Hereby we

know that we are of the truth, and shall assure our hearts before him' (1 John 3:14, 19). The scope of the whole of that Epistle is, to propose such sure marks to believers, by which they may 'know that they have eternal life' (1 John 5:13).

3. We have many examples of the attainment of this assurance in the history of the personal experience of the saints. The saints described in Scripture were in the habit of expressing their assurance of salvation. 'As for me,' said David, 'I will behold thy face in righteousness; I shall be satisfied, when I awake, with thy likeness' (Psalm 17:15). 'Surely goodness and mercy shall follow me all the days of my life: and I will dwell in the house of the LORD for ever' (Psalm 23:6). 'Thou shalt guide me with thy counsel, and afterward receive me to glory' (Psalm 73:24). Job, too, in the midst of his accumulated afflictions, spake the language of assurance: 'I know that my Redeemer liveth...' (Job 19:25). The experience of New Testament believers is still more plainly expressed. The Apostle Paul may serve as an example. These are his triumphant assertions in behalf of all the saints: 'We are more than conquerors through him that loved us. For I am persuaded, that neither death nor life, nor angels, nor principalities, nor powers, nor things present, nor things to come, nor height, nor depth, nor any other creature, shall be able to separate us from the love of God which is in Christ Jesus our Lord' (Romans 8:37-39; see also, 2 Corinthians 5:1). Upon another occasion he declares his assurance that he had believed in Christ, and his full persuasion of his future felicity: 'I know whom I have believed, and I am persuaded that he is able to keep that which I have committed unto him against that day' (2 Timothy 1:12). So confident was he that, when 'absent from the body', he should be 'present with the Lord', that he expresses his willingness, nay, his ardent desire, in consequence of his assurance, to be released from the body, that he might immediately enter upon the heavenly enjoyment: 'I am now ready to be offered, and the time of my departure is at hand. I have fought a good fight, I have finished my course, I have kept the faith. Henceforth there is laid up for me a crown of righteousness, which the Lord, the righteous judge, shall give me at that day' (2 Timothy 4:6-8; see also 2 Corinthians 5:8; Philippians 1:23). These examples must be sufficient to establish the general principle that an assurance of salvation is in this life attainable by believers.

2. This assurance is 'founded upon the divine truth of the promises of salvation, the inward evidence of those graces unto which
these promises are made, and the testimony of the Spirit of adoption witnessing with our spirits that we are the children of God.'
It is not founded upon any of these things singly, but upon all of
them combined. The promises of salvation in the Word furnish us
with the distinguishing characters of true Christians, and infallibly assure us that all in whom these characters are found shall be
saved. The inward evidences of grace assure us that we possess
these characters; and we are now in a gracious state, and 'shall be
saved with an everlasting salvation'.

> 'Assurance is generally attained by a sort of sacred syllogism, or
> reasoning in this manner: Whosoever believeth in the Lord Jesus
> Christ is in a state of grace, and shall be saved (Acts 16:31; Romans
> 9:33). But I believe in him; therefore, I am in a state of grace, and
> shall be saved. So long as we believe the Scriptures of truth, the first
> of these propositions cannot be called in question. All the difficulty
> respects the second, viz., Whether we truly believe in Christ. For it
> cannot be denied that a man may think himself to be something when
> he is nothing, and so deceive himself (Galatians 6:3). As little can it,
> that the mental eyes may be holden, as sometimes the bodily have
> (Luke 24:16); and in such a case, even he that feareth the Lord must
> walk in darkness (Isaiah 1:10); not knowing that he is in Christ, though
> he certainly is. It is not sufficient that the man is conscious of certain
> acts, as of faith, repentance, love to God and all his saints. In order to
> reach the heights of holy assurance, he must be satisfied as to the
> specific nature of these acts, that they are unfeigned, and not hypo-
> critical. But how he can attain to this without the assistance of the
> Holy Spirit is inconceivable. He who gave faith and repentance must
> also make him know the things which are freely given him of God (1
> Corinthians 2:12). As the sun cannot be seen but by his own light,
> neither can we know, but by the Spirit, that we have the Spirit.'[1]

Some have taught, that every man who believes in Christ must
be immediately conscious that he does so; and that this
consciousness is the first evidence which a man has that he is in a
justified state. Our Confession is altogether silent concerning this
evidence; or rather, it plainly indicates that this consciousness is
by no means an inseparable concomitant of true faith. This
consciousness is the same thing that many theological writers have

1. Bell's Notes to Witsius' *Irenical Animadversions*, pp. 305, 306.

termed 'the reflex act of faith'. By this they meant a consciousness of the direct act of faith, or a knowledge that one has believed, arising from reflection. Now, by declaring that the 'assurance of grace and salvation' is not essential to faith, our Confession teaches that a person may believe in Christ, and may be justified by his faith, before he attain the assurance that he is in a justified state; or, in other words, he may believe in Christ and not be immediately conscious that he has truly believed to the saving of his soul. Faith admits of different degrees, and the evidence of it will be proportioned to its strength. When large communications of the Spirit are given, by means of which faith becomes very strong, then it may carry along with it the most convincing evidence of its truth. Doubtless the faith of many of the saints recorded in Scripture, as of Abraham, the centurion, and the woman of Canaan, was such as left no room to doubt of it. But this will not warrant us to assert that every believer must be instantly conscious of his believing in Christ, and that his faith is unfeigned.

'If faith consisted merely in an assent of the understanding to the truth of a proposition, on perceiving the evidence on which it rests, there could be no doubt of the person being conscious or certain of it; but if the heart be in any sense the proper seat of saving faith, more uncertainty will attend the evidence arising from consciousness. If no opposite dispositions to God and to the way of salvation by grace existed in the soul, the matter would be very easy; but that is not the case. The heart, in regeneration, is not altogether delivered from the deceit occasioned by sin; so that it constantly attempts to deceive and mislead the soul. There is not one gracious spiritual disposition or exercise of the heart but may be, in some degree, counterfeited by the mere working of natural principles; and the remaining deceit of the heart may so operate as to render it very difficult for the believer to discriminate the one from the other. Many morally serious persons are deceived in this way, mistaking those affections which they sometimes feel, and which are excited by various causes, for the work of grace. It must, indeed, be past a doubt that the saving operations of the Spirit must produce very different effects on the soul from any other cause whatever; and, therefore, his work may certainly be discriminated from every other. Still, however, considerable difficulty will remain where faith is weak. Nor can it be otherwise, while there is in the believer's members a law warring against the law in his mind; and while the flesh lusts against the Spirit, preventing him from doing the things that he would.

Nor is the inference fairly drawn from the case of the primitive Christians, who seemed to have no hesitation about the truth of their faith, and declared readily that they believed. Much larger measures of grace seem then to have been given, and given to all, than are given in general, and since that time.'[2]

There can be no question in regard to the reality of the *witnessing of the Spirit*; for an inspired apostle expressly declares: 'The Spirit itself beareth witness with our spirit, that we are the children of God' (Romans 8:16). There are different opinions, however, in regard to the manner in which the Spirit gives this testimony. Some have thought that the Spirit witnesses the believer's adoption by inward revelation, or by way of immediate suggestion. 'The Spirit,' says one, 'by himself, witnesses in a distinct way from that which is by water and blood, by shedding abroad the love of God upon the heart in a soul-ravishing way.' 'This is evident,' it is added, 'from the experience of the saints. Many of them have been brought to assurance in this immediate way; and not merely by reflection upon marks, and signs, and qualifications within, which is the Spirit's witnessing by water or sanctification.'[3] The greater parts of divines, however, concur in the opinion that the Spirit witnesses by means of his operations, or by the effects produced by him in the hearts of believers. They reject the idea of an *immediate* testimony, and hold that the *work* of the Spirit is the *testimony* which he gives, assuring believers of their adoption and consequent safety.

President Edwards speaks very decidedly and strongly against the opinion that the Spirit witnesses by way of immediate suggestion or revelation, and declares that many mischiefs have arisen from this false and delusive notion. 'What has misled many,' says he, 'in their notion of that influence of the Spirit of God we are speaking of is the word 'witness', its being called the *witness* of the Spirit. Hence they have taken it, not to be any effect or work of the Spirit upon the heart, giving evidence from whence men may argue that they are the children of God; but an inward immediate suggestion, as though God inwardly spoke to the man, and testified to him, and told him that he was his child, by a kind of secret voice, or impression: not observing the manner in which the word *witness*

---

2. Thomson's (of Quarrelwood) Sermons, vol. 2, p. 540.
3. Ralph Erskine's *Sermons*, Ser. 143, vol. 9, pp. 199, 200.

or *testimony* is often used in the New Testament; where such terms often signify, not only a mere declaring and asserting a thing to be true, but holding forth evidence from whence a thing may be argued and proved to be true. Thus (Hebrews 2:4), God is said to bear witness with signs and wonders and divers miracles and gifts of the Holy Ghost. Now these miracles, here spoken of, are called God's witness, not because they are of the nature of assertions, but evidences and proofs. So also Acts 14:3; John 5:36; 10:25. So the water and the blood are said to bear witness (1 John 5:8), not that they spake or asserted anything, but they were proofs and evidences.' 'Indeed the apostle, when in that (Romans 8:16), he speaks of the Spirit bearing witness with our spirit that we are the children of God, does sufficiently explain himself, if his words were but attended to. What is here expressed is connected with the two preceding verses, as resulting from what the apostle had there said, as every reader may see. The three verses together are thus: "For as many as are led by the Spirit of God, they are the sons of God; for ye have not received the Spirit of bondage again to fear; but ye have received the Spirit of adoption, whereby we cry, Abba, Father: the Spirit itself beareth witness with our spirit that we are the children of God." Here what the apostle says, if we take it together, plainly shows that what he has respect to, when he speaks of the Spirit's giving us witness or evidence that we are God's children, is his dwelling in us, and leading us, as a spirit of adoption, or spirit of a child, disposing us to behave towards God as to a Father.'[4]

More recent authors take the same view of this subject, and it is satisfactory to find such harmony among the most eminent theological writers upon a point so interesting. 'The Spirit bears testimony to the sonship of believers,' says Dr. Dick, 'when he brings to light, by his operations upon their souls, the evidences of their adoption; and thus makes their relation to God as manifest as if he assured them of it with an audible voice.'[5] Says Dr. Chalmers:

> There is one very obvious way in which the Spirit may bear witness with our spirit that we are the children of God; or in which, according to the translation of many, the Spirit may bear witness to, or

---

4. Edwards' *Treatise Concerning Religious Affections*, pp. 131, 137. See also Flavel's *4th Sac. Med.*, vol. 2, p. 455, 456; McLeod's (New York) *Life and Power of True Godliness*, p. 204.
5. Dick's *Theological Lectures*, vol. 3. p. 415.

attest to our spirit that we are God's children. It is he who worketh a work of grace in our souls, and that work may become manifest to our own consciences. We may read the lineaments of our own renovated character, and it may be regarded as an exercise of our own spirit, that by which we become acquainted with the new features of the new characteristics that have been formed upon ourselves. As we may, furthermore, read in the Bible, what be the Scriptures marks of the new creature; and as all Scripture is given by inspiration of God, this is one way in which a joint testimony may be made out between God's Spirit and our spirit upon the subject; or in which a communication may be made to pass from the one to the other, so that they both shall concur in one and the same sentence – that we are indeed God's children. The part that the Spirit of God hath had in this matter is, that he both graves upon us the lineaments of a living epistle of Christ Jesus, and tells us in the epistle of a written revelation what these lineaments are. The part which our own spirit has is, that, with the eye of consciousness, we read what is in ourselves; and, with the eye of the understanding, we read what is in the Book of God's testimony. And upon our perceiving that such as the marks of grace which we find to be within, so are the marks of grace which we observe in the description of that Word without that the Spirit hath indited, we arrive at the conclusion that we are born of God. But what is more, it is the word of the Spirit to make one see more clearly in both of these directions, to open one's eyes both that he might behold the things contained in the Bible with brighter manifestation, and, also that he might behold the things which lie deeply, and to most, undiscoverably, hidden in the arcana of their own hearts.

I could not, without making my own doctrine outstrip my own experience, vouch for any other intimation of the Spirit of God than that which he gives in the act of making the Word of God clear unto you, and the state of your own heart clear unto you. From the one you draw what are its promises – from the other, what are your own personal characteristics; and the application of the first to the second may conduct to a most legitimate argument, that you personally are one of the saved and that not a tardy or elaborate argument either, but with an evidence quick and powerful as the light of intuition.[6]

Section 3
This infallible assurance doth not so belong to the essence of faith, but that a true believer may wait long, and conflict with many difficulties, before he be partaker or it (1 John 5:13; Isaiah 50:10; Mark 9:24; Psalm 88; 77:1-12): yet, being enabled by the Spirit to know the things which

6. Chalmers *Lectures on the Romans*, vol. 3, pp. 64-66, 68.

are freely given him of God, he may, without extraordinary revelation, in the right use of ordinary means, attain thereunto (1 Corinthians 2:12; 1 John 4:13; Hebrews 6:11, 12; Ephesians 3:17-19). And, therefore, it is the duty of every one to give all diligence to make his calling and election sure (2 Peter 1:10); that thereby his heart may be enlarged in peace and joy in the Holy Ghost, in love and thankfulness to God, and in strength and cheerfulness in the duties of obedience (Romans 5:1, 2, 5; 14:17; 15:13; Ephesians 1:3, 4; Psalms 4:6, 7; 119:32), the proper fruits of this assurance: so far is it from inclining men to looseness (1 John 2:1, 2; Romans 6:1, 2; Titus 2:11, 12, 14; 2 Corinthians 7:1; Romans 8:1, 12; 1 John 3:2, 3; Psalm 130:4; 1 John 1:6, 7).

Section 4
True believers may have the assurance of their salvation divers ways shaken, diminished, and intermitted; as, by negligence in preserving of it: by falling into some special sin, which woundeth the conscience, and grieveth the Spirit; by some sudden or vehement temptation; by God's withdrawing the light of his countenance, and suffering even such as fear him to walk in darkness, and to have no light (Canticles 5:2, 3, 6; Psalm 51:8, 12, 14; Ephesians 4:30, 31; Psalm 77:1-10; Matthew 26:69-72; Psalms 31:22; 88. Isaiah 50:10); yet are they never utterly destitute of that seed of God, and life of faith, that love of Christ and the brethren, that sincerity of heart and conscience of duty, out of which by the operation of the Spirit, this assurance may in due time be revived (1 John 3:9; Luke 22:32; Job 13:15; Psalm 73:15; 51:8, 12; Isaiah 50:10), and by the which, in the meantime, they are supported from utter despair (Micah 7:7-9; Jeremiah 32:40; Isaiah 54:7-10; Psalm 22:1; 88).

Exposition
That the assurance that one is in a gracious state does not belong to the essence of faith requires no proof. This assurance arises from the perception of the fruits and evidences of faith; and it is manifest that faith must exist before its evidences can be discerned. All faith is founded on testimony; but there is no testimony in the Scriptures declaring to any man that he is in a state of grace; this, therefore cannot be object of faith. This kind of assurance, as has been already shown, is ordinarily obtained by reflection, or by a process of reasoning. But although the assurance described in this chapter is not essential to faith, yet there is an assurance which belongs to the essence of faith, and this our Confession recognises in the chapter which treats of saving faith. It makes the principal acts of saving faith to consist in 'accepting, receiving, and resting' on Christ for salvation; and it is impossible for one to *rest* on

Christ for salvation without believing or trusting that he shall be saved by him. Whoever rests upon a person for doing a certain thing in his favour, must have a persuasion, or assurance, that he will do that thing for him. Indeed, assurance is so essential to faith that without it there can be no faith, human or divine. To believe a report is to be persuaded or assured of the truth of the report; to believe a promise is to be persuaded or assured that the promiser will do as he has said. In like manner, to believe in Christ for salvation is to be persuaded or assured that we shall be saved through the grace of our Lord Jesus Christ.

That assurance which is essential to faith, is generally termed *the assurance of faith*; and the assurance of grace and salvation is termed *the assurance of sense*. By some the former is called an *objective* and the latter a *subjective* assurance. There is a marked distinction between them; the former having for its object the faithfulness of God in the gospel testimony; whereas the latter has for its object the existence of a gracious work in the soul. The former arises from a single view of what is contained in the Word of God; the latter, from a combined view of his Word without us and of his work within us. The former is an assurance that God is presently giving Christ, with his salvation to us, in the free offer and promise of the gospel; the latter is an assurance that Christ and his salvation are already ours in real possession and enjoyment. *That* is inseparable from saving faith; *this* is both separable, and often actually separated, from the exercise of true faith.

There are two extremes in reference to this subject which ought to be avoided. The one is that there is no assurance in the direct act of faith, and that assurance can only be derived from the marks and evidences of a gracious state; the other is that the assurance of personal salvation is so essential to saving faith that no one can be a genuine believer who has any doubt of his own salvation. We apprehend, on the one hand, that while the assurance which arises from marks and evidences of a gracious state does not belong to the essence of faith, yet there is an assurance in the direct act of faith, founded upon nothing about the person himself, but solely upon the Word of God; and, on the other hand, that though there is an assurance essential to faith, yet the believer may be often perplexed with doubts and fears concerning his personal salvation, because there is still much unbelief, and other corruptions, remaining in him, and these frequently prevail against him.

It will be sufficient briefly to state the other truths contained in these sections.

1. As the assurance of their gracious state is attainable by believers in the due use of ordinary means, so it is their duty to give diligence and use their utmost endeavours to obtain it. This is incumbent upon them by the command of God, and it is necessary to their own comfort, though not to their safety.

2. This assurance it not the attainment of all believers; and, after it has been enjoyed, it may be weakened, and even lost for a season. It is liable to be shaken by bodily infirmity, by their own negligence, by temptation, by that visitation of God which the Scriptures call his hiding his face from his people, and by occasional transgression.

3. Although believers may forfeit their assurance, yet they are never entirely destitute of gracious habits and dispositions, nor left to sink into utter despair; and their assurance may, by the operation of the Spirit, be in due time revived.

4. This assurance, instead of encouraging believers to indulge in sin, excites them to the vigorous pursuit of holiness. Such as boast of their assurance, and yet can deliberately practise known sin, are only vain pretenders. True assurance cannot be attained or preserved without close walking with God in all his commandments and ordinances blameless. We must judge of the tendency of the assurance of salvation by what the apostles of our Lord have said concerning it; and they uniformly improve it as a motive to holiness (Romans 13:11-14; 1 Corinthians 15:58; 1 John 3:2, 3).

CHAPTER 19

THE LAW OF GOD

Section 1
God gave to Adam a law, as a covenant of works, by which he bound him, and all his posterity, to personal, entire, exact, and perpetual obedience; promised life upon the fulfilling, and threatened death upon the breach of it; and endued him with power and ability to keep it (Genesis 1:26, 27; 2:17; Romans 2:14, 15; 10:5; 5:12, 19; Galatians 3:10, 12; Ecclesiastes 7:29; Job 28:28).

Exposition
God having formed man an intelligent creature, and a subject of moral government, he gave him a law for the rule of his conduct. This law was founded in the infinitely righteous nature of God, and the moral relations necessarily subsisting between him and man. It was originally written on the heart of man, as he was endowed with such a perfect knowledge of his Maker's will as was sufficient to inform him concerning the whole extent of his duty, in the circumstances in which he was placed, and was also furnished with power and ability to yield all that obedience which was required of him. This is included in the moral image of God, after which man was created (Genesis 1:27). The law, as thus inscribed on the heart of the first man, is often styled *the law of creation*, because it was the will of the sovereign Creator, revealed to the reasonable creature, by impressing it upon his mind and heart at his creation. It is also called *the moral law*, because it was a revelation of the will of God, as his moral governor, and was the standard and rule of man's moral actions. Adam was originally placed under this law in its natural form, as merely directing and obliging him to perfect obedience. He was brought under it in a *covenant form*, when an express threatening of death, and a gracious promise of life, was annexed to it; and then a *positive* precept was added, enjoining him not to eat of the fruit of the tree of knowledge, as the test of his obedience to the whole law (Genesis 2:16, 17). That this covenant was made with the first man, not as a single person, but as the federal representative of all his natural posterity, has been formerly shown (see page 125). The

law, as invested with a covenant form, is called, by the Apostle Paul, 'The law of works' (Romans 3:27); that is, the law as a covenant of works. In this form, the law is to be viewed as not only prescribing duty, but as promising life as the reward of obedience, and denouncing death as the punishment of transgression. This law 'which was ordained to life' is now become 'weak through the flesh', or through the corruption of our fallen nature. It prescribes terms which we are incapable of performing; and instead of being encouraged to seek life by our own obedience to the law as a covenant, we are required to renounce all hopes of salvation in that way and to seek it by faith in Christ. But all men are naturally under the law as a broken covenant, obnoxious to its penalty, and bound to yield obedience to its commands. The covenant being made with Adam, not only for himself, but also for all his posterity, when he violated it, he left them all under it as a broken covenant. Most miserable, therefore, is the condition of all men by nature; for 'as many as are of the works of the law are under the curse' (Galatians 3:10). Truly infatuated are they who seek for righteousness by the works of the law; for 'by the deeds of the law shall no flesh be justified in the sight of God' (Romans 3:20).

Section 2

This law, after his fall, continued to be a perfect rule of righteousness; and, as such, was delivered by God upon Mount Sinai in ten commandments, and written in two tables (James 1:25; 2:8, 10-12; Romans 13:8, 9; Deuteronomy 5:32; 10:4; Exodus 34:1); the first four commandments containing our duty towards God, and the other six our duty to man (Matthew 22:37-40).

Exposition

Upon the fall of man, the law, considered as a covenant of works, was disannulled and set aside; but, considered as moral, it contained to be a perfect rule of righteousness. That fair copy of the law, which had been inscribed on the heart of the first man in his creation, was, by the fall, greatly defaced, although not totally obliterated. Some faint impressions of it still remain on the minds of all reasonable creatures. Its general principles, such as, that God is to be worshipped, that parents ought to be honoured, that we should do to others what we would reasonably wish that they should do to us – such general principles as these are still, in some degree, engraven on the minds of all men (Romans 2:14, 15). But the original edition of the law being greatly obliterated, God was graciously pleased to give a new and complete copy of it. He delivered it to the Israelites from Mount Sinai, with awful solemnity. In this promulgation of the law, he summed it up in ten commandments; and, therefore, it is commonly styled the Law of the Ten Commandments. These commandments were written by the finger of God himself on two tables of stone (Exodus 32:15, 16; 34:1). The first four commandments contain our duty to God, and the other six our duty to man; and they are summed up by our Saviour in the two great commandments, of loving God with all our hearts, and our neighbour as ourselves (Matthew 22:37-40).

The Church of Rome assign only three precepts to the first table, and seven to the second. They join together the first and second commandments, and that for an obvious reason. Standing separately, the second forbids the use of images in the worship of God, and plainly condemns the practice of that Church; but viewed as an appendage to the first precept, it only forbids, as they pretend, the worship of the images of false gods; and, consequently, leaves them at liberty to worship the images which they have consecrated to the honour of the true God and his saints. Having thus turned two precepts into one, in order to make up the number of ten, they split the last precept of the decalogue into two, making 'Thou shalt not covet thy neighbour's house', one, and the words which follow, another.

This division cannot be vindicated. The two first precepts obviously relate to distinct things. The first points out the object of worship, viz., the living and true God, and no other. The second prescribes the means of worship not by images or any other plan of human invention, but by ordinances which are divinely appointed. The tenth precept is as clearly one and indivisible. The whole of it relates to one subject – covetousness, or unlawful desire; and if it ought to be divided into two, because the words 'Thou shalt not covet' are twice repeated, it would follow that it should be divided into as many commands as there are different classes of objects specified; for the words 'Thou shalt not covet' must be understood as prefixed to each of these objects. The Apostle Paul plainly speaks of it as one precept, when he says: 'I had not known lust, except the law had said, Thou shalt not covet' (Romans 7:7).

It may be remarked, that the law of the ten commandments was promulgated to Israel from Sinai in the form of a covenant of works. Not that it was the design of God to renew a covenant of works with Israel, or to put them upon seeking life by their own obedience to the law; but the law was published to them as a covenant of works, to show them that without a perfect right-eousness, answering to all the demands of the law, they could not be justified before God; and that, finding themselves wholly des-titute of that righteousness, they might be excited to take hold of the covenant of grace, in which a perfect righteousness for their justification is graciously provided. The Sinai transaction was a mixed dispensation. In it the covenant of grace was published, as appears from these words in the preface standing before the com-mandments: 'I am the Lord *thy God*, which have brought thee out of the land of Egypt, out of the house of bondage'; and from the promulgation of the ceremonial law at the same time. But the moral law, as a covenant of works, was also displayed, to con-vince the Israelites of their sinfulness and misery, to teach them the necessity of an atonement, and lead them to embrace by faith the blessed Mediator, the Seed promised to Abraham, in whom all the families of the earth were to be blessed. The law, there-fore, was published at Sinai as a covenant of works, in subservi-ence to the covenant of grace. And the law is still published in subservience to the gospel, as 'a schoolmaster to bring sinners to Christ, that they may be justified by faith' (Galatians 3:24).

Section 3
Besides this law, commonly called Moral, God was pleased to give to the people of Israel, as a Church under age, ceremonial laws, containing several typical ordinances: partly of worship, prefiguring Christ, his graces, actions, sufferings, and benefits (Hebrews 9; 10:1; Galatians 4:1-3; Colossians 2:17); and partly holding forth divers instructions of moral duties (1 Corinthians 5:7; 2 Corinthians 6:17. Jude 23). All which cer-emonial laws are now abrogated under the New Testament (Colossians 2:14, 16, 17; Daniel 9:27; Ephesians 2:15, 16).

Section 4
To them, also, as a body politic, he gave sundry judicial laws, which expired together with the state of that people, not obliging any other now, further than the general equity thereof may require (Exodus 21; 22:1-29; Genesis 49:10; 1 Peter 2:13, 14; Matthew 5:17, 38, 39; 1 Cor-inthians 9:8-10).

Section 5

The moral law doth for ever bind all, as well justified persons as others, to the obedience thereof (Romans 13:8-10; Ephesians 6:2; 1 John 2:3, 4, 7, 8); and that not only in regard of the matter contained in it, but also in respect of the authority of God, the Creator, who gave it (James 2:10, 11). Neither doth Christ in the gospel any way dissolve, but much strengthen this obligation (Matthew 5:17-19; James 2:8. Romans 3:31).

Exposition

Besides the *moral* law, God gave to Israel *ceremonial* and *judicial* laws; the two latter are of limited and temporary use; the former is of universal and perpetual obligation.

The *ceremonial* law respected the Jews in their ecclesiastical capacity, or as a Church, and prescribed the rites and carnal ordinances which were to be observed by them in the external worship of God. These ceremonies were chiefly designed to prefigure Christ, and lead them to the knowledge of the way of salvation through him (Hebrews 10:1). This law is abrogated under the New Testament dispensation. This appears:

1. From the nature of the law itself. It was given to the Jews to separate them from the idolatrous rites of other nations, and to preserve their religion uncorrupted. But when the gospel was preached to all nations, and Jews and Gentiles were gathered into one body under Christ their Head, the wall of separation was taken down (Ephesians 2:14, 15).

2. Because these ceremonies were only figures of good things to come, imposed upon the Jews until the time of reformation, and were abrogated by Christ, in whom they were realized and substantiated (Hebrews 9:9-12).

3. Because these ceremonies were given to the Israelites to typify and represent Christ and his death; and, since Christ has come, and has, by his death and satisfaction, accomplished all that they prefigured, these types must be abolished (Colossians 2:17).

4. Because many of these rites were restricted to the temple of Jerusalem, and the temple being now destroyed, these rites must cease along with it.

5. Because the apostles expressly taught that the ceremonial law is abrogated under the Christian dispensation (Acts 15:24). One chief design of the Epistle to the Hebrews is, to prove that this law must necessarily be disannulled (Hebrews 7:12).

2. The *judicial* law respected the Jews in their political capacity, or as a nation, and consisted of those institutions which God prescribed to them for their civil government. This law, as far as the Jewish polity was peculiar, has also been entirely abolished; but as far as it contains any statute founded in the law of nature common to all nations, it is still obligatory.

3. The *moral* law is so called because it relates to moral actions, and to distinguish it from the positive laws, which were only of temporary obligation. This law has no relation to times and places, or to one nation more than another; but being founded in the relations of men to their Creator, and to one another, it retains its authority under all dispensations. In opposition to the Antinomians, who say that believers are released from the obligation of the moral law, our Confession teaches that this law is perpetually binding on justified persons, as well as others. Believers are, indeed, delivered from this law in its covenant form; but they are still under it as a rule of life, in the hand of the Mediator, being 'not without law to God, but under the law to Christ' (1 Corinthians 9:21). Christ, in the most solemn and explicit manner, declared, that he 'came not to destroy the law, but to fulfil it' (Matthew 5:17). He fulfilled it, as a covenant, by his own perfect obedience, and his most grievous suffering in the room of his people; and its heavenly precepts he has enforced upon their minds, by the most cogent motives, as a perfect rule of duty. The gospel, instead of weakening the obligation of the law, confirms and strengthens its authority, and enforces obedience to its precepts by the strongest motives: 'Do we make void the law through faith? God forbid; nay, we establish the law' (Romans 3:31). Although the moral law is to believers divested of its covenant form, it remains immutably the same, in regard both to its matter and its authority. And as the law was binding on the first man as a rule of life, antecedent to any covenant-transaction between God and him, we may easily understand that the law may be entirely divested of its covenant form, while it continues in full force as a rule of moral conduct.

Section 6
Although true believers be not under the law as a covenant of works, to be thereby justified or condemned (Romans 6:14; Galatians 2:16; 3:13; 4:4, 5; Acts 13:39; Romans 8:1): yet is it of great use to them, as well as to others: in that, as a rule of life, informing them of the will of God and their duty, it directs and binds them to walk accordingly (Romans 7:12, 22, 25; Psalm 119:4-6; 1 Corinthians 7:19; Galatians 5:14, 16, 18-23); discovering also the sinful pollutions of their nature, hearts, and lives (Romans 7:7; 3:20); so as examining themselves thereby, they may come to further conviction of, humiliation for, and hatred against sin (James 1:23-25; Romans 7:9, 14, 24); together with a clearer sight of the need they have of Christ, and the perfection of his obedience (Galatians 3:24; Romans 7:24, 25; 8:3, 4). It is likewise of use to the regenerate, to restrain their corruptions, in that it forbids sin (James 2:11; Psalm 119:101, 104, 128); and the threatenings of it serve to show what even their sins deserve, and what afflictions in this life they may expect for them, although freed from the curse thereof threatened in the law (Ezra 4:13, 14; Psalm 89:30-34). The promises of it, in like manner, show them God's approbation of obedience, and what blessings they may expect upon the performance thereof (Leviticus 26:1-14; 2 Corinthians 6:16; Ephesians 6:2, 3; Psalm 37:11; Matthew 5:5; Psalm 19:11), although not as due to them by the law as a covenant of works (Galatians 2:16; Luke 17:10): so as a man's doing good, and refraining from evil, because the law encourageth to the one and deterreth from the other, is no evidence of his being under the law, and not under grace (Romans 6:12, 14; 1 Peter 3:8-12; Psalm 34:12-16; Hebrews 12:28, 29).

Section 7
Neither are the fore-mentioned uses of the law contrary to the grace of the gospel, but do sweetly comply with it (Galatians 3:21); the Spirit of Christ subduing and enabling the will of man to do that freely and cheerfully which the will of God revealed in the law requireth to be done (Ezekiel 36:27; Hebrews 8:10; Jeremiah 31:33).

Exposition
It is here affirmed, that true believers are completely delivered from the law, as a covenant of works. Christ, as their representative and surety, endured the curse of the law in all its bitterness, and in its utmost extent, in his sufferings unto death, and thus set them completely free from its condemning power (Galatians 3:13; Romans 8:1). But had Christ only endured the curse of the law, and still left his people under its commanding power as a covenant, this would only have restored them to the same uncertain

state of probation in which Adam originally stood, and every transgression would have again involved them under the curse. Christ,
however, not only sustained the full infliction of the penalty of
the law, he also yielded perfect obedience to its precepts, and
thus obtained for his people deliverance from its commanding, as
well as its condemning power. To show the complete nature of
this freedom, we are told that they are dead to the law through the
body of Christ; that Christ is the end of the law of righteousness
to every one that believeth; and that they are not under the law,
but under grace (Romans 7:4; 10:4, 6:14).

The doctrine of the believer's freedom from the law, as a covenant, has no tendency to licentiousness; for it has already been
established, that they are under the obligation of the law as a rule
of life; and here it is further shown that the law is of manifold use
to them, as well as to others: 'The law is good,' says the Apostle
Paul, 'if a man use it lawfully' (1 Timothy 1:8); that is, if he use it
in a suitableness to the state wherein he is, either as a believer or
an unbeliever. The law serves numerous and important purposes,
both to the unregenerate and to the regenerate. Some of these
uses may be briefly stated.

First, To the *unregenerate* the moral law is of use in the following respects:

1. To restrain them from much sin (1 Timothy 1:9).

2. To convince them of their sinfulness and misery (Romans
3:20; 7:9).

3. To discover to them their absolute need of Christ, and drive
them to him as their all-sufficient Saviour (Galatians 3:24).

4. To render them inexcusable, if they continue in their sins,
and finally reject the only Saviour of lost sinners (Romans 1:20;
2:15; John 3:18, 36).

Second, The moral law is of use to the *regenerate* in the
following respects:

1. To render Christ more precious to them, and excite their
gratitude to him who so loved them as to obey its precepts and
suffer its penalty, that he might deliver them from it as a *covenant*
(Galatians 3:13; 4:4, 5).

2. To show them the will of God, and regulate their conduct
(Micah 6:8).

3. To serve as a standard of self-examination, in order to
discover the pollutions of their hearts and lives – to keep them

self-abased – to lead them to a constant dependence upon Christ, and to excite them to a progressive advancement in holiness (Philippians 3:10-14).

4. To serve as a test of their sincerity, that they may assure their hearts that they are of the truth, and that they delight in the law of God after the inward man, notwithstanding their manifold defects in duty (1 John 3:19; Romans 7:22, 25; 2 Corinthians 1:12).

CHAPTER 20

CHRISTIAN LIBERTY,
AND LIBERTY OF CONSCIENCE

Section 1

The liberty which Christ hath purchased for believers under the gospel, consists in their freedom from the guilt of sin, the condemning wrath of God, the curse of the moral law (Titus 2:14; 1 Thessalonians 1:10; Galatians 3:13); and in their being delivered from this present evil world, bondage to Satan, and dominion of sin (Galatians 1:4; Colossians 1:13; Acts 26:18; Romans 6:14), from the evil of afflictions, the sting of death, the victory of the grave, and everlasting damnation (Romans 8:28; Psalm 119:71; 1 Corinthians 15:54-57; Romans 8:1); as also in their free access to God (Romans 5:1, 2), and their yielding obedience unto him, not out of slavish fear, but a childlike love, and willing mind (Romans 8:14, 15; 1 John 4:18). All which were common also to believers under the law (Galatians 3:9, 14); but under the New Testament, the liberty of Christians is further enlarged in their freedom from the yoke of the ceremonial law, to which the Jewish Church was subjected (Galatians 4:1-3, 6, 7; 5:1. Acts 15:10, 11), and in greater boldness of access to the throne of grace (Hebrews 4:14, 16; 10:19-22), and in fuller communications of the free Spirit of God than believers under the law did ordinarily partake of (John 7:38, 39. 2 Corinthians 3:13, 17, 18).

Exposition

Civil liberty is justly esteemed an invaluable privilege, and no sacrifice is deemed too great in order to recover it when lost, or to secure it when enjoyed. But valuable as civil liberty is, it cannot be questioned that the liberty wherewith Christ makes his people free is much to be preferred. In proportion to the value of the soul above the body, so must the liberty that respects the one surpass that which merely relates to the other. Those whom Christ makes free are free indeed (John 8:36). Christian liberty may be considered, either as common to believers in every age, or as a special immunity of the children of God under the New Testament dispensation. That liberty which is common to believers in all ages consists in their freedom:

1. *From the guilt and the dominion of sin.* By the *guilt* of sin is meant an obligation to suffer eternal punishment on account of

sin. From this believers are freed by an act of pardoning mercy, which is passed upon the ground of Christ's blood. 'They have redemption through his blood, the forgiveness of sins, according to the riches of his grace' (Ephesians 1:7). But sin is not only accompanied with guilt, it also exercises a rigorous *dominion* over the sinner. From the reigning power of sin Christ delivers his people in the day of their regeneration; and although sin still dwells in them, its power is gradually weakened in their progressive sanctification, and its very being shall in due time be abolished. Hence the Apostle Paul thus addresses believers: 'Sin shall not have dominion over you'; 'Being made free from sin, and become servants unto God, ye have your fruit unto holiness, and the end everlasting life' (Romans 6:14, 22).

2. *From the condemning wrath of God.* To the wrath of God all men are naturally obnoxious. Being children of disobedience, they are also children of wrath (Ephesians 2:2, 3). But, upon the ground of the righteousness of Christ imputed to them, believers are completely freed from divine wrath. 'There is now no condemnation to them that are in Christ Jesus' (Romans 8:1). God may hide his face from them, but his judicial wrath is for ever turned away from them (Isaiah 54:9, 10; Romans 5:10).

3. *From the curse of the law as a broken covenant.* Under that curse all men lie naturally; for it is written: 'Cursed is every one that continueth not in all things which are written in the book of the law to do them' (Galatians 3:10). But Christ, having endured that curse as the Surety of his people, delivers from it all who are found in him. Hence the Apostle Paul saith: 'Christ hath redeemed us from the curse of the law, being made a curse for us' (Galatians 3:13). Though believers are under the moral law as a rule of life, they are completely freed from it as a covenant of works – freed from both its commanding and condemning power; and, therefore, they cannot be subjected to its curse on account of their transgressions. 'Ye are not under the law, but under grace' (Romans 6:14). 'Now we are delivered from the law, that being dead wherein we were held' (Romans 7:6).

4. *From this present evil world.* The world is another tyrannical master, under whose power and influence all men naturally are. But believers are freed from the power of this fascinating and destructive foe. This freedom Christ has obtained for them, and bestows upon them. 'He gave himself for our sins, that he might

deliver us from this present evil world, according to the will of God and our Father' (Galatians 1:4). Through the powerful influence of his cross, believers are crucified unto the world, and the world unto them (Galatians 6:14).

5. *From bondage to Satan.* All men are by nature the captives of Satan, who is, therefore, called 'the god of this world'. Having taken them in his snare, they are become his prey, and are 'taken captive by him at his will'. But Christ 'was manifested to destroy the works of the devil'; and 'through death he destroyed him that had the power of death, that is, the devil'. In the gospel he proclaims liberty to the captives (Isaiah 61:1); and, in the day of their effectual calling, he actually delivers his people from the power of Satan (Colossians 1:13). While in the present world, indeed, they are exposed to the assaults of this adversary (1 Peter 5:8); but he shall never regain his dominion over them, and, in due time, they shall be completely freed from his temptations, and placed beyond the reach of his influence; for the promise is: 'The God of peace shall bruise Satan under your feet shortly' (Romans 16:20).

6. *From the evil of afflictions.* Christ does not grant to believers an entire exemption from the troubles that are common to men, but he frees them from all the penal evil of afflictions. The cup of their affliction may be large and deep, but there is not one drop of judicial wrath mingled in it. Their afflictions are designed for their profit; and, through the divine blessing, they are rendered, in various respects, highly beneficial to them. Hence the children of God have often acknowledged that it was good for them to have been afflicted (Psalm 119:71); and, though they may sometimes be at a loss to perceive how their trials are to be rendered profitable to them, yet they have the fullest assurance that all things shall work together for their good (Romans 8:28. See also Hebrews 12:6-11; 2 Corinthians 4:17).

7. *From the sting of death.* As death means the dissolution of the union between the soul and the body, believers are not exempted from its stroke (Hebrews 9:28; Psalm 89:48). Christ, however, delivers his people from death, considered as the effect of the law-curse, and the harbinger of everlasting destruction (John 11:25, 26). He has extracted the sting of death, and rendered it powerless to do his people any real harm (1 Corinthians 15:56). Instead of doing believers any real injury, death has a commission

to confer upon them unspeakable good. It is the termination of all their sorrows, their release from warfare, and their departure to be with Christ (Philippians 1:21, 23).

8. *From the victory of the grave*. The bodies of believers must be laid in the grave, and see corruption. To them, however, the grave is not a prison, but a bed of rest; and they shall not always remain under the power of corruption, but shall be raised up, glorious and immortal, at the last day (Job 19:26, 27). 'Now is Christ risen from the dead, and is become the first-fruits of them that slept' (1 Corinthians 15:20). His resurrection is the pledge and earnest of the resurrection of all that sleep in him. In due time the promise will be fully accomplished: 'I will ransom them from the power of the grave; I will redeem them from death' (Hosea 13:14); and 'then the saying shall be brought to pass, Death is swallowed up in victory' (1 Corinthians 15:54).

9. *From everlasting damnation*. The full punishment due to sin is never inflicted upon any in this life, but at last 'the wicked shall be turned into hell' (Psalm 9:17). At the great day, a sentence of condemnation shall be solemnly pronounced upon them, and they shall be led away 'into everlasting fire, prepared for the devil and his angels' (Matthew 25:41). But believers are secured against coming into condemnation, and are delivered from the wrath to come (John 5:24; 1 Thessalonians 1:10). When the great day of God's wrath is come, they shall behold and see the reward of the wicked; but it shall not come nigh unto them.

10. *Believers have also free access to God*. They have liberty of access to God as a gracious Father, and may pour out their hearts, and vent their complaints unto him, with filial freedom. 'In Christ Jesus we have boldness and access with confidence, by the faith of him' (Ephesians 3:12).

11. *Believers have freedom of spirit in the service of God*. The obedience which wicked men pay to God is like that of slaves to a tyrant, whom they hate, and whose only motive to obedience is a fear of punishment. But believers are delivered from a slavish fear of wrath, and serve God from a generous principle of love, and with a willing mind. 'Where the Spirit of the Lord is, there is liberty' (2 Corinthians 3:17. See also Luke 1:74, 75; 2 Corinthians 5:14; 1 John 4:18).

The liberty which has now been described, belonged to believers under the law, as well as under the present dispensation;

but, under the New Testament, the liberty of Christians has been enlarged in several particulars, which are next to be briefly noticed.

1. *Christians are now freed from the yoke of the ceremonial law.* The Jewish Church was kept 'in bondage under the elements of the world' (Galatians 4:3); but that burdensome yoke is not imposed on the Christian Church (Acts 15:10). The ancient ceremonies were abrogated, in point of obligation, by the death of Christ; and though, for a time, the use of them was indifferent, yet upon the full promulgation of the gospel, and the destruction of the temple of Jerusalem, the observance of them became unlawful; and the Apostle Paul exhorted Christians to 'stand fast in the liberty wherewith Christ had made them free, and not be entangled again with the yoke of bondage' (Galatians 5:1).

2. *Christians have now greater boldness of access to the throne of grace.* The Apostle Paul frequently mentions liberty, confidence, and boldness, in their access to God, as an especial privilege of believers under the New Testament, in opposition to the state of those who lived under the Old (See Hebrews 4:16; 10:19; 1 John 3:21; 4:17; 5:14).

3. *Christians enjoy fuller communications of the free Spirit of God than were ordinarily granted to believers under the law.* The Spirit had, no doubt, been dispensed to the Church under the Old Testament; but the more extensive and copious effusion of the Spirit was reserved to New Testament times. Hence the Spirit is said not to have been given before that Jesus was glorified (John 7:39). The plentiful effusion of the Spirit was frequently foretold as the great privilege of gospel times (Isaiah 44:3; Joel 2:28, 29). Accordingly, upon the ascension of Christ, and the commencement of the Christian dispensation, the extraordinary and miraculous gifts of the Spirit were communicated, not only to the apostles, but often to common believers; and the ordinary gifts and gracious influences of the Spirit are still conferred in richer abundance than under the former dispensation. Hence the Apostle Paul represents it as an eminent part of the glory of the New Testament dispensation, that it is 'the ministration of the Spirit' (2 Corinthians 3:8).

How excellent is that liberty we have been describing! If civil liberty be highly prized, sure the glorious liberty of the children of God is eminently precious. How highly are believers indebted to the Lord Jesus Christ, who obtained this freedom for them at the incalculable price of his own precious blood! Sure their hearts should overflow with gratitude to their generous Deliverer, who gave his own life a ransom for them. Since he has emancipated them from the most degrading servitude, and set them free from those cruel masters who formerly tyrannized over them, ought they not to take upon them his yoke, which is easy, and his burden which is light? Every true Christian will reckon it his highest privilege, as well as his incumbent duty, to be the devoted servant of Christ, whose service is perfect freedom.

Section 2

God alone is Lord of the conscience (James 4:12. Romans 14:4), and hath left it free from the doctrines and commandments of men which are in anything contrary to his Word, or beside it, in matters of faith or worship (Acts 4:19; 5:29; 1 Corinthians 7:23; Matthew 23:8-10; 2 Corinthians 1:24; Matthew 15:9). So that to believe such doctrines, or to obey such commandments out of conscience, is to betray true liberty of conscience (Colossians 2:20, 22, 23; Galatians 1:10; 2:4, 5; 5:1); and the requiring of an implicit faith, and an absolute and blind obedience, is to destroy liberty of conscience and reason also (Romans 10:17; 14:23; Isaiah 8:20; Acts 17:11; John 4:22; Hosea 5:11; Revelation 13:12, 16, 17; Jeremiah 8:9).

Exposition

In this section the doctrine of liberty of conscience is laid down in most explicit terms. The conscience, in all matters of faith and duty, is subject to the authority of God alone, and entirely free from all subjection to the traditions and commandments of men. To believe any doctrine, or obey any commandment, contrary to, or beside, the Word of God, out of submission to human authority, is to betray true liberty of conscience. And be the power and authority whose it will – be it that of a magistrate or a minister – of a husband, a master, or a parent – that would require an implicit faith and an absolute blind obedience, it would destroy liberty of conscience.

The rights of conscience have been frequently invaded by rulers, both civil and ecclesiastical. By the Church of Rome the statements of our Confession are directly contradicted, both in doctrine and in practice. They teach that the Pope, and the bishops in their own dioceses, may, by their own authority, enact laws which bind the conscience, and which cannot be transgressed without incurring the same penalties which are annexed to every breach of the divine law. And they have actually imposed many articles of faith, and enjoined numberless rites and ceremonies, as necessary in the worship of God, which have no foundation in Scripture; and they require implicit faith in all their decrees, and a blind obedience to all their commands. Against the tyrannical usurpations and encroachments of that Church this section is principally levelled.

No person on earth can have authority to dictate to conscience; for this would be to assume a prerogative which belongs to none but the supreme Lord and Legislator. 'There is one Lawgiver, who is able to save and to destroy' (James 4:12). Such a power was prohibited by Jesus Christ among his followers: 'The kings of the Gentiles exercise lordship over them, but ye shall not be so' (Luke 22:25). It was disclaimed by the inspired apostles: 'Not that we have dominion over your faith,' said the Apostle of the Gentiles, 'but are the helpers of your joy' (2 Corinthians 1:24).

From the principles laid down in this section, it manifestly follows, that a right of private judgment about matters of religion belongs to every man, and ought to be exercised by every Christian. Christians are expressly required to examine and prove every doctrine by the unerring rule of the Word of God (Isaiah 8:20; 1 John 4:1). They ought to be ready to render a reason of the hope which is in them (1 Peter 3:15); and this none can do who receive the doctrines and commandments of men with implicit faith and blind obedience. Whatsoever is not done in faith, nor accompanied with a personal persuasion of the obligation or lawfulness of it in the sight of God, is pronounced to be sin (Romans 14:23).

It follows no less clearly, from the principles here laid down, that when lawful superiors command what is contrary to the Word of God, or beside it, in matters of faith and worship, their commands do not bind the conscience. The obedience which the Scriptures command us to render to lawful superiors – whether parents, or husband, or magistrates – is not unlimited; there are cases in which disobedience becomes a duty. No one doubts that the precept, 'Children, obey your parent in all things,' is a command to obey them only in the exercise of their rightful parental authority, and imposes no obligation to implicit and passive obedience. The case is equally plain with regard to the command, 'Wives submit to your own husbands'. And it cannot be questioned that the obedience due to magistrates is also limited. The precept, 'Let every soul be subject to the higher powers,' must be understood as a command to obey magistrates only in the exercise of their rightful authority, and in all things lawful. The same inspired teachers who enjoined in such general terms obedience to rulers, themselves uniformly and openly disobeyed them whenever their commands were inconsistent with other and higher obligations. 'We ought to obey God rather than men' (Acts 5:29), was the principle which they avowed, and on which they acted. When the apostles were charged by the Jewish Council to speak no more in the name of Jesus, their unhesitating answer was: 'Whether it be right in the sight of God to hearken unto you more than unto God, judge ye. For we cannot but speak the things which we have seen and heard' (Acts 4:19, 20). No command to do anything morally wrong can be binding on the conscience.

From the principles here laid down, some have inferred that civil authority is wholly inapplicable to matters of religion. Nothing, however, can be farther from the design of the Confession than to countenance this notion. That there is a lawful exercise of civil power about religious matters the compilers of the Confession clearly teach, in the fourth section of this chapter, and also in chapter 23. And as it was not their design, in this section, to condemn this exercise of civil authority, so no such doctrine can justly be inferred from the words; for, 'if they condemn all exercise of civil authority', to use the language of Dr. M'Crie, 'then they condemn also all exercise of every other species of human authority about these things, whether ecclesiastical, parental, etc. Is it not equally true, that God hath left the conscience "free from the doctrines and commandments of men, which are in anything contrary to his Word, or beside it, in matters of faith or worship", whether these be the doctrines and commandments of ministers or magistrates, of master or parents? Is not "an implicit faith", or "an absolute and blind obedience", unreasonable and sinful, whether it be yielded to synods or parliaments? The design of the words is, to teach the subordination of all human power to the sovereignty and laws of God, particularly in matters of faith and worship. Nay, they seem in that passage to be more immediately levelled against invasions by Church authority, which have been fully as frequent and pernicious in religion as those of civil rulers; such as the assumed lordship of popes, councils, prelates, and convocations, in devising new articles of faith, decreeing and imposing unscriptural rights and ceremonies, canons, etc., here called "the doctrines and commandments of men", in contradistinction from divine institutions; as the traditons and superstitions of the Scribes and Pharisees, superadded to the divine law, are called by our Lord. If civil rulers concur in these impositions, or if they shall attempt the like by their own sole authority, and the claim of an ecclesiastical supremacy, this doctrine equally condemns their tyranny, and teaches, that no error, will-worship, or any species of false religion, by whomsoever commanded in Churches or States, can lay any obligation on conscience, which is immediately subject to God alone. But no such thing is taught, as that men's consciences are set free from obedience to any human authority, when acting in entire consistency with the Word of God, and enjoining nothing beside it, or beyond its own proper limits; which authority of any kind may certainly do.'[1]

Section 3
They who, upon pretence of Christian liberty, do practise any sin, or cherish any lust, do thereby destroy the end of Christian liberty; which is, that, being delivered out of the hands of our enemies, we might serve the Lord without fear, in holiness, and righteousness before him, all the days of our life (Galatians 5:13; 1 Peter 2:16; 2 Peter 2:19; John 8:34; Luke 1:74, 75).

Section 4
And because the powers which God hath ordained, and the liberty which Christ hath purchased, are not intended by God to destroy, but mutually to uphold and preserve one another; they who, upon pretence of Christian liberty, shall oppose any lawful power, or the lawful exercise of it, whether it be civil or ecclesiastical, resist the ordinance of God (Matthew 12:25; 1 Peter 2:13, 14, 16; Romans 13:1-8; Hebrews 13:17). And for their publishing of such opinions, or maintaining of such practices, as are contrary to the light of nature, or to the known principles of Christianity, whether concerning faith, worship, or conversation; or to the power of godliness; or such erroneous opinions or practices, as either in their own nature, or in the manner of publishing or maintaining them, are destructive to the external peace and order which Christ hath established in the Church; they may lawfully be called to account, and

1. M'Crie's Statement, pp. 100, 101.

proceeded against by the censures of the Church (Romans 1:32; 1 Corinthians 5:1, 5, 11, 13; 2 John 10,11; 2 Thessalonians 3:14; 1 Timothy 6:3-5; Titus 1:10, 11, 13; 3:10; Matthew 18:15-17; 1 Timothy 1:19, 20; Revelation 2:2, 14, 15, 20; 3:9), and by the power of the civil magistrate (Deuteronomy 13:6-12; Romans 13:3, 4; 2 John 10, 11; Ezra 7:23, 25-28; Revelation 17:12, 16, 17; Nehemiah 13:15, 17, 21, 22, 25, 30; 2 Kings 23:5, 6, 9, 20, 21; 2 Chronicles 34:33; 15:12, 13, 16; Daniel 3:29; 1 Timothy 2:2; Isaiah 49:23; Zechariah 13:2, 3).

Exposition

The liberty pleaded for in our Confession is not absolute and uncontrollable. To assert that men have a right to think and act as they please, without respect to the moral law, and without being responsible to God, would be atheistical. And, if men are considered as socially united, and as placed under government, their natural rights, in religious as well as in civil things, must be liable to restraint and regulations, so far as the interests and ends of society require. Accordingly, the Confession, in the above sections, proceeds to guard the doctrine of liberty of conscience against abuse, *first*, in reference to the authority of God in his law; and, *secondly*, in reference to the authorities on earth, civil and ecclesiastical. With respect to the former, it declares, that 'they who, upon pretence of Christian liberty, do practise any sin, or cherish any lust, do thereby destroy the end of Christian liberty.' God has not liberated the conscience from the obligation of his own law; on the contrary, he requires every one to yield implicit and prompt obedience to all things whatsoever he has commanded. To plead for a liberty to practise any known sin, is to plead for licentiousness; and for persons to indulge themselves in any corrupt affections and practices, under a pretence of Christian liberty, is to 'use their liberty for an occasion to the flesh'. With respect to the latter, the Confession mentions certain things for which persons of a certain description may be proceeded against, both by the civil and ecclesiastical authorities. It is to be observed, however, that the intention of this section is not to lay down the extent of the provinces of these powers, but only to remove the plea of conscience; and it ought to be understood, in consistency with their acting each in its own province, without the one interfering with the causes which come under the cognizance of the other. Although civil rulers may restrain, and, when occasion requires, may punish the more flagrant violations of the first table of the moral law, such as blasphemy, the publishing of blasphemous opinions, and the open and gross profanation of the Sabbath, yet they are to repress these evils, not formally as sins, which is the prerogative of God, nor as scandals, in which light they come under the cognizance of the Church, but as crimes and injuries done to society.

All sound Presbyterians disclaim all intolerant or compulsory measures with regard to matters purely religious. They maintain that no man should be punished or molested on account of his religious opinions or observations, provided there is nothing in these hurtful to the general interests of society, or dangerous to the lawful institutions of the country in which he lives. The section now under consideration, however, has sometimes been represented as arming the civil magistrate with a power to punish good and peaceable subjects purely on account of their religious opinions and practices, or as favourable to persecution for conscience' sake. In vindicating the Confession from this serious charge, we shall avail ourselves of the judicious remarks of Dr. M'Crie. 'The design of section fourth,' says that eminent author, 'is to guard against the abuse of the doctrine' of liberty of conscience "in reference to public authority. 'And because the powers which God hath ordained, and the liberty which Christ hath purchased, are not intended by God to destroy, but mutually to uphold and preserve one another, they who, upon pretence of Christian liberty, shall oppose any lawful power, or the lawful exercise of it, whether it be civil of ecclesiastical, resist the ordinance of God." He who is the Lord of the conscience has also instituted the authorities in Church and State; and it would be in the highest degree absurd to suppose that he has planted in the breast of every individual a power to resist, counteract, and nullify his own ordinances. When public and private claims interfere and clash, the latter must give way to the former; and when any lawful authority is proceeding lawfully within its line of duty, it must be understood as possessing a rightful power to remove out of the way everything which necessarily obstructs its progress. The Confession proceeds, accordingly to state: "And for their publishing of such opinions, or maintaining of such practices, as are contrary to the light of nature, or to the known principles of Christianity, whether concerning faith, worship, or conversation, or to the power of godliness; or such erroneous opinions or practices as, either in their own nature or in the manner of publishing and maintaining them, are destructive to the external peace and order which Christ hath established in the Church; they may lawfully be called to account, and proceeded against by the censures of the Church, and by the power of the civil magistrate." Now, this does not say that all who publish such opinions, and maintain such practices as are mentioned, may be proceeded against, or punished (if the substitution of this word shall be insisted for) by the civil magistrate; nor does it say that any good and peaceable subject shall be made liable to this process simply on the ground of religious opinions published, and practices maintained by him.

'For, in the *first* place, persons of a particular character are spoken of in this paragraph, and these are very different from good and peaceable subjects. They are described in the former sentence as "they who *oppose* lawful power, or the lawful exercise of it", and "*resist* the ordinance of God". The same persons are spoken of in the sentence under consideration, as appears from the copulative and the relative. It is not said "*Any one* for publishing" etc., but, "they who *oppose* any lawful power" etc., "for *their* publishing" etc.

'In the *second* place, this sentence specifies some of the ways in which these persons may become chargeable with the opposition mentioned, and consequently '*may* be called to account'; but it does not assert that even they must or ought to be prosecuted for every avowed opinion or practice of the kind referred to. All that it necessarily implies is, that they may be found opposing lawful powers, or the lawful exercise of them in the things specified; and that they are not entitled to plead a general irresponsibility in matters of that kind. Notwithstanding such a plea, "they may be called to account, and proceeded against".

'For, be it observed, it is not the design of this paragraph to state the objects of Church censure or civil prosecution; its proper and professed object is to interpose a check on the abuse of liberty of conscience, as operating to the prejudice of just and lawful authority. It is not sin as *sin*, but as *scandal*, or injurious to the spiritual interests of Christians, that is the proper object of Church censure; and it is not for sins as such, but for *crimes*, that persons become liable to punishment by magistrates. The compilers of the Confession were quite aware of these distinctions, which were then common.

'Some think that if the process of the magistrate had been limited to offences "contrary to the light of nature", it would have been perfectly justifiable; but the truth is, that it would have been so only on the interpretation now given. To render an action the proper object of magistratical punishment, it is not enough that it be contrary to the law of God, whether natural or revealed; it must, in one way or another, strike against the public good of society. He who "provides not for his own, especially those of his own house", sins against "the light of nature", as also does he who is "a lover of pleasures more than of God"; but there are few who will plead that magistrates are bound to proceed against, and punish every idler and belly-god.

'On the other hand, there are opinions and practices "contrary to the known principles of Christianity", or grafted upon them, which, either in their own nature, or from the circumstances with which they may be clothed, may prove so injurious to the welfare of society in general, or of particular nations, or of their just proceedings, or of lawful institutions established in them, as to subject their publishers and maintainers to warrantable coercion and punishment. As one point to which these may relate, I may mention the external observance and sanctification of the Lord's day, which can be known only from "the principles of Christianity", and is connected with all the particulars specified by the Confession, "faith, worship, conversation, the power of godliness, and the external order and peace of the Church". That many other instances of a similar description can be produced, will be denied by no sober-thinking person who is well acquainted with Popish tenets and practices, and with those which prevailed among the English sectaries during the sitting of the Westminster Assembly; and he who does not deny this, cannot be entitled, I should think, upon any principles of fair construction, to fix the stigma of persecution on the passage in question.'[2]

---

2. M'Crie's Appendix to *Discourses on the Unity of the Church*, pp. 134-137.

CHAPTER 21

RELIGIOUS WORSHIP,
AND THE SABBATH-DAY

Section 1
The light of nature showeth that there is a God, who hath lordship and sovereignty over all; is good, and doeth good unto all; and is, therefore, to be feared, loved, praised, called upon, trusted in, and served, with all the heart, and with all the soul, and with all the might (Romans 1:20; Acts 17:24; Psalm 119:68; Jeremiah 10:7; Psalms 31:23; 18:3; Romans 10:12; Psalm 62:8; Joshua 24:14; Mark 12:33). But the acceptable way of worshipping the true God is instituted by himself, and so limited by his own revealed will, that he may not be worshipped according to the imaginations and devices of men, or the suggestions of Satan, under any visible representation, or any other way not prescribed in the Holy Scripture (Deuteronomy 12:32; Matthew 15:9; Acts 17:25; Matthew 4:9, 10; Deuteronomy 15:1-20; Exodus 20:4-6; Colossians 2:23).

Exposition
Religious worship consists in that homage and honour which we give to God, as a being of infinite perfection; whereby we profess our subjection to, and confidence in him, as our chief good and only happiness. It may be viewed as either internal or external; the former consisting in that inward homage which we owe to God, such as loving, believing, fearing, trusting in him, and other elicit acts of the mind; the latter consisting in the outward expression of that homage, by the observance of his instituted ordinances.

Concerning the external worship of God, our Confession affirms, in the first place, that God can be worshipped acceptably only in the way of his own appointment. As God is the sole object of religious worship, so it is his prerogative to prescribe the mode of it. Divine institution must, therefore, be our rule of worship; and whatever may be imagined to be useful and decent, must be examined and determined by this rule. It is not left to human prudence to make any alterations in, or additions to, God's own appointments. 'What thing soever I command you,' saith the Lord, 'observe to do it; thou shalt not add thereto, nor diminish from it' (Deuteronomy 12:32). To introduce into the worship of God what may be deemed significant ceremonies, under the pretext of beautifying the worship, and exciting the devotion of the worshippers, is to be guilty of superstition and will-worship.

In the second place, our Confession particularly condemns the worshipping of God 'under any visible representation'. The worshipping of God in or by images is one of the worst corruptions of the Church of Rome. God is a spiritual, invisible, and incomprehensible being, and cannot, therefore, be represented by any corporeal likeness or figure. 'To whom will ye liken me, or shall I be equal? saith the Holy One' (Isaiah 40:25). 'We ought not to think that the Godhead is like unto gold, or silver, or stone, graven by art and man's device' (Acts 17:29). The Israelites were expressly forbidden to make any image of God. In Deuteronomy 4:15, 16, Moses insists that 'they saw no manner of similitude on the day that the LORD spake to them in Horeb, lest they should corrupt themselves, and make them a graven image'. And, therefore, he charges them (verse 23) 'to take heed lest they should forget the covenant of the LORD their God, and make them a graven image'. The Scripture forbids the worshipping of God by images, although they may not be intended as proper similitudes, but only as emblematical representations of God. Every visible form which is designed to recall God to our thoughts, and to excite our devotions, and before which we perform our religious offices, is expressly prohibited in the second commandment (Exodus 20:4). The Church of Rome, being sensible that this precept condemns their doctrine and practice, make it an appendage to the first commandment, and leave it out in their catechism and books of devotion.

In the third place, our Confession not only condemns the worshipping of God by images, but also the worshipping him 'in any other way not prescribed in the Holy Scripture'. Not only has the Church of Rome corrupted the worship of God by a multitude of insignificant ceremonies, but even some Protestant Churches retain many of the usages of Popery, and enjoin the wearing of particular vestments by the ministers of religion, the observation of numerous festival days, the erection of altars in churches, the sign of the cross in baptism, bowing at the name of Jesus, and kneeling at the Lord's Supper. These practices we justly reckon superstitious, because there is no scriptural warrant for them, and they are the inventions of men. It were well if those who enjoin and those who observe them would consider the words of God concerning the Jews: 'In vain do they worship me, teaching for doctrines the commandments of men' (Matthew 15:9).

Section 2
Religious worship is to be given to God, the Father, Son, and Holy Ghost; and to him alone (Matthew 4:10; John 5:23; 2 Corinthians 13:14): not to angels, saints, or any other creature (Colossians 2:18; Revelation 19:10; Romans 1:25): and, since the fall, not without a Mediator; nor in the mediation of any other but of Christ alone (John 14:6; 1 Timothy 2:5; Ephesians 2:18; Colossians 3:17).

Exposition
In this section the object of religious worship is defined.

1. Our Confession affirms that religious worship is to be given to God alone. While the first commandment forbids us to have any other gods before him, it requires us to worship him alone. Most explicit, too, was the answer which Christ gave to Satan, when he would have our Saviour to fall down and worship him. 'It is written,' he replied, 'Thou shalt worship the Lord thy God, and him only shalt thou serve' (Matthew 4:10). And when the Apostle John attempted to offer religious worship to an angel, either through surprise, or through a mistake of him for Jesus Christ, the angel said unto him, 'See thou do it not; worship God' (Revelation 22:8, 9); thereby intimating that God alone is to be worshipped.

There can be only one true God, but there are three distinct persons in the Godhead; these three persons are designated the Father, the Son, and the Holy Ghost; and religious worship is due to each of these persons. Although Christians usually address their supplications to the Father, in the name of the Son, and by the assistance of the Holy Ghost, yet divine worship may be performed to any of the adorable Three immediately. And it must ever be remembered, that when any one of the persons of the Godhead is immediately addressed, the other two are included. These divine persons are only one object of worship, because they are only one Being – one God.

2. In opposition to the Papists, who maintain, that not only God, but good angels and departed saints, being canonized by the Pope, ought to be worshipped, even in a religious manner, our Confession affirms that neither angels, nor saints, nor any other creature, ought to receive religious worship. The worshipping of

angels is expressly forbidden by the Apostle Paul: 'Let no man beguile you of your reward, in a voluntary humility and worshipping of angels' (Colossians 2:18). And when the Apostle John was going to worship the angel, he absolutely refused it, and ordered him to direct his worship to God himself: 'I fell at his feet to worship him; and he said unto me, See thou do it not: I am thy fellow-servant; worship God' (Revelation 19:10). Papists are likewise guilty of gross idolatry, in worshipping saints departed, especially the Virgin Mary. To the saints they pray, make vows, swear by them, consecrate altars and temples to them, offer incense, and, in short, render to them all the honours which are paid to God himself. They, no doubt, pretend that the worship which they give to the saints is not precisely the same in kind and degree with that which they give to God; but, however, they may distinguish in theory, the greater part make no distinction in practice. To render any kind of religious worship to departed saints cannot be vindicated by Scripture. Christians are desired to remember them that had the rule over them (Hebrews 13:17), but no intimation is given of worshipping them. Several of the apostles and first Christians, particularly James the Great and Stephen, had suffered martyrdom when the Epistles were written; but no mention is made of offering prayers to them. The invocation of saints implies either that they are everywhere, or that they know all things; but omnipresence and omniscience are divine perfections, incommunicable to any creature.

Our Confession condemns the worshipping not only of angels and saints, but also of 'any other creature'. And Papists have a multiplicity of objects of worship besides those here specified. They not only worship departed saints themselves, but even their *relics*. The Council of Trent authorised the adoration of relics; and they continue in high esteem among the Papists to the present day. But as God effectually guarded against the superstition into which the Jews might have fallen with respect to the remains of Moses, by taking care that his body should be buried in such a manner that 'no man knew of his sepulchre' (Deuteronomy 34:6); so this certainly justifies us in doing no further honour to the bodies of saints than merely interring them. We know that the early Christians took no further care about Stephen's body than to bury it with decency (Acts 8:2). And as the worshipping of relics is directly contrary to the practice of the primitive Christians, so it is utterly irreconcilable with common sense.

It was also decreed by the Council of Trent, that 'due honour and veneration' be given to the images of Christ, of the blessed Virgin, and other saints.[1] Papists, accordingly, bow down to images, kiss them, offer incense, and pray to them. They may tell us that they do not terminate their worship on the image itself, but worship God in and by it. The same thing might have been said both by enlightened heathens and by the Jews, yet this did not exempt them from the charge of idolatry. The Israelites professed to worship Jehovah by the golden calf (Exodus 32:5); and the calves set up at Dan and Bethel, by Jeroboam, were intended only as means whereby to worship the true God (1 Kings 12:26). Not only the worshipping of images themselves, but the use of them in worship, even when the true God is worshipped in and by them, is called idolatry in Scripture.

This section likewise refers to the medium by which acceptable worship must be offered to God. In the state of innocence man had liberty of access to God at all times, and needed none to mediate between him and his Creator; but, since the fall, no acceptable worship can be given to God without a mediator. And, in opposition to Papists, who maintain that angels, departed saints, and chiefly the Virgin Mary, are mediators and intercessors between God and man, our Confession affirms, that there is no other mediator but Christ alone. The Scripture expressly assures us that 'there is one God, and one Mediator between God and man, the man Christ Jesus' (1 Timothy 2:5). Christ declares of himself, 'I am the way; no man cometh to the Father but by me' (John 14:6); and 'by him we have access to the Father' (Ephesians 2:18).

Papists grant that Jesus Christ is the alone mediator of *redemption*; but they join angels and saints with him as mediators of *intercession*. On this point, indeed, they are not agreed among themselves. Some hold that, along with our now glorified Mediator, the holy angels and departed saints intercede with God for us. Others hold that they only act as mediators between Christ and us. The Scripture, however, gives no warrant for these distinctions. It represents the intercession of Christ as founded upon the invaluable merit of his atoning sacrifice. He who is our Advocate with the Father is also the propitiation for our sins

1. Con. Trid., Sess. 25.

(1 John 2:1, 2). He is Mediator of intercession, because he is Mediator of redemption; and upon this account his intercession is effectual. Glorified saints are indebted to free grace for their own admission into heaven, and they have no merit to apply to others. To solicit their intercession supposes that they hear our prayers and are acquainted with our circumstances; but this is a gratuitous assumption. To employ them to intercede for us with God, is highly derogatory to the honour of Christ; for it implies that he is either unmindful of his office, or that he has not interest enough to obtain from God the blessings we need. To employ them to intercede for us with Christ himself is also dishonouring to him; for it must imply, that there are more disposed 'to sympathize with us than our merciful High Priest, who is touched with a feeling of our infirmities, and was, in all points, tempted like as we are'.

While the doctrine of the Church of Rome upon this subject degrades the Lord Jesus Christ, it invests departed saints with the honours and attributes of Deity. It must import that they are omnipresent and omniscient; for how could the Virgin Mary, for example, otherwise have any knowledge of the prayers which are addressed to her at the same time in ten thousand places, and, it may be, by millions of individuals? Protestants, therefore, with good reason, reject the notion of angelical and human intercessors, and rely solely on the intercession of that glorious Mediator whom the Father always heareth.

Section 3
Prayer with thanksgiving, being one special part of religious worship (Philippians 4:6), is by God required of all men (Psalm 65:2); and, that it may be accepted, it is to be made in the name of the Son (John 14:13, 14; 1 Peter 2:5), by the help of his Spirit (Romans 8:26), according to his will (1 John 5:14), with understanding, reverence, humility, fervency, faith, love and perseverance (Psalm 47:7; Ecclesiastes 5:1, 2; Hebrews 12:28; Genesis 18:27; James 5:16; 1:6, 7; Mark 11:24; Matthew 6:12, 14, 15; Colossians 4:2; Ephesians 6:18); and, if vocal, in a known tongue (1 Corinthians 14:14).

Section 4
Prayer is to be made for things lawful (1 John 5:14), and for all sorts of men living, or that shall live hereafter (1 Timothy 2:1, 2; John 17:20; 2 Samuel 7:29; Ruth 4:12); but not for the dead (2 Samuel 12:21-23; Luke 16:25, 26; Revelation 14:13), nor for those of whom it may be known that they have sinned the sin unto death (1 John 5:16).

Exposition

Our Confession having given a general description of religious worship, in regard to its object, and the manner in which it ought to be performed, proceeds now to give a more particular account of the several parts of religious worship; and, in the sections under our consideration, it treats of prayer, which is one special part of that worship we owe to God. Prayer, when taken in its most extensive sense, includes: adoration, or a devout celebration of the perfections of God, and of his works, in which they are displayed; confession of our sins to God; thanksgiving for the favours which we have received from him; and petition for the blessings of which we stand in need. But prayer, in the strict sense of the word, consists in petition alone; and in this light we shall view it in the observations we have to offer in illustration of the statements of the Confession.

1. *Prayer is a duty incumbent on all men.* As dependent creatures we owe this homage to God. 'In him we live, and move, and have our being'; and 'from him cometh every good gift, and every perfect gift'. What, then, can be more reasonable than to acknowledge our constant dependence on him, and make daily application to him for the supply of our wants?

That God knows our wants before we tell him of them, and that his infinite goodness will prompt him to bestow what is conducive to our happiness, have been sometimes urged as arguments against the necessity and utility of prayer. But, although prayer is certainly not necessary to give information to God, and is not intended to excite the divine benevolence, yet it does not follow that it is superfluous; because there may be other reasons of great importance for which it is required. It may be designed to impress our own minds more deeply with a sense of our wants, and to bring them into that state in which alone it is proper that the blessings we solicit should be bestowed upon us. Besides, prayer is the divinely appointed means of obtaining from our heavenly Father the blessings we need. He has commanded us to ask, and promised we shall receive (Matthew 7:7). He has given us many exceeding great and precious promises, and he has said: 'For this will I be inquired of by the house of Israel, to do it for them' (Ezekiel 36:37).

It has also been alleged, 'that wicked and unregenerate men ought not to pray unto God at all'. This error was broached by certain sectaries, at the very period when our Confession was compiled;[2] and it has been revived in our own day. It is maintained that, because unbelievers cannot pray acceptably, they ought not to pray at all. It will be readily admitted that the prayer of faith can alone be acceptable; still we must hold that all men are bound to pray to God.

(1) Prayer is a duty required by the mere light of nature, and must, therefore, be incumbent on all men (Jonah 1:5, 6, 14).

(2) Prayer is a duty enjoined upon men indiscriminately, and universally in the Word of God (Psalm 65:2; Philippians 4:6; 1 Thessalonians 5:17).

(3) If unbelievers, or unregenerate men ought not to pray, then their omission of prayer would not be their sin; but their neglect of prayer is always represented in Scripture as highly criminal (Psalm 10:4; Jeremiah 10:25).

(4) The Apostle Peter required Simon Magus to pray unto God, though he was then 'in the gall of bitterness, and in the bond of iniquity' (Acts 8:22, 23).

(5) Prayer is an appointed means of grace which all men ought to improve. Though it is not for our praying, yet it is in the way of prayer, as God's instituted order, that we may expect any blessing from him (Matthew 7:7). Every one that needs and desires any good thing from God is, therefore, bound to ask it by prayer.

(6) Though the prayer as well as the ploughing of the wicked be sinful, because not done by them in a right manner, yet the matter of it being lawful and good in itself, their neglect of it is a greater abomination (Proverbs 15:8; 21:4). For these reasons we must maintain, agreeably to our Confession, that 'prayer is by God required of all men'.

2. *Prayer is to be made for things that are lawful, or according to the will of God.* As our petitions ought to be regulated by the revealed will of God, his Word must be the rule of prayer. Nor by this rule are our prayers circumscribed within narrow limits; for nothing really necessary for us can be pointed out which is not contained in some divine declarations or promise. We are warranted to ask temporal mercies of God; for 'our heavenly Father knoweth that we have need of these things' (Matthew 6:32); but spiritual mercies ought to have the preference in our requests; for thus saith our Saviour: 'Seek ye first the kingdom of God, and his

---

2. Edward's *Gangraena,* part i., p. 27.

righteousness, and all these things shall be added unto you' (Matthew 6:33). If we regulate our petitions by the Word of God, then we may feel the utmost confidence that there is an entire harmony between his will and our desires; and we may take the full encouragement of that beautiful and comprehensive promise: 'If ye abide in me, and my words abide in you, ye shall ask what you will, and it shall be done unto you' (John 15:7; see also, 1 John 5:14).

3. *Prayer is to be made in the name of Christ.* Our Saviour frequently enjoins us to ask all things in his name, and assures us that all our lawful desires and requests, presented in his name, shall be granted (John 14:13, 14; 16:23, 24). It is not enough, however, that we merely introduce the name of Christ into our prayers, or that we conclude them with the bare words: 'All that we ask is for Christ's sake.' To pray in the name of Christ is to draw all our encouragement to pray from Christ alone, to engage in this duty in dependence upon his strength, and to rely upon his merit and intercession alone for access to God, and for acceptance and a gracious answer to our prayers.

4. *Prayer is to be made in dependence upon the assistance of the Holy Spirit.* This is frequently mentioned in Scripture as requisite to acceptable prayer (Ephesians 6:18; Jude 20). We know not what to pray for as we ought, so that, without the assistance of the Spirit, we are in danger of asking amiss in regard to the matter of our requests. Neither do we know how to pray as we ought. But the Spirit is promised to help our infirmities, by enlightening our minds in the knowledge of our needs, bringing to our remembrance the promises which are our encouragement to ask of God the supply of our wants, and exciting within us those affections and graces which are necessary to acceptable prayer (Romans 8:26, 29).

5. If we would have our prayers accepted of God, *they must be offered up in a right manner*, which includes a variety of things. We must pray:

1. With *understanding* (Psalm 47:7); with some knowledge of God, the alone object of prayer; of our wants, the subject-matter of prayer; of the person and work of Christ, the alone medium of acceptable prayer; and of the promises, which are our encouragement in prayer.

2. With *reverence* (Hebrews 12:28), arising from a deep

sense of the infinite majesty and unspotted holiness of God.

3. With *humility* (Genesis 18:27), arising from a deep impression of our own unworthiness and sinfulness.

4. With *fervency* (James 5:16), arising from a lively apprehension of our own wants, and of the invaluable nature of the blessings which we ask of God.

5. With *faith* (James 1:6), believing that we shall receive what we ask according to the will of God.

6. With *love* (1 Timothy 2:8), cherishing an ardent desire after God's presence with us, and an affectionate regard to all those for whom we ought to pray.

7. With *importunity and perseverance* (Matthew 15:22-28; Ephesians 6:18), pressing our suit, and renewing our petition again and again, until a gracious answer is obtained.

8. *Hopefully*, waiting upon God, with submission to his will, and looking for an answer to our supplications (Psalm 5:3; Micah 7:7).

6. *Prayer, at least when public and social, ought to be offered up in a known tongue*. This condemns the doctrine and practice of the Church of Rome, which maintains that it is not needful that public prayers be in a known tongue, and still continues to perform her service in the Latin language, which has ceased to be vernacular for a thousand years. This practice is so contrary to common sense, that no argument can be necessary to support the statement of our Confession in opposition to it. It is sufficient to observe, that the Apostle Paul occupies nearly the whole of the 14th chapter of the First Epistle to the Corinthians in showing that public prayers ought to be offered up in the vulgar tongue. He would rather speak five words which the people could understand, than ten thousand in an unknown tongue. He lays down this general rule: 'Let all things be done unto edifying'. But how can the people be edified by worship performed in a language which they do not understand?

7. *Prayer is to be made 'for all sorts of men living, or that shall live hereafter; but not for the dead, nor for those of whom it may be known that they have sinned the sin unto death'*. We ought to pray 'for the whole Church of Christ upon earth – for magistrates and ministers; our brethren, yea, our enemies'.[3] And as Christ

3. *The Larger Catechism*, Question 183.

prayed for those that should afterwards believe on him (John 17:20), so we should pray for the advancement of his kingdom in the world until his second coming (Psalm 102:18).

The statement that we are not to pray for the dead is levelled against the Church of Rome, which maintains that prayers and masses ought to be performed for departed souls, and may really profit them. In Scripture we find no precept requiring us to pray for the dead, nor any promise that God will hear our prayers for them, nor any example of prayer being offered on their behalf; for when Paul prayed that 'Onesiphorus might find mercy of the Lord in that day' (2 Timothy 1:18), it cannot be proved that Onesiphorus was then dead. David ceased praying for his child when once it was removed by death (2 Samuel 12:22, 23). The state of the dead is unalterably fixed, and therefore our prayers cannot profit them (Luke 16:22-26).

The statement, that we are not to pray for those who are known to have sinned the sin unto death, is founded on the express words of the Apostle John: 'If any man see his brother sin a sin which is not unto death, he shall ask, and he shall give him life for them that sin not unto death. There is a sin unto death: I do not say that he shall pray for it' (1 John 5:16). The sin unto death most probably is the sin against the Holy Ghost, which alone is pronounced to be unpardonable; and the irremissible nature of that sin is evidently the reason why prayer is forbidden for the person who is known to be guilty of it.

Section 5

The reading of the Scriptures with godly fear (Acts 15:21; Revelation 1:3); the sound preaching (2 Timothy 4:2), and conscionable hearing of the Word, in obedience unto God, with understanding, faith, and reverence (James 1:22; Acts 10:33; Matthew 13:19; Hebrews 4:2; Isaiah 66:2); singing of psalms with grace in the heart (Colossians 3:16; Ephesians 5:19; James 5:13); as also the due administration and worthy receiving of the sacraments instituted by Christ; are all parts of the ordinary religious worship of God (Matthew 28:19; 1 Corinthians 11:23-29; Acts 2:42): besides religious oaths (Deuteronomy 6:13; Nehemiah 10:29), and vows (Isaiah 19:21; Ecclesiastes 5:4, 5), solemn fastings (Joel 2:12; Esther 4:16; Matthew 9:15; 1 Corinthians 7:5), and thanksgivings upon special occasions (Psalm 107; Esther 9:22), which are, in their several times and seasons, to be used in an holy and religious manner (Hebrews 12:28).

Exposition

Our Confession having explained the duty of prayer, proceeds to enumerate the other ordinances of religious worship; some of which are ordinary and stated, others extraordinary and occasional.

1. *The reading of the Scriptures.* The reading of the Word of God ought to be attended to in public (Nehemiah 8:8; Luke 4:16); in families (Deuteronomy 6:6-9; Psalm 78:5); and in secret (John 5:39).

'The Holy Scriptures are to be read with a high and reverent esteem of them; with a firm persuasion that they are the very Word of God, and that he only can enable us to understand them; with desire to know, believe, and obey the will of God revealed in them; with diligence and attention to the matter and scope of them; with meditation, application, self-denial and prayer.'[4]

2. *The preaching and hearing of the Word.* The preaching of the Word is a divine ordinance, and appointed to continue in the Church to the end of the world (1 Corinthians 1:21; Matthew 28:20). That the office of the ministry is of divine institution, and a distinct office in the Church, appears from the following considerations:

(1) Peculiar titles are in Scripture given to the ministers of the gospel. They are called pastors, teachers, stewards of the mysteries of God, bishops or overseers of the flock, and angels of the Churches.

(2) Peculiar duties are assigned to them. They are to preach the Word, to rebuke and to instruct gainsayers (2 Timothy 4:2; 2:25); to administer the sacraments (Matthew 28:19; 1 Corinthians 11:23); to watch over the flock, as those that must give an account (Hebrews 13:17); to give attendance to reading, to exhortation, to doctrine; to meditate upon these things, and give themselves wholly to them (1 Timothy 2:13, 15).

(3) Peculiar duties are required of the people in reference to their ministers. They are called to know and acknowledge them that labour among them, and are over them in the Lord (1 Thessalonians 5:12); to esteem them highly in love for their work's sake (1 Thessalonians 5:13); and to obey them that have the rule over them, and submit themselves (Hebrew 13:17); to provide for their maintenance (Galatians 6:6); and to pray for them

---

4. *The Larger Catechism*, Question 157.

(2 Thessalonians 3:1). These things clearly prove that the ministry is a distinct office in the Church.

Though all may and ought to read the Word of God, yet it is to be preached 'only by such as are sufficiently gifted, and also duly approved and called to that office'.[5] Christians should improve their gifts and opportunities in a private way for mutual admonition and edification; but none, whatever gifts they may possess, are warranted to preach the gospel unless they have the call of Christ for that purpose. The apostles received their call immediately from Christ himself, and they were empowered to commit that sacred trust to inferior teachers; these, again, were commanded to commit it to faithful men who should be able to teach others; and none have a right to preach the gospel, in ordinary cases, but those who are thus authorised by Christ through the medium of persons already vested with official power in the Church. In the primitive Church, those who preached the Word were solemnly set apart to their office by 'the laying on of the hands of the presbytery' (1 Timothy 4:14).

A regular call to preach the gospel is necessary, on account of the people; for all the success of a minister's labours depends on the blessing of Christ, and the people have no warrant to expect this blessing upon the labours of those who are not the servants of Christ (Jeremiah 23:32).

This call is no less necessary for the comfort and encouragement of ministers themselves; for as the work of the ministry is a work of peculiar difficulty and danger, so none are warranted to expect divine support and protection in the discharge of that work, but those who act under a divine commission (Romans 10:14, 15; Acts 26:16, 17).

3. *Singing of psalms.* This was enjoined, under the Old Testament, as a part of the ordinary worship of God, and it is distinguished from ceremonial worship (Psalm 69:30, 31). It is not abrogated under the New Testament, but rather confirmed (Ephesians 5:19; Colossians 3:16). It is sanctioned by the example of Christ and his apostles (Matthew 26:30; Acts 16:25). The Psalms of David were especially intended by God for the use of the Church, in the exercise of public praise, under the former dispensation; and they are equally adapted to the use of the Church under the present dispensation. Although the apostles insist much upon the aboli-

5. *Ibid.*, Question 158.

tion of ritual institutions, they give no intimation that the Psalms of David are unsuitable for gospel-worship; and had it been intended that they should be set aside in New Testament times, there is reason to think that another psalmody would have been provided in their room. In the Book of Psalms there are various passages which seem to indicate that they were intended by the Spirit for the use of the Church in all ages. 'I will extol thee, my God, O King,' says David, 'and I will bless thy name for ever and ever' (Psalm 145:1). This intimates, as the excellent Henry remarks, 'that the Psalms which David penned should be made use of in praising God by the Church to the end of time'. We ought to praise God with our lips as well as with our spirits, and should exert ourselves to do it 'skilfully' (Psalm 33:3). As this is a part of public worship in which the whole congregation should unite their voices, persons ought to cultivate sacred music, that they may be able to join in this exercise with becoming harmony. But the chief thing is to sing with understanding, and with affections of heart corresponding to the matter sung (Psalm 47:7; 1 Corinthians 16:15; Psalm 108:1).

4. *The due administration and worthy receiving of the sacraments instituted by Christ.* As subsequent chapters treat fully of these ordinances, we pass them at present.

5. *Religious oaths and vows.* These will come under our consideration in the next chapter.

6. *Solemn fasting and thanksgivings.* Stated festival-days, commonly called *holy-days*, have no warrant in the Word of God; but a day may be set apart, by competent authority, for fasting or thanksgiving, when extraordinary dispensations of Providence administer cause for them. When judgements are threatened or inflicted, or when some special blessing is to be sought and obtained, fasting is eminently seasonable. When some remarkable mercy or deliverance has been received, there is a special call to thanksgiving. The views of the compilers of our Confession respecting these ordinances may be found in 'The Directory for the Public Worship of God'.

Section 6
Neither prayer, nor any other part of religious worship, is, now under the gospel, either tied unto, or made more acceptable by, any place in which it is performed, or towards which it is directed (John 4:21): but

God is to be worshipped everywhere (Malachi 1:11; 1 Timothy 2:8), in spirit and in truth (John 4:23, 24); as in private families (Jeremiah 10:25; Deuteronomy 6:6, 7; Job 1:5; 2 Samuel 6:18, 20; 1 Peter 3:7; Acts 10:2), daily (Matthew 6:11), and in secret each one by himself (Matthew 6:6; Ephesians 6:18); so more solemnly in the public assemblies, which are not carelessly or wilfully to be neglected or forsaken, when God, by his Word or providence, calleth thereunto (Isaiah 56:6, 7; Hebrews 10:25; Proverbs 1:20, 21, 24; 8:34; Acts 13:42; Luke 4:16; Acts 2:42).

Exposition

Under the gospel, all difference of places for religious worship is abolished. We are required to 'worship the Father in spirit and in truth' (John 4:21); without respect of places; and 'to pray everywhere, lifting up holy hands without wrath and doubting' (1 Timothy 2:8). This condemns the practice of consecrating churches, and ascribing holiness to them; and also the superstitious opinion that religious services are more acceptable to God and beneficial to men in one place than another.

1. *Religious worship ought to be performed in private families daily.* This is a duty which the light of nature very plainly teaches. And the heathens will rise up in judgment against the prayerless families of professed Christians; for besides their tutelar deities, who were supposed to preside over cities and nations, and who had public honours paid to them in that character, they had their household gods, whom every private family worshipped at home as their immediate guardians and benefactors.

But the light of Scripture gives a more clear discovery of the obligation of this duty. It is recommended by the example of the saints recorded in Scripture; and good examples as really bind us to the duty as express precepts. We find Abraham rearing up altars wherever he came; and his attention to family religion was expressly commended by God (Genesis 18:19). We have the examples of Joshua (24:15); of Job (1:5); and of David (2 Samuel 6:20). But we have a still more engaging example of family worship on record in Scripture than any of these, even the example of our Saviour himself, who, though he had no house of his own, yet he had a family (Matthew 10:25). Now we find him retiring from the crowd that followed him, and praying with his own family: 'As he was alone praying, his disciples were with him' (Luke 9:18).

The practice of family worship tends to promote even the temporal prosperity of families; for it is the blessing of God that maketh rich and prosperous; and what more likely way to obtain that blessing, than for a whole family to join in prayer and ask it daily of God? (Proverbs 3:33). Much more does family worship tend to promote the spiritual and eternal interests of families; while it is also the most effectual means to propagate religion from generation to generation.

On the other hand, the neglect of this duty will bring the curse of God upon families; for 'the curse of the LORD is in the house of the wicked' (Proverbs 3:33). How awful is that text (Jeremiah 10:25): 'Pour out thy fury upon the heathen that know thee not, and upon the families that call not upon thy name.' Let the head of every family, then, adopt the excellent resolution of Joshua: 'As for me and my house, we will serve the LORD' (Josh. 24:15).

2. *Religious worship ought to be performed in secret, each one by himself.* In Matthew 6:6, our Saviour plainly inculcates the duty of secret prayer upon all his disciples, and directs them how to perform it in a right manner, particularly to choose some secret place of retirement for their secret devotions. This duty is also most strongly recommended by the Saviour's example (Matthew 14:23; Mark 1:35). It has been practiced by the saints of God in every age. We have the example of Jacob (Genesis 32:24); of Daniel (Daniel 6:10); of David (Psalms 55:3, 5:17); or Hezekiah (Isaiah 38:2). Secret prayer, indeed, is inseparable from the state of grace; it is one of the first, one of the plainest and strongest symptoms of spiritual life. No sooner was Saul of Tarsus converted, than it was said of him, 'Behold he prayeth' (Acts 9:11). This is an eminent means to promote genuine piety; and the regular and conscientious practice of this duty is one of the best evidences of Christian sincerity. But not only ought Christians to engage in secret prayer at least every morning and evening, they may also, on other occasions, even when employed in their daily occupations, frequently lift up their souls to God in devout and fervent ejaculations. Of this species of prayer we have many examples in the Word of God (Exodus 14:15; 1 Samuel 1:13; Nehemiah 2:4; 1 Chronicles 5:20).

3. *Christians ought to assemble together, at stated seasons, for public worship.* Under the former dispensation, all the males of God's chosen people were enjoined 'to appear three times in the year before the Lord God' (Exodus 23:17). But all their worship of a public nature was not confined to the temple, or to the

celebration of the sacred feasts; they had synagogues erected throughout the land, in which they assembled, at least on the Sabbath-days, for the service of the Lord (Acts 15:21). Jesus Christ, while he was on earth, not only went up to Jerusalem at the celebration of the great feasts, but also attended regularly to the service of the synagogue on the Sabbath-days. 'He came to Nazareth, where he had been brought up, and, as his custom was, he went into the synagogue on the Sabbath-day' (Luke 4:16). His example lays a strong obligation upon those who profess to be his followers, to be regular and conscientious in their attendance upon the public worship of God. The primitive Christians did not satisfy themselves with worshipping God in secret and in their families, but whenever they had an opportunity they assembled together for public worship (Acts 2:46). God is eminently honoured by the social worship of his people; and he delights to honour the ordinances of his public worship, by making them means of grace. Most commonly it is by means of these ordinances that sinners are awakened and converted, and that saints are edified and comforted. Christians ought, therefore, to put a high value upon the public worship of God, diligently to improve their opportunities of 'going up to the house of the Lord', and to beware of 'forsaking the assembling of themselves together, as the manner of some is' (Hebrews 10:25).

Section 7

As it is of the law of nature that, in general, a due proportion of time be set apart for the worship of God; so, in his Word, by a positive, moral and perpetual commandment, binding all men in all ages, he hath particularly appointed one day in seven for a Sabbath, to be kept holy unto him (Exodus 20:8, 10, 11; Isaiah 56:2, 4, 6, 7): which from the beginning of the world to the resurrection of Christ, was the last day of the week; and, from the resurrection of Christ, was changed into the first day of the week (Genesis 2:2, 3; 1 Corinthians 16:1, 2; Acts 20:7), which in Scripture is called the Lord's-day (Revelation 1:10), and is to be continued to the end of the world as the Christian Sabbath (Exodus 20:8, 10; Matthew 5:17, 18).

Exposition

Our Confession next treats of the *time* consecrated to the worship of God.

It is a dictate of the law of nature, that a due proportion of our time should be employed in the immediate worship of God. The right of determining what exact proportion of time, and what particular day of the week should be set apart for this purpose, belongs to God. He has, accordingly, interposed his authority, and appointed that a seventh part of our time should be appropriated to his service. From the beginning of the world to the resurrection of Christ, he enjoined that the seventh day of the week should be employed in his worship, for the special purpose of commemorating his rest from the work of creation. The particular day, however, might be altered by the authority, and according to the pleasure, of the Lawgiver. And from the resurrection of Christ, in order to commemorate the work of redemption in combination with the work of creation, the Sabbath was changed from the seventh to the first day of the week; which is to be continued to the end of the world as the Christian Sabbath.

From these remarks it will be obvious that the Sabbath is partly a moral and partly a positive institution. So far as it requires that a certain portion of our time should be devoted to the worship of God, it is moral, being founded in the relation subsisting between God and man. So far as it appropriates the seventh part of our time, and determines the particular day to be set apart for the service of God, it is of positive institution, being founded in the will and appointment of God. But it ought to be observed, that a positive institution, when once enacted and revealed by God, may be of perpetual obligation, and, in this sense, may be called moral. Hence it is usual to speak of 'the morality of the Sabbath', and to distinguish betwixt what is *moral natural* and what is *moral positive* in the fourth precept of the decalogue. As it requires that some stated portion of our time should be consecrated to the worship of God, it is moral natural; and as it enacts that a seventh portion of our time, rather than any other proportion, shall be set apart for this purpose, it is moral positive. We call it a POSITIVE institution, because the observing of one day in seven as a Sabbath flows from the sovereign appointment of God; and we call it MORAL positive, because the divine appointment is of universal and perpetual obligation; and the Sabbath is thus distinguished from ceremonial institutions, which were peculiar to the Jews, and were abrogated at the death of Christ. The morality of the Sabbath, therefore, consists in its binding obligation upon all men, in all ages.

That the appointment of one day in seven for a Sabbath is of universal and perpetual obligation, appears from the following considerations:

1. *From the original institution of the Sabbath.* Of this we have an account (Genesis 2:1-3). At this time none of the human race were in being but our first parents; and since the Sabbath was instituted for them, it must be obligatory on all their posterity to the end of the world. There is, unquestionably, as much reason and as much need for all the sons of Adam, in all ages and nations, in their feeble and sinful state, to have a day appointed for their own rest, and for the worship of God, as there was for Adam in Paradise, and in a state of innocence.

The Sabbath, as then appointed, could not be a ceremonial institution; for while man retained his integrity, there was no need of any types to shadow forth Christ. This reasoning can only be overturned by denying that the Sabbath was instituted in the beginning, and proving that it was first given to the Israelites in the wilderness. This, accordingly, has been attempted by various writers, but the proof entirely fails. There is no reason to think that, in Genesis, Moses records the institution of the Sabbath by anticipation. The manner of the narrative would naturally lead any reader to suppose that he is relating what took place when the work of creation was finished. Although there is no record of the observation of the Sabbath for a period of 2,500 years, or until after Israel came out of Egypt, yet it cannot be inferred from this that the Sabbath was not instituted from the beginning, or that it was not observed in antediluvian and patriarchal times; for neither is there any record of its observation during a period of about 500 years, containing the histories of Joshua, of the Judges, particularly Samuel, and of Saul; nor is there a single instance of circumcision on record from the time that Israel entered into Canaan until the circumcision of John the Baptist. In Exodus 16:23, the Sabbath is evidently mentioned, not as a new institution, but as one already known. And when the law was promulgated to Israel, at Mount Sinai, the Sabbath was spoken of as an institution with which they were formerly acquainted, but which had been too much neglected or forgotten. Probably in Egypt the observance of it had been in a great measure suspended; and therefore they were called to 'REMEMBER the Sabbath-day, to keep it holy'. It may be observed, too, that the division of time into weeks of seven days, which subsisted in the age of the patriarchs, cannot be satisfactorily accounted for, but by the previous institution of the Sabbath.

2. The binding obligation of the Sabbath may be argued from *the place which the fourth commandment occupies in the decalogue*. It is inserted in the very middle of the moral precepts which God delivered to mankind as a perpetual rule of their lives. It is one of those commands that were spoken by the voice of God himself, that were twice written on tables of stone by the finger of God, and that were laid up in the ark of the covenant. None of these things can be said of any ceremonial institution.

3. All the reasons annexed to this commandment, as promulgated from Mount Sinai, are *moral in their nature*. These reasons had no special reference to the Jews, but equally respect all men, in all nations and in all ages. And hence we find that strangers, as well as the Jews, were obliged to observe the Sabbath; but they were not bound to observe ceremonial institutions (Exodus 20:10, 11).

4. That the observation of the Sabbath was to continue after the abolition of the Jewish Sabbath, is implied *in the words of Jesus Christ*: 'Pray ye that your flight be not in the winter, neither on the Sabbath-day' (Matthew 24:20). Christ is there speaking, not of the Jewish, but of the Christian Sabbath; for he refers to a flight which should happen at the destruction of Jerusalem; and this did not take place until forty years after the Jewish Sabbath was abolished. But though the Sabbath was then to be changed from the seventh to the first day of the week, yet the words of Christ certainly intimate that the Sabbath was still to be continued.

5. The perpetuity of the Sabbath is clearly taught in Isaiah 56:6-8. Whoever examines the passage will find that the prophet is speaking of New Testament times. Under the gospel dispensation, therefore, the Sabbath was still to continue a divine institution; it was still to be a duty to keep it from polluting it; and the keeping of it was to be blessed, according to the declarations of the unerring Spirit of prophecy.

The morality of the Sabbath is not affected by the change of the day. The substance of the institution consists in the separation of a seventh portion of our time to the immediate worship of God; and the particular day is a thing perfectly circumstantial. It is not said, 'Remember the *seventh* day'; but 'Remember the *Sabbath-*

day, to keep it holy'. Neither is it said, 'God blessed the *seventh* day'; but 'God blessed the *Sabbath*-day, and hallowed it'. But as the seventh day of the week was, by divine appointment, originally appropriated to the worship of God, the day could only be altered by 'the Lord of the Sabbath'. It is admitted that we have no express precept for the alteration of the day, but we have convincing evidence that the Sabbath was changed from the seventh to the first day of the week at the resurrection of Christ.

1. That the first day of the week should be the Christian Sabbath was foretold in the Old Testament Scriptures: 'This is the day which the Lord hath made' (Psalm 118:24); not which he has created – for so he has made all other days – but which he has consecrated to himself, or made into a holy day. And the day referred to is the day of Christ's resurrection, when 'the stone which the builders refused was become the head stone of the corner'. Compare Acts 4:10, 11; see also Ezekiel 43:27, where the *eighth* day is mentioned as the day on which spiritual sacrifices were to be offered up to the Lord; and the Christian Sabbath may be called the *eighth* day, because the first day of the week now is the eighth day in order from the creation.

2. After his resurrection, Christ repeatedly met with his disciples on the first day of the week (see John 20:19, 26). Though Christ appeared to several of the disciples on other days, yet it is only expressly recorded that on the first day of the week he met with them when assembled together. From this we may conclude that the disciples had already begun to assemble on the first day of the week, and that Christ approved of the practice. Many are of the opinion that he continued to meet with them upon that day of the week till his ascension, 'speaking to them of the things pertaining to the kingdom of God' (Acts 1:3).

3. The apostles and primitive Christians statedly met on that day for the celebration of divine ordinances. We read that 'upon the first day of the week, when the disciples came together to break bread, Paul preached unto them' (Acts 20:7); where their meeting together on that day is not spoken of as a thing extraordinary, or merely occasional, but as a stated ordinary practice. From 1 Corinthians 16:1, 2, it appears that the primitive Christians, on the first day of the week, contributed for the relief of their needy brethren, and this by an express apostolical injunction. Thus the collection for the poor, which was made in the Jewish synagogues

on the Sabbath, seems to have been transferred, by apostolical authority, to the first day of the week among Christians.

4. In early times the Christian Sabbath was well known by the distinguishing title of 'the *Lord's* day' (Revelation 1:10), the day which Jesus Christ peculiarly claimed as his own, and which was consecrated to his honour.

5. The first day of the week has been uniformly observed as the Christian Sabbath, from the apostolic age down to the present time; and God has remarkably honoured that day by conferring precious blessings on his people, when employed in the religious observance of it.

There is an adequate reason for the change of the Sabbath from the seventh to the first day of the week. As the seventh day was kept holy from the beginning of the world to the resurrection of Christ, in commemoration of the work of creation, so it is reasonable that, since the resurrection of Christ, the first day of the week should be sanctified, in commemoration of the greater and more glorious work of redemption. And as there will be no new work of the Almighty of superior or equal importance, it is fit that this day should continue to the end of the world, as the Christian Sabbath.

Section 8

This Sabbath is then kept holy unto the Lord, when men, after a due preparing of their hearts, and ordering of their common affairs beforehand, do not only observe an holy rest all the day from their own works, words, and thoughts about their worldly employments and recreations (Exodus 20:8; 16:23, 25, 26, 29, 30; 31:15-17; Isaiah 58:13; Nehemiah 13:15-19, 21, 22); but also are taken up the whole time in the public and private exercises of his worship, and in the duties of necessity and mercy (Isaiah 58:13; Matthew 12:1-13).

Exposition

This section points out what is requisite to the proper sanctification of the Sabbath. After due preparation beforehand, the Sabbath is to be kept holy, by resting from all worldly employments and recreations – by spending the whole time in holy exercises, and in the duties of necessity and mercy.

1. Persons should endeavour so to dispose of their common affairs beforehand, that the Sabbath may not be entrenched upon by the cares and business of this world, and to prepare their hearts for engaging in the exercises appropriate to the Lord's day.

2. As the Sabbath is a day of holy rest, persons ought to abstain, during the whole day, from their worldly employments – from all manual labour, and also from the labours of the mind about secular studies – and from all unnecessary words and thoughts about such subjects. They are also required to abstain from those innocent recreations which are lawful on other days, because these would engross a portion of the time which is sacred to other purposes, and would indispose them for the proper duties of the Sabbath. To engage on that day in such recreations or amusements as are in themselves sinful must be attended with highly aggravated guilt.

3. Persons ought to spend the whole time of the Sabbath, when they are awake, in holy exercises – in prayer, in religious reading, and meditation – in the instruction of their families, and pious conversation with them – and in attendance upon the public ordinances of grace. It is very wrong to appropriate a few hours of the Sabbath to religious exercises, and to employ all the rest in a worldy manner. A Sabbath day is of the same duration as the other six days of the week, and the same proportion of time that we spend in our own works on the other days should be devoted on the Sabbath to the public or private exercises of God's worship.

4. Works of necessity and mercy are allowed on the Sabbath. By the former are meant works which could not have been done on the preceding day, and cannot be delayed till the day following. By the latter are meant those works which are performed from compassion to our fellow-creatures. Under these heads are included such works as these: travelling to and from the house of God; defending a town or city that is invaded by enemies; working a vessel at sea; quenching a fire, and removing goods which would be destroyed by it, or by a sudden inundation; feeding cattle, and preserving their lives from danger; visiting the sick, and ministering to their comfort and necessities; and taking care of children. In short, there is nothing of this kind forbidden, though it may, in a great measure, sometimes hinder the proper work of the day; for 'God will have mercy, and not sacrifice'. Jesus healed the sick on the Sabbath day, and his disciples rubbed out the corn from the ears, when they were hungry; and though the Pharisees reproved them, yet the Lord pronounced them blameless.

'The Sabbath was made for man.' It is not an arbitrary appointment, but a most benevolent institution – designed for the benefit and advantage of man. Viewed merely as a day of cessation from labour, it must be regarded as a merciful and beneficial institution. It is intended to give to the labouring classes of mankind an opportunity of resting from toil; and the return of the hepdomadal rest is found to be absolutely necessary for the preservation of health and strength. Every member of the community ought to be secured in the full enjoyment of that day of rest which God in his goodness, and by his authority, has allowed him.

But the Sabbath is not merely a season of rest from the fatigues and anxieties of secular business – it is a cessation from ordinary labour, that we may attend with greater diligence to the duties of religion. And surely one whole day in seven is not too much for the immediate service of God, for the improvement of our souls, and for preparation for eternity. Scotland has long been honourably distinguished for its decent observance of the Sabbath. It is to be deplored, however, that in this respect a sad deterioration is taking place. Sabbath profanation has of late years been making progress with fearful rapidity, and as this is the fertile source of numerous other evils, we know of nothing more injurious to the best interests of our country. The proper observation of the Sabbath is a principal means of promoting the temporal welfare of individuals and of nations, of elevating the tone of public morals, of advancing the interests of religion, and of drawing down the divine favour and blessing. The desecration of the Sabbath, on the other hand, is detrimental to the temporal interests of men – demoralizes the community, lays waste religion, and calls down the displeasure and judgments of God upon a nation. Every one, therefore, should exert all his influence to arrest the progress of this increasing evil, and should resolve that, whatever others do, he will 'keep the Sabbath from polluting it'. They who honour God by a strict and diligent observation of that day which he claims as his special property, shall obtain the blessing of the Lord, according to that comprehensive promise: 'If thou turn away thy foot from the Sabbath, from doing thy pleasure on my holy day; and call the Sabbath a delight, the holy of the LORD, honourable; and shalt honour him, not doing thine own ways, nor finding thine own pleasure, nor speaking thine own words: then shalt thou delight thyself in the LORD; and I will cause thee to ride upon the high places of the earth, and feed thee with the heritage of Jacob thy father; for the mouth of the LORD hath spoken it' (Isaiah 58:13, 14).

CHAPTER 22

LAWFUL OATHS AND VOWS

Section 1
A lawful oath is a part of religious worship (Deuteronomy 10:20), wherein, upon just occasion, the person swearing solemnly calleth God to witness what he asserteth or promiseth; and to judge him according to the truth of falsehood of what he sweareth (Exodus 20:7; Leviticus 19:12; 2 Corinthians 1:23; 2 Chronicles 6:22, 23).

Section 2
The name of God only is that by which men ought to swear, and therein it is to be used with all holy fear and reverence (Deuteronomy 6:13): therefore to swear vainly or rashly by that glorious and dreadful name, or to swear at all by any other thing, is sinful, and to be abhorred (Exodus 20:7; Jeremiah 5:7; Matthew 5:34, 37; James 5:12). Yet as, in matters of weight and moment, an oath is warranted by the Word of God under the New Testament as well as under the Old (Hebrews 6:16; 2 Corinthians 1:23; Isaiah 65:16); so a lawful oath being imposed by lawful authority, in such matters, ought to be taken (1 Kings 8:31; Nehemiah 13:25; Ezra 10:5).

Section 3
Whosoever taketh an oath, ought duly to consider the weightiness of so solemn an act, and therein to avouch nothing but what he is fully persuaded is the truth (Exodus 20:7; Jeremiah 4:2). Neither may any man bind himself by oath to anything but what is good and just, and what he believeth so to be, and what he is able and resolved to perform (Genesis 24:2, 3, 5, 6, 8, 9). Yet it is a sin to refuse an oath touching anything that is good and just, being imposed by lawful authority (Numbers 5:19, 21; Nehemiah 5:12; Exodus 22:7-11).

Section 4
An oath is to be taken in the plain and common sense of the words, without equivocation or mental reservation (Jeremiah 4:2. Psalm 24:4). It cannot oblige to sin; but in anything not sinful, being taken, it binds to performance, although to a man's own hurt (1 Samuel 25:22, 32-34; Psalm 15:4); nor is it to be violated, although made to heretics or infidels (Ezekiel 17:16, 18, 19; Joshua 9:18. 19; 2 Samuel 21:1).

Exposition
These sections embrace the following points: *first*, The nature of a lawful oath; *secondly*, By whose name men ought to swear; *thirdly*, The warrantableness of taking an oath; *fourthly*, The manner in which an oath ought to be taken; and, *fifthly*, The binding obligation of an oath.

1. An oath is a solemn act of religious worship, in which the person swearing calls God to witness his sincerity in what he asserts or promises, and to judge him according to the truth or falsehood of what he swears. When a person swears to facts past or present, this is called an *assertory* oath; when one swears that he will perform a certain deed or deeds in time to come, this is called a *promissory* oath. An oath may relate to matters civil or ecclesiastical, and according to its matter, may be denominated a civil or ecclesiastical oath; but to whatsoever matter it may be applied, the oath itself retains its high place among the solemnities of religion.

2. An oath is only to be taken in the name of God. We are expressly commanded to 'swear by his name' (Deuteronomy 6:13); and to 'swear by them that are no gods' is represented as highly criminal (Jeremiah 5:7). Swearing by the name of God implies a belief and acknowledgement of his omniscience, omnipotence, and justice; it follows, therefore, that to swear by any other besides him, must be utterly unlawful, and no less than idolatry.

3. An oath may be warrantably taken on weighty occasions, when imposed by lawful authority. The Quakers, and some others, deny the lawfulness of swearing an oath in any case, under the New Testament. But their opinion is refuted by a variety of arguments. An oath for confirmation is warranted by the third precept of the moral law; for while that precept prohibits the taking of God's name in vain, it sanctions swearing by the name of God on lawful occasions.

The practice is confirmed by numerous approved examples under the Old Testament. Abraham sware to Abimelech that he would not deal falsely with him (Genesis 21:23, 24). A king of the same name desired that an oath might be between Isaac and him; and they sware one to another (Genesis 26:31). In like manner Jacob sware to Laban (Genesis 31:53); and Joseph sware to his father (Genesis 47:31). All these examples occurred before the Mosaic law was given to the Jews, and therefore an oath can be no peculiarity of the Mosaic dispensation. But that law expressly recognised the warrantableness of taking an oath (Leviticus 5:1), and under that dispensation we have various examples of holy men swearing by the name of God. Thus Jonathan required David to swear unto him (1 Samuel 20:17); and David also sware unto Saul (1 Samuel 24:21, 22).

The taking of an oath being no part of the judicial, or of the ceremonial law, it must be equally warrantable under the present dispensation, unless expressly prohibited in the New Testament. But there is much in the New Testament to confirm the practice. The Apostle Paul frequently appeals to God in these and similar expressions: 'God is my witness'; 'I say the truth in Christ, I lie not' (Romans 1:9; 9:1): 'I call God for a record upon my soul' (2 Corinthians 1:23). Christ himself answered the question of the high priest, when he adjured him by the living God; which was the common form of administering an oath among the Jews. The writer to the Hebrews speaks of the oath which God sware to Abraham, 'who, because he could swear by no greater, sware by himself'; and he adds, 'An oath for confirmation is an end of all strife' (Hebrews 6:13, 16); plainly showing that he sanctioned the practice. It must be evident, therefore, that our Saviour's words, 'Swear not at all' (Matthew 5:34), and the similar words of the Apostle James (5:12), do not absolutely prohibit all swearing on necessary and solemn occasions; but only forbid the practice of swearing in common conversation, and particularly of swearing by creatures.

It must be remarked, however, that an appeal to God in trivial matters, and the frequent and unnecessary repetition of the same oath, is a taking the name of God in vain. And it may also be observed, that as the lifting up of the hand is the usual mode of swearing mentioned in Scripture (Genesis 14:22; Revelation 10:5, 6), so it ought to be preferred; and all superstitious forms ought to be rejected.

4. An oath ought to be taken 'in truth, in righteousness, and in judgment' (Jeremiah 4:2). *In truth*; that is, with an entire correspondence between the sentiments of the mind and the words of the oath, in their common obvious meaning, and as understood by those who administer it; without any equivocation and mental reservation. To allow of mental reservation in swearing, as the Church of Rome in certain cases does, is to defect the very end of an oath, to destroy all confidence among men, and to involve the

swearer in the heinous sin of perjury. *In righteousness*; that is, in things lawful and possible for us at the time of swearing, and with a fixed intention to perform what we pledge ourselves to do. *In judgment*; that is, deliberately and reverently, well considering whether the matter of the oath be good and just, and whether the ends proposed be sufficient to justify us in interposing the glorious and dreadful name of God for a pledge of the truth of our declarations.

5. A lawful oath binds to performance. Oaths engaging persons to what is sinful are in themselves null and void; and they who have rashly taken such oaths ought to repent of and renounce them, instead of adding the sin of keeping to the sin of making them, as Herod most wickedly did in beheading John the Baptist for the sake of his oath (Mark 6:23, 26). But a lawful oath is binding, though the performance may be prejudicial to a man's temporal interest; and it is the character of a good man, that though 'he swears to his own hurt, he changes not' (Psalm 15:4). It is a detestable principle of the Romish Church, that 'faith is not to be kept with heretics'.

Section 5
A vow is of the like nature with a promissory oath, and ought to be made with the like religious care, and to be performed with the like faithfulness (Isaiah 19:21; Ecclesiastes 5:4-6; Psalm 61:8; 66:13, 14).

Section 6
It is not to be made to any creature, but to God alone (Psalm 76:11; Jeremiah 44:25, 26): and that it may be accepted, it is to be made voluntarily, out of faith and conscience of duty, in way of thankfulness for mercy received, or for the obtaining of what we want; whereby we more strictly bind ourselves to necessary duties, or to other things, so far and so long as they may fitly conduce thereunto (Deuteronomy 23:21-23; Psalm 1:14; Genesis 28:20-22; 1 Samuel 1:11; Psalm 66:13, 14; 132:2-5).

Section 7
No man may vow to do anything forbidden in the Word of God, or what would hinder any duty therein commanded, or which is not in his own power, and for the performance whereof he hath no promise of ability from God (Acts 23:12, 14; Mark 6:26; Numbers 30:5, 8, 12, 13). In which respects Popish monastical vows of perpetual single life, professed poverty, and regular obedience, are so far from being degrees of higher

perfection, that they are superstitious and sinful snares, in which no Christian may entangle himself (Matthew 19:11, 12; 1 Corinthians 7:2, 9; Ephesians 4:28; 1 Peter 4:2; 1 Corinthians 7:23).

Exposition

These sections relate to the nature, the matter, and the obligation of a vow.

A vow is a solemn promise made to God, and may be either personal or social. Although a vow is 'of the like nature with a promissory oath', yet they admit of being distinguished. In an *oath*, man is generally the party, and God is invoked as the witness; in a *vow*, God is both the party and the witness. A vow is to be made to God alone; and, therefore, to make vows to saints departed, as Papists do, is superstitious and idolatrous. Vows ought to be entered into voluntarily, and in the exercise of faith, or in dependence upon the grace of Christ for enabling us to perform them (Philippians 4:13; 2 Corinthians 12:9).

Persons may bind themselves by a vow, either to necessary duties or to other things not expressly required, so far and so long as they may be conducive to the better performance of these duties. But no man may vow to do anything which is either unlawful or which is not in his own power, and for the performance of which he has no promise of ability from God.

A vow has an intrinsic obligation, distinct from the obligation of the law of God. In the law, God *binds us* by his authoritative command; in a vow, we *bind ourselves* by our own voluntary engagement. To represent a vow as laying no new or superadded obligation on the conscience, or to maintain, as some Popish writers do, that a vow does not bind us in moral duties commanded by the law of God, because our vow cannot add any obligation to his law, is manifestly absurd. It is equally contrary to Scripture and to the common sense of mankind. The law of God obliges; this is the primary obligation. But a vow also obliges; this is the secondary obligation. And subordinate things oppose not each other. The performance of vows is frequently and strictly enjoined in the Word of God. 'When thou shalt vow a vow unto the LORD thy God,' says Moses, 'thou shalt not slack to pay it; for the LORD thy God will surely require it of thee; and it would be sin in thee' (Deuteronomy 23:21; see also Ecclesiastes 5:4; Psalms 50:14; 76:11).

CHAPTER 23

THE CIVIL MAGISTRATE

Section 1
God, the supreme Lord and King of all the world, hath ordained civil magistrates to be under him over the people, for his own glory and the public good; and, to this end, hath armed them with the power of the sword, for the defence and encouragement of them that are good, and for the punishment of evildoers (Romans 13:1-4; 1 Peter 2:13, 14).

Section 2
It is lawful for Christians to accept and execute the office of a magistrate, when called thereunto (Proverbs 8:15, 16; Romans 13:1, 2, 4): in the managing whereof, as they ought especially to maintain piety, justice, and peace, according to the wholesome laws of each commonwealth (Psalm 2:10-12; 1 Timothy 2:2; Psalm 82:3, 4; 2 Samuel 23:3; 1 Peter 2:13); so, for that end, they may lawfully, now under the New Testament, wage war upon just and necessary occasions (Luke 3:14; Romans 13:4; Matthew 8:9, 10; Acts 10:1, 2; Revelation 17:14, 16).

Exposition
The Sacred Scriptures are a perfect 'rule of faith and manners'. They prescribe the duty incumbent upon men in every station and relation, whether as members of the Church or of the commonwealth – whether as rulers or as subjects. Any summary of Christian doctrine, therefore, which did not exhibit the duty of civil rulers, especially in reference to religion and the kingdom of Christ, would be extremely defective. This subject, accordingly, occupies a prominent place in the Confessions of all the Reformed Churches; and the harmony of these Confessions is a strong presumptive proof that the doctrine of the Holy Scriptures on this interesting topic is neither ambiguous nor 'hard to be understood'.

It is true that sects have sprung up, at various periods, which have held principles subversive of all civil government, and hostile especially to all interference of the civil magistrate about matters of religion. The German Anabaptists who, in the sixteenth century, produced such dreadful commotions, maintained that, 'in the kingdom of Christ civil magistrates were absolutely useless'. And even after their principles were modified by Menno, they 'neither admitted civil rulers into their communion, nor allowed any of their members to perform the functions of magistracy'. They also denied 'the lawfulness of repelling force by force, and considered war, in all its shapes, as unchristian and unjust'.[1] Similar sentiments were broached by the English sectaries at the period when the Westminster Assembly was sitting. Among the many pernicious errors vented at that time, we find the following: 'That 'tis not lawful for a Christian to be a magistrate; but, upon turning Christian, he should lay down his magistracy: That it is unlawful for Christians to fight, and take up arms for their laws and civil liberties.'[2] It is well known that the lawfulness of war is still denied by the Society of Friends, or Quakers.

In opposition to such opinions, our Confession here teaches:

1. That magistracy or civil government is the ordinance of God.

2. That magistrates are appointed for the promotion of the public good, in subordination to the glory of God.

3. That Christians may lawfully accept the office of a magistrate.

4. That magistrates ought to maintain piety as well as peace and justice.

5. That they may lawfully, now under the New Testament, wage war upon just and necessary occasions.

1. Magistracy, or civil government, is the ordinance of God. Several eminent writers have supposed that government is founded in the social compact; but it has been more generally held that government is founded in the will of God.[3] When it is asserted that magistracy is a divine institution, it is not meant that it is of direct and express divine appointment, like the office of the gospel ministry. Nothing more is intended than that government is agreeable to the will of God. It is his will that the happiness of mankind be promoted. But government is indispensable to their

---

1. Mosheim's Eccl. Hist., cent. xvi., sect. 3, part 2, chap. 3. cap. 5, 16.

2. Edwards' *Gangraena*, part i., pp. 29, 30.

3. Among those who have pleaded for a social compact as the foundation of government, the venerable name of Locke may be specified; and among those who have advocated the opposite opinion, we may refer to Paley 'Moral and political Philosophy', book vi., chap. 3, and to Dwight (Ser. 113).

happiness – to the preservation of peace and order, to the safety of life, liberty, and property. Nay, it is necessary to the very existence of any considerable number of mankind in a social state. The deduction natively follows, that it is the will of God that government should exist; and this deduction of reason is amply confirmed by the express declaration of an inspired apostle: 'There is no power but of God; the powers that be are ordained of God. Whosoever, therefore, resisteth the power, resisteth the ordinance of God' (Romans 13:1, 2). It is to be observed, that magistracy was instituted by God, as the moral Governor of the world, and is not derived from Christ as Mediator. This forms an important distinction between the civil and the ecclesiastical powers.

> The King of nations hath instituted the civil power; the King of saints hath instituted the ecclesiastical power. I mean, the most high God, possessor of heaven and earth, who exerciseth sovereignty over the workmanship of his own hands, and so over all mankind, hath instituted magistrates to be in his stead, as gods upon earth; but *Jesus Christ*, as Mediator and King of the Church, whom his Father hath set upon his holy hill of Zion (Psalm 2:6), to reign over the house of Jacob for ever (Luke 1:33), who hath the key of the house of David upon his shoulder (Isaiah 22:22), hath instituted an ecclesiastical power and government in the hands of Church officers, whom, in his name, he sendeth forth.[4]

It may be further remarked, that, although God has instituted civil government, yet he has not enjoined any one form of government as obligatory upon all communities; he has left it free to the several countries to choose that form which they think fittest for themselves; and in this respect the Apostle Peter calls it 'the ordinance of man' (1 Peter 2:13).

2. Magistrates are appointed for the promotion of the public good, in subordination to the glory of God. Magistrates are called 'the ministers of God for good' (Romans 13:4). They are invested with dignity and power, not for their own honour and advantage, but for promoting the welfare of society; especially 'for the punishment of evil-doers, and for the praise of them that do well'. As this is the design of civil government, so this end is in some measure gained even by the worst of governments. But when this

---

4. George Gillespie, *Aaron's Rod*, p. 185.

design is systematically and notoriously disregarded – when rulers become habitual tyrants, invading and overthrowing the liberties and privileges of the nation– the governed must have a right to remedy the evil. This is a principle essential to true liberty, and it was acted upon in our own country at the Revolution.

3. Christians may lawfully accept of the office of a magistrate. It cannot be questioned that, under the former dispensation, some of the most pious men, such as David, Josiah and Hezekiah, exercised this office with the divine approbation. There are also many predictions which clearly intimate that Christians should execute this office under the New Testament dispensation (Isaiah 44:23; Psalm 72:10, 11). Those who consider it unlawful for Christians to bear such an office, chiefly rest their opinion upon the example of Christ (Luke 12:14), and upon his declaration to his disciples (Matthew 20:25, 26). But though Christ came not to exercise temporal dominion, and though he repressed the ambitious temper which then manifested itself among his apostles, and interdicted them and the ministers of the gospel in succeeding ages from holding such an office, this does not exclude *all* Christians from executing that function. Were it unlawful for Christians to accept of the office of a magistrate, it would follow, either that there must be no magistrate at all in Christian countries – which would involve them in anarchy and dissolution – or else, that magistrates who are not Christians must be established among them; and who does not perceive the absurdity of this?[5]

4. Christians magistrates ought to maintain piety, as well as justice and peace. The apostle exhorts, that prayers be made by Christians 'for kings, and for all that are in authority; that we may lead a quiet and peaceable life in all godliness and honesty' (2 Timothy 2:1).

What Christians are here to pray for, that magistrates must be bound to promote as their end; and this is not simply a 'quiet and peaceable life', but 'in all godliness and honesty'. Rulers are not, in their official capacity, to be indifferent to *godliness* any more than to *honesty*; both are to be countenanced and promoted by them (Ezra 6:8-10)'.[6]

---

5. Calvin's Inst., book iv., chap. 20, sect. 4, 5. Doddridge's Lectures, vol. ii. p. 253.
6. M'Crie's Statement, p. 139.

5. Christian magistrates may lawfully, now under the New Testament, wage war upon just and necessary occasions. War must be regarded as a great evil, but in the present state of the world it is sometimes necessary; and if a nation were to adopt and act upon the principle that war is absolutely unlawful, it would soon become a prey to its ambitious neighbours. Under the Old Testament, wars were undertaken by the express command and with approbation of God; but he could never command and approve of what is morally wrong. In the New Testament, too, there are various circumstances stated which countenance the lawfulness of magistrates waging war, and of Christians bearing arms. When the soldiers inquired of John what they should do, he said unto them, 'Do violence to no man, neither accuse any falsely'; but he did not command them to relinquish their profession, as unlawful; on the contrary, the precept which he added, 'Be content with your wages', supposed them to continue in their situation (Luke 3:14). The first Gentile convert who was received into the Christian Church was a centurion; but Peter, when he baptized him, did not require him to give up his situation in the Roman army (Acts 10). To determine the several cases in which war may be justifiable would be out of place here; it may, however, be generally stated that aggressive wars, or such as are undertaken to gratify views of ambition or worldly aggrandizement, cannot be justified; but that defensive wars, or those which, as to the first occasion of them, are defensive, though in their progress they must often be offensive, are lawful.

Section 3

The civil magistrate may not assume to himself the administration of the Word and sacraments, or the power of the keys of the kingdom of heaven (2 Chronicles 26:18; Matthew 18:17; 16:19; 1 Corinthians 12:28, 29; Ephesians 4:1, 12; 1 Corinthians 4:1, 2; Romans 10:15; Hebrews 5:4); yet he hath authority, and it is his duty, to take order, that unity and peace be preserved in the Church, that the truth of God be kept pure and entire, that all blasphemies and heresies be suppressed, all corruptions and abuses in worship and discipline prevented or reformed, and all ordinances of God duly settled, administered, and observed (Isaiah 49:23; Psalm 122:9; Ezra 7:23, 25-28; Leviticus 24:16; Deuteronomy 13:5, 6, 12; 2 Kings 18:4; 1 Chronicles 13:1-9; 2 Kings 24:1-26; 2 Chronicles 34:33; 15:12, 13). For the better effecting whereof, he hath power to call synods, to be present at them, and to provide that whatsoever is transacted in them be according to the mind of God (2 Chronicles 19:8-11; 29, 30. Matthew 2:4, 5).

Exposition
In this section it was manifestly the object of the compilers of our Confession to guard equally against Erastian and Sectarian principles. In opposition to Erastian principles, according to which the government and discipline of the Church are devolved upon the civil magistrate, they declare that the magistrate may not take upon himself either the ministerial dispensation of the Word and sacraments, or any part of the government of the Church. But while they deny to the magistrate all ministerial or judicial power in the Church, in opposition to Erastians, yet, to guard against the other extreme, they assert, in opposition to the Sectarians of that age, that it is his duty to employ his influence and authority, in every way competent to him, for the good of the Church, and the advancement of the interests of true religion.

It is somewhat remarkable that parties holding the most opposite view in regard to the power of the civil magistrate about religion and the connection between Church and State have concurred in representing this section of our Confession as allowing to the civil magistrate a controlling power in and over the Church. The defenders of the recent interferences of the civil courts in matters strictly ecclesiastical, now homologated by the State of Legislature, have appealed to this section as sanctioning these interferences. The opponents of all civil establishments of religion, on the other hand, have put the same construction on this section, and have alleged that it does allow to the civil magistrate an Erastian power in and over the Church.

'This, if true, would be very strange, considering that the Assembly who compiled it were engaged in a dispute against this very claim with the Parliament under whose protection they sat; and that, owing to their steady refusal to concede that power to the State (in which they were supported by the whole body of Presbyterians), the erection of presbyteries and synods in England was suspended.'[7]

Independently of this important fact, it would be easy to adduce numerous declarations from the Confession itself more than sufficient to repel the imputation. These declarations will come

7. M'Crie's *Appendix*, p. 138.

under our consideration afterwards, and at present we only remark, that the Confession must be presumed to be consistent with itself; and if some detached phrases in this section may be thought to admit of a construction unfavourable to the freedom and independence of the Church, yet if these phrases are susceptible of an interpretation which harmonizes with other explicit declarations respecting the independence of the Church and the sole headship of Christ over it, that interpretation ought certainly to be received as their true and intended import.

Before proceeding to explain the several clauses of this section, it will be proper to offer a few general remarks.

In the *first* place, it may be observed that by the civil magistrate is here meant the State, or supreme civil power of the nation. In the Confession, and in theological writing in general, the civil magistrate means, not the sovereign, acting singly and exclusively, but the government of the country, or the power which is entitled to frame the national laws, and to regulate national measures.

In the *second* place, it is unquestionable that what the Confession here teaches respecting the duty of the civil magistrate belongs to him *as a magistrate*; for it says, 'He hath authority' to do what is ascribed to him. He is to discharge the duty here assigned to him, not merely by his advice and example, as a Christian placed in an exalted station, but by his official authority and influence as a magistrate.

But, in the *third* place, it is not less evident that our Confession here speaks of such a magistrate as is also a *Christian*, making a profession of the true religion. To suppose that any other than a Christian magistrate can do the things here ascribed to the magistrate, is an absurdity too gross to be imputed to the Confession.

In the *fourth* place, our Confession here teaches, that the advancement of religion, and the promotion of the interests of the Church of Christ, form an important part of the official duty of Christian magistrates. Although the proper and immediate end of civil government, in subordination to God's glory, is the temporal good of men, yet the advancement of religion is an end which civil rulers, in the exercise of their civil authority, are bound to aim at; for even this direct end of their office cannot be gained without the aids of religion. And although magistracy has its foundation in natural principles, yet it greatly enlarges the sphere of the operation of that power which they possess, as civil rulers, from the law of nature. That law binds the subjects of God's moral government, jointly and severally, to embrace and reduce to practice whatsoever God is pleased to reveal as the rule of their faith and duty. And therefore nations and their rulers, when favoured with divine revelation, should give their public countenance to the true religion; remove everything out of their civil constitution inconsistent with it, or tending to retard its progress; support and protect its functionaries in the discharge of their duty; and provide, in every way competent to them, that its salutary influence have free course, and be diffused through all order and departments of society. The compilers of our Confession had not imbibed the doctrine, that the exercise of the magistrate's authority must be limited to the secular affairs of men, and that it is no part of his duty, in his official capacity, to aim at the promotion of the true religion. 'Certainly,' said an eminent member of the Westminster Assembly, 'there is much power and authority, which by the Word of God, and by the Confessions of Faith of the Reformed Churches, both belong to the Christian magistrate, in matters of religion.'[8]

But while our Confession undeniably teaches that the civil magistrate is authorised to do something about religion and the Church of Christ, yet it lays certain restrictions and limitations upon the exercise of his authority in regard to these matters.

According to our Confession, the civil magistrate must not assume a lordly supremacy over the Church; for 'there is no other head of the Church, but the Lord Jesus Christ' (Chapter 25, section 6). He must not interfere with her internal government; for 'the Lord Jesus, as king and head of his Church, hath therein appointed a government in the hand of Church-officers, distinct from the civil magistrate'; and 'to these officers the keys of the kingdom of heaven are committed' (Chapter 30, section 1, 2). He must not, as a magistrate, sustain himself a public judge of true or false religion, so as to dictate to his subjects in matters purely religious; for 'it belongeth to synods and councils ministerially to determine controversies of faith and cases of conscience' (Chapter 31, section 3).

In the first paragraph of the section now under consideration, there is another important limitation of the power of the civil magistrate in regard to the Church. It is expressly declared that he

8. George Gillespie, *Aaron's Rod*, p. 181.

may not take upon himself the administration of her ordinances of worship: 'He may not assume to himself the administration of the Word and sacraments.' Neither may he take upon himself the administration of the government and discipline of the Church: 'He may not assume to himself the power of the keys of the kingdom of heaven'. The *keys*, in the most extensive sense, include the whole ecclesiastical power, in distinction from the *sword*, or the civil power.[9] But 'the power of the keys', taken in its more limited sense, as it must be here, where it is distinguished from the administration of the Word and sacraments, just means the ordinary power of government, in the administration of the affairs of the Church; and more particularly, the right of authoritatively and judicially determining all questions that may arise as to the admission of men to ordinances and to office in the Church of Christ, and the infliction and relaxation of Church censures.[10]

This is not the only restriction laid upon the power of the civil magistrate is the present section. It is also plainly intimated, that, in the execution of the duty here intrusted to him, he must be regulated by the Word of God. He is not to act arbitrarily, but must be guided by the standard of God's Word. In regard to one important branch of the functions here assigned to him – that which concerns synods – it is expressly declared, that he is to see that 'what is transacted in them be according to the mind of God' – the mind of God, as revealed in his Word, being thus distinctly prescribed as a rule to him, as it is to the ordinary members of synods.[11] This principle was admitted by the Erastians of former times; for they conceded to their opponents, 'that the Christian magistrate, in ordering and disposing of ecclesiastical causes and matters of religion, is tied to keep close to the rule of the Word of God; and that as he may not assume an arbitrary government of the State, so far less of the Church'.[12]

It may be further added, that, according to our Confession, the civil magistrate is bound to act, in his official capacity 'according to the wholesome laws of each commonwealth' (Sect. 2). Now,

---

9. The civil power is called the power of the sword, and the other (the ecclesiastical), the power of the keys – Second Book of Discipline, chap. i.)
10. Cunningham's *Remarks on the Twenty-third Chapter of the Confession of Faith*, p. 12.
11. *Ibid.*, pp. 15-19.
12. Gillespie, *Aaron's Rod*, p. 173.

as our Confession of Faith is founded upon the Word of God, so it is embodied in our Statute-Book; and, therefore, when civil rulers assume a proper jurisdiction in ecclesiastical matters, which the Confession has denied to them, their proceedings must be inconsistent at once with the Word of God and law of the land.

Keeping these remarks in view, it will not be difficult to explain, in full consistency with the liberty and independence of the Church, this section of our Confession. The civil magistrate, it is declared, 'hath authority, and it is his duty, to take order' etc. This cannot mean that he is to accomplish the objects specified by all the ways in which it may be attempted; for, in the introductory clause, some of these are carefully excepted. It cannot mean that he has a rightful jurisdiction in these matters, and is entitled to judge and determine them, not only for himself, but for the regulation of the conduct of others; for this would be to usurp the keys of the kingdom of heaven. It can only imply that the matters specified are objects which he is entitled and bound to aim at, and to effect by such method as are competent to him, without invading the jurisdiction of the Church.

The Confession specifies certain means which the civil magistrate may lawfully employ for effecting the objects mentioned: 'For the better effecting whereof, he hath power to call synods.' From this it cannot be inferred that ministers have not a power to meet of themselves in synods and assemblies, without being called by the civil magistrate; for in Chapter 31 it is expressly declared that they have such power 'of themselves, and by virtue of their office'. The General Assembly of the Church of Scotland, indeed, were of the opinion that, in the chapter now referred to, the Confession is not sufficiently explicit in regard to the intrinsic power of the Church to call her own assemblies; and accordingly, in their Act of 1647, by which the Confession was approved, they expressly declare that they understood that part of it 'only of kirks not settled or constituted in point of government'; and that explanation must apply equally to the section now before us. Our Confession, then, does not assert that the magistrate may exercise this power on all occasions, and in all circumstances, or whenever there are any evils of a religious kind to correct. It is sufficient that there may be times and circumstances in which he may warrantably exercise this power. When the state of the nation as well as of the Church may be convulsed, and its convulsions may be in a great degree owing to religious disorders, it is surely a high duty incumbent on him to take such a step, provided he finds it practicable and advisable. And such was the state of matters when the Westminster Assembly was convoked by the Parliament of England.

After stating that the magistrate has power to call synods, it is added, 'To be present at them, and to provide that whatsoever is transacted in them be according to the mind of God'.

'Not to insist here that these words ought, in fair construction, to be understood of such synods as have been convoked by the magistrate, what reasonable objection can be made to his being present? May he not claim a right to be present at any public meeting within his dominions? – may he not be present in a synod to witness their proceedings, to preserve their external peace, to redress their grievances, or (why not?) to receive their advice or admonitions? But, if it be supposed that his presence is necessary to give validity to their proceedings, and that he sits as preses of their meeting, or as director of their deliberations and votes, I shall only say, that the words of the Confession give not the slightest countenance to such claims, which are utterly inconsistent with the common principles of Presbyterians, and, in particular, with the well-known and avowed principles of the Church of Scotland.

'A similar answer may be given to the objection against the last clause of the paragraph. May not any Christian, whatever his station be, "provide that whatsoever is transacted", even in synods, "be according to the mind of God?" If the legislature or government of a nation have a special care about religion, or if there is any particular duty at all which they have to discharge respecting it, and particularly, if they have power in any case to call synods, must it not in a special manner be incumbent on them to see to this? Now does this imply that they are in possession of any ecclesiastical powers, or that they pass a public judgement on true and false religion. Their private judgment is sufficient to regulate them in their public managements in this as well as on many other subjects about which they exercise their authority, without sustaining themselves as the proper judges of them, as in the case of many arts and sciences which they patronize and encourage. Must not Christian rulers, judges, and magistrates, provide that "whatsoever is transacted" by themselves "be according to the mind of God?" Is it not highly fit that they should be satisfied, and that they should, by every proper means, provide that the determinations of synods be according to the mind of God, if they are afterwards to legalize them, or if they are to use their authority for removing all external obstructions out of the way of their being carried into effect; both of which they may do, without imposing them on the consciences of their subjects? And, in fine, are there not various ways in which they may provide, as here stated, without assuming a power foreign to their office, or intruding on the proper business of synods, or ecclesiastical courts? But if it be supposed that the magistrate, as the proper judge in such matters, is to control the deliberations of the ecclesiastical assembly – to prescribe and dictate to them what their decisions shall be; or that, when they have deliberated and decided, he may receive appeals from their decisions, or may bring the whole before his tribunal, and review, alter, and reverse their sentences, I have only to say, as formerly, that the words of the Confession give not the slightest countenance to such claims, which are utterly inconsistent with the common principles of Presbyterians, and, in particular, with the well-known and avowed principles and contendings of the Church of Scotland.'[13]

Section 4

It is the duty of people to pray for magistrates (1 Timothy 2:1, 2), to honour their persons (1 Peter 2:17), to pay them tribute and other dues (Romans 13:6, 7), to obey their lawful commands, and to be subject to their authority, for conscience' sake (Romans 13:5. Titus 3:1). Infidelity, or difference in religion, doth not make void the magistrate's just and legal authority, nor free the people from their due obedience to him (1 Peter 2:13, 14, 16): from which ecclesiastical persons are not exempted (Romans 13:1; 1 Kings 2:35; Acts 25:9-11; 2 Peter 2:1, 10, 11; Jude 8-11); much less hath the Pope any power or jurisdiction over them in their dominions or over any of their people; and least of all to deprive them of their dominions or lives, if he shall judge them to be heretics, or upon any other pretence whatsoever (2 Thessalonians 2:4; Revelation 13:15-17).

Exposition

1. This section, in the first place, states the duty of subjects towards their rulers; and the proofs adduced by the compilers of our Confession clearly show that it is their duty to pray for the divine blessing upon them, to honour their persons, to pay them tribute, and to yield them a conscientious subjection and obedience in all their lawful commands.

2. It is affirmed, in opposition to a Popish tenet, that 'infidelity, or difference in religion, doth not make void the magistrate's just and legal authority, nor free the people from their due obedience

---

13. McCrie's Appendix, pp. 142, 143.

to him'. Christ himself paid tribute to Caesar, and his apostles inculcated upon Christians subjection to 'the higher powers' then existing, although all these powers were heathen. It must be admitted, however, that nations favoured with supernatural revelation ought, in choosing their rulers, to have a respect to religious qualifications. And nations that have made great attainments in reformation, and pledged themselves, by national vows to the Most High, to hold fast their attainments, certainly ought, in setting up magistrates, to look out for those who will concur with them in the maintenance of the true religion, and rule them by laws subservient to its advancement. On this principle our Reformers acted; for they provided, by their deed of civil constitution, that the sovereign over these realms should be of the same religion with the people, and co-operate with them in prosecuting the ends of the national covenants. But where a magistrate has authority, by the will and consent of the body politic, or majority of the nation (this being what renders his authority 'just and legal', according to the Word of God), 'infidelity, or difference in religion, does not make void his authority', nor release individuals, or a minority, from subjection and obedience to him in all lawful commands. With this principle, so clearly laid down in our Confession, accords the practice of 'our reforming fathers in Scotland under Queen Mary, and of their successors during the first establishment of Episcopacy, and after the Restoration, down to the time at which the government degenerated into an open and avowed tyranny.'

3. It is affirmed that 'ecclesiastical persons are not exempted' from due obedience to the civil magistrate. This is an explicit denial of the Popish doctrine of the exemption of the persons and property of ecclesiastics from the jurisdiction of the ordinary criminal and civil tribunals. Our Confession decidedly maintains that the civil magistrate may not claim authority to control or over-rule the office-bearers of the Church in the discharge of their proper functions; but it no less clearly teaches that ecclesiastical persons are not exempted from his authority in matters that fall under his rightful jurisdiction, as being of a civil nature. The apostolic injunction is general, and extends to all sorts of persons: 'Let every soul be subject unto the higher powers' (Romans 13:1). The expression *every soul* is very emphatic, and seems intended to bring the idea of the universality of the obligation more strongly

out than the use of the ordinary phrase, *every one*, would have done. The civil and ecclesiastical authorities have separate and distinct jurisdictions. In ecclesiastical matters, civil rulers have no rightful jurisdiction; and in civil matters, ecclesiastical persons, as they are members of the commonwealth, are equally bound with others to be subject to the ruling authorities.

4. It is further affirmed, that the Pope hath no power or jurisdiction over magistrates in their dominions, or over any of their people. The Popes, when in the plenitude of their power, usurped a supremacy over the whole earth, in temporals as well as in spirituals. They pretended to have authority, by divine right, over kings and their dominions, and claimed a power to dispose of crowns and kingdoms at their pleasure. This arrogant claim they have, in innumerable instances, reduced to practice. They have deposed and excommunicated kings, on the ground of pretended heresy or schism – absolved their subjects from their allegiance, and transferred their dominions to others. Since the Reformation, however, the exorbitant power of the Pope has been greatly restrained. Protestants disclaim his authority, not only in temporal, but also in spiritual matters; and even in the most of those countries where his spiritual authority is still acknowledged, his temporal supremacy is disowned; but since Papists boast of the unchangeableness of their Church, and since the Roman Pontiffs lay claim to infallibility, it cannot be supposed that they have renounced their right to universal dominion; and should they again attain to power, it may be presumed that their ancient extravagant principles would be openly avowed, and their universal supremacy enforced as rigorously as in the darker ages. Every friend of civil and religious liberty ought, therefore, strenuously to resist every encroachment of 'the Man of Sin, who opposeth and exalteth himself above all that is called god'.

CHAPTER 24

MARRIAGE AND DIVORCE

Section 1
Marriage is to be between one man and one woman: neither is it lawful for any man to have more than one wife, nor for any woman to have more than one husband at the same time (Genesis 2:24; Matthew 19:5, 6; Proverbs 2:17).

Section 2
Marriage was ordained for the mutual help of husband and wife (Genesis 2:18); and the increase of mankind with a legitimate issue, and of the Church with an holy seed (Malachi 2:15); and for preventing of uncleanness (1 Corinthians 7:2, 9).

Exposition
Marriage is an ordinance of God, designed for the mutual help of husband and wife, for the honourable propagation of the human race, and for other important purposes connected with the comfort and improvement of the species. It was instituted before the entrance of sin, and must, therefore, be a holy ordinance, and no hindrance to men in the service of God. The Lord saw that 'it was not good for Adam', even in Paradise, 'to be alone', and that 'there was no help meet for him' to be found among all the other creatures. He was therefore pleased to form the woman from his side, as 'bone of his bone, and flesh of his flesh', and, having brought her to Adam, he joined them together as husband and wife, and thus gave an example to be imitated by their descendants. As God made no more than one woman for Adam, he thereby plainly indicated his will that every man should have only one wife, and every woman only one husband. In this manner Malachi explains the fact, when he says: 'And did not he make one?' – namely one woman – 'yet had he the residue of the Spirit. And wherefore one? That he might seek a godly seed' (Malachi 2:15).

Polygamy was first introduced by Lamech, an abandoned descendant of Cain (Genesis 4:19) and, though practised by the patriarchs and other pious men, it is contrary both to the divine institution and to the law of nature. As God in his providence maintains so near an equality between the males and females born into the world, it is manifestly his intention that one woman only should be assigned to one man; and wherever polygamy has prevailed, it has been attended with numerous evils, both to the parties themselves and to the public. It promotes jealousies and contentions among the wives of the same husband; produces distracted affections, or the loss of all affection in the husband himself; tends to the degradation of the female character, to the neglect of children and manifold other evils. The words of Christ plainly imply a prohibition of polygamy; for if 'whosoever putteth away his wife [except it be for incontinence], and *marrieth* another, committeth adultery' (Matthew 19:9), he who marrieth another *without* putting away the first, must be no less guilty of adultery.

Section 3

It is lawful for all sorts of people to marry who are able with judgment to give their consent (Hebrews 13:4; 1 Timothy 4:3; 1 Corinthians 7:36-38; Genesis 24:57, 58): yet it is the duty of Christians to marry only in the Lord (1 Corinthians 7:39). And therefore such as profess the true reformed religion should not marry with infidels, Papists, or other idolaters: neither should such as are godly be unequally yoked, by marrying with such as are notoriously wicked in their life, or maintain damnable heresies (Genesis 34:14; Exodus 34:16; Deuteronomy 7:3, 4; 1 Kings 11:4; Nehemiah 13:25-27; Malachi 2:11, 12; 2 Corinthians 6:14).

Exposition

The Church of Rome forbids the marriage of the clergy, and of all under the celibate vow. This is one of 'the doctrines of devils' which is mentioned as characteristic of the great apostasy: 'Now the Spirit speaketh expressly, that in the latter times some shall depart from the faith, giving heed to seducing spirits, and *doctrines of devils*, speaking lies to hypocrisy, having their conscience seared with a hot iron; *forbidding to marry...*' (1 Timothy 4:1-3). It is a doctrine in direct opposition to the Word of God, which allows 'all sorts of people to marry, who are able with judgment to give their consent'. An apostle declares that 'marriage is honourable in *all*' (Hebrews 13:4), without excepting those who are employed in the public offices of religion. Under the Old Testament, the prophets, the priests and all those who attended more immediately upon the service of God were permitted to marry. Under the New Testament, also, the ministers of religion have an express allowance to enter into the marriage state. That the Apostle Peter was a married man is evident from Matthew 8:14. Philip the evangelist 'had four daughters, virgins, which did prophesy' (Acts 21:9). Paul claimed a right to 'lead about a sister, a wife, as well as the other apostles' (1 Corinthians 9:5). And it is repeatedly mentioned that 'a bishop must be blameless, the husband of one wife' (1 Timothy 3:2; Titus 1:6). It is thus evident that the ministers of religion have the same liberty in this matter that other men enjoy. The constrained celibacy of the Romish clergy is one of the chief causes of the abandoned profligacy which has ever existed in that Church.

Under the former dispensation, the people of God were expressly prohibited entering into marriages with heathens, and especially with the Canaanites (Exodus 34:12-16; Deuteronomy 7:3). Such marriages were reckoned in themselves null, and so Ezra and Nehemiah caused the Jews to put away their heathenish wives (Ezra 10; Nehemiah 13).

Upon the introduction of the gospel, it must have frequently happened that a husband or a wife embraced the Christian faith, while their partner continued attached to idolatry. In this case, the Apostle Paul determines that the believing husband or wife should continue with the unbeliever: 'If any brother hath a wife that believeth not, and she be pleased to dwell with him, let him not put her away. And the woman which hath an husband that believeth not, and he be pleased to dwell with her, let her not leave him' (1 Corinthians 7:12, 13). The apostle thus decides, that after marriage, if either the husband or the wife embrace the Christian religion, the other party still continuing a heathen, this difference in religion is not a sufficient ground for a separation. If the idolatrous party is still willing to live with the party converted, it is the duty of the believer cheerfully and faithfully to perform his or her obligations, notwithstanding their different sentiments regarding religion.

But if a Christian man or woman have their choice to make, they are required to marry 'only in the Lord'. The intermarrying of the professors of the true with those of a false religion, or of believers with those who are evidently strangers to true godliness, is prohibited, at least in ordinary cases: 'Be ye not unequally yoked together with unbelievers' (2 Corinthians 6:14). The disregard of this rule is productive of many evils. The Christian who unites himself to such a partner exposes himself to many powerful temptations. He must necessarily mingle in the society of those whose views and pursuits are of a character entirely opposite to his own. His opportunities of religious improvement will be greatly lessened. Family worship can scarcely be maintained. His endeavours to train up his children in the fear of God will be counteracted by the example and instructions of his unbelieving partner. Instead of an help meet for him in his Christian warfare, she will prove a snare to his soul. From this cause, many have apostatized from the faith, and others who have maintained their integrity have pierced themselves through with many sorrows.

Section 4
Marriage ought not to be within the degrees of consanguinity or affinity forbidden in the Word (Leviticus 18; 1 Corinthians 5:1; Amos 2:7); nor can such incestuous marriages ever be made lawful by any law of man or consent of parties, so as those persons may live together as man and wife (Mark 6:18; Leviticus 18:24-28). The man may not marry any of his wife's kindred nearer in blood than he may of his own (Leviticus 20:19-21), nor the woman of her husband's kindred nearer in blood than of her own.

Section 5
Adultery or fornication committed after a contract, being detected before marriage, giveth just occasion to the innocent party to dissolve that contract (Matthew 1:18-20). In the case of adultery after marriage, it is lawful for the innocent party to sue out a divorce (Matthew 5:31, 32), and, after the divorce, to marry another, as if the offending party were dead (Matthew 19:9; Romans 7:2, 3).

Section 6
Although the corruption of man be such as is apt to study arguments unduly to put asunder those whom God hath joined together in marriage; yet nothing but adultery, or such wilful desertion as can no way be remedied by the Church or civil magistrate, is cause sufficient of dissolving the bond of marriage (Matthew 19:8, 9; 1 Corinthians 7:15; Matthew 19:6): wherein a public and orderly course of proceeding is to be observed, and the persons concerned in it not left to their own wills and discretion in their own case (Deuteronomy 24:1-4).

Exposition
In the Mosaic law marriage was expressly forbidden within certain degrees of consanguinity or affinity (Leviticus 18); and by the laws of our country the prohibition is extended to the same degrees. Marriages contracted within these degrees are in themselves justly deemed invalid, and may properly be dissolved.

Moses permitted the Jews, 'because of the hardness of their

hearts', to put away their wives, to prevent greater evils; but in the New Testament, a divorce is only permitted in case of adultery, or of wilful and obstinate desertion. There can be no question that adultery is a just ground for 'the innocent party to sue out a divorce, and, after the divorce, to marry another, as if the offending party were dead'; for Christ has plainly decided this case: 'I say unto you, That whosoever shall put away his wife, saving for the cause of fornication, causeth her to commit adultery; and whosoever shall marry her that is divorced, committeth adultery' (Matthew 5:32).

But whether the wilful and obstinate desertion of one of the parties sets the other party at liberty to marry again, may admit of dispute. Many divines of great name have maintained the affirmative, and have thought the case to be expressly determined by the Apostle Paul: 'If the unbelieving depart, let him depart. A brother or a sister is not under bondage in such cases' (1 Corinthians 7:15). At verse 11, the apostle plainly declares that the party who wilfully and obstinately deserted the other was not at liberty to marry again during the other's life. But at verse 15, he appears to declare that the party who was deserted, after using due means for the return of the party deserting, was free to marry again.[1] And the decision seems just; for by irreclaimable desertion the marriage bond is broken, and the ends for which marriage was appointed are effectually defeated; and it is not reasonable that the innocent party should be denied all relief. Our Confession, accordingly, teaches that not only adultery, but also 'such wilful desertion as can no way be remedied by the Church or civil magistrate, is cause sufficient for dissolving the bond of marriage'; and the law of Scotland also allows of divorce in case of wilful and irreclaimable desertion.

It ought to be observed, however, that even adultery does not, *ipso facto*, dissolve the bond of marriage, nor may it be dissolved by consent of parties. The violation of the marriage vow only invests the injured party with a right to demand the dissolution of it by the competent authority; and if he chooses to exercise that right, the divorce must be effected 'by a public and orderly course of proceeding'.

---

1. This view of the text has been warmly opposed by Dr. Dwight (Sermon cxxi.); but the interpretation given above has been the general opinion of enlightened statesmen as well as theologians in this country.

CHAPTER 25

THE CHURCH

Section 1
The catholic or universal Church, which is invisible, consists of the whole number of the elect that have been, are, or shall be, gathered into one, under Christ the head thereof; and is the spouse, the body, the fulness of him that filleth all in all (Ephesians 1:10, 22, 23; 5:23, 27, 32; Colossians 1:18).

Section 2
The visible Church, which is also catholic or universal under the gospel (not confined to one nation, as before, under the law), consists of all those throughout the world that profess the true religion (1 Corinthians 1:2; 12:12, 13; Psalm 2:8; Revelation 7:9; Romans 15:9-12), together with their children (1 Corinthians 7:14; Acts 2:39; Ezekiel 16:20, 21; Romans 11:16; Genesis 3:15; 17:7); and is the kingdom of the Lord Jesus Christ (Matthew 13:47; Isaiah 9:7), the house and family of God (Ephesians 2:19; 3:15), out of which there is no ordinary possibility of salvation (Acts 2:47).

Section 3
Unto this catholic visible Church Christ hath given the ministry, oracles, and ordinances of God, for the gathering and perfecting of the saints in this life to the end of the world; and doth by his own presence and Spirit, according to his promise, make them effectual thereunto (1 Corinthians 12:28. Ephesians 4:11-13. Matthew 28:19, 20. Isaiah 59:21).

Exposition
The Greek work *ekklesia*, which we render 'church', is derived from a word which signifies to *call out*, and denotes an assembly called out and convened for any particular purpose. In democratic states it was applied to the assemblies of the people, who were called out by a public herald, and gathered into a certain place, in order to deliberate together. To specify the various meanings which this word bears in the New Testament is at present unnecessary; it is sufficient for our purpose to remark, that the term is used to denote an assembly or society of men, called by the gospel out of the world which lieth in wickedness, into the faith and fellowship of Jesus Christ. But there is a twofold calling; the one *external*, merely by the Word – the other *internal*, by the Holy Spirit, which

is peculiar to the elect. Hence the Church may be considered under a twofold aspect or form; the one external or visible – the other internal or invisible.

The Church, viewed as invisible, consists according to our Confession 'of the whole number of the elect that have been, are, or shall be, gathered into one, under Christ, the head thereof'. Of this Church the apostle speaks:

> Christ loved the church, and gave himself for it; that he might sanctify and cleanse it, with the washing of water by the word, that he might present it to himself a glorious church, not having spot or wrinkle, or any such thing; but that it should be holy and without blemish (Ephesians 5:25-27).

Of the members of this Church some have already finished their course, and are now perfected spirits in heaven; others are still living upon earth, and engaged in the Christian warfare; which diversity of condition has given occasion for the ordinary distinction between the Church *triumphant*, and the Church *militant*. The invisible Church, viewed as comprehending the whole number of the elect, will not be completed until that day when 'the Lord shall make up his jewels'. This Church, viewed as actually existing on earth at any particular period, is composed of those who have been called by divine grace into the fellowship of the gospel, and sanctified by the truth; and these constitute one Church, because, however distant in place, and diversified in circumstances, they are vitally united to Christ as their head, and to one another as members of the same body, by the bond of the Spirit and of faith. 'By one Spirit are we all baptized into one body, whether we be Jews or Gentiles, whether we be bond or free; and have been all made to drink into one Spirit' (1 Corinthians 12:13).

> This Church is said to be invisible, because it cannot be discovered by the eye. It is not separated from the world in respect of place, but of state. It lies hidden in the visible Church, from which it cannot be certainly distinguished. The qualifications of its members are internal; their faith and love are not the objects of sense. Towards our fellow-men we can exercise only the judgment of charity, founded on probable grounds; but we are liable to err, and, from various causes, may suppose saints to be hypocrites, and hypocrites to be saints. It is unseen by every eye but that which 'searches the heart and tries the

reins of the children of men'. 'The Lord,' and he only, 'knows them that are his.'[1]

The visible Church, according to our Confession, consists 'of all those throughout the world that profess the true religion, together with their children'. Of this Church the Apostle Paul speaks in 1 Corinthians 12:28: 'God hath set some in the Church, first apostles, secondarily prophets, thirdly teachers, after that miracles, then gifts of healings, helps, governments, diversities of tongues.'

This Church is called visible, not only because the persons who compose it are not angels or separate spirits, but men dwelling in mortal flesh, but because, as a society, it falls under the observation of our senses. The members are known; their assemblies are public; we may be present in them, and observe the celebration of the several parts of their worship. It is distinguishable, like any other society; and we can say, Here is the Church of Christ; but there is the Church of the Jews or of the Mohammedans. Nothing more is necessary to discover it than the use of our senses. Having learned, by the perusal of the Scriptures, what are the discriminating characters of the Church, wherever we perceive a society whose creed and observances are, upon the whole, conformable to this pattern, we are authorized to say, This is the Church, or rather, a part of the Church.[2]

When we speak of the visible and invisible Church, this is not to be understood as if there were two Churches, or as if one part of the Church were visible and another invisible. The former includes the latter, but they are not co-extensive; the same individuals who constitute the Church considered as invisible, belong also to the Church considered as visible; but many who belong to the visible, are not comprehended in the invisible Church.

The ministry and ordinances of the gospel, which Christ has given to the visible Church, are designed for the gathering of sinners into the Church invisible, and for the perfecting of the saints; and, by the concurring influences of his Spirit, they are made effectual to these ends. This is clearly taught by the Apostle Paul:

1. Dick's *Lectures on Theology*, vol. iv., pp. 309, 310.
2. Ibid., pp. 308, 309.

> He gave some, apostles; and some, prophets; and some, evangelists; and some, pastors and teachers; for the perfecting of the saints, for the work of the ministry, for the edifying of the body of Christ: till we all come in the unity of the faith, and of the knowledge of the Son of God, unto a perfect man, unto the measure of the stature of the fulness of Christ (Ephesians 4:11-13).

This being the design for which a gospel ministry was appointed in the Church, it will certainly be continued until all the elect are gathered to Christ, and every one of them brought to perfection. So much is implied in the promise of Christ: 'Lo, I am with you alway, even unto the end of the world' (Matthew 28:20). This also secures the success of the gospel. At some periods few may seem to be gathered unto Christ; but, from time to time, some are 'added to the Church of such as shall be saved'. All that the Father gave to Christ shall come unto him, and none of them shall be lost. 'Other sheep I have,' says Christ, 'which are not of this fold; them also I must bring, and they shall hear my voice; and there shall be one fold and one Shepherd' (John 10:16).

The epithet 'catholic' – which is here applied to the visible Church – does not occur in Scripture, but has been used from an early period, although not always in the same sense. As employed in our Confession, it is synonymous with the term universal. It is well known that the Church of Rome arrogantly claims to be the catholic Church, and pronounces all beyond her pale, or who do not submit to the usurped supremacy of the Pope, to be heretics, and accursed of God. It might be easily shown that her pretensions are unfounded and presumptuous – that in no age has she realized the character of universal. But the true Church of Christ is not confined to any country or sect; it comprehends all who profess the true religion and observe the ordinances of the gospel; and the several particular Churches, when regularly constituted in the different parts of the Christian world, are integral parts of the catholic or universal Church.

Having given a general explanation of these sections, the several propositions which they embrace may be more particularly considered.

1. There is a universal invisible Church, comprehending the whole body of believers, or all the elect of God, as called out of the world unto the fellowship of Jesus Christ. This is denied by

Papists, who maintain that the catholic Church is absolutely visible – as really as any of the kingdoms of this world, and consists not merely of the elect effectually called, but of unbelievers and manifest sinners – even all who profess subjection to the See of Rome. But the Church of which we now speak consists of such only as are true believers. These, it must be admitted, are not visible; and, consequently, the Church which they constitute must be invisible. As men, believers are the objects of sense; but as believers, they come not under the cognizance of the senses. In the visible Church they are mingled with hypocritical professors, and the one cannot be certainly and infallibly distinguished from the other. The Scripture teaches us that there is a Church which is the spouse of Christ, and whose glory is internal (Psalm 45:13); which is the mystical body of Christ, conjoined with him by spiritual bonds (Ephesians 1:23); and the individual members of which are joined together in one body by one Spirit (1 Corinthians 12:13). But these things cannot be discerned by the senses, and we must, therefore, believe that there is a catholic or universal invisible Church, composed of true believers.

2. There is a universal visible Church, consisting of the whole body of professing Christians, dispersed throughout all parts of the world. This is denied by the Independents, who confine the idea of a visible Church to a single congregation, which ordinarily assembles in one place for public worship. But, in various places of the New Testament, the word Church (as applied to the visible Church) cannot be restricted to any particular congregational Church. When we are told that 'Saul made havock of the church' (Acts 8:3), and that 'he persecuted the church of God, and wasted it' (Galatians 1:13), it cannot be supposed that it was only a single congregation that was exposed to his fury. It is related (Acts 9:31), that, after his conversion, 'the churches had rest throughout all Judea, and Galilee, and Samaria'; which certainly intimates that formerly they had suffered by his blind zeal; yet they are all spoken of as one Church persecuted by him.

All Christians throughout the world are united together in such a way as to constitute them one Church. This is evident from the various designations given to the catholic visible Church. It is called 'a body', in allusion to the natural body, consisting of various members, all so connected together as to form one body. It is termed 'the kingdom of God'; but a kingdom is one, though made up of many provinces and subordinate governments. It is designated 'the house of God'; which implies that, though made up of many parts, it is but one spiritual family.

As it is impossible that the whole body of professing Christians can meet together in one place for the observance of the ordinances of religion, it is necessary that particular Churches or congregations should be formed for this purpose; but these particular Churches constitute several integral parts of the one catholic or universal visible Church.[3]

This visible Church comprehends hypocrites and formal professors, as well as those that are effectually called and regenerated. On this account the Church is compared to a *floor*, in which there is not only wheat but also chaff (Matthew 3:12); to a *field*, where tares as well as good seed are sown (Matthew 13:24, 25); to a *net*, which gathers bad fish together with the good (verse 47); to a *great house*, in which are vessels of every kind, some to honour and some to dishonour (2 Timothy 2:20).

Such being the state of the visible Church, as exhibited in Scripture, there can be no warrant to exact from persons positive marks of their regeneration, as indispensable to their admission to the fellowship of the Church, and to require from them an account of their religious experience for the purpose of forming some judgment about their spiritual state. Christ has not authorized the office-bearers of the Church to make an entire separation between true believers and formal professors of religion (Matthew 13:30). This is a task to which they are altogether incompetent; for, as the servants of the husbandman could not, for a considerable time, distinguish the tares from the wheat, so the servants of Christ cannot infallibly distinguish hypocrites from sincere believers. They can only judge of persons by their external deportment; and this cannot furnish evidence sufficient to enable them to pronounce an unerring judgment about their spiritual state before God. The ground of admission to the fellowship and privileges of the visible Church is a scriptural profession. Of this alone the office-bearers of the Church are capable of judging; and to proceed upon a judgment about their spiritual state as it is in the sight of God, would be to assume the prerogative of him who alone 'searcheth the heart'.

3. Whytock's *Essays on the Church*, essay ii.

3. The children of professing Christians are members of the visible Church. This is denied by Antipaedobaptists; and many Independents, though they admit infants to baptism, hesitate about what account is to be made of them; whether they are to be considered as Church members, or only as put under the care of the Church in order to their preparation for that state.

> It is a considerable presumption in favour of the Church state of the infants of Church members, that, in civil society, the privilege of children is the same with that of their parents. The kingdoms of this world consist of infants as well as adults; and shall we think that infants are excluded from a place in the kingdom of Christ? The children of British subjects are entitled to the same privileges as their parents, although, in the meantime, they be not capable of an understanding, or full enjoyment of them. Is it not, therefore, reasonable to suppose that the constitution of Christ's kingdom is every whit as favourable to the privilege of infants? We are not, however, left to supposition and analogy in this matter; their privilege may be clearly established from the Word of God. God's covenant with his Church extends to parents and their children. Infants were members of the Church under the Old Testament, and there is no word of their exclusion under the New; nay, in the New Testament there are various testimonies that the privilege of Church membership extends to infants still.[4]

Our Lord himself asserts it most expressly: 'Jesus said, Suffer little children to come unto me, and forbid them not: for of such is the kingdom of God' (Luke 18:16). If, by 'the kingdom of God', as some contend, be here meant the state of glory, we might strongly infer that children, being heirs of glory, ought to be acknowledged as members of the visible Church. But it is more probable that, in this passage, by 'the kingdom of God' is to be understood the Church on earth; and our Lord assigns as the reason why children should be suffered to come to him, that he recognised them as members of his Church.

4. There is no ordinary possibility of salvation out of the visible Church. This is widely different from the doctrine of the Romish Church, which affirms that the Roman Catholic is the *only* Church, and that there is no salvation out of that Church. The same arrogant pretensions are frequently put forth by proud, uncharitable Prelatists, in the southern part of the island; who, assuming that

---

4. Whytock's *Essays on the Church*, essay ix.

their own society is 'the Church', pronounce all who do not submit to the government of bishops to be schismatics, and hand them over to the uncovenanted mercies of God; or, in other words, exclude them from all hope of salvation. But we are not so presumptuous as to confine the possibility of salvation within the limits of any particular Church, neither do we absolutely affirm that there is no possibility of salvation out of the universal visible Church.

Our Confession, in terms remarkably guarded, only asserts, that 'out of the visible Church there is no *ordinary* possibility of salvation'. There is, then, a possibility of salvation without its pale; for a person may, by some means, such as by the perusal of the Scriptures, be brought to the knowledge of the truth, and have no opportunity of joining himself to the Church; but such cases are extraordinary: and, as God usually works by means, there is no *ordinary* possibility of salvation out of the visible Church, because those who are out of the Church are destitute of the ordinary means of salvation.

Section 4
This catholic Church hath been sometimes more, sometimes less visible (Romans 11:3, 4; Revelation 12:6, 14). And particular Churches, which are members thereof, are more or less pure, according as the doctrine of the gospel is taught and embraced, ordinances administered, and public worship performed more or less purely in them (Revelation 2; 3; 1 Corinthians 5:6, 7).

Section 5
The purest Churches under heaven are subject to mixture and error (1 Corinthians 13:12; Revelation 2; 3; Matthew 13:24-30, 47); and some have so degenerated as to become no Churches of Christ, but synagogues of Satan (Revelation 18:2; Romans 11:18-22). Nevertheless, there shall be always a Church on earth, to worship God according to his will (Matthew 16:18; Psalm 72:17; 102:28; Matthew 28:19, 20).

Exposition
1. The catholic Church has been sometimes more, sometimes less visible. It has been already shown that the Church, as to its external state, is visible, and it will afterwards appear that the Church shall never perish. But though the visible Church always exists in some part of the world, it is not always equally flourishing and equally conspicuous. As the moon waxes and wanes, so the Church

sometimes shines forth with splendour, and at other times is so obscured as to be scarcely discernible. It may be so reduced in numbers, and the few that remain faithful may be so scattered, or compelled to hide themselves, through the violence of persecution, that the most discerning Christian shall scarcely perceive the form of a visible Church.

This we maintain in opposition to the doctrine of the Church of Rome, that the Church has been, is, and shall be, most gloriously visible to the whole world. This doctrine is refuted by the history of the Church, both under the Old and the New Testament. Under the former dispensation, so general was the defection to idolatry, and so violent the rage of persecution, during the reign of Ahab, that Elijah supposed he was the only worshipper of the true God that survived. God had indeed reserved to himself seven thousand men who had not bowed the knee to the image of Baal – but they were 'hidden ones'; and Elijah, having failed to discover them, came to this conclusion: 'I, even I, only am left' (1 Kings 19:10). Under the latter dispensation, we read of a period when two wings of a great eagle were given to the woman (that is, to the Church), that she might fly into the wilderness, to hide herself (Revelation 12:14). The Church is always liable to be oppressed by persecutions, or corrupted by errors; and both of these must obscure her brightness and glory.

2. The purest Churches under heaven are subject both to mixture and error. Papists strenuously maintain that the Church cannot err; but as they are not agreed among themselves where this infallibility resides – whether in the Pope or in a general council, or in both united –we may regard this as affording indubitable evidence that the claim is preposterous and unfounded. If any individual or Church were really invested with a privilege so important and distinguished as infallibility, it would certainly have been clearly announced where it is lodged. We need only appeal to history for innumerable proofs that particular Churches have erred, and that no Church has erred so egregiously as the Church of Rome. 'The faith once delivered to the saints' will be preserved by some society or other, greater or less, in all generations; but no particular Church is secured against error.

3. A true Church shall always be preserved upon earth. Often has the Church been greatly reduced as to numbers, and particular Churches have become so corrupt that they might rather be

considered as synagogues of Satan; but never has the Church of Christ been annihilated. And as the Church has subsisted from its first erection in Paradise to the present hour, so it will continue throughout all subsequent ages, till the second coming of Christ. Earthly kingdoms may be overturned, and the mightiest empires laid in ruins; but neither power nor policy can ever accomplish the utter destruction of the Church. There is, indeed, no security for the permanent continuance of the Church in any particular country where it has been once planted; but we have the most solid ground for assurance that, in one place or another, Christ shall have a seed to serve him and to perpetuate his name as long as sun and moon endure. Hitherto the Church has, for the most part, been subjected to persecution from the powers of this world; but, though like a bush burning, she has not been consumed. Power and stratagem may be combined to effect her ruin, but in vain; she is 'built upon a rock, and the gates of hell shall not prevail against her'.

Section 6

There is no other head of the Church but the Lord Jesus Christ (Colossians 1:18; Ephesians 1:22): nor can the Pope of Rome in any sense be head thereof; but is that Antichrist, that man of sin and son of perdition, that exalteth himself in the Church against Christ, and all that is called God (Matthew 23:8-10; 2 Thessalonians 2:3, 4, 8, 9; Revelation 13:6).

Exposition

That the Lord Jesus Christ is the alone head of the Church must be maintained, not only in opposition to Papists, who affirm that the Pope of Rome, as the successor of Peter and the vicegerent of Christ, is the head of the universal Church; but also in opposition to Erastians, who make the supreme magistrate the head of the Church within his own dominions.

A universal headship or dominion belongs to Christ. As God, he has a natural and essential right to rule and dispose of all creatures at his pleasure, and for the manifestation of his own glory. As mediator, he has a universal headship by donation from the Father. It is said the Father 'gave him to be the head over all things to the Church' (Ephesians 1:22); where, it is to be observed, the apostle is not treating of Christ's headship over the Church, but of his universal headship as Mediator. He is constituted head 'over all things'; but this power is delegated to him that he may over-rule all things for the good of the Church; and therefore he is said to be head 'over all things *to the Church*', or for her benefit. But Christ has a peculiar headship over the Church, which is his body. This is expressly asserted: 'He is the head of the body, the Church' (Colossians 1:18). Here he is compared to the head of the natural body; and in Ephesians 5:23, he is declared to be the head of the Church, as the husband is the head of the wife.

To the visible Church Christ is a head of government and direction. He is the 'Ruler in Israel', and 'the government shall be upon his shoulder' (Isaiah 9:6). 'Yet have I set my King,' says Jehovah, 'upon my holy hill of Zion' (Psalm 2:6). To him it belongs to enact laws for his Church – to institute the ordinances of worship, and the form of government to be observed by her – to appoint her office bearers, and to prescribe the manner of their admission into office. To the Church invisible Christ is not only a head of government and direction, but also of vital influence. Hence he is called 'the head, from which all the body, by joints and bands, having nourishment ministered, and knit together, increaseth with the increase of God' (Colossians 2:19). Christ is the sole and exclusive head of the Church, whether considered as visible or as invisible. His authority alone is to be acknowledged by the Church, as her supreme Lawgiver. Her language must ever be: 'The Holy One of Israel is our king.' Let men distinguish as they will, but as a body with more heads than one would be a monster in nature, so the Scripture clearly shows that the body of Christ, which is the Church, is no such monster. As there is 'one body', so there is only 'one Lord'. Christ has not delegated his authority either to popes or princes; and though he is now in heaven as to his bodily presence, yet he needs no depute to act for him in the Church below. Before he ascended up on high, he gave this precious promise to his disciples: 'Lo, I am with you alway, even unto the end of the world': and 'where two or three are gathered together in his name, there he is in the midst of them' (Matthew 28:20, 18:20).

Daring encroachments have been often made upon this royal prerogative of Christ, both by ecclesiastical and civil powers. Long has the *Man of Sin* and Son of *Perdition* blasphemously arrogated universal headship and lordly dominion; and when the Reformation took place in England, the headship over the Church was only transferred from the Roman Pontiff to the British

Sovereign. Henry VIII. was recognised as 'supreme head of the Church of England'; and it was enacted, 'that the king, his heirs, etc., shall be taken, accepted, and reputed, the only supreme head on earth of the Church of England, called *Anglicana Ecclesia*; and shall have and enjoy, annexed and united to the imperial crown of this realm, as well the title and style thereof as all honours, dignities, immunities, profits, and commodities to the said dignity of supreme head of the said Church belonging and appertaining'.[5] It was also enacted, that his majesty hath full authority to exercise 'ecclesiastical jurisdiction'; and 'that the archbishops and bishops, have no manner of jurisdiction ecclesiastical, but by, under, and from the royal majesty'.[6] In the commencement of Queen Elizabeth's reign, the metaphorical term *head* was changed into *supreme governor*; but both terms signify the same thing. No part of the power or authority which had been possessed by her royal predecessors was relinquished; for, at the same time, it was enacted, that 'all jurisdictions – *spiritual* and *ecclesiastical* –should for ever be united and annexed to the imperial crown'.

This sacrilegious usurpation of spiritual authority, and impious invasion of Christ's sovereignty, is sanctioned by the Church of England in her 37th Article. It runs thus: 'The queen's majesty hath the chief power in this realm of England, and other her dominions; under whom the chief government of all estates of this realm, whether they be ecclesiastical or civil, *in all causes* doth appertain.' Some Churchmen, indeed, seem to be ashamed of recognising the sovereign as *head* or *supreme governor* of the Church, and have attempted to palliate or explain away the real import of the title. But the attempt is vain; of the spiritual jurisdiction which the title involves, and of the Erastian bondage under which the Church of England is held, numerous proofs can be easily adduced. Who knows not, for example, that the appointment of all her bishops belongs to the sovereign – that her clergy cannot meet in convocation without the permission of her majesty; and that the convocation has actually been suspended, or virtually abolished, for upwards of a century? That a Church so completely fettered is utterly powerless for the suppression of heresy and for the exercise of discipline recent events have too clearly demonstrated.

5. The 26th, Henry VIII., cap. 1.
6. The 37th, Henry VIII. cap. 17.

The Church of Scotland, at the era of the Reformation, nobly asserted, and practically vindicated, the sole headship of Christ. This was especially the grand and leading principle of the Second Reformation; and it was in the way of contending for the royal prerogatives of Christ, as her alone king and head, and resisting the Erastian encroachments of aspiring princes upon her spiritual liberties, that many of her sons suffered bonds and exile, and shed their blood in fields and on scaffolds. Though the sole headship of Christ is explicitly asserted in our Confession of Faith, yet it is deeply to be regretted that this vital principle was not more effectually guarded in the Revolution Settlement. The Act 1592, upon which the Church was erected at this time, contained no acknowledgement of the headship of Christ; and it was not formally asserted by any act of the General Assembly. Though a regal supremacy was neither directly claimed by the Crown nor conceded by the Church, yet it was not long till it was virtually exercised. The meetings of the General Assembly were repeatedly dissolved and prorogued by the sovereign (during 1691-95) and, in 1703, when the Assembly had prepared the draft of an act for the purpose of asserting the supremacy of Christ, the intrinsic power of the Church, and the divine right of the Presbyterian government, it was abruptly dissolved by her majesty's commissioner, without any recorded protest.

> But ecclesiastical independence was still more invaded, and spiritual interests more effectually subjected to secular dominion, by the restoration of the power of lay-patrons, after it had been repeatedly abolished. The power of patronage, when it is of any real effect in the settlement of the vacant churches, flows from the same spring with the ecclesiastical supremacy, and can neither be vindicated nor condemned, but on the same principles with it; and is indeed, when exercised by the Crown, a branch of it.[7]

Without referring particularly to those recent struggles of the Church to vindicate her spiritual independence, which have issued in the disruption of the Scottish Establishment, there is nothing, it may be remarked, more clearly evinced by these events than the determined resolution of the State to retain and exercise an Erastian power over the Church. But the Christian people of Scotland have given the most unequivocal proofs of their continued and firm

7. Bruce's *Dissertation on the Supremacy of Civil Powers*, p. 105.

attachment to the sole supremacy of Christ as 'king in Zion' – a truth in defence of which their ancestors 'loved not their lives unto the death'. They cannot contend or suffer in a nobler cause. Those who assume a headship over the Church of Christ, are guilty of an impious usurpation of his prerogatives; and his faithful subjects are bound to display their loyalty to him by asserting his sole right to reign and rule in his own Church, and by giving no countenance to a claim so degrading to the Church, and so dishonouring to her alone king and head.

CHAPTER 26

COMMUNION OF SAINTS

Section 1

All saints that are united to Jesus Christ, their head, by his Spirit, and by faith, have fellowship with him in his graces, sufferings, death, resurrection and glory (1 John 1:3; Ephesians 3:16-19; John 1:16; Ephesians 2:5, 6; Philippians 3:10; Romans 6:5, 6; 2 Timothy 2:12). And being united to one another in love, they have communion in each other's gifts and graces (Ephesians 4:15, 16; 1 Corinthians 12:7; 3:21-23; Colossians 2:19); and are obliged to the performance of such duties, public and private, as do conduce to their mutual good, both in the inward and outward man (1 Thessalonians 5:11, 14; Romans 1:11, 12, 14; 1 John 3:16-18; Galatians 6:10).

Section 2

Saints, by profession, are bound to maintain an holy fellowship and communion in the worship of God, and in performing such other spiritual services as tend to their mutual edification (Hebrews 10:24, 25; Acts 2:42, 46; Isaiah 2:3; 1 Corinthians 11:20); as also in relieving each other in outward things, according to their several abilities and necessities. Which communion, as God offereth opportunity, is to be extended unto all those who in every place call upon the name of the Lord Jesus (Acts 2:44, 45; 1 John 3:17; 2 Corinthians 8, 9; Acts 11:29, 30).

Exposition

Communion is founded in union. The above sections embrace: *First,* The union of the saints to Jesus Christ, and their communion with him; *Secondly,* The union and communion of real saints with one another; *Thirdly,* The union of saints by profession, and the communion which they are bound to maintain.

1. *All saints are united to Jesus Christ.* This is not an essential union, such as subsists between the sacred persons of the Godhead; nor a personal union, such as exists between the divine and human natures in the person of Christ; nor merely a political union, like that between a king and his subjects; nor a mere moral union, like that between two friends. Between Christ and believers there is a legal union, like that betwixt a surety and the person for

whom he engages. This union was formed from all eternity, when Christ was appointed their federal head. But, besides this, there is a spiritual union formed between them in time, of which our Confession here treats. It is a profound mystery, and, for this reason, is usually denominated a mystical union. But, though deeply mysterious, its reality cannot be questioned. Sometimes it is expressed in Scripture by believers being in Christ: 'There is now, therefore, no condemnation to them which are in Christ Jesus' (Romans 8:1). At other times Christ is said to be in believers: 'Know ye not your own-selves, how that Jesus Christ is in you, except ye be reprobates' (2 Corinthians 13:5). Sometimes both modes of expression are joined together: 'Abide in me, and I in you' (John 15:4). This union is exhibited and illustrated in Scripture by various similitudes. It is compared to the union between a tree and its branches (John 15:5), to the union between the building and the foundation by which it is supported (1 Peter 2:4, 6), to the union between husband and wife (Ephesians 5:31, 32), and to the union between the head and the members of the body (Ephesians 4:15, 16). These similitudes, though they come far short of the union which they represent, yet clearly import its reality.

In all unions, there is something which binds together the things or persons united. As the union between Christ and his people is spiritual in its nature, so are its bonds; and these are the Holy Spirit on Christ's part, and faith on their part. Christ apprehends them by his Spirit, and they receive him by that faith which his Spirit produces in them. Hence he is said to dwell in their hearts by faith. So close and intimate is this union, that Christ and believers are said to be one spirit: 'He that is joined to the Lord is one spirit' with him (1 Corinthians 6:17). But it is the crowning excellence of this union, that it can never be dissolved. The Holy Spirit will never depart from any in whom he has taken up his residence (John 14:16, 17). Satan and all his agents, with all their combined strength and subtilty, cannot separate one soul from Christ (Romans 8:38, 39). Death will break all other ties, and separate the soul from the body, but it cannot dissolve the union between Christ and believers. Hence they are said to 'die in the Lord', and to 'sleep in Jesus' (Revelation 14:13; 1 Thessalonians 4:14).

Being thus united to Christ, believers have fellowship with him in his sufferings and death, and are therefore said to be 'crucified and dead with Christ' (Romans 6:6, 8). They have also fellowship with Christ in his resurrection; for they are 'raised up together with him', and have communion with him in his life (Ephesians 2:6; Galatians 2:20). They have fellowship with him in his victories. He spoiled principalities and powers, overcame the world, destroyed death, and vanquished the grave for them; and they shall be made more than conquerors over all these enemies, through him (Romans 8:37). They have communion with him in all the benefits which he purchased; hence they are said to be 'made partakers of Christ' (Hebrews 3:14), and to be 'complete in him who is the head of all principality and power' (Colossians 2:10); they have an interest in his righteousness, by which he fulfilled the law in their room, and are thus entitled to the blessing of justification; they are adopted into the family of heaven, and made heirs of God, and joint heirs with his Son Jesus Christ; they are sanctified in soul, body, and spirit, being enabled by his grace to die more and more unto sin, and live unto righteousness; they now sit in heavenly places with Christ as their representing head; and, in due time, they shall be glorified in their own persons together with him (Ephesians 2:6; Colossians 2:4). In short, all things are theirs, as the Apostle Paul asserts; and he founds their title to all things upon their union to Christ: 'All things are yours; whether Paul, or Apollos, or Cephas, or the world, or life, or death, or things present, or thing to come; all are yours; and ye are Christ's; and Christ is God's' (1 Corinthians 3:22, 23).

2. All real saints are united to one another, and have communion among themselves. They form one body, are all united to Christ as their common head, and are partakers of one Spirit. They have all obtained like precious faith; and their faith, as to the leading doctrines of the gospel, is substantially the same. They are also united in love, which is called 'the bond of perfectness'. So perfectly were the primitive Christians knit together by this bond, that they were 'of one heart and of one soul' (Acts 4:32). There is nothing which our Saviour more earnestly inculcated upon his followers than mutual love; he represented it as the best proof to themselves, and the most decisive evidence to others, that they were his genuine disciples: 'A new commandment I give unto you, That ye love one another; as I have loved you, that ye also love one another. By this shall all men know that ye are my

disciples, if ye love one another (John 13:34, 35). As the saints 'love our Lord Jesus Christ in sincerity', so they love all in whom they can perceive the image of Christ. Being thus united to one another, they have communion with each other in their gifts and graces. As the natural body consists of many members – some of superior, and others of inferior use, and each member is serviceable to its fellow-members, and contributes to the good of the whole – so the mystical body of Christ is composed of many members, endued with different gifts and graces; and the several members ought to be profitable to each other, and promote the benefit of the whole Church. They are obliged to the performance of such duties as conduce to their mutual good. They ought to be 'kindly affectioned one to another', to 'bear one anothers burdens, and so fulfil the law of Christ', to 'rejoice with them that rejoice, and weep with them that weep', to offer up fervent 'supplication for all saints', and, 'as they have opportunity, do good to all men, especially to them who are of the household of faith'.

3. Saints by profession are also united in one body, and bound to maintain a holy fellowship and communion with each other. Professed saints compose the Church considered as visible; and of this society unity is an essential attribute. This union is not confined to those who live together, and can assemble in one place for the observance of religious ordinances; but extends to 'all that in every place call upon the name of Jesus Christ our Lord, both theirs and ours'. The visible bonds of this unity are specified by the Apostle Paul: 'There is one body and one Spirit, even as ye are called in one hope of your calling; one Lord, one faith, one baptism; one God and Father of all, who is above all, and through all, and in you all' (Ephesians 4:4-6). Our Confession mentions three things in which professed saints are bound to hold fellowship and communion with one another:

First, they ought to *assemble together for joining in the public worship of God*. This species of communion was assiduously maintained by the early Christians: 'They continued steadfastly in the apostles' doctrine, and fellowship, and in breaking of bread, and in prayers' (Acts 2:42). When some, at a later period, had become negligent in cultivating this communion, the apostle warned them against 'forsaking the assembling of themselves together, as the manner of some is'.

The institutions of the gospel were intended as a bond of union among Christians; and by the joint celebration of them communion is maintained and expressed. 'By one Spirit we are all baptized into one body'; and 'being many, we are one bread and one body; for we are all partakers of that one bread' in the sacramental communion (1 Corinthians 10:17; 12:13). It is not necessary to this unity that Christians should all meet for worship in the same place – this is physically impossible; nor are we to conceive of Church communion as local. It consists in their celebrating the same holy ordinances – in their performing acts of worship the same in kind, wherever they assemble; and in their being disposed and ready to embrace every proper occurring opportunity to join with all 'those who in every place call on the name of Jesus Christ the Lord, both theirs and ours'. Thus it was in the primitive Church; and thus it would still be if catholic unity were preserved, and if the institutions of Christ, along with the faith to which they relate, were everywhere preserved pure and entire'.[1]

Secondly, professed saints ought *to perform such other spiritual services as tend to their mutual edification*. They are enjoined to 'follow after the things wherewith one may edify another' (Romans 14:19). Among the 'services which tend to mutual edification', may be mentioned mutual prayer; spiritual conference; admonishing, exhorting, and provoking one another to love and good works; comforting the feeble-minded, supporting the weak, visiting and encouraging the afflicted (Malachi 3:16; Colossians 3:16; 1 Thessalonians 5:11, 14; Hebrews 10:24).

Thirdly, professed saints *ought to relieve each other in outward things*, according to their several abilities and opportunities. Not a few who are 'rich in faith, and heirs of the kingdom which God hath promised to them that love him', are poor in this world (James 2:5). Their Christian brethren, who have 'this world's good', ought to sympathize with them, and minister to their necessities (1 John 3:17). Sometimes Christians in one country suffer 'the spoiling of their goods', and are reduced to great straits, through the violence of persecution; in such cases, their brethren in other places ought to contribute liberally for their relief. This duty was nobly exemplified by the primitive Christians: 'It pleased them of Macedonia and Achaia to make a certain contribution for the poor saints which were at Jerusalem' (Romans 15:25). If professing Christians in one district are unable of themselves to provide for

1. M'Crie on the *Unity of the Church*, pp. 19, 20.

the regular dispensation of public religious ordinances among them, it is no less the duty of their brethren who are placed in more favourable circumstances to afford them pecuniary aid. Thus the strong should support the weak, that the abundance of the one may be a supply for the want of the other, that there may be equality. Ministering to the saints is expressly called 'fellowship' (2 Corinthians 8:4). To this kind of communion the concluding sentence of this section of our Confession may, perhaps, more especially refer: 'Which communion, as God offereth opportunity, is to be extended unto all those who, in every place, call upon the name of the Lord Jesus.' This sentence is closely connected with the clause immediately preceding, which relates to 'relieving each other in outward things'; and the whole of the Scripture proofs adduced refer either to the Church of Jerusalem – which 'had all things common' – or to the saints in one place 'sending relief' to those in distant places who were impoverished by persecution.

It will be admitted, however, that Christian communion of a more extensive nature, including all those services which tend to mutual edification, ought to be maintained with all that call on the name of the Lord Jesus, as opportunity permits; nay, were the visible catholic Church what it ought to be, according to the rule of God's Word, one in profession, the members of this or that particular Church would be entitled to enjoy, and bound to hold, Church communion wherever Providence might order their lot. If professed Christians throughout the world, instead of being divided into diverse and opposing sections, were cemented into one holy brotherhood, then, whoever was admitted into the fellowship of the Church in one place, would be recognised as a member of the catholic Church, and would be entitled to claim the privilege of communion in any particular Church where his lot was cast. On the other hand, whoever was laid under censure in a particular Church, would be considered under the same in all others; and would not be received into communion till the sentence were reversed by the same power, or by a still higher authority. Thus it ought to be: and thus it would be, were that unity which should characterize the visible Church, fully realized. But in the present state of the Church, divided and subdivided as it is into an almost countless number of sections, all of them contending for some peculiar principle or practice which they deem important, and by which they are not only distinguished from, but opposed to, other denominations, such extended Church communion cannot be consistently maintained. It will scarcely be questioned that separation from corrupt Churches becomes, in certain cases, warrantable and necessary; but 'where communion is lawful, it will not be easy to vindicate separation from the charge of schism'.[2] If a particular Church is organized for the special purpose of vindicating the sole headship of Christ and the spiritual independence of his Church – were the members of that Church to join in all the intimacies of communion with another Church which had either avowedly or practically surrendered these distinguishing principles, they would virtually declare that they have no scriptural and conscientious grounds for separation, and expose themselves to the charge of unnecessarily rending that body which Christ so fervently prayed might be 'one'.

Section 3

This communion which the saints have with Christ, doth not make them in any wise partakers of the substance of his Godhead, or to be equal with Christ in any respect: either of which to affirm is impious and blasphemous (Colossians 1:18, 19; 1 Corinthians 8:6; Isaiah 42:8; 1 Timothy 6:15, 16; Psalm 45:7; Hebrews 1:8, 9). Nor doth their communion one with another, as saints, take away or infringe the title of property which each man hath in his goods and possessions (Exodus 20:5; Ephesians 4:28; Acts 5:4).

Exposition

This section guards against two heretical opinions: the one relating to the saints' communion with Christ; the other, to their communion with one another. Certain mystics have employed impious and blasphemous terms in reference to the saints' union and communion with Christ, as if they were *deifed* or *christified*. They have not scrupled to use the phrases of being 'godded in God', and 'christed in Christ', and other expressions equally wild. In the beginning of the sixteenth century, the Anabaptists of Germany, among other absurd and dangerous tenets, contended for the necessity of a community of goods among Christians. This doctrine never made much progress in this country, and modern Anabaptists entirely reject it. In opposition to these extravagant notions, our Confession teaches:

---

2. M'Crie on the *Unity of the Church*, p. 95.

1. That the saints' communion with Christ does not involve a participation of the substance of his Godhead, nor constitute an equality between him and them in any respect. The union that subsists between Christ and believers leaves them distinct persons; and the communion which believers have with Christ does not raise them to an equality with him in dignity. They cannot participate in his divine excellences, which are incommunicable; neither can they share with him in the glory of his mediatory work. He had none to cooperate with him in that arduous work, and he alone must bear the glory; as the saints are not deified, neither are they exalted to be mediators and saviours in conjunction with Christ.

2. That the saints' communion with one another does not take away or infringe upon the rights of private property. The perpetual obligation of the eighth commandment, the admonitions of the New Testament to charity and hospitality, the particular precepts addressed to the high and to the low, to the rich and to the poor – all plainly prove that, under the gospel, each man retains a property in his goods and possessions. We are told, indeed, that in the primitive Church 'all that believed had all things common, and sold their possessions and goods, and parted them to all men, as every man had need' (Acts 2:44, 45). From this 'it has been supposed that there was a real community of goods among the Christians of Jerusalem; or that every man, renouncing all right in his property, delivered it over to a public stock, to which all had an equal claim. It appears, however, from the story of Ananias and Sapphira (Acts 5:4), that the disciples were under no obligation, or bound by no positive law, to dispose of their property for the benefit of the Church; and that, after it was sold, they could retain the whole, or any part of the price, provided that they did not, like those unhappy persons, practise dissimulation and deceit; and it is further evident, from the passage we have quoted, that although in many instances they laid down the price at the apostles' feet, intrusting them with the distribution, yet they sometimes reserved it in their own hands, and gave it to the indigent, according to their own ideas of their need. These considerations seem to prove, that there was not an actual community of goods in the primitive Church; but that, in consequence of the fervent charity which united their hearts and interests, 'no man', as Luke informs us in the fourth chapter, 'said

that ought of the things which he possessed was his own', or appropriated them to his own use, but readily parted with them for the supply of his brethren. There is no evidence that the conduct of the Church of Jerusalem was followed by any other Church, even in the apostolic age; but as far as it is an example of generous love triumphing over the selfish affections, and exciting men to pursue the welfare of others as their own, it is worthy to be imitated to the end of the world.'[3]

3. Dick's *Lectures on the Acts of the Apostles*, lect. iii.

CHAPTER 27

THE SACRAMENTS

Section 1
Sacraments are holy signs and seals of the covenant of grace (Romans 4:11; Genesis 17:7, 10), immediately instituted by God (Matthew 28:19; 1 Corinthians 11:23), to represent Christ and his benefits, and to confirm our interest in him (1 Corinthians 10:16; 11:25, 26; Galatians 3:27, 17); as also to put a visible difference between those that belong unto the Church and the rest of the world (Romans 15:8; Exodus 12:48; Genesis 34:14); and solemnly to engage them to the service of God in Christ, according to his Word (Romans 6:3, 4; 1 Corinthians 10:16, 21).

Exposition
The word 'sacrament' is not found in the Scriptures, but is derived from the Latin language. It was used by the Romans to signify their military oath, or the oath by which soldiers bound themselves to be faithful to their general, and not to desert his standard; and it is supposed to have been applied to the symbolical institutions of the Church, because in these we, as it were, enlist in the service of Christ, the Captain of our salvation, and engage to follow him whithersoever he leads us. But it may be remarked, that the early Christian writers employed the term sacrament (*sacramentum*) as equivalent to the scriptural term mystery ($\mu\upsilon\sigma\tau\eta\rho\iota o\nu$); and in the Vulgate the latter word is always translated by the former. There is reason to think that the term *mysteries* was early applied to baptism and the Lord's supper, partly because, under external symbols, spiritual blessings were vailed, and partly also on account of the secrecy with which Christians, in times of persecution, were obliged to celebrate them; and as Latins used the word sacrament as synonymous with mystery, it has been thought that we are in this way to account for its application to these symbolical institutions.

The express institution of God is essentially requisite to constitute a sacrament. No ordinances ought to be observed in the Christian Church but such as have been appointed by Christ, her alone king and head. He only can have authority to institute sacraments, who has power to confer the blessings which are thereby represented and applied. No rite, therefore, can deserve the name of a sacrament, unless it bear the stamp of divine institution.

Socinians represent the sacraments as being merely solemn badges by which the disciples of Jesus are discriminated from other men. It is readily granted that they are badges of the disciples of Christ, by which they are distinguished from Jews, Mohammedans and Heathens; but this is not their chief design. They are principally 'signs and seals of the covenant of grace'. Circumcision is expressly called a sign and seal of the righteousness of faith (Romans 4:11); and the same description is equally applicable to the sacraments of the New Testament. As signs, they represent and exhibit Christ and the blessings of the new covenant to us; as seals, they ratify our right to them, and confirm our faith.

The principal uses and ends of the sacraments are: to represent Christ and his benefits; to confirm the believer's interest in Christ and his blessings; to distinguish between the members of the visible Church, and those that are without; and solemnly to engage them to the service of God in Christ, according to his Word.

Section 2
There is in every sacrament a spiritual relation, or sacramental union, between the sign and the thing signified; whence it comes to pass that the names and effects of the one are attributed to the other (Genesis 17:10; Matthew 26:27, 28; Titus 3:5).

Exposition
The parts of a sacrament are two: the sign and the thing signified. The sign is something sensible and visible – that may be seen and handled. Thus, the outward sign in baptism is *water*, which is visible to us; and the outward signs in the Lord's supper are *bread* and *wine*, which are also visible, and which we can handle and taste. The things signified are Christ and the benefits of the new covenant. These are called the matter of the sacrament. The form consists in the spiritual relation or sacramental union, established between the sign and the thing signified by the divine institution. Though there is some analogy or resemblance between the outward signs and the things signified, yet their sacramental union depends entirely upon the institution of Christ.

'From this union arises what has been called sacramental phraseology, or certain expressions in which the names of the sign and the thing signified are exchanged. Thus, the name of the sign is given to the thing signified, when Christ is called "our passover"; and the name of the thing signified is given to the sign, when the bread is called the body of Christ. The foundation of this interchange is the sacramental union, which so couples them together that the one may be predicated of the other'.[1]

Section 3

The grace which is exhibited in or by the sacraments, rightly used, is not conferred by any power in them: neither doth the efficacy of a sacrament depend upon the piety or intention of him that doth administer it (Romans 2:28, 29; 1 Peter 3:21), but upon the work of the Spirit (Matthew 3:11; 1 Corinthians 12:13), and the word of institution; which contains, together with a precept authorizing the use thereof, a promise of benefit to worthy receivers (Matthew 26:27, 28; 28:19, 20).

Exposition

This section is levelled against two tenets of the Church of Rome. That Church holds that the sacraments, when rightly administered, are of themselves effectual to confer grace; and that the *intention* of the priest or administrator is essential to a sacrament; so that if a priest goes through all the forms of administering baptism or the Lord's supper, and does not in his own mind *intend* to administer it, it is in fact no sacrament. That the sacraments themselves cannot confer saving grace is evident; for if they had this power in themselves, they would be equally effectual to all who receive them. But many are partakers of the sacraments, who are not partakers of the grace of God. Simon Magus was baptized, and yet remained in the gall of bitterness, and in the bond of iniquity (Acts 8:13, 23). That the efficacy of the sacraments does not depend upon the *intention* of the administrator is not less evident; for this would place the administrator in God's stead, whose sole prerogative it is to render the sacraments effectual for the purposes designed by them. Besides, in this case, no one could be certain that he had received the sacraments; because he could not be absolutely certain of the intention of another. In opposition to these absurd tenets, we maintain that the efficacy of the sacraments depends upon the working of the Spirit on the souls of the receivers; and upon the word of institution, which contains

---

1. Dick's *Lectures on Theology*, vol. iv, p. 118.

a precept authorizing the use of these ordinances, and a promise of benefit by them to the worthy receivers.

Section 4
There be only two sacraments ordained by Christ our Lord in the gospel; that is to say, baptism and the supper of the Lord; neither of which may be dispensed by any but a minister of the Word, lawfully ordained (Matthew 28:19; 1 Corinthians 11:20, 23; 4:1; Hebrews 5:4).

Exposition
We acknowledge only two sacraments instituted by Christ in the gospel, and these are baptism and the Lord's supper; the former being the sign and seal of our spiritual birth, and the latter of our spiritual nourishment. The Church of Rome has added five spurious sacraments: ordination, marriage, confirmation, penance, and extreme unction. None of these have any divine appointment as *sacraments*; and the three last, as used by Papists, have no warrant at all from Scripture. None of them are seals of the covenant of grace, and, therefore, they are no sacraments, but are to be considered as gross corruptions of the purity and simplicity of the Christian ritual. In opposition, also, to the Church of Rome, which permits laymen and women to administer the sacrament of baptism in cases of necessity, our Confession asserts that none but a minister of the Word, lawfully ordained, has any warrant to dispense the sacraments.

Section 5
The sacraments of the Old Testament, in regard of the spiritual things thereby signified and exhibited, were, for substance, the same with those of the New (1 Corinthians 10:1-4).

Exposition
The ordinary sacraments of the Old Testament were circumcision and the passover; the former being now superceded by baptism, and the latter by the Lord's supper. The sacraments of the Old Testament represented Christ *as to come*, while those of the New Testament represent Christ *as already come*; and by the latter spiritual blessings are exhibited in a more clear and plain manner than by the former. But in opposition to the Church of Rome, which asserts that the sacraments of the Old Testament were no more than shadows of that grace which those of the New Testament

actually confer, we maintain that, in respect of the spiritual blessings signified and exhibited, the sacraments of the Old Testament were substantially the same with those of the New. Both were signs and seals of the same righteousness of faith (Romans 4:11). Both agree in the word of promise (Genesis 17:7; Acts 2:38, 39).

CHAPTER 28

BAPTISM

Section 1

Baptism is a sacrament of the New Testament, ordained by Jesus Christ (Matthew 28:19), not only for the solemn admission of the party baptized into the visible Church (1 Corinthians 12:13), but also to be unto him a sign and seal of the covenant of grace (Romans 4:11; Colossians 2:11, 12), of his ingrafting into Christ (Galatians 3:27; Romans 6:5), of regeneration (Titus 3:5), of remission of sins (Mark 1:4), and of his giving up unto God through Jesus Christ, to walk in newness of life (Romans 6:3, 4): which sacrament is, by Christ's own appointment, to be continued in his Church until the end of the world (Matthew 28:19, 20).

Exposition

This section, in the *first* place, affirms that baptism is a sacrament of the New Testament, instituted by Christ, and to be continued in his Church until the end of the world; and *secondly*, declares the ends of baptism.

1. Baptism is a sacrament of the New Testament, instituted by Christ. John, the harbinger of Christ, was the first who administered baptism by divine authority. The Lord 'sent him to baptize with water'; and 'there went out unto him all the land of Judea, and they of Jerusalem, and were all baptized of him in the river of Jordan, confessing their sins' (John 1:33; Mark 1:4). Jesus, after he entered on his public ministry, employed his apostles to baptize those who came to him; for 'Jesus himself baptized not, but his disciples' (John 4:2). The baptism of John was a sign of faith in Christ as shortly to be revealed; whereas the baptism of the disciples of Jesus was an expression of faith in him as already come.

But baptism was not formally appointed as a perpetual ordinance in the New Testament Church until after the resurrection of Christ, when he gave the following commission to his disciples: 'Go ye, therefore, and teach', or make disciples of, 'all nations, baptizing them in the name of the Father, and of the Son, and of the Holy Ghost; teaching them to observe all things whatsoever I have commanded you: and, lo, I am with you alway, even unto the end of the world' (Matthew 28:19, 20). These words not only contain an express institution of baptism, but also a plain intimation of the will of Christ that this ordinance should be continued in the Church in all succeeding ages; for he promised to be with his disciples in executing his commission, not only to the end of that age, but 'to the end of the world'. Baptism has, accordingly, continued to be practised by all sects of Christians, with the exception of the Quakers. It appears to them that, as it is the distinguishing character of the gospel to be the dispensation of the Spirit, the baptism of water was only a temporary institution, and is now superseded by the baptism of the Spirit. But it cannot be questioned, that the apostles did use the baptism of water after the dispensation of the Spirit had commenced. The Apostle Peter makes a distinction between being baptized in the name of Christ and receiving the Holy Ghost; and he actually dispensed baptism to those who had previously received the Holy Ghost (Acts 2:38; 10:47). It appears, therefore, to have been the judgment of Peter, that the baptism of the Spirit does not supercede the baptism of water.

2. This section declares the ends of baptism: (1) It is a solemn admission of the party baptized into the visible Church, and to all its privileges.

> 'It supposes the party to have a right to these privileges before, and does not *make* them members of the visible Church, but *admits* them solemnly thereto. And therefore it is neither to be called nor accounted *christening* – that is, making them Christians: for the infants of believing parents are born within the covenant, and so are Christians and visible Church members; and by baptism this right of theirs is acknowledged, and they are solemnly admitted to the privileges of Church membership.'[1]

(2) It is a sign and seal of the covenant of grace, and of the benefits of that covenant. These benefits are, ingrafting into Christ, or union with him; the remission of sins by virtue of the blood of Christ; and regeneration by the Spirit of Christ. It is not intended that remission of sins and regeneration are inseparably connected with baptism; for our Confession, in a subsequent section, expressly guards against the opinion 'that all that are baptized are undoubtedly regenerated'.

---

1. Boston's *Complete Body of Divinity*, vol. iii, p. 307.

(3) It is a sign and seal of the party baptized being devoted to God, and engaged to walk in newness of life. Baptism is a dedicating ordinance, in which the party baptized is solemnly given up to God to be his and for him, now, wholly, and for ever. He is, as it were, enlisted under Christ's banner, to fight against the devil, the world, and the flesh. He is bound to renounce every other lord and master, and to 'serve God in holiness and righteousness all the days of his life'.

Section 2

The outward element to be used in this sacrament is water, wherewith the party is to be baptized in the name of the Father, and of the Son, and of the Holy Ghost, by a minister of the gospel, lawfully called thereunto (Matthew 3:11; John 1:33; Matthew 28:19, 20).

Exposition

This section embraces the following points:

1. That the outward element to be used in the sacrament of baptism is water. This outward sign represents the blood and Spirit of Christ (Revelation 1:5; Titus 3:5). As water has a cleansing virtue for removing defilements from the body, so the blood of Christ removes the guilt of sin and cleanses the defiled conscience, and the Spirit of Christ purifies the soul from the pollution of sin.

2. That baptism is to be administered in the name of the Father, and of the Son, and of the Holy Ghost. To be baptized in the name of the Father, and of the Son, and of the Holy Ghost, signifies that we are baptized by the authority of the persons of the Holy Trinity; that we are baptized into the faith and profession of the blessed Trinity; and that we are solemnly devoted to the service of these divine persons.

3. That baptism is to be dispensed by a lawfully ordained minister of the gospel. They only have authority to administer baptism who have received a commission from Christ to preach the gospel (Matthew 28:19). We have no account of any one dispensing the ordinance in the primitive Church, but such as were called, either ordinarily or extraordinarily, to the work of the ministry. It is the unfounded opinion that baptism is absolutely necessary to salvation, that has led the Church of Rome to permit this rite to be performed by laymen and women in cases of urgent necessity.

Section 3

Dipping of the person into the water is not necessary; but baptism is rightly administered by pouring or sprinkling water upon the person (Hebrews 9:10, 19-22; Acts 2:41; 16:33; Mark 7:4).

Exposition

This section relates to the *mode* of administering baptism. This is a subject which has occasioned much controversy among Christians, and the dispute is still carried on with unabated zeal. A large and respectable body of Christians strenuously contend that baptism can only be valid when performed by immersion, or by dipping the whole body under water. Our Confession does not deny that baptism may be lawfully performed by immersion; but maintains that it is rightly administered by pouring or sprinkling water on the person. No conclusion can be drawn from the word *baptize*, or from the original term; for it has been most satisfactorily proved that it signifies to wash with water in any way. Several instances of the administration of baptism are recorded in the New Testament; and in some of these cases it is not credible that baptism was performed by immersion. When three thousand were baptized in one day, it cannot be conceived that the apostles were capable of dipping all this multitude in so short a space of time. When whole families were baptized in their own houses, it cannot be thought that, on every occasion, a sufficient quantity of water could be found for immersion. Besides, the application of the spiritual benefit signified by baptism is in Scripture frequently expressed by sprinkling and pouring out (Isaiah 44:3; Ezekiel 36:25; Hebrews 10:22; 12:24; Titus 3:5, 6). It may be added, that baptism by immersion cannot, in some cases, be dispensed with convenience or decorum; nor in some countries, and at certain seasons, without endangering the health of the body. This affords, at least, a strong presumption against the absolute necessity of dipping the person into the water; and from all these considerations we must conclude that it is sufficient and most expedient to administer baptism by sprinkling or pouring water on the person.

Section 4

Not only those that do actually profess faith in and obedience unto Christ (Mark 16:15, 16; Acts 8:37, 38), but also the infants of one or both believing parents are to be baptized (Genesis 17:7, 9; Galatians 3:9, 14; Colossians 2:11, 12; Acts 2:38, 39; Romans 4:11, 12; 1 Corinthians 7:14; Matthew 28:19; Mark 10:13-16; Luke 18:15).

Exposition

This section relates to the *subjects* of baptism. That baptism is to
be administered to all *adult* persons who profess their faith and
obedience to Christ, and who have not been baptized in their
infancy, is admitted by all who acknowledge the divine institution
of this ordinance.

But there are many who confidently assert that baptism ought
to be confined to adults. These were originally called Anabaptists,
because they rebaptized those who have received baptism in their
infancy, and Antipaedobaptists, because they were opposed to
the baptism of infants. They now assume the name of Baptists;
but this designation we cannot concede to them, if it be intended
to insinuate that others do not baptize, and are not baptized,
agreeably to the principles of the gospel.[2] Our Confession affirms,
that 'the infants of one or both believing parents are to be baptized'.
This might be confirmed by numerous arguments; but only a few
of them can be here stated with the utmost brevity.

1. The infants of believing parents are to be considered as within
the covenant, and therefore entitled to receive its seal. The
covenant which God made with Abraham was substantially the
same with that under which believers now are. This appears by
comparing Genesis 17:7, where the covenant made with Abraham
is expressed, with Hebrews 8:10, when the new covenant is
expressed. In the one, the promise is: 'I will establish my covenant
between me and thee, and thy seed after thee, in their generations,
for an everlasting covenant, to be a God unto thee, and to thy seed
after thee'; and in the other: 'I will be to them a God, and they
shall be to me a people.' We thus find, that when God established
his covenant with Abraham, he embraced his infant seed in that
covenant; and that the promise made to Abraham and to his seed
is still indorsed to us is evident from the express declaration of
the Apostle Peter: 'The promise is unto you, and to your children'
(Acts 2:39). If children are included in the covenant, we conclude
that they have a right to baptism, the seal of the covenant.

2. Infants were the subjects of circumcision under the Old
Testament dispensation; and as baptism under the New Testament
has come in the room of circumcision, we conclude that infants
have a right to baptism under the present dispensation. That under
the Old Testament, the infants of God's professing people were

2. Dwight, Sermon 147.

to be circumcised, cannot be doubted; for the command is express: 'Every man-child among you shall be circumcised' (Genesis 17:10). That baptism has now come in the room of circumcision is evident from Colossians 2:11, where it is called 'the circumcision of Christ'. It must therefore follow, either that the privileges of the Church are now greatly abridged, or else that the children of the members of the Church now are to be admitted to baptism, as they were to circumcision under the former dispensation.

3. That the children of professing Christians are members of the visible Church, and therefore entitled to baptism, appears from the words of our Saviour: 'Suffer little children to come unto me, and forbid them not; for of such is the kingdom of God' (Luke 18:16). By 'the kingdom of God', we apprehend is to be here understood the Church on earth; and if children are members of the visible Church, it cannot be denied that they have a right to baptism, the sign of admission. But if by 'the kingdom of God' be understood the state of glory, the inference is strong that, being heirs of eternal life, they ought not to be denied that ordinance which is the seal of their title to it.

4. The warrantableness of infant baptism may be inferred from the commission of the apostles to baptize 'all nations', which certainly includes infants; and from the practice of the apostles, who baptized 'households', upon a profession of faith by their domestic heads. Paul baptized Lydia 'and her household', the Philippian jailer 'and all his', and 'the household of Stephanas' (Acts 16:15, 33; 1 Corinthians 1:16).

'Now, though we are not certain that there were young children in any of these families, it is highly probable there were. At any rate, the great principle of *family baptism*, of receiving all the younger members of households *on the faith of their domestic head* seems to be plainly and decisively established. This furnishes ground on which the advocate of infant baptism may stand with unwavering confidence.'[3]

5. That the infants of believing parents ought to be baptized; and that it is sufficient if one of the parents be a member of the visible Church, is evident from 1 Corinthians 7:14: 'For the unbelieving husband is sanctified by the wife, and the unbelieving

3. Miller on *Infant Baptism*.

wife is sanctified by the husband: else were your children unclean; but now are they holy.'

> 'The word *unclean*, in almost all instances in the Scriptures, denotes *that which may not be offered to God, or may not come into his temple*. Of this character were the heathen universally; and they were, therefore, customarily and proverbially, denominated unclean by the *Jews*. The unbelievers here spoken of were heathen, and were, therefore, unclean. In this sense, the children born of two heathen parents are here pronounced to be unclean also, as being, in the proper sense, heathen. *To be holy*, as here used, is the converse of being unclean, and denotes *that which may be offered to God. To be sanctified*, as referring to the objects here mentioned, *is to be separated for religious purposes, consecrated to God* – as were the first-born, and vessels of the temple; or to be in a proper condition to appear before God. In this text it denotes, that the unbelieving parent is so purified by means of his relation to the believing parent, that their mutual offspring are not unclean, but may be offered unto God. There is no other sense in which a Jew could have written this text, without some qualification of these words. The only appointed way in which children may be offered to God is baptism. The children of believing parents are, therefore, to be offered to God in baptism.'[4]

The objections usually brought forward against the warrantableness of infant baptism, are either frivolous in themselves, or proceed from mistaken views of the ordinance. Is it urged that in the New Testament we have no express injunction to baptize the infants of professing Christians? This, we reply, is precisely what might have been expected, because the Church-membership of the children of God's professing people was fully established under the Old Testament, and their admission by the rite of circumcision was a privilege well known, and universally extended to them; so that, unless it had been designed to abridge the privileges of the children of believing parents under the New Testament, there was no occasion for any explicit injunction to baptize their children. But no hint is given in the New Testament that the privilege of infants, which had been so long enjoyed under the former dispensation, was to be withdrawn; and as the privilege is not revoked, it must be continued.

Is it asked, What benefit can infants derive from baptism? With equal propriety, we reply, it might have been asked, What benefit

---

4. Dwight's Theology, Sermon 158.

can a child, eight days old, derive from circumcision? To put such a question is almost impious, because it implies an impeachment of the wisdom of God. He appointed circumcision to be administered to infants under the Old Testament; and with equal propriety is baptism administered to them under the New Testament.

Is it objected, that we have no express example of the baptism of infants under the New Testament? All the cases of baptism recorded in the New Testament, we reply, are cases in which it was administered to converts from Judaism or Paganism to Christianity; and if we do not find it explicitly stated, that any infant born of Christian parents was baptized, as little do we find any example of those who were born of Christian parents being baptized in adult age. This entirely accords with our practice at the present day. We baptize adult converts from among Jews or Heathens; and as the apostles baptized 'households' on the faith of their domestic heads, we also consider ourselves warranted to baptize the children of professing Christians. But those who defer the baptism of the children of professing Christians until they arrive at adult age, have no precedent or example for their practice; for, though the Book of the Acts contains the history of the Church for upwards of thirty years, in which time the children of those who were first baptized by the apostles must have reached maturity, yet we have no record of the baptism of a single individual born of Christian parents. From this silence, we justly infer that they must have been baptized in their infancy; and we defy the advocates of adult baptism to adduce a single scriptural example of their practice.

Is it urged, that infants cannot profess their faith in Christ? We reply, that when faith, or the profession of it, is spoken of as a prerequisite to baptism, it is always supposed that the subjects of it are capable of instruction; and that if this proved anything, it would prove too much; for this objection, if valid against infant baptism, must also be valid against infant salvation, since the Scripture connects faith and the profession of it, in the case of adults, with the one as well as the other.

Section 5

Although it be a great sin to contemn or neglect this ordinance (Luke 7:30; Exodus 4:24-26), yet grace and salvation are not so inseparably annexed unto it, as that no person can be regenerated or saved without it (Romans 4:11; Acts 10:2, 4, 22, 31, 45, 47), or that all that are baptized are undoubtedly regenerated (Acts 8:13, 23).

Exposition
This section affirms:

1. That baptism is not of such absolute necessity to salvation, that none can be saved without it. God has not made baptism and faith equally necessary (Mark 16:16). The penitent thief was saved without being baptized. But baptism is an instituted means of salvation, and the contempt of it must be a great sin on the part of the parents, though the neglect cannot be ascribed to the child before he arrives at maturity, and cannot, therefore, involve him in the guilt.

2. That baptism is not regeneration, nor are all who are baptized undoubtedly regenerated. That the baptism of water is regeneration, and that every person duly baptized is born again, is the doctrine of the Church of Rome; and this doctrine has been embraced by many in Protestant Churches, and receives too much countenance from the Liturgy of the Church of England. It is a very dangerous doctrine; and that it has no warrant from Scripture appears from the case of Simon Magus, who after baptism remained 'in the gall of bitterness, and in the bond of iniquity' (Acts 8:13, 23). Paul, writing to the Corinthians, says: 'I thank God that I baptized none of you, but Crispus and Gaius.' But if baptism be regeneration, his meaning must be: 'I thank God that I regenerated none of you.' And could Paul really give thanks to God on this account? How absurd the idea! 'Christ,' says he, 'sent me not to baptize.' But can it be thought that Christ did not send the chief of the apostles to promote the great work of regeneration? Unquestionably Paul made a great difference between baptism and regeneration.

Section 6
The efficacy of baptism is not tied to that moment of time wherein it is administered (John 3:5, 8); yet notwithstanding, by the right use of this ordinance, the grace promised is not only offered, but really exhibited and conferred by the Holy Ghost, to such (whether of age or infants) as that grace belongeth unto, according to the counsel of God's own will, in his appointed time (Galatians 3:27; Titus 3:5; Ephesians 5:25, 26; Acts 2:38, 41).

Section 7

The sacrament of baptism is but once to be administered to any person (Titus 3:5).

Exposition

1. The efficacy of baptism is not confined to the moment of administration; but though not effectual at the time it is administered, it may afterwards be effectual, through the working of the Spirit (John 2:5, 8).

2. Baptism is not to be administered to any person oftener than once. This is plain from the nature of the ordinance. It is a solemn admission of the person baptized as a member of the visible Church; and though those that 'walk disorderly' are to be cast out, yet there is no hint in Scripture that, when re-admitted, they are to be baptized again. The thing signified by baptism cannot be repeated, and the engagements come under can never be disannulled.

It may be remarked, that the *naming* of the baptized person is no part of this institution. The custom of publishing the child's name at baptism probably arose from the practice of the Jews at their circumcision (Luke 1:59-63). It belongs to the parent to give a name to his child, and this may be done before baptism. There may be a propriety in publishing the name of the person baptized, who is then admitted a member of the visible Church; but this is by no means essential to baptism, nor even any part of the ordinance.

We ought to improve our baptism, especially when we are present at the administration of it to others:

'by serious and thankful consideration of the nature of it, and of the ends for which Christ instituted it, the privileges and benefits conferred and sealed thereby, and our solemn vow made therein; by being humbled for our sinful defilement, our falling short of, and walking contrary to, the grace of baptism, and our engagements; by growing up to assurance of pardon of sin, and of all other blessings sealed to us in that sacrament; by drawing strength from the death and resurrection of Christ, into whom we are baptized, for the mortifying of sin and quickening of grace; and by endeavouring to live by faith, to have our conversation in holiness and righteousness, as those that have therein given up their name to Christ, and to walk in brotherly love, as being baptized by the same Spirit into one body.'[5]

5. *The Larger Catechism*, Question 167.

CHAPTER 29

THE LORD'S SUPPER

Section 1

Our Lord Jesus, in the night wherein he was betrayed, instituted the sacrament of his body and blood, called the Lord's Supper, to be observed in his Church unto the end of the world, for the perpetual remembrance of the sacrifice of himself in his death, the sealing all benefits thereof unto true believers, their spiritual nourishment and growth in him, their further engagement in and to all duties which they owe unto him, and to be a bond and pledge of their communion with him, and with each other, as members of his mystical body (1 Corinthians 11:23-26; 10:16, 17, 21; 12:13).

Exposition

This chapter treats of the Lord's supper; and the present section declares: (1) The author of this sacrament; (2) The time of its institution; (3) Its permanent continuance in the Church; (4) The uses and ends for which it is designed.

1. The author of this sacrament is the Lord Jesus Christ. It is the prerogative of Christ, as king and head of the Church, to institute religious ordinances; and we are not at liberty to add to, or to diminish from his appointments. The institution of this ordinance by our Saviour is recorded by the three first Evangelists (Matthew 26:26-28; Mark 14:22-24; Luke 22:19, 20), and by the Apostle Paul, who declares that he 'had received of the Lord that which he delivered' to the Church (1 Corinthians 11:23-26).

2. This sacrament was instituted by our Lord Jesus 'the same night in which he was betrayed'. It was when Jesus was eating the passover with his disciples that he instituted this sacred ordinance; from which circumstance we infer that the one was changed into the other, and that the latter was henceforth to supply the place of the former. This also accounts for the designation usually given to this sacrament. Being instituted by the Lord Jesus Christ, and being appointed by him immediately after eating the passover, which was always celebrated in the evening, it is with the utmost propriety called the *Lord's supper*. When we reflect on the time of the institution of this ordinance, we have a striking view of the fortitude with which Jesus met his unparalleled sufferings, and of the singular love which he cherished towards his people; and we ought to feel the sacred obligation laid upon us to keep this feast. On that night the Jewish rulers and the chief priests were met in close cabal, to concert measures for apprehending Jesus, and bringing him to an ignominious death. In that night he was to be perfidiously betrayed by one of his own disciples, denied by another, and abandoned by them all to the rage of his malicious foes. He was to be smitten by the sword of Justice, and forsaken of his God – to be cruelly mocked and scourged – to be led away to a cross, and there to pour out his soul unto death. Of all this Jesus was fully apprized; yet in the immediate view of the dreadful sufferings he was about to undergo, such was the calm serenity of his mind, such his matchless love to his people, and such his concern for their spiritual benefit, that he instituted this ordinance for their encouragement and consolation in all succeeding ages. Did he remember them in such affecting circumstances? And shall not this engage them to remember him? Shall they undervalue, by a wilful neglect, an ordinance which he settled immediately before his death, and disregard the dying command of that friend who laid down his life for them?

3. The sacrament of the Lord's supper is to be observed in the Church to the end of the world. This is plainly implied in the words of the Apostle Paul: 'For as often as ye eat this bread, and drink this cup, ye do show the Lord's death *till he come*' (1 Corinthians 11:26). So universally has it been understood that the observance of this ordinance is obligatory upon all Christians to the end of the world, that, with the exception only of the Quakers, it has been observed in the Christian Church from the earliest times to the present day.

4. The ends and uses of this sacrament are various.

(1) It was instituted to be a memorial of the death of Christ. That it is a commemorative ordinance, appears from the Saviour's words: 'This do in remembrance of me'; and that it is especially a memorial of his death, is evident from his words in distributing the elements. While he gave the bread to his disciples, he said: 'This is my body, which is *broken* for you'; and of the cup he said: 'This cup is the New Testament *in my blood.*' The ordinance is eminently fitted to bring to our remembrance the reality and the painful nature of the death of Christ – to remind us of the

vicarious nature of his death, of its acceptableness to God as a satisfaction for our sins, and of its present and perpetual efficacy. And we should remember his death with a lively and appropriating faith; with ardent love to him who first loved us; with deep contrition for our sins, the procuring cause of his death; with holy joy in God; and with the warmest gratitude to Christ, who gave himself for us an offering and a sacrifice to God for a sweet-smelling savour.

(2) This sacrament seals the benefits of Christ's death unto true believers. It seals not the truth of Christ's death, nor the truth of their faith; but it seals the right and interest of faith, as the seal affixed to a deed seals the right and interest of the person in the property conveyed by that deed.

(3) It promotes the spiritual nourishment and growth of believers. A devout participation of this ordinance is fitted to confirm and invigorate their faith, to enflame their love, to deepen their godly sorrow, to enliven their joy, and to enlarge and strengthen their hopes of the Saviour's second coming, and of the glory then to be revealed.

(4) It is a sign and pledge of the believers' communion with Christ. This is evident from the words of Paul: 'The cup of blessing which we bless, is it not the communion of the blood of Christ? The bread which we break, is it not the communion of the body of Christ?' (1 Corinthians 10:16). These words certainly import that, in the holy supper, believers have communion with Christ in the fruits of his sufferings and death.

(5) It is an emblem of the saints' communion with each other. All true saints are members of one body, and in the holy supper they have communion, not merely with those who sit along with them at the same table, but 'with all that in every place call on the name of Jesus Christ', their common Lord. 'We being many,' says Paul, 'are one bread, and one body; for we are all partakers of that one bread' (1 Corinthians 10:17). This ordinance is very expressive of the communion of saints, and has a powerful tendency to cherish it. They meet together at the same table, as brethren and children of the same family, to partake of the same spiritual feast.

(6) In this ordinance believers engage themselves to all the duties which they owe to Christ, They acknowledge him as their master, and engage to do whatsoever he has commanded them.

Persons may come under engagements by performing certain significant actions, as well as by express words. Submission to the ordinance of circumcision, under the former dispensation, made a man 'a debtor to do the whole law'. Baptism, in like manner, under the Christian dispensation, involves an engagement to be the Lord's; and Christians, in partaking of the Lord's supper, renew this engagement. They acknowledge that they are not their own, but are bought with a price, and bind themselves to glorify God with their bodies and spirits which are his.

Section 2
In this sacrament Christ is not offered up to his Father, nor any real sacrifice made at all for remission of sins of the quick or dead (Hebrews 9:22, 25, 26, 28); but only a commemoration of that one offering up of himself by himself, upon the cross, once for all, and a spiritual oblation of all possible praise unto God for the same (1 Corinthians 11:24-26; Matthew 26:26, 27); so that the Popish sacrifice of the mass, as they call it, is most abominably injurious to Christ's one only sacrifice, the alone propitiation for the sins of the elect (Hebrews 7:23, 24, 27; 10:11, 12, 14, 18).

Section 3
The Lord Jesus hath, in this ordinance, appointed his ministers to declare his word of institution to the people, to pray, and bless the elements of bread and wine, and thereby to set them apart from a common to a holy use; and to take and break the bread, to take the cup, and (they communicating also themselves) to give both to the communicants (Matthew 26:26-28; Mark 14:22-24; Luke 22:19, 20; 1 Corinthians 11:23-26); but to none who are not then present in the congregation (Acts 20:7; 1 Corinthians 11:20).

Section 4
Private masses, or receiving this sacrament by a priest, or any other alone (1 Corinthians 10:6); as likewise the denial of the cup to the people (Mark 14:23; 1 Corinthians 11:25-29); worshipping the elements, the lifting them up, or carrying them about for adoration, and the reserving them for any pretended religious use; are all contrary to the nature of this sacrament, and to the institution of Christ (Matthew 15:9).

Section 5
The outward elements in this sacrament, duly set apart to the uses ordained by Christ, have such relation to him crucified, as that truly, yet sacramentally only, they are sometimes called by the name of the things they represent, to wit, the body and blood of Christ (Matthew 26:26-

28); albeit, in substance and nature, they still remain truly and only bread and wine, as they were before (1 Corinthians 11:26-28; Matthew 26:29).

Section 6

That doctrine which maintains a change of the substance of bread and wine into the substance of Christ's body and blood (commonly called Transubstantiation), by consecration of a priest, or by any other way, is repugnant not to Scripture alone, but even to common sense and reason; overthroweth the nature of the sacrament; and hath been, and is, the cause of manifold superstitions, yea, of gross idolatries (Acts 3:21; 1 Corinthians 11:24-26; Luke 24:6, 39).

Exposition

In these sections certain dangerous errors and superstitious practices of the Church of Rome are condemned; and we have placed all these sections together, that we may include the leading error, called transubstantiation, which has given rise to the absurd doctrine of the sacrifice of the mass, and the various other tenets and practices here rejected.

1. The Church of Rome holds that the words, 'This is my body', and 'This is my blood', are to be understood in their most literal sense; and that the priest, by pronouncing these words, with a good intention, changes the substance of the bread and wine into the real body and blood of Jesus Christ; which change is known by the name of *transubstantiation*. This doctrine receives no support from Scripture, but is founded on a gross perversion of its language. The words, 'This is my body', and 'This is my blood', were manifestly used by our Saviour in a figurative sense; and must have been so understood by the apostles, to whom they were immediately addressed. Such figurative expressions are of frequent occurrence in the Scripture. No one supposes that, when our Lord said, 'I am the vine', 'I am the way', 'I am the door', he meant us to understand that he is literally a vine, a way, and a door; and no satisfactory reason can be assigned for understanding the words of institution in a literal sense. Our Saviour plainly meant that the bread and wine *signify* or *represent* his body and blood; and nothing is more common in scripture than to affix to a type or symbol the name of the thing signified by it; thus circumcision is called God's covenant (Genesis 17:10); the paschal lamb, the passover (Exodus 12:11); and the smitten rock, Christ (1 Corinthians 10:4). But, not only is the doctrine of transubstantiation destitute

of any support from the inspired writings, it is *repugnant to Scripture*; for the Apostle Paul gives to the elements after blessing the very same names they had before it; which certainly intimates that there is no change of their substance (1 Corinthians 11:26, 28). It is also contradicted by *our senses*; for we see and taste that the bread and wine after blessing, and when we actually receive them, still continue to be bread and wine, without any change or alteration whatever. It is equally repugnant to *reason*; for this tells us that Christ's body cannot be both in heaven and on earth at the same time; but according to the Popish doctrine of transubstantiation, though the body of Christ remains in heaven, it is also present, not in one place on earth only, but in a thousand places – wherever the priest has, with a good intention, pronounced the words of institution. This doctrine likewise *overthrows the nature of the sacrament*. Two things are necessary to a sacrament – a sign and a thing signified – an object presented to our senses, and some promised blessing which is represented and sealed by it. But by transubstantiation the sign is annihilated, and the thing signified is put in its place.

Transubstantiation is not only contrary to Scripture, and reason, and common sense, but *it has been, and is, the cause of manifold superstitions, yea, of gross idolatries*. In the fourth section, several of these superstitious and idolatrous practices are specified. Conceiving that the bread and wine are changed into the real body and blood of Christ, Papists reserve part of the consecrated wafers, for the purpose of giving them to the sick, or other absent persons, at some future time. In direct opposition to the command of Christ, 'Drink ye all of it', they deny the cup to the people; on the pretence that, as the bread is changed into the body of Christ, they partake, by concomitancy, of the blood together with the body. When the priest is supposed to have changed the bread into the body of Christ, he adores it with bended knee, and rising, lifts it up, that it may be seen and adored by the people – which is called the elevation of the host; it is also carried about in solemn procession, that it may receive the homage of all who meet it; and, in short, it is worshipped as if it were Christ himself. All these practices are declared by our Confession to be 'contrary to the nature of this sacrament, and to the institution of Christ'. They were unknown in the primitive ages of the Church, and have evidently originated in the absurd doctrine of transubstantiation.

2. In the Church of Rome, the priest being supposed to have changed the bread and wine into the very body and blood of Christ, it is also conceived that, in laying upon the altar what has been thus transubstantiated, he offers to God a sacrifice which, although it be distinguished from all others by being without the shedding of blood, is a true, proper, and propitiatory sacrifice for the living and the dead. This is called the sacrifice of the mass. As this is founded upon the doctrine of transubstantiation, if the one be unscriptural so must the other. But we may adduce a few of those pointed declarations of Scripture, by which this particular doctrine is refuted. '*Once* in the end of the world hath he appeared, to put away sin by the sacrifice of himself.' 'Christ was *once* offered, to bear the sins of many.' 'We are sanctified through the offering of the body of Jesus Christ *once* for all.' 'By *one* offering he hath perfected for ever them that are sanctified' (Hebrews 9:26, 28; 10:10, 14). These texts, and they might easily be greatly multiplied, clearly prove that the one sacrifice of Christ, once offered by himself, is sufficient and perfect; and we are expressly told that 'there remaineth no more sacrifice for sins' (Hebrews 10:26). In the language of our Confession, therefore, 'the Popish sacrifice of the mass is most abominably injurious to Christ's one only sacrifice – the alone propitiation for all the sins of the elect'.

3. The right manner of dispensing the sacrament of the supper is here declared.

(1) The minister is to read the word of institution to the people, to pray, and bless the elements of bread and wine, and thereby to set them apart from a common to a holy use. In instituting this sacrament, according to the evangelist Matthew, 'Jesus took bread, and blessed *it*, and brake *it*' (Matthew 26:26). Some have observed, that it is not necessary for us to understand this as signifying that Jesus blessed *the bread*, for the pronoun *it* is a supplement; and as the word rendered *blessed* sometimes means *to give thanks*, especially as the evangelist Luke employs the phrase, 'he gave thanks', they conclude that the two expressions are in this case synonymous; and that we are to understand that Jesus blessed, not the bread, but God, or gave thanks to his Father. We are of opinion, however, that the pronoun *it* has been very properly introduced by our translators after the word *blessed*, as it is unquestionably repeated with the utmost propriety after the word *brake*; and we conceive that the order of the words requires us to

understand that Jesus blessed *the bread*. Nor is there any more difficulty in apprehending how Jesus blessed the bread, than in apprehending how God blessed the seventh or the Sabbath-day (Genesis 2:3; Exodus 20:11). Indeed, the two cases are exactly analogous; God blessed the seventh day by setting it apart to a holy use, or appointing it to be a day of sacred rest; Christ blessed the bread, by setting it apart from a common to a holy use, or appointing it to be the visible symbol of his body. And while it belonged exclusively to Christ, as the Head of the Church, to appoint bread and wine to be the symbols of his body and blood, yet we are persuaded that the servants of Christ, in administering the Lord's supper, are warranted, according to the institution and example of Christ, to set apart by solemn prayer so much of the elements as shall be used from a common to a holy use. That there is a sense in which the servants of Christ may be said to *bless* the elements, seems plain from 1 Corinthians 10:16, where Paul denominates the sacramental cup 'The cup of blessing *which we bless*'. It is not pretended that any real change is thereby made upon the elements, but only a relative change, so that they are not to be looked upon as common bread and wine, but as the sacred symbols of Christ's body and blood.

(2) The minister is also to take and break the bread. The *breaking* of the bread is an essential part of this ordinance, and, when it is wanting, the sacrament is not celebrated according to the original institution. It is, indeed, so essential, that the Lord's supper is sometimes designated from it alone, the whole being denominated from a part. The 'breaking of bread' is mentioned among the institutions of the gospel (Acts 2:42); and in Acts 20:7 we are told that, 'upon the first day of the week, the disciples came together to break bread': in both of which passages the celebration of the Lord's supper is doubtless meant by the 'breaking of bread'. The rite is significant, and we are left in no doubt about the meaning of the action. Our Saviour himself explained it when he said, 'This is my body, which is broken for you'; intimating that the broken bread is a figure of his body as wounded, bruised, and crucified, to make atonement for our sins. As an unbroken Christ could not profit sinners, so unbroken bread cannot fully represent to faith the food of the soul. Wherefore, to divide the bread into small pieces called wafers, and put a wafer into the mouth of each of the communicants, as is done in the

Church of Rome, is grossly to corrupt this ordinance, for it takes away the significant action of breaking the bread.

(3) The minister is further to take the cup, and give both the elements to the communicant. The cup, as a well as the bread, is an essential element in this ordinance – the one representing the blood, and the other representing the body of Christ. To give both the elements to all the communicants, was the universal practice of the Church of God for about 1400 years; but the Church of Rome then departed from the primitive institution, and the practice of the ancient Church, by withholding the cup from the laity.

The Council of Constance decreed, 'That though Christ did administer this venerable sacrament to his disciples under both the kinds of bread and wine, yet notwithstanding this, the custom of communicating under one kind only is now to be taken for a law'. And, 'Though, in the primitive Church, this sacrament was received by the faithful under both kinds, yet, notwithstanding this, the custom that is introduced of communicating under one kind only for the laity is now to be taken for a law' (Anno 1414, Sess. 13).

The Council of Trent also declared, 'That the laity, and the clergy not officiating, are not bound by any divine precept, to receive the sacrament of the eucharist under both kinds.' 'And further declares, that although our Redeemer in the last supper instituted this sacrament in two kinds, and so delivered it to the apostles, yet under one kind only, whole and entire Christ and the true sacrament are taken; and that, therefore, those who receive only one kind are deprived of no grace necessary to salvation' (Anno 1545, Sess. 21).

The Church of Rome, it will be remarked, acknowledges both kinds, the bread and the wine, to have been instituted by Christ, and the ordinance to have been thus celebrated in primitive times; she is, therefore, guilty of an avowed opposition to the authority of Christ, has sacrilegiously mutilated this holy sacrament, and infringed the privileges of the Christian people. The command of Christ to drink the wine is as express as the command to eat the bread; nay, as foreseeing how, in after ages, this ordinance would be dismembered by the prohibition of the cup to the laity, he is even more explicit in his injunction concerning the cup than the bread. Of the bread, he simply said, 'Take, eat'; but when he gave the cup, he said, 'Drink ye all of it' (Matthew 26:26, 27). According to the divine institution, therefore, both the elements are to be given to all the communicants. And as really as the bread and wine are given to the communicants, so Christ gives himself, with all his benefits, to the worthy receivers; and in taking these elements – in eating the bread and drinking the wine – they profess to receive Christ by faith, and to rest their hope of pardon and salvation solely upon his death.

Section 7
Worthy receivers, outwardly partaking of the visible elements in this sacrament (1 Corinthians 11:28), do then also inwardly by faith, really and indeed, yet not carnally and corporally, but spiritually, receive and feed upon Christ crucified, and all benefits of his death: the body and blood of Christ being then not corporally or carnally in, with, or under the bread and wine; yet as really, but spiritually, present to the faith of believers in that ordinance as the elements themselves are to their outward senses (1 Corinthians 10:16).

Section 8
Although ignorant and wicked men receive the outward elements in this sacrament, yet they receive not the thing signified thereby; but by their unworthy coming thereunto are guilty of the body and blood of the Lord, to their own damnation. Wherefore all ignorant and ungodly persons, as they are unfit to enjoy communion with him, so are they unworthy of the Lord's table, and cannot, without great sin against Christ, while they remain such, partake of these holy mysteries (1 Corinthians 11:27-29; 2 Corinthians 6:14-16), or be admitted thereunto (1 Corinthians 5:6, 7, 13; 2 Thessalonians 3:6, 14, 15; Matthew 7:6).

Exposition
In the preceding sections we have a strong condemnation of the Popish doctrine respecting the sacrament of the Lord's supper, and here we have an explicit condemnation of the Lutheran doctrine. The Lutherans hold, that although the bread and wine are not changed into the body and blood of Christ, yet that his real body and blood are received by the communicants along with the symbols. This is called *consubstantiation*, to signify that the substance of the body and blood of Christ is present *in*, *with*, or *under* the substance of the elements.

'This opinion, although free from some of the absurdities of transubstantiation, appears to us to labour under so many palpable difficulties, that we are disposed to wonder at its being held by men of a philosophical mind. It is fair, however, to mention, that the doctrine of the real presence is, in the Lutheran Church, merely a speculative opinion, having no influence upon the practice of those by whom it is adopted. It appears to them that this opinion furnishes the best method of explaining a Scripture expression; but they do not consider the presence of the body and blood of Christ with the bread and wine as imparting to the sacrament any physical virtue, by which the benefit derived from it is independent of the disposition of him by whom it is received; or as giving it the nature of a sacrifice; or as rendering the bread and wine an object of adoration to Christians. And their doctrine being thus separated from the three great practical errors of the Church of Rome, receives, even from those who account it false and irrational, a kind of indulgence very different from that which is shown to the doctrine of transubstantiation.'[1]

While our Confession rejects the doctrine of the Papists and of the Lutherans, respecting the Lord's supper, it teaches that 'the body and blood of Christ are as really, but spiritually, present to the faith of believers in that ordinance, as the elements themselves are to their outward senses'. Christ is not present in body at his table; and, therefore, we cannot see him there after the flesh; but he is present spiritually, and may be discerned by faith. From this it follows that the participation of Christ's body and blood, in the holy supper, is spiritual. There is an external representation and confirmation of it, in participating of the sacred and instituted elements, which symbolize the broken body and shed blood of Christ. And while the worthy receivers outwardly partake of the visible elements in this sacrament, they inwardly, by faith, receive and feed upon Christ crucified, and the benefits of his death.

From the nature and ends of this sacrament, it is manifest that the ignorant and ungodly are unfit for partaking of it. They may receive the outward elements; but they receive not the thing signified thereby. As they are unfit for communion with Christ, so they are unworthy of occupying a seat at his table. They cannot venture to approach to it without contracting a great sin, and exposing themselves to the judgments of God. The Scripture declares, that 'whosoever shall eat this bread, and drink this cup of the Lord unworthily, shall be guilty of the body and blood of the Lord'; and that such 'eat and drink damnation to themselves' (1 Corinthians 11:27, 29). Not that all unworthy communicants

---

1. Hill's *Lectures*, vol. ii., p. 352.

must necessarily perish eternally. The word in our version unhappily rendered 'damnation' properly signifies *judgment*; and the judgment intended must be determined by the context. That the judgments inflicted on the Corinthians were chiefly of a temporal nature is evident from the words that are immediately added: 'For this cause many are weak and sickly among you, and many sleep.' Temporal judgments may be still inflicted for the profanation of this ordinance, but those of a spiritual nature are chiefly to be dreaded; and this sin, if unrepented, must, like other sins, expose to eternal punishment. This being the case, it must be the duty of the office-bearers of the Church to be careful in excluding the ignorant and ungodly from this ordinance. All were not permitted to eat of the passover; neither ought there to be a promiscuous admission of all to the Lord's table. To admit the immoral and scandalous is to profane the ordinance and to corrupt the communion of the Church. But those who have a right to this ordinance in the judgment of the office-bearers of the Church, who can only judge of their knowledge and external conduct, may have no right to it in the sight of God. Every one, therefore, ought impartially and faithfully to examine himself as to his state before God, and his consequent right to partake of that feast which he has prepared for his children. The injunction of the apostle is express, and he enjoins self-examination as a means of preventing the sin of unworthy communicating: 'But let a man examine himself, and so let him eat of that bread, and drink of that cup' (1 Corinthians 11:28).

CHAPTER 30

CHURCH CENSURES

Section 1

The Lord Jesus, as king and head of his Church, hath therein appointed a government in the hand of Church officers, distinct from the civil magistrate (Isaiah 9:6, 7; 1 Timothy 5:17; 1 Thessalonians 5:12; Acts 20:17, 18; Hebrews 13:7, 17, 24; 1 Corinthians 12:28; Matthew 28:18-20).

Exposition

To suppose, as some have done, that the government of the Church is ambulatory, or that no particular form has been appointed by Christ, but that he has left it to be moulded according to the wisdom or caprice of men, and varied according to the external circumstances of the Church, is to impeach the love of Christ to his Church, and his fidelity to Him who hath appointed him to 'reign over the house of Jacob'. No human society can subsist without government; how absurd, then, to suppose that the Church of Christ, the most perfect of all societies, has been left by her king destitute of what is essential to the very being of society! Under the Old Testament a most perfect form of government was prescribed to the Church; but order and discipline are as necessary to the Christian as they were to the Jewish Church. And can it be reasonably supposed, that while the government of the latter was minutely prescribed, that of the former has been totally neglected? All sects of Christians, indeed, plead the authority of Scripture for that form of government which they prefer; and thus they implicitly acknowledge that the outlines, at least, of some particular form may be found in the Scriptures.

Even the advocates of the divine right of ecclesiastical government differ widely respecting the precise form of it which has been appointed by Christ. Papists, conceiving that the Bishop of Rome, as the successor of Peter, and the vicegerent of Christ, is the visible head of the whole Church, maintain that in him the supreme government of the universal Church is reposed, and that from him all other bishops derive their authority. Episcopalians, holding a distinction of rank among the ministers of religion, vest the government of the Church in bishops, archbishops, etc. Independents, conceiving that every congregation forms a complete Church, and has an independent power of jurisdiction within itself, lodge the government of the Church in the assembly of the faithful. Presbyterians, holding, in opposition to Episcopalians, that all the ministers of the Word are on a level, in respect of office and authority; and, in opposition to Independents, that particular congregations are only parts of the one Church, maintain that the government of the Church is committed, under Christ, to the presbytery, or the teaching and ruling elders; and that there is a subordination of courts, in which the sentence of inferior courts may be reviewed, and either affirmed or reversed. It would be out of place here to examine the claims of these different systems. That the Presbyterial form is 'founded upon, and agreeable to, the Word of God', is, in our judgment, fully established in 'the Form of Church Government' drawn up by the Westminster Assembly.

It is only necessary to advert to the opinion of the Erastians, who maintain that the external government of the Church belongs to the civil magistrate. This opinion is directly opposed to all that the Scriptures say about the spiritual nature of the kingdom of Christ. That remarkable declaration of Christ, 'My kingdom is not of this world', plainly shows that his kingdom, though in the world, is totally and specifically distinct from all others in it; and when he forbade the exercise of such dominion over his subjects as the kings of the Gentiles exercised, the different nature of the government to take place in it was clearly pointed out. Among the various office-bearers which Christ has 'set in the Church', the civil magistrate is never mentioned. And were it true that it belongs to the civil magistrate to model the government of the Church, Christ must have left his Church more than three hundred years without any government; for it was not till the fourth century that the Church received any countenance from the civil powers.

> The formal and specific difference betwixt the Church and the kingdoms of the world, and consequently, between civil and ecclesiastical authority, in respect of origin, ends, subjects, laws, privileges, means, extent, etc., has, by many writers, been very particularly explained. No doubt, the Church on earth hath some things in common with other societies, and the authority in both may

often have the same objects, materially considered; they admit also of a mutual respect, and reciprocal acts and duties towards each other; but none of these are inconsistent with their formal distinction; but rather suppose it; so that all the power and peculiar acting of each, whatever matters they respect, must ever be of the same nature with that of the society they belong to – in the one wholly spiritual, and in the other always and wholly secular. When following their proper line, and keeping within their proper sphere, they can never jar or impede one another by interference: like two straight and parallel lines, they can never meet or be confounded together. Whatever dangers have arisen, or may arise, from abuse, none can arise merely from the distinct and independent nature and acting of these societies; so that there can be no reason for subjecting one of them to the other. The common plea of the necessity of one undivided supreme power in all states, and of the danger of an '*imperiun in imperio*', applies only to societies and powers of the same nature and order, and is impertinently urged for a supremacy of temporal rulers over a Church of Christ, whose authority is of a different kind.[1]

Section 2
To these officers the keys of the kingdom of heaven are committed; by virtue whereof they have power respectively to retain and remit sins, to shut that kingdom against the impenitent, both by the Word and censures; and to open it unto penitent sinners, by the ministry of the gospel and by absolution from censures, as occasion shall require (Matthew 16:19; 18:17, 18; John 20:21-23; 2 Corinthians 2:6-8).

Section 3
Church censures are necessary for the reclaiming and gaining of offending brethren: for deterring of others from the like offences; for purging out of that leaven which might infect the whole lump; for vindicating the honour of Christ, and the holy profession of the gospel; and for preventing the wrath of God, which might justly fall upon the Church, if they should suffer his covenant, and the seals thereof, to be profaned by notorious and obstinate offenders (1 Corinthians 5; 1 Timothy 5:20; Matthew 7:9; 1 Timothy 1:20; 1 Corinthians 11:27; Jude 23).

Section 4
For the better attaining of these ends, the officers of the Church are to proceed by admonition, suspension from the sacrament of the Lord's supper for a season, and by excommunication from the Church, according to the nature of the crime and demerit of the person (1 Thessalonians

---

1. Bruce on the *Supremacy of Civil Powers*, p. 23.

5:12; 2 Thessalonians 3:6, 14, 15; 1 Corinthians 5:4, 5, 13; Matthew 18:17; Titus 3:10).

Exposition

In opposition to the Erastians, who assign the power of inflicting the censures of the Church to the civil magistrate, our Confession here affirms, that the keys of the kingdom of heaven are committed to the officers whom Christ has appointed in his Church. 'I will give unto thee the keys of the kingdom of heaven,' said Christ to Peter, 'and whatsoever thou shalt loose on earth shalt be loosed in heaven' (Matthew 16:19). By 'the keys of the kingdom of heaven', we are to understand the power and authority of exercising government and discipline in the Church; in virtue of which, those intrusted with these keys have power to 'bind and loose', by inflicting and removing censures; and their proceedings, when conducted agreeably to Scripture, are ratified in heaven. Presbyterians maintain that these keys were given to Peter, as an apostle and elder; and, therefore, that the gift extends to all the apostles, and after them, to all ordinary elders, to the end of time. The same thing that is expressed in the above passage by *binding* and *loosing*, is elsewhere expressed by *remitting* and *retaining sins*. But Christ addressed these words to all the apostles: 'Peace be unto you; as the Father hath sent me, so send I you. Whose soever sins ye remit, they are remitted unto them; and whose soever sins ye retain, they are retained' (John 20:21, 23). It is true that this power is ascribed to the Church: 'Tell it unto the Church ...' (Matthew 18:17); but by the *Church*, in this passage, is to be understood the *rulers* or *elders* of the Church; and this text further confirms the doctrine of our Confession, that the power of discipline is committed solely to the office-bearers of the Church. The Church and the State may take up the same cases, but under a different consideration; it is only when viewed as crimes against the State that they come under the cognizance of civil rulers, and are to be punished with civil pains; viewed as scandals against religious society, they come under the cognizance of the rulers of the Church, and can only be removed by ecclesiastical censures.

Church censures are necessary for vindicating the honour of Christ and his religion – maintaining the purity of his worship – reclaiming offenders – deterring others from the like offences – removing contagion from the Church – and preventing the wrath of God, which might justly fall upon the Church, if they should suffer the seals of his covenant to be profaned by notorious and obstinate offenders.

The censures of the Church are spiritual in their nature and effects. They are appointed by Christ for the benefit of offenders, and have a tendency, as means, to promote their recovery, and not their destruction. As offences differ in degrees of guilt and circumstances of aggravation, the Church is to proceed according to the nature and degree of the offence committed. In some cases a simple *admonition* will suffice (Titus 3:10). A greater degree of guilt will call for a *rebuke*, solemnly administered in the name of Jesus Christ (Titus 1:13; 1 Timothy 5:20). Scandals of greater magnitude will require the *suspension* of the offender from the sacrament of the Lord's supper for a season (2 Thessalonians 3:14). This is called *the lesser excommunication*; and the highest censure which the Church has the power to inflict is called *the greater excommunication* (Matthew 18:17). We have an example in the case of the incestuous man, who was delivered 'unto Satan for the destruction of the flesh, that the spirit might be saved in the day of the Lord Jesus' (1 Corinthians 5:5). It does not, according to the Popish notion, consist in literally delivering up the offender to the devil, but in casting him out of the Church into the world, which is described in Scripture as Satan's kingdom.

CHAPTER 31

SYNODS AND COUNCILS

Section 1
For the better government and further edification of the Church, there
ought to be such assemblies as are commonly called synods or councils
(Acts 15:2, 4, 6).

Exposition
The General Assembly of the Church of Scotland, in their act
approving of the Confession of Faith, 1647, inserted a caveat:
'That the not mentioning in this Confession the several sorts of
ecclesiastical officers and assemblies, shall be no prejudice to the
truth of Christ in these particulars, to be expressed fully in the
Directory of Government.' The views of the Church of Scotland,
and also of the Westminster Assembly, on this subject, are
therefore to be more fully ascertained in 'The Form of Presbyterial
Church Government', agreed upon by that Assembly, and usually
bound up with the Confession of Faith. In that document they
declare: 'It is lawful and agreeable to the Word of God, that the
Church be governed by several sorts of assemblies, which are
congregational, classical, and synodical'; and also: 'That synodical
assemblies may lawfully be of several sorts, as provincial, national,
and oecumenical'; and further, that 'It is lawful, and agreeable to
the Word of God, that there be a subordination of congregational,
classical provincial, and national assemblies, for the government
of the Church.' Here we have a distinct specification of the several
sorts of ecclesiastical assemblies, and also an explicit statement
of the due subordination of the judicatories of the Church; which
we are now accustomed to denominate kirk-sessions, presbyteries,
provincial synods, and General Assemblies. At present, however,
we have only to notice the statement in the section of the
Confession under consideration. In opposition to the Independents,
who maintain that every congregation has an independent power
of government within itself, and deny all subordination of
judicatories, our Confession asserts that, 'for the better government
and further edification of the Church' (that is, for attaining the
end better than can be accomplished in smaller meetings of Church

officers), 'there ought to be such assemblies as are commonly called synods or councils'. Of this we have an example in the synod which met at Jerusalem to settle the question about circumcision.

> 'The question, whether or not the Gentiles who made a profession of the Christian religion were bound to submit to circumcision, was of common concern, and could only be settled by the judgment and decision of office-bearers delegated from the Church as a whole; and we find that the judgment or decision of these office-bearers, when met judicially to consider the question, was considered as binding upon the whole Church. Nor is it any valid objection to this court forming a model for the imitation of the Church in after ages, that it was composed partly of apostles; for the apostles were also elders, as every higher office in the Church includes the official power belonging to inferior offices, and we do not find that, in the whole discussion, the apostles, as judges, claimed any superiority over their brethren, who are called elders. At any rate, the decision was promulgated as the joint decision of both (Acts 15:21-31).'[1]

Section 2

As magistrates may lawfully call a synod of ministers, and other fit persons, to consult and advise with about matters of religion (Isaiah 49:23; 1 Timothy 2:1, 2; 2 Chronicles 19:8-11; 29, 30; Matthew 2:4, 5; Proverbs 11:14); so if magistrates be open enemies to the Church, the ministers of Christ of themselves, by virtue of their office, or they, with other fit persons upon delegation from their Churches, may meet together in such assemblies (Acts 15:2, 4. 22, 23, 25).

Exposition

The Assembly of the Church of Scotland, in the act by which they adopted the Confession, make a special reference to this section, and expressly declare that they understood it 'only of kirks not settled or constituted in point of government'; and while they admit that 'in such kirks a synod of ministers, and other fit persons, may be called by the magistrates' authority and nomination, without any other call, to consult and advise with about matters of religion', they assert that this 'ought not to be done in kirks constituted and settled', and that it is always free to the ministers and ruling elders 'to assemble together synodically, as well *pro re nata* as at the ordinary times, upon delegation from the

---

1. Stevenson on the *Offices of Christ*, pp. 347, 348.

Churches, by the intrinsical power received from Christ, as often as it is necessary for the good of the Church so to assemble, in case the magistrate, to the detriment of the Church, withhold or deny his consent.' Our Reformers, it is well known, were ever jealous of the least encroachment upon the independence of the Church. Her intrinsic power to convene her own Assemblies occupied a prominent place in all their contendings with the Crown. Their maxim was: 'Take from us the freedom of Assemblies, and take from us the Evangel.' At the period of the first Reformation this power was both claimed and exercised. The Church held her first Assembly, in 1560, solely in virtue of her own proper authority, under Christ her head; and for at least twenty years – during which time there were no fewer than thirty-nine or forty Assemblies – the sovereign was not present, either in person or by a representative, as afterwards became the custom. At the era of the second Reformation, the intrinsic power of the Church was nobly vindicated by the famous Assembly held in Glasgow in 1638. Although the king's commissioner dissolved the Assembly in his master's name, and discharged their further proceedings, under the highest penalties, yet the Assembly, claiming an intrinsical power from the Lord Jesus Christ, continued their sessions and proceeded with the important business for which they had met. It must be acknowledged, however, that in the Act of 1592 – which has been considered as the *Magna Charta* of the Established Church, and which the Act of 1690 revived and confirmed – the right of the Church to appoint her own Assemblies was not sufficiently secured. This right is conceded only when neither the king nor his commissioner is present. Accordingly, immediately after the Revolution, the Assemblies of the Church were often abruptly dissolved, and repeatedly adjourned, by the royal authority.

'This point (the power of freely meeting and dissolving by the Church's own authority), that so often was contested between the Crown and the Presbyterian courts in Scotland, is of far greater importance to ecclesiastical independence and liberty than at first it may appear to be. Without this being retained and secured, a little reflection may show that the exercise of any other powers they may claim, may be rendered, by the will of a superior, not only precarious, but altogether nugatory and void. It is well known that this arbitrary exercise of prerogative, in calling and dissolving Parliaments, had rendered them powerless, and they were in danger by it of being utterly abolished; nor did the nation reckon their civil liberties at all secure, till annual or regular meetings of Parliament were secured by law. The danger would be equal and the effect similar, if ecclesiastical assemblies were made, in this respect, wholly dependent on the Crown; of which the history of the English Convocation affords a striking evidence.'[2]

Section 3
It belongeth to synods and councils ministerially to determine controversies of faith and cases of conscience; to set down rules and directions for the better ordering of the public worship of God and government of his Church; to receive complaints in cases of mal-administration, and authoritatively to determine the same: which decrees and determinations, if consonant to the Word of God, are to be received with reverence and submission, not only for their agreement with the Word, but also for the power whereby they are made, as being an ordinance of God, appointed thereunto in his Word (Acts 15:15, 19, 24, 27-31; 16:4; Matthew 18:17-20).

Exposition
This section is evidently intended as a decision upon another important principle in the controversy with Independents, who, while they admitted that congregations might, in difficult cases, *consult* with advantage synods of ministers, denied to these synods any *authority* over the congregations. Presbyterians readily grant that the power of Church rulers is purely *ministerial*. Christ is the alone Lord and Lawgiver in his Church; so that their business is only to apply and enforce the laws which he has enacted. Their deliberations, however, are to be considered, not as merely consultative, but authoritative; and, so far as their decisions accord with the laws of Christ, laid down in his Word, being formed in his name, and by authority conferred by him, they must be binding upon the conscience. The Synod of Jerusalem did not merely give a counsel or advice, but pronounced an authoritative decision upon the case referred to them. The 'ordained decrees', 'laid a burden' upon the Churches, and enjoined them to observe certain 'necessary things'; and their decision was cheerfully submitted to by the Churches concerned (Acts 15:28; 16:4).

---

2. Bruce on the *Supremacy of Civil Powers*, p. 103.

Section 4

All synods or councils since the apostles' times, whether general or particular, may err, and many have erred; therefore they are not to be made the rule of faith or practice, but to be used as an help in both (Ephesians 2:20; Acts 17:11; 1 Corinthians 2:5; 2 Corinthians 1:24).

Exposition

Although Papists maintain that infallibility is lodged somewhere in the Church, they are not agreed among themselves whether it resides in the Pope, or in a general council, or in both united. It is here affirmed that all councils *may* err. Councils being composed of men, every one of whom is fallible, they must also be liable to error when collected together. It is also asserted that many of them *have* erred; and this is sufficiently evident from the fact, that different general councils have made decrees directly opposite to each other. In the Arian controversy, several councils decreed in opposition to that of Nice. The Eutychian heresy was approved in the second Council of Ephesus, and soon after condemned in the Council of Chalcedon. The worship of images was condemned in the Council of Constantinople, and was approved in the second Nicene Council, and again condemned at Francfort. Finally, the authority of councils was declared, at Constance and Basil, to be superior to that of the Pope; but this decision was reversed in the Lateran.[3] (3. Burnet on the Thirty-Nine Articles, Art. 21.)

Section 5

Synods and councils are to handle or conclude nothing but that which is ecclesiastical; and are not to intermeddle with civil affairs, which concern the commonwealth, unless by way of humble petition, in cases extraordinary, or by way of advice for satisfaction of conscience, if they be thereunto required by the civil magistrate (Luke 12:13, 14; John 18:36).

Exposition

While our Confession denounces any Erastian interference of the civil magistrate in matters purely spiritual and ecclesiastical, it no less explicitly disavows all Popish claims, on the part of the synods and councils of the Church, to intermeddle with civil affairs, unless by way of petition, in extraordinary cases, or by way of advice, when required by the civil magistrate. Our Reformers appear to have clearly perceived the proper limits of the civil and ecclesiastical jurisdiction, and to have been very

370 EXPOSITION OF THE WESTMINSTER CONFESSION OF FAITH

careful that they should be strictly observed. 'The power and policy ecclesiastical,' say they, 'is different and distinct in its own nature from that power and policy which is called civil power, and appertaineth to the civil government of the commonwealth; albeit they be both of God, and tend to one end, if they be rightly used, viz., to advance the glory of God, and to have godly and good subjects.' 'Diligence should be taken, chiefly by the moderator, that only ecclesiastical things be handled in the Assemblies, and that there be no meddling with anything pertaining to the civil jurisdiction.'[3] Church and State may co-operate in the advancement of objects common to both; but each of them must be careful to act within its own proper sphere – the one never intermeddling with the affairs which properly belong to the province of the other.

---

3. Second Book of Discipline, chaps. i. and vii.

CHAPTER 32

THE STATE OF MEN AFTER DEATH,
AND
THE RESURRECTION OF THE DEAD

Section 1

The bodies of men after death return to dust, and see corruption (Genesis 3:19; Acts 13:36); but their souls (which neither die nor sleep) having an immortal subsistence, immediately return to God who gave them (Luke 23:43; Ecclesiastes 12:7). The souls of the righteous, being then made perfect in holiness, are received into the highest heavens, where they behold the face of God in light and glory, waiting for the full redemption of their bodies (Hebrews 12:23; 2 Corinthians 5:1, 6, 8; Philippians 1:23; Acts 3:21; Ephesians 4:10); and the souls of the wicked are cast into hell, where they remain in torments and utter darkness, reserved to the judgment of the great day (Luke 16:23, 24; Acts 1:25; Jude 6,7; 1 Peter 3:19). Besides these two places for souls separated from their bodies, the Scripture acknowledgeth none.

Exposition

1. It is here supposed that death is an event common to all men. 'It is appointed unto men once to die' (Hebrews 9:27). This is the immutable appointment of Heaven, which cannot be reversed, and which none can frustrate. When meditating upon this subject, the royal Psalmist exclaimed: 'What man is he that liveth, and shall not see death? shall he deliver his soul from the hand of the grave?' (Psalm 89:48). Job speaks of death as an event which certainly awaited him, and of the grave as the common receptacle of all mankind: 'I know that thou wilt bring me to death, and to the house appointed for all living' (Job 30:26). Our own observation abundantly confirms the declaration of Scripture. Nor are we at a loss to account for the introduction of death into our world, and its universal prevalence over the human race: 'As by one man sin entered into the world, and death by sin; so death passed upon all men, for that all have sinned' (Romans 5:12).

There is, indeed, a vast difference between the death of the righteous and that of the wicked. To the latter, death is the effect of the law-curse, and the harbinger of everlasting destruction; but to the former, death is not the proper punishment of sin, but the termination of all sin and sorrow, and an entrance into life eternal. To them death is divested of its sting, and rendered powerless to do them any real injury. Not only is it disarmed of its power to hurt them – it is compelled to perform a friendly part to them. It is their release from warfare, their deliverance from woe, their departure to be with Christ. But although death is no real loss, but rather great gain to the righteous; yet, as it consists in the dissolution of the union between the soul and the body, it is an event from which they are not exempted.

God could, no doubt, if he pleased, easily save his saints from natural death. Of this he gave a proof in the case of Enoch and of Elijah. For good reasons, however, he has determined otherwise.

(1) That the righteous, as well as others, should be subjected to temporal death, is best adapted to the present plan of the divine government, and seems necessary, if not to the preservation, at least to the comfort of human society. According to the plan of the divine government, rewards and punishments are principally reserved for a future world. But if the righteous were exempted from death, while the wicked fell under its stroke, this would be a manifestation of the final destiny of every man that is removed out of this world. Death, therefore, happens to the righteous in the same outward form, and attended with the same external circumstances, as it happens to the wicked, that there may be no visible distinction between them.

(2) Were the righteous to be distinguished from the wicked by being translated to heaven without tasting of death, this would introduce great confusion into society. Without producing any salutary effect upon the wicked, it would render them more regardless of character, and remove one powerful stimulus – the prospect of future fame – which animates them to noble exertions for the benefit of society. It would also greatly affect the character and the happiness of the living. Were the parent singled out as the object of the divine displeasure, by being subjected to death, this would fix a brand of infamy upon his children; or if the child were taken away in a manner so expressive of its future destiny, this would pierce the heart of the parent, especially if serious, with inexpressible anguish. No class, indeed, would be more affected by such a state of things than the righteous themselves. Hence death is the common lot of the godly and of the wicked.

(3) This arrangement affords occasion for a richer display of the power and grace of God. As the hour of death is the most trying to men, so the power and grace of God are most gloriously displayed, in supporting his people in that solemn hour; in enabling them, in the exercise of faith and hope, to rise superior to the fear of death, and to triumph over this last enemy as conquerors. And how illustriously will his power be displayed in raising up their bodies at the last day!

(4) Another reason, we conceive, why the righteous are subjected to temporal death, is, that they may be conformed to Christ, their glorious head. He tasted of death before he was crowned with glory and honour; and they also must enter into glory through 'the valley of the shadow of death'.

2. The bodies of men after death return to the dust, and see corruption. So humiliating and deeply affecting is the change which death produces on the human body, that it becomes obnoxious to the view, and necessity compels the living to remove it from their sight. It is committed to the grave, in which it putrefies; and after a certain time is reduced to dust, so that it cannot be distinguished from the vegetable mould with which it is mingled. These things, however, are offensive only to the living; they occasion no uneasiness to the dead. To the wicked, indeed, the grave is a prison, where they are kept in close confinement until the resurrection; but to believers it is a place of rest, where, exempted from all pain and weariness, they shall enjoy profound repose till the resurrection morn, when, awakened as from a long refreshing sleep, they shall rise, with renovated life and vigour, to enjoy everlasting felicity.

3. The souls of men survive the dissolution of their bodies, and have an immortal subsistence. Some have held that death is the utter extinction of man's being; others, that the soul shall sleep between death and the resurrection, alike inactive and unconscious as the body that is then dissolved into dust. In opposition to these notions, equally absurd and uncomfortable, our Confession affirms, and the Scripture clearly teaches, that the souls of men subsist in a disembodied state, after such a manner as to be capable of exercising those powers and faculties which are essential to them. 'Fear not them which kill the body, but are not able to kill

the soul' (Matthew 10:28). These are the words of him who made man, and who perfectly knows the constituent parts of his nature; and he affirms, not only that the soul is distinct from the body – not only that it does not, in fact, die with the body, but that it is impossible to kill the soul by any created power. Our Saviour taught the same doctrine in parabolical language: 'It came to pass that the beggar died, and was carried by the angels into Abraham's bosom. The rich man also died and was buried; and in hell he lift up his eyes, being in torments' (Luke 16:22, 23). Both the beggar and the man of wealth died; both left their bodies in the dust; but the souls of both retained their existence and their consciousness after their separation from their bodies. No doubt the death of the righteous is frequently described in Scripture as a *sleep*; but such language is obviously figurative, and gives no countenance to the notion that the soul falls asleep when disunited from the body. When the dead are said to be asleep, a metaphor is used, founded upon the striking resemblance between death and sleep; and, at the same time, by another figure of speech, a part is spoken of as the whole. They are said to sleep, and to be unconscious and inactive, because these things are true of their bodies.

4. The souls of the righteous, immediately after death, are admitted into the happiness of the heavenly state. Some, who allow that the souls of believers possess consciousness, and experience happiness in their disembodied state, conceive that at death their souls pass into an *intermediate* state, and that they will enter into *heaven* only when the final judgment takes place. The Church of Rome maintains that the souls of the saints, on leaving their bodies, must pass for a time into a place called *purgatory*, that they may be purified by fire from the stains of sin, which had not been washed out during the present life. That Church further teaches, that the pains and suffering of purgatory may be alleviated and shortened by the prayers of men here on earth; by the intercession of the saints in heaven; and, above all, by the sacrifice of the mass, offered by the priests in the name of sinners; and that, as soon as souls are released from purgatory, they are immediately admitted to eternal happiness. Of this doctrine there is no trace in the Bible; it is a cunningly devised fable, invented by designing men to impose upon the credulous, and to fill their own treasures. The Scripture speaks only of a *heaven* and a *hell*, into one of

which all departed souls have entered; and accordingly, our Confession affirms: 'Besides these two places for souls separated from their bodies, the Scripture acknowledgeth none.'

The *immediate* admission of the souls of the righteous into heaven is confirmed by numerous passages of Scripture. Our Lord's promise to the penitent thief: 'Today shalt thou be with me in paradise' (Luke 23:43), implies that, ere that day was finished, his soul should be in the same place with the soul of Christ, and should enjoy all the felicity which the word 'paradise' suggests. When Stephen, with his expiring breath, called upon God, saying, 'Lord Jesus, receive my spirit' (Acts 7:59), he manifestly expected that his soul should immediately pass into the presence of his Saviour. The same thing is implied in the language of Paul: 'For me to live is Christ, and to die is gain. I am in a strait betwixt two, having a desire to depart, and to be with Christ, which is far better' (Philippians 1:21, 23). Certainly if he had not expected to be admitted into the presence of Christ until the resurrection, he would not have judged it *gain* to die; and, instead of desiring, he would have been loath to depart; for while he was in the body he was honourably engaged in the service of Christ, and enjoyed delightful communion with him. But the apostle tells us that the reason of his desire to depart was, that he might be with Christ – in a state of blessedness far superior to anything found in this present world. The same apostle says: 'We are confident, I say, and willing rather to be absent from the body, and to be present with the Lord' (2 Corinthians 5:8). No words could express in a clearer manner the immediate transition of the soul from its present habitation into the presence of Christ. The believer's absence from the body and his presence with Christ are closely connected; the latter succeeds the former without any interval. Accordingly, the Apostle John hears a voice from heaven, saying to him: 'Write, Blessed are the dead which die in the Lord, *from henceforth*' (Revelation 14:13) – that is, they are blessed from the time of their death.

If the souls of believers are admitted into heaven immediately after death, it is evident that a wonderful change must then take place upon them, in order to qualify them for the new state into which they are introduced. Unless they were completely freed from every stain of impurity, they would be unfit for the society of the heavenly world, and incapable of enjoying the felicities of that world. Our Confession accordingly asserts, that their souls are then 'made perfect in holiness'; and in Scripture the souls of departed saints are called 'the spirits of just men made perfect' (Hebrews 12:23).

5. The souls of the wicked are at death cast into hell. While some have maintained that the souls of the wicked shall never be tormented in hell, others have held that they shall not be adjudged to that place of torment till after the resurrection; but, according to the representation of our Saviour, as soon as the rich man died, 'in hell he lifted up his eyes, being in torments' (Luke 16:23). The spirits of those who in the time of Noah were disobedient, were, when the Apostle Peter wrote his epistle, shut up in the prison of hell (1 Peter 3:19).

Section 2
At the last day, such as are found alive shall not die, but be changed (1 Thessalonians 4:17; 1 Corinthians 15:51, 52): and all the dead shall be raised up with the selfsame bodies, and none other, although with different qualities, which shall be united again to their souls for ever (Job 19:26, 27; 1 Corinthians 15:42-44).

Section 3
The bodies of the unjust shall, by the power of Christ, be raised to dishonour; the bodies of the just, by his Spirit, unto honour, and be made conformable to his own glorious body (Acts 24:15; John 5:28, 29; 1 Corinthians 15:43; Philippians 3:21).

Exposition
1. *Such as remain alive upon the earth at the last day shall not die, but undergo a wonderful change.* This truth was first revealed to the Church in Paul's First Epistle to the Corinthians: 'Behold I show you a mystery; we shall not all sleep, but we shall all be changed' (15:51). When Christ shall descend from heaven to judge the world, some will be found alive upon the earth; these shall not die, and sleep for a short time in the dust of the earth; but they will experience a change equivalent to that which shall pass on those who shall then be raised from the grave; and, as we are informed, the dead saints will be raised before the living are changed. 'The dead in Christ shall rise first: then we which are alive and remain, shall be caught up together with them in the clouds, to meet the Lord in the air: and so shall we ever be with the Lord' (1 Thessalonians 4:16, 17).

2. *There shall be a general resurrection of the dead.* This is a doctrine which unassisted reason could not discover. The wisest of the heathen philosophers derided it. When Paul preached at Athens, which was called the Eye of Greece, the Epicurean and Stoic philosophers mocked when he spake of the resurrection of the dead. But it cannot be reckoned an incredible thing that God should raise the dead. If he be omnipotent and omniscient, as he certainly is, otherwise he would cease to be God, this cannot be considered impossible. He who formed the human body out of dust, and breathed into it the breath of life, must be able to raise and animate it again after it has been reduced to dust. To the power of God our Saviour referred, as an answer to all the cavils which might be brought forward against the doctrine of the resurrection. To the Sadducees, a sect of the Jews who denied this doctrine, he said: 'Ye do err, not knowing the Scriptures, nor the power of God' (Matthew 22:29).

But it is only by the revelation of the will of God that we are infallibly assured of the certainty of the resurrection. It was revealed in the writings of the Old Testament. Job expressed the strongest confidence of the resurrection of his body (Job 19:25). The prediction of the Prophet Daniel is equally explicit (Daniel 12:2). This doctrine held a prominent place in the discourses of our Lord's declaration: 'The hour is coming in the which all that are in the graves shall hear his voice, and shall come forth ...' (John 5:28, 29). After our Lord's ascension this was the grand theme of the testimony of his apostles, as upon it the truth of the whole system of Christianity rested. Hence Paul thus argued with the Corinthians: 'Now, if Christ be preached that he rose from the dead, how say some among you that there is no resurrection of the dead? But if there be no resurrection of the dead, then is Christ not risen. And if Christ be not risen, then is our preaching vain, and your faith is also vain' (1 Corinthians 15:12-14).

The resurrection of the saints is firmly established by the resurrection of Christ himself. In the chapter to which we have now referred, the apostle shows the infallible evidence which he and his brethren had for the resurrection of Christ, and then argues that the resurrection of believers necessarily follows from the admission that Christ their head is risen. The grave cannot always retain what is so intimately connected with the living Redeemer. 'Now is Christ risen from the dead, and become the first-fruits of them that slept' (1 Corinthians 15:20. See also 1 Thessalonians 4:14; Romans 8:11).

3. *The dead shall be raised with the selfsame bodies, although with very different qualities.* The very term *resurrection* implies that the same bodies shall be raised that fell by death; for if God should form new bodies, and unite them to departed souls, it would not be a resurrection, but a new creation. Our Saviour declares: 'All that are in the graves shall come forth'; this certainly implies that the same bodies which were committed to the graves shall be raised; for, if new bodies were to be produced, and united to their souls, they could not, with truth, be said to come out of their graves. The Apostle Paul affirms, that the same body shall be raised which is sown in corruption, and declares: 'This corruptible must put on incorruption, and this mortal must put on immortality'; pointing, as it were, to that corruptible and mortal body which he then carried about. But, though the bodies of the saints will be the same in all essentials as to substance, they will be vastly changed as to qualities. 'Flesh and blood,' in their present state of grossness and frailty, 'cannot inherit the kingdom of God, neither doth corruption inherit incorruption.' The resurrection-body, therefore, shall be wonderfully changed, in respect to qualities, that it may be fitted for the employments and felicities of the heavenly state. 'It is sown in corruption, it is raised in incorruption; it is sown in dishonour, it is raised in glory; it is sown in weakness, it is raised in power; it is sown a natural body, it is raised a spiritual body' (1 Corinthians 15:42-44). With regard to the wicked, the Scriptures give us no specific information with respect to the state and qualities of their bodies. All that we learn is, that they shall rise 'to shame and everlasting contempt'; from which it is evident that they shall be raised to dishonour.

How solicitous should we be to obtain the resurrection of the just! This was Paul's great desire, and the object of his earnest pursuit (Philippians 3:11). If we would attain to a blessed resurrection, let it be our concern to be 'found in Christ'. United to him by the inhabitation of his Spirit and by a living faith, we need not be slavishly afraid of death or of the grave; for Christ is 'the resurrection and the life, and he that believeth in him, though he were dead, yet shall he live; and whosoever liveth and believeth in him shall never die'.

CHAPTER 33

THE LAST JUDGMENT

Section 1
God hath appointed a day wherein he will judge the world in
righteousness by Jesus Christ (Acts 17:31), to whom all power and
judgment is given of the Father (John 5:22, 27). In which day, not only
the apostate angels shall be judged (1 Corinthians 6:3; Jude 6; 2 Peter
2:4), but likewise all persons that have lived upon earth shall appear
before the tribunal of Christ, to give an account of their thoughts, words,
and deeds, and to receive according to what they have done in the body,
whether good or evil (2 Corinthians 5:10; Ecclesiastes 12:14; Romans
2:16; 14:10, 12; Matthew 12:36, 37).

Section 2
The end of God's appointing this day is for the manifestation of the
glory of his mercy in the eternal salvation of the elect, and of his justice
in the damnation of the reprobate, who are wicked and disobedient. For
then shall the righteous go into everlasting life, and receive that fulness
of joy and refreshing which shall come from the presence of the Lord;
but the wicked, who know not God, and obey not the gospel of Jesus
Christ, shall be cast into eternal torments, and be punished with
everlasting destruction from the presence of the Lord, and from the glory
of his power (Matthew 25:31-46; Romans 2:5, 6; 9:22, 23; Matthew
25:21; Acts 3:19; 2 Thessalonians 1:7-10).

Exposition
There is a particular judgment which passes upon every individual
immediately after death; for 'it is appointed unto men once to die,
but after this the judgment' (Hebrews 9:27). There is also a general
judgment, which shall take place after the resurrection of the dead,
at the last day. The present sections: (1) declare the certainty of a
future judgment; (2) affirm that the administration of this judgment
is committed to Jesus Christ; (3) point out the parties who shall
appear before his tribunal; (4) the matters to be tried; and, (5) the
sentence to be pronounced.

1. The *certainty* of a future judgment. We are told that Paul
reasoned before Felix of judgment to come (Acts 24:25). He
proved this truth by arguments drawn from the nature and reason

of things; and such arguments are not to be overlooked by us, though *our* faith stands upon a more sure foundation.

(1) The certainty of a future judgment appears from the dictates of conscience. Men, even when destitute of supernatural revelation, apprehend an essential difference between good and evil. When they do what is right, their conscience approves and commends their conduct; and when they do what is wrong, their conscience reproaches and condemns them. If they have committed some atrocious crime, conscience stings them with remorse; and this it does although the crime be secret, and concealed from every human eye. Whence does this arise, but from an awful foreboding of future retribution? The Apostle Paul, accordingly, shows that all mankind have a witness in themselves that there shall be a future judgment (Romans 2:15).

(2) Reason infers a future judgment from the state of things in this world. Here we take for granted these two fundamental principles of religion – the being of God, and his providence in the government of the world. All who acknowledge these truths must, and do, believe that God is infinitely just and merciful; and that he cannot be otherwise. From this it necessarily results that it must be well with the righteous, and ill with the wicked. But the most superficial view of the present state of things is sufficient to convince us that God does not, in this world, dispense prosperity only to the good, and adversity only to the evil. 'There be just men, unto whom it happeneth according to the work of the wicked; again, there be wicked men, to whom it happeneth according to the work of the righteous' (Ecclesiastes 8:14). The promiscuous dispensations of Providence have perplexed the minds of men in every age, and tried the faith of the children of God (Psalm 73:4-17; Jeremiah 12:1, 2; Habakkuk 1:13). But reason rightly exercised would lead us to the conclusion that, upon the supposition of the being and providence of God, there must be a day coming when these things will be brought under review, and when a wide and visible difference shall be made between him that serveth God and him that serveth him not.

(3) God has given testimony to this truth in all the extraordinary judgments which he has executed since the beginning of the world. Though much wickedness remains unpunished and undiscovered in this world, yet God sometimes executes judgment upon daring offenders, to show that he judgeth in the earth, and to give warning

to men of a judgment to come. In signal judgments, 'the wrath of God is revealed from heaven against the ungodliness of men'; and an intimation is given of what he will further do hereafter (2 Peter 2:5, 6; 3:5, 7).

(4) That there is a judgment to come is confirmed by the most explicit testimonies of scripture. Enoch predicted the approach of this day of universal decision as a salutary admonition to that profligate age in which he lived (Jude 14, 15). Solomon addressed this solemn warning to the voluptuous: 'Know that for all these things God will bring thee into judgment' (Ecclesiastes 11:9). Job put his friends in mind that there is a judgment; and the Psalmist frequently represents it in very solemn language (Job 19:29; Psalms 50:3-6; 98:9). Our Lord, during his personal ministry, frequently foretold his coming to judgment; and the testimonies to this truth in the writing of his apostles are numerous (Matthew 25:31-46; Romans 14:10, 12; 2 Corinthians 5:10).

(5) This truth is confirmed by the resurrection of Christ. The Apostle Paul, having affirmed that 'God will judge the world in righteousness by that man whom he hath ordained', adds, 'whereof he hath given assurance to all men, in that he hath raised him from the dead' (Acts 17:31). The resurrection of Christ is a specimen and pledge of a general resurrection – that grand preparative for the judgment. It is an incontestable proof of our Lord's divine mission, and is, therefore, an authentic attestation of all his claims. In the days of his humiliation, when he was accused and condemned before the tribunal of men, he plainly warned them of a future judgment, and declared that he himself would be the judge: 'Hereafter shall ye see the Son of man sitting on the right hand of power, and coming in the clouds of heaven' (Matthew 26:64). Now, since God hath raised him from the dead, although he was condemned as a blasphemer for this very declaration, is not this an undeniable proof from heaven of the truth of what he then asserted?

2. The administration of the future judgment is committed to Jesus Christ: 'He is ordained of God to be the judge of quick and dead' (Acts 10:42). It is, indeed, frequently said, that 'God shall judge the world'; and the Psalmist declares, 'None else is judge but God' (Psalm 50:6). How are these declarations to be reconciled? The words of Paul enable us to solve the difficulty. He has told us

that 'God will judge the world in righteousness by that man whom he hath ordained' (Acts 17:31). It thus appears that God the Father judges the world by the Son. The supreme judiciary power is in the Godhead, and the exercise of that power is committed to Christ, as mediator (John 5:22).

There is a peculiar fitness and propriety in this constitution:

(1) It is fit that this high office should be conferred upon Christ, as an honorary reward for his extreme abasement and ignominious sufferings.

(2) Inasmuch as men are to be judged after the resurrection in an embodied state, it is fit they should have a visible judge.

(3) It is also fit that Christ should be the supreme judge, as it must contribute greatly to the consolation of the saints that they shall be judged by him who is a partaker of their nature, who redeemed them to God by his blood, and who is their advocate with the Father.

(4) It may be added, that hereby the condemnation of the wicked will be rendered more conspicuously just; for if a Mediator – a Saviour – the Friend of sinners – condemn them, they must be worthy of condemnation indeed.

3. We are next to consider the parties who shall appear before the tribunal of Christ. The Scripture says nothing of the judgment of good angels, but it clearly teaches that the apostate angels will be judged (Jude 4; 2 Peter 2:4). That men universally shall stand before the judgment-seat of Christ is expressly declared (2 Corinthians 5:10). We are told that Christ 'shall judge the quick and the dead at his appearing' (2 Timothy 4:1). This expression, 'the quick and the dead', comprehends all mankind. By *the dead*, are to be understood all who died before the period of Christ's coming to judgment; and by *the quick*, such as shall then be found alive.

4. The matter to be tried. This is expressed in the most comprehensive terms: 'God shall bring every work into judgment, with every secret thing, whether it be good, of whether it be evil' (Ecclesiastes 12:14). All the works of the sons of men will be tried, and they shall receive according to what they have done in the body, whether good or evil. Not only the actions of the life, but also the *words* of men shall be judged; for our Saviour has

assured us that 'for every idle word which men shall speak, they shall give an account in the day of judgment' (Matthew 12:36). And not only the actions and words, but also the very thoughts of men shall be brought into judgment; for we are told 'God shall judge the secrets of men by Jesus Christ' (Romans 2:16).

5. The sentence to be pronounced will be answerable to the several states in which mankind shall be found. They shall receive their doom according to their works (Revelation 20:13). It is to be remarked, that the good works of the righteous will be produced in that day, not as the grounds of their acquittal, and of their being adjudged to eternal life, but as the evidences of their gracious state, as being interested in the righteousness of Christ. But the evil deeds of the wicked will be brought forward, not only as evidences of their being strangers to Christ, but also as the grounds of their condemnation. To the glorious company on his right hand the King will say: 'Come, ye blessed of my Father, inherit the kingdom prepared for you from the foundation of the world.' How different the sentence that will be passed on the guilty crowd on his left hand! To them he will say: 'Depart from me, ye cursed, into everlasting fire, prepared for the devil and his angels.' The sentence shall no sooner be passed than it shall be executed. While fallen angels and wicked men shall be driven from the presence of the Judge into the pit of eternal perdition, the righteous shall be conducted into heavenly mansions, and 'shall go no more out'. 'These shall go away into everlasting punishment; but the righteous into life eternal.' The same expression being applied to the happiness of the righteous and the punishment of the wicked, we may conclude that both will be of equal duration.

Section 3
As Christ would have us to be certainly persuaded that there shall be a day of judgment, both to deter all men from sin, and for the greater consolation of the godly in their adversity (2 Peter 3:11, 14; 2 Corinthians 5:10, 11; 2 Thessalonians 1:5-7; Luke 21:27, 28; Romans 8:23-25); so will he have that day unknown to men, that they may shake off all carnal security, and be always watchful, because they know not at what hour the Lord will come; and may be ever prepared to say, Come, Lord Jesus, come quickly. Amen (Matthew 24:36, 42-44; Mark 13:35-37; Luke 12:35, 36; Revelation 22:20).

Exposition

The day of the eternal judgment is fixed in the counsels of God; but, that we may be kept habitually watchful, the knowledge of that day is wisely concealed from us. Though a long series of ages may elapse before Christ shall come in the clouds of heaven to judge the world, let every one remember that the day of his own death is equally important to him as the day of the universal judgment; for where death leaves him, judgment will find him. Let him, therefore, 'be diligent, that he may be found of God in peace, without spot and blameless'. Let every reader study to improve the talents with which he is intrusted, and be solicitous to obtain the approbation of his Master in heaven. How highly will he commend all those who have been diligent and faithful in his service! He will bestow upon them that best of plaudits: 'Well done, good and faithful servant'; and will introduce them into 'the joy of their Lord'. Well may the genuine believer 'love the appearing' of Christ; for when Christ shall appear, he also shall appear with him in glory. And since Christ proclaims in his Word, 'Surely I come quickly', let every Christian joyfully respond, 'Amen. Even so, come Lord Jesus.'

APPENDIX 1

ACT

APPROVING THE CONFESSION OF FAITH

Assembly at Edinburgh, August 27, 1647. Sess. 23.

A Confession of Faith for the Kirks of God in the three kingdoms, being the chiefest part of that uniformity in religion, which by the Solemn League and Covenant, we are bound to endeavour: And there being accordingly a Confession of Faith agreed upon by the Assembly of Divines sitting at Westminster, with the assistance of Commissioners from the Kirk of Scotland; which Confession was sent from our Commissioners at London to the Commissioners of the Kirk met at Edinburgh in January last, and hath been in this Assembly twice publicly read over, examined, and considered; copies thereof being also printed, that it might be particularly perused by all the members of this Assembly, unto whom frequent intimation was publicly made, to put in their doubts and objections, if they had any: And the said Confession being, upon due examination thereof, found by the Assembly to be most agreeable to the Word of God, and in nothing contrary to the received doctrine, worship, discipline, and government of this Kirk. And, lastly, It being so necessary, and so much longed for, that the said Confession be, with all possible diligence and expedition, approved and established in both kingdoms, as a principal part of the intended uniformity in religion, and as a special means for the more effectual suppressing of the many dangerous errors and heresies of these times; the General Assembly doth therefore, after mature deliberation, agree unto, and approve the said Confession, as to the truth of the matter (judging it to be most orthodox, and grounded upon the Word of God); and also, as to the point of uniformity, agreeing for our part, that it be a common Confession of Faith for the three kingdoms. The Assembly doth also bless the Lord, and thankfully acknowledge his great mercy, in that so excellent a Confession of Faith is prepared, and thus far agreed upon in both kingdoms; which we look upon as a great strengthening of the true Reformed religion against the common enemies thereof. But, lest our intention and meaning be in some particulars misunderstood, it is hereby expressly declared and provided, That the not mentioning in this Confession the several sorts of ecclesiastical officers and assemblies, shall be no prejudice to the truth of Christ in these particulars, to be expressed fully in the Directory of Government. It is further declared, That the Assembly understandeth some parts of the second article of the thirty-one chapter only of kirks not settled, or constituted in point of government: And that although, in such kirks, a synod of Ministers, and other fit persons, may be called by the Magistrate's authority and nomination, without any other call, to consult and advise with about matters of religion; and although, likewise, the Ministers of Christ, without delegation from their churches, may of themselves, and by virtue of their office, meet together synodically in such kirks not yet constituted, yet neither of these ought to be done in kirks constituted and settled; it being always free to the Magistrate to advise with synods of Ministers and Ruling Elders, meeting upon delegation from their churches, either ordinarily, or, being indicted by his authority, occasionally, and *pro re nata*; it being also free to assemble together synodically, as well *pro re nata* as at the ordinary times, upon delegation from the churches, by the intrinsical power received from Christ, as often as it is necessary for the good of the Church so to assemble, in case the Magistrate, to the detriment of the Church, withhold or deny his consent; the necessity of occasional assemblies being first remonstrate unto him by humble supplication.

A. Ker.

SCRIPTURE INDEX

SELECTED INDEX OF THEMES

Reformed Theological Writings
R. A. Finlayson

This volume contains a selection of doctrinal studies, divided into three sections:

General theology
The God of Israel; God In Three Persons; God the Father; The Person of Christ; The Love of the Spirit in Man's Redemption; The Holy Spirit in the Life of Christ; The Messianic Psalms; The Terminology of the Atonement; The Ascension; The Holy Spirit in the Life of the Christian; The Assurance of Faith; The Holy Spirit in the Life of the Church; The Church – The Body of Christ; The Authority of the Church; The Church in Augustine; Disruption Principles; The Reformed Doctrine of the Sacraments; The Theology of the Lord's Day, The Christian Sabbath; The Last Things.

Issues Facing Evangelicals
Christianity and Humanism; How Liberal Theology Infected Scotland; Neo-Orthodoxy; Neo-Liberalism and Neo-Fundamentalism; The Ecumenical Movement; Modern Theology and the Christian Message.

The Westminster Confession of Faith
The Significance of the Westminster Confession; The Doctrine of Scripture in the Westminster Confession of Faith; The Doctrine of God in the Westminster Confession of Faith; Particular Redemption in the Westminster Confession of Faith; Efficacious Grace in the Westminster Confession of Faith; Predestination in the Westminster Confession of Faith; The Doctrine of Man in the Westminster Confession of Faith.

R. A. Finlayson was for many years the leading theologian of the Free Church of Scotland and one of the most effective preachers and speakers of his time; those who were students in the 1950s deeply appreciated his visits to Christian Unions and IVF conferences. This volume contains posthumously edited theological lectures which illustrate his brilliant gift for simple, logical and yet warm-hearted presentation of Christian doctrine (I Howard Marshall).

272 pages   ISBN 1 85792 259 X   large format

Also by Christian Focus

Puritan Profiles

Biographical profiles of 54 leading Puritans who influenced the putting together of the Westminster Confession of Faith. The author, William Barker, is Professor of Church History at Westminster Theological Seminary, Philadelphia. Puritans described include:

William Twisse	Thomas Hill
John White	John Arrowsmith
Cornelius Burgess	Thomas Gataker
Charles Herle	Robert Harris
Herbert Palmer	Thomas Young
William Gouge	Joshua Hoyle
James Ussher	Thomas Temple
Daniel Featley	Anthony Tuckney
John Selden	Edward Reynolds
Thomas Coleman	Edmund Staunton
John Lightfoot	William Spurstowe
Thomas Goodwin	John Wallis
Philip Nye	Edmund Calamy
Jeremiah Burroughes	Simeon Ashe
William Bridge	Thomas Case
Sidrach Simpson	Lazarus Seaman
Alexander Henderson	Matthew Newcomen
Samuel Rutherford	John Ley
Robert Baillie	George Walker
George Gillespie	John Cotton
Archibald Johnston	Thomas Hooker
John Maitland	John Davenport
Stephen Marshall	Sir Henry Vane
Joseph Caryl	Richard Baxter
Obadiah Sedgwick	John Owen
Richard Vines	John Milton
Jeremiah Whitaker	John Bunyan

Hardback   ISBN 1 8579 219 17   320 pages